Chick Flicks

Chick Flicks

Theories

B. Ruby Rich

and

Memories

DUKE UNIVERSITY PRESS

of the

DURHAM AND LONDON, 1998

Feminist

Film

Movement

For permission to reprint materials first published elsewhere, the author would like to thank the following: Chicago *Reader* for "Laboring Under No Illusions" (7 Apr. 1978), "Voodoo Verité" (15 Sept. 1978), and "Femicide Investigation: Thriller" (21 Mar. 1980); Linda Williams and *Film Quarterly* for "The Right of Re-Vision: Michelle Citron's 'Daughter Rite'" (vol. 35, no. 1, fall 1981); *Discourse* for "She Says, He Says: The Power of the Narrator in Modernist Film Politics" (no. 6, fall 1983); *Village Voice* for "Anti-Porn: Soft Issue, Hard World" (vol. 27, no. 29, 20 July 1982), "Lady Killers: It's Only a Movie, Guys" (vol. 29, no. 32, 7 Aug. 1984), "Julie Christie Goes to Washington" (26 Feb. 1985), "Good Girls, Bad Girls" (15 Apr. 1986), and "Avant to Live: Or, I Was a Teenage Film Buff" (Dec. 1991); the Walker Art Center for "Yvonne Rainer" (Jan. 1981); the Film Center of the Art Institute with the Chicago *Tribune* for "The Personal Film" from *Films by Women, Chicago '74* (1974); *Jump Cut* for "In the Name of Feminist Film Criticism" (vol. 19, 1979) and "From Repressive Tolerance to Erotic Liberation: Maedchen in Uniform" (no. 24/25, Mar. 1981); *Feminist Review* for "Feminism and Sexuality in the Eighties" (vol. 12, no. 3, fall 1986); and *New Art Examiner* for "Sex and Cinema" (vol. 6, no. 10, summer 1979).

This ability to forget, itself the result of a long and terrible education by experience, is an indispensable requirement of mental and spiritual hygiene without which . . . life would be unbearable; but it is also the mental faculty that sustains submissiveness and renunciation. . . . Against this surrender to time, the restoration of remembrance to its rights, as a vehicle of liberation, is one of the noblest tasks of thought.

— Herbert Marcuse, *Eros and Civilization*

You know, they straightened out the Mississippi River in places, to make room for houses and livable acreage. Occasionally the river floods these places. "Floods" is the word they use, but in fact it is not flooding; it is remembering. Remembering where it used to be. All water has a perfect memory and is forever trying to get back to where it was. Writers are like that: remembering where we were, what valley we ran through, what the banks were like, the light that was there and the route back to our original place.

— Toni Morrison, "The Site of Memory"
in *Out There*

Who remembers all that? History throws its empty bottles out the window.

— Chris Marker, *Sans Soleil*

Contents

Acknowledgments

Every author owes a debt to the people who have surrounded a work in progress and offered support of an artistic, financial, moral, or psychological nature. This book owes a particularly large set of debts, as it has gestated over such a long period and has come about in large part thanks to the friends and colleagues who urged me to persevere in the face of my perennial excuses and postponements.

First, I would like to thank the circle of friends who have pushed me onward with all the fervor of a coach, mentor, and best friend combined. Without their belief, enthusiasm, and wise counsel, I couldn't have done this. Special thanks, then, for their long-term friendship and wise counsel and professional companionship, to Joan Braderman, Rosa Linda Fregoso, Martha Gever, Faye Ginsburg, Herman Gray, Bill Horrigan, Kate Horsfield, Lillian Jimenez, Isaac Julien, Judith Mayne, Sheila McLaughlin, Kathy McNicholas, Monica Melamid, Mark Nash, Yvonne Rainer, Carrie Rickey, Tony Safford, Hollis Sigler, Deborah Silverfine, Helga Stephenson, Sharon Thompson, Michelle Yasmine Valladares, and Martella Wilson. Special thanks to my designated elder, Loretta Szeliga, who never stopped inquiring after this manuscript even when many of fainter heart might have ceased. I have been blessed with wonderful friends and generous supporters and I owe them these thanks and many more.

Along the way, when I needed help or encouragement, information or practical assistance, there were others who provided all that and more. Thanks to Siew-Hwa Beh, Nancy Bereano, Hali Breindel, Patricia Erens, Marcia Festen, Karola Gramann, Bill Nichols, Sally Potter, Robert Stricker, Lynne Tillman, Warner Wada, Virginia Wright Wexman, Mary Wings, Meg Wolitzer, Elizabeth Young, and Tomas Ybarra-Frausto for their time, conversation, or assistance, and, above all, for the reassurance that this volume ought to see the light of day. At the University of California, Berkeley, my great thanks to my former student Catherine Zimmer for convincing me that her generation has something at stake in the histories told here; to my filmmaking students Cynthia Tsai and Sarah Harbin for reassuring me that a new generation will carry the torch; and to the staff and faculty in the Film Program, and the Rhetoric, Women's Studies, and Undergraduate Interdisciplinary Departments for their collegial support.

Thanks also to the friends, scholars, and editors (including some mentioned above) who read the manuscript when I first submitted it, offered much-needed and welcomed support, and made useful suggestions: Rhona Berenstein, Philip Dodd, Janet Franzendini, Jane Gaines, Mikah Kleit, Willis Regier, Michael Renov, Robert Sklar, and Linda Williams. For their belief in this work and its future, thanks above all to my editor at Duke University Press, Ken Wissoker, and to Richard Morrison.

Finally, there are several people whose material support was so decisive in the realization of this project that they require separate acknowledgment. First, my great thanks to Woody Wickham, who believed in the worth of what I was doing almost before I did and invited me to spend a couple of months at the John D. and Catherine T. MacArthur Foundation as a Distinguished Visitor. The inestimable leisure of that time allowed me for the first time to break the bonds of journalism and experience the very different feeling of a book's tempo and demands. The early support of the MacArthur staff that attended my reading of a few of the early pieces was invaluable for ensuring the merit of this work for a larger public. Without Woody's generous offer, I might never have started.

Once started, however, I stalled. It is thanks to Faye Ginsburg that I was able to finish. She first invited me to apply to her Center for Media, Culture and History at New York University, where I was selected as a Rockefeller Fellow in the Humanities during the 1995–96 academic year; after my arrival, she and Fred Myers and their daughter Samantha offered much-needed hospitality that went well beyond the call of duty. In addition to the fellowship's financial support, which again offered a refuge from the deadline rituals of journalism, I was thrilled and inspired by the intellectual comradeship that I encountered at NYU. My thanks to the staff of the Center: Barbara Abrash, Sarah Berry, and Ruth VonGoeler for all their assistance during my stay. During my NYU months and the many months since then, I've also benefited from the friendship and humor of my NYU friends Lisa Duggan and José Muñoz.

Special thanks are due to the band of NYU and NYC friends and colleagues who came out on a blizzarding night to hear my sole public reading of this material. In contrast to my initial reluctance to expose this material, I received back an evening of such extraordinary energy, warmth, and enthusiasm that it propelled me to completion during the long months of solitary work that followed. Thank you, then, to Bambi Schieffelin, Wanda Bershen, Shu-Lea Cheang, Laura Cottingham, Charlayne Haynes, Ernie Larson, Sherry Millner, Yvonne Rainer, Sylvie Thouard, Rose Troche, Robin Vaxal, and others already thanked above or below. Thanks, too, to the other members of the queer reading group that met during my year at NYU in stimulating conversation.

Some important debts have been left to the end. Special thanks to Margaret Pavel for her gifts of sanguine courage and her guidance through the minefields of personal obstacles that so often blocked my way. Thanks to Linda Youtt-Schneider for her early assistance in the same direction. And for material assistance on the preparation of this manuscript and its innumerable details, thanks to my assistant, Elizabeth Sanín, for her intelligent optimism and considerable labors.

Finally, thanks to my partner, Lourdes Portillo, and to my stepsons, Antonio, Karim, and Carlos Scarlata, who shared my life throughout my writing of this text and provided a constant spur and challenge to the work that I do. If ideas must be tested to gather strength, then this text owes its muscles to my family.

And to my birth family, thanks as well, for their part in shaping the mind and spirit on which I rely: to my late parents, Abraham and Lillian Rich, my sister Susan Rich, and my sister Cheryl Koeber and her family, my brother-in-law Douglas and my very excellent nephew Zachary.

Finally, lest I or you ever forget, thanks to the filmmakers. Without their work, there would be no subject and far less inspiration.

Preface:

Jews without

Books

The aim of this book is both modest and grandiose: to bring history, theory, and experience back into better communication with one another, and to marshal the trio into a synthesis that exposes its process and preserves its parts in as rough-edged, disparate, even contradictory a form as possible. To this end, the shape is somewhat unusual, with texts that are more parallel than sequential. In a sense, this form has to do with the particular and peculiar intersections of memory and history and my attempt to integrate the two.

While constructing this volume, I decided that a collection of my own essays, much as I value them, would be inadequate or even irrelevant without some recollection of the times that spawned them, along with the details of the culture — people, places, and experiences — that formed me, their author, into a critic, journalist, and independent thinker. What I've ended up with, then, is a book that insists on the connection between the writer's life and her text, between a writer's text and her era, between an era past and an era present. It's no accident that the volume takes this form, and no accident that I've only been able to complete it now, after the deaths of both my mother and father. Let me explain.

I grew up in Boston in the fifties and sixties, reinvented myself in Chicago in the seventies, then arrived in New York City in the winter of 1980–81. It was there that I made an interesting discovery: people assumed (and eventually told me) that I must be the product of an Upper West Side kind of Jewish family with intellectual parents, a houseful of books, and an education to match. I was perceived, then, as an heir to knowledge—intellectual royalty, as it were—rather than the upstart entrepreneur in the field of learning that I actually was.

In fact, I grew up in a lower-middle-class family, and only just. My parents' parents were all immigrants, his from the shtetls of Shepetovka and hers from one outside of Vilna; my grandparents all landed at Ellis Island in flight from some pogrom or another in typical search of a better life in America. My mother's father was an itinerant housepainter with a ladder over his shoulder who traveled around by foot and streetcar during the Depression in search of work. He fell prey to a combination of lead paint and cigarettes and died of lung cancer when I was five. My father's father was a failed shopkeeper who ran a tiny grocery store, then lost it during the Depression when the customers to whom he extended credit shopped elsewhere with the paltry cash that eventually came their way. He fell victim to stress and bad luck and died of colon cancer before my parents were married. My grandmothers were old-world wives and mothers, cooking gefilte fish and tending the children and worrying: my mother's mother, about us; my father's mother, about herself.

My parents raised themselves up a rung on the class ladder. My father worked his way through Northeastern University, which at that time was a cooperative college geared to working-class students' economic needs; by alternating semesters of school with full-time work, he earned his degree as an engineer. My mother had taken a business course in high school and worked as a bookkeeper until the arrival of children, after which she became a housekeeper, PTA member, Girl Scout troop leader, Hadassah volunteer: a Jewish version of an Ozzie and Harriet mom. When my father hit the wall of space-program cutbacks under Nixon and got laid off—a brutal shock to a middle-aged man with two children in college who'd voted Republican all his life and risen to be Grand Master of his Masonic Lodge—she returned to bookkeeping to get by.

Notions of my class privilege were laughably off-base. My family's house was devoid of culture and learning; that was something that was left to school. The only things I ever saw my parents read were the daily *Boston Herald,* the weekly *Jewish Advocate,* the monthly *Reader's Digest* and *National Geographic,* and once in a while a coffee-table volume on, say, prominent Jews in world history. Literature entered the home exclusively in the form of Reader's Digest Condensed Books. My access to a wider world of literature was composed of equal parts of the following: the Bookmobile's visits to my elementary school; trips across town, once I was a bit older, to the branch library, located on the second floor above a Rexall Drugstore with garish windows filled with color blowups illustrating psoriasis and other skin diseases that could be cured by the products inside; and the regular appearance at home of each new volume of condensed books selected as worthy of my parents' attention by the mysterious staff of *Reader's Digest*.

Yet writing was important to me; in fact, it saved my life. I was devastated by the death of my grandfather. I have no memories of my childhood after his death, no memories at all for several years that have gone undocumented, including my first day of school. My depression must have been intense. But the memories start up again when I enter third grade, where the extraordinary Florence Gorman, the only Jew and the only divorcee among the Irish Catholic spinster schoolteachers of the Harriet A. Baldwin Elementary School, took our class on excursions to the theater. It was she who encouraged me and my best friend Leslie to expand the stories we'd begun to write together in our little office in Leslie's house. We had our own miniature rolltop desk and Underwood typewriter and even a character file of fictive biographies so we wouldn't make mistakes as we extended our fiction series of a boy (!) and his dog and their adventures.

When I graduated from the Baldwin School after the sixth grade, I entered Girls' Latin School, a precursor to today's magnet schools that modeled itself on a Bostonian notion of British public school education and sought to save inner-city girls from the horrors that awaited us without its intervention. There, the much feared English teacher Zabelle Tamizian put me through an education that I retrospectively identify as a paradigmatically feminist one. From her locked glass-windowed cabinet she lent me the bound illustrated works of Alexandre Dumas, editions of *The Three Musketeers* and *The Count of Monte Cristo;* the books of Elizabeth Gaskell, *Cranford* among them; and biographies such as *With a Sword in Her Hand! Biography of a Suffragist*. In other words, she bequeathed to me a world of (male) adventure, (female) socialization, and a clear ideology of equality. Though the school was a rigid and old-fashioned one that taught by rote and governed by intimidation, the teachers believed in the transformative power of education for girls. Their message to us was clear: The road upward was paved with study, the road downward with sex. Read books, apply yourself, stay chaste, and even working-class girls could get into Radcliffe and jump class. But hang out with boys, become a girl of loose virtue, and you'd be barefoot, pregnant, and exiled to the local high school of dead-end horror in a jiffy.

When I was fifteen, the course of my life was drastically altered by my parents' decision to move three-quarters of a mile down the road from

Brighton, where I was part of the Boston Public School system, to slightly suburban Brookline, with its higher social status. Thus did we join the great postwar migration out of the cities to the land of better schools, prosperous synagogues, and Jewish nirvana. (It was a belated move, for economic reasons; my parents' friends had already left the old neighborhood and I lost classmates constantly to the new geographic quadrants of their family aspirations.) After the death of my beloved grandfather, this move turned out to be the next most traumatic event of my young life.

Brookline High School prided itself on modernity: boys and girls mixed together, teachers sometimes were called by their first name, nobody stood when called on or did anything as quaint as "recite" a passage. The school was absolutely dedicated to creative thinking and to the most up-to-date, experimental teaching methods, a veritable laboratory in which the Harvard School of Education could test its theories in practice. From Annette Busse, the English teacher of legendary learning and high standards, I learned how to be a scholar and formed the desire to be a poet, learned how to analyze literature and felt important in the exercise of that power.

I learned lots of things at Brookline High School, but above all, I learned about class. I discovered, for instance, that there were people who lived in houses of two stories that were all theirs. Their houses were nothing like the two-family and three-family dwellings, dubbed triple-deckers or Irish schooners in Boston jargon, that came cozily packed with neighbors above or below and that constituted the lifelong habitat of my parents and grandparents. I learned there were families that had pianos in the living room, where mothers had something called professions and teenage daughters listened to classical music, rode horses, or dressed in John Meyer matching sets of clothing in the fashionable color of the season.

I learned that books weren't actually meant to be condensed, that classical music wasn't the Top 40 of earlier decades as I'd thought, and that there were clothes that never arrived in Filene's Basement (the original basement, not today's modern stores; this was back when women clawed each other over sweaters and stripped right in front of you to try on clothing in the middle of the mob). My first huge fight with my parents transpired around this time, when they chastised me for wasting my babysitting money on the purchase of a book. Why buy a book when you can take it out of the library, ran their reasoning, and why own one permanently when you'd have no use for it again after reading it? Their thrift was a direct assault on my fledgling aspiration. Though my memory of this incident is bruising, I eventually fought back. Within a few years, I scored a triumph of adolescent snobbery: convincing my parents to switch from subscribing to the Reader's Digest Condensed Books to the Book of the Month Club. At least the books came whole. Later still, I delighted in the discovery of Mike Gold's informative book, *Jews without Money,* and hereby adapt its title to describe my own history and family: Jews without books.

Over the years, I've written hundreds of articles but remained steadfastly phobic about writing books. It's only during the final preparation of this volume that I've begun to acknowledge the full impact on this adult writer of that particular upbringing. And to realize that it's no accident that this volume is structured as a sort of intellectual's version of the condensed-book model, updated to accommodate my kind of material.

I don't know what my parents would have thought of this volume. Perhaps its long postponement was strategic. My father dismissed his lack of reading by explaining that books other than his Masonic manuals put him to sleep. My mother, who complained of trouble following most of my writing, nevertheless kept my magazine articles carefully stacked and itemized on a shelf in the living room for easy access, all ready to retrieve for her friends, display for my mother being always the better part of valor. Incredulous and deeply touched, I discovered the collection after her death. Perhaps this volume would have made it onto the coffee table.

Introduction

This book has been prompted by my conviction that the present landscape of feminism and film has been deprived of its own history, substituting a canon of texts for a set of lived experiences long since forgotten, shelved, or denied by those who went through them. For veterans of the early years of the seventies, this void has diminished the sense of accomplishment and importance achieved in that period and has undermined the sense of self-worth that ought to have infused the intervening decades with pride of contribution. For the younger generations that have come of age in the academy over the past two decades, this historical amnesia has canceled out a birthright that would have been helpful in terms of avoiding the repetition of certain errors, learning how to negotiate across difference, and reconciling the personal with the professional — if not always the political. For filmmakers, recalling the past can suggest remedies for the market excesses of the present, even a sense of relief that it wasn't always so.

My subject here is cinefeminism, a term that was sometimes used to describe the broad field of feminism and film that began in the seventies with the flourishing of film festivals and the simultaneous invention of theoretical approaches to classic Hollywood representations of women, eventually expanding to other films as well. It's a discipline that began as a movement, drawing its strength from the political breakthroughs of the women's liberation movement as well as from the intellectual and ideological lessons of the New Left. On the film front, it was fed by the energies of the Nouvelle Vague, Czech New Wave, New Latin American Cinema, and, closer to home, by the activist Newsreel collectives. Some people followed Jean-Luc Godard, some Maya Deren, some Fernando Solanas and Octavio Getino. On the theoretical front, the operative names were Louis Althusser, Umberto Eco, Christian Metz, and Charles Propp, with Chairman Mao and Julio Garcia Espinosa as alternative models.

Over the decades, of course, cinefeminism evolved into something rather different—feminist film theory—with theoretical legitimacy, currency, and prestige. It was one singular contribution that set in motion the sea change of realignment: the appearance in *Screen* magazine in the autumn of 1975 of an article by Laura Mulvey entitled "Visual Pleasure and Narrative Cinema." The thousands of subsequent articles that footnoted Mulvey soon constituted a veritable cottage industry and effectively transformed the nature of the field, once so varied, into one concerned with the controlling power of the male gaze, the fetishization of the female body, and the collusion of narrative cinema with gender subjugation. One of my aims here is to recover a sense of the field before it was entirely captivated by textual analysis, theoreticism, and academic concerns; before it was recuperated into a range of specializations that today often prevent the open communication among women that once had been possible and enriching; before psychoanalysis achieved analytical dominance as the only approach of value; before nostalgia and amnesia competed in our minds to trivialize or ignore a terrain that had inexplicably vanished from history.

Because this volume doubles as a tracking of my own intellectual and personal concerns during a lengthy history, it also encompasses my attempts to interrogate changing interests and shifts in popular culture. I have a method to my madness, and it's called autobiography—certainly not the most obvious or natural choice, but for me the only one possible. Perhaps it's understandable. To house a selection of ephemeral pieces spanning more than a decade in one volume may appear adequate enough reason to undertake publication, at the very least saving people the trouble of hoarding old Xeroxes; not so. For me, a quixotically utopian attempt to recapture history is the only mission that makes this project relevant, or even necessary: I'm driven by the desire to situate these pieces within the historical context of their time, to tease out the thread of circumstance and polemic that gave rise to them in the first place. I want to recapture an era's long-forgotten intellectual trajectories and struggles and try to read them back through the convex reflecting mirror of the present. Only an autobiographical frame could contain what I have to say.

I believe in the utility of memory and the need to learn from history, but there's something else at stake, too: a reminder that the person and the text are linked. I believe it's important for us to understand the kind of evolutionary processes that gave rise to some of the early feminist film texts and the kind of laboratory of speculation within which we were working. Lives, friendships, and quarrels all inform the development of intellectual thought, despite the way in which intellectual histories tend to obscure such connections. It's a shame, really. Bloomsbury Britain, Weimar Germany, Paris *avant la guerre*, Mexico between the wars, Shanghai in the twenties: these fabled sites should not be the only monuments to creative synergy among individuals, ideas, art, and politics. Autobiography has an intrinsic connection to history, just as anecdote does to analysis. All of our lives count: it's all history, if only we remember.

I have labored in the fields of film and video for twenty-five years of my life in one capacity or another, some of which I attempt to chronicle in the pages that follow. Knowledge can be acquired and exhibited in a variety of ways. To read and then to write: that's the standard intellectual route. In the years of my own formation, though, there were many other options. Journals and journeys, conferences and conversations, partying and politicking, going to movies and going to bed. I spent the seventies in Chicago; my friends and colleagues may not have fit the fantasy scene of expatriates living the high life on the Left Bank, but we did conduct our lives with a glamor and style of our own invention, in community if not always in concert, and we developed our ideas hand in hand with our lived experience. As a critic and a film exhibitor, I tried to get audiences for the work I believed in and to combat insularity. I wanted them to understand why they should be interested in the work I was championing and what was at stake in its structures or ideas or images that was relevant to their lives and our shared times.

I was engaged in a process of reinvention of my self in the world, as well, moving from living with a man to living with a woman, functioning as a curator and later as a critic, learning to lecture and teach and, above all, learning the difficult female lesson of how to internalize authority to command respect in the world. It was the era of women's studies departments being founded, histories being recovered, new languages and customs developed, and I was very much in sync with the era.

There was, at that moment and in that place, a constructed sense of shared film culture. It wasn't exactly concrete, but neither am I imagining things. During the writing of this text, I had occasion to spend time in Chicago once again, and found myself constantly encountering individuals whose lives had been marked by that time, stimulated and changed and enriched, and who testify still to its cultural realness.

In the eighties, battle lines shifted and so did lifestyles. Much was gained and much was lost. I left Chicago for New York City on the cusp of the changes: New Year's Day 1981. The kind of feminist world I'd inhabited became less coherent, more effervescent perhaps: it was everywhere, or nowhere. The political world I'd already explored in a long trip through Latin America and a subsequent trip to Cuba, through community-based screenings in Chicago's barrio, and by working on "solidarity" committees changed, too; I kept traveling to Cuba and Latin America, but increasingly I went as a professional committed to cultural exchange and scholarly research.

My interests soon focused on the emerging independent feature sector, institutional politics, popular culture, and the interrelation of works of representation and belief systems. I moved from film exhibition to criticism, theory, administration and funding, teaching, lecturing, always searching for that magical magnetic connection that originally drew me in: the connection between self and public, between idea and practice, between the individual and the social, the ideological and the marketable. To use my favorite subway metaphor, I've always liked the energy of the third rail, which is indispensable to locomotion, not despite but precisely because of its dangerous power. When I began to work as a bureaucrat in a system of public funding, I was able to harness power to my version of the public good, even as all such potential began to diminish under the assault on culture by ravaged state economies and underemployed cold warriors eager for new targets. The New York State Council on the Arts, where I served throughout the eighties, was a beacon of light in the cultural darkness, thanks in no small part to its "Chairman" Kitty Carlisle Hart. Whether funding films by Yvonne Rainer or Sheila McLaughlin, channeling distribution funds to Women Make Movies, or encouraging prestigious venues to show more films made by women and people of color in general, the service occupation of public philanthropy didn't always seem as far away from the old world of upstart polemicist as it might have.

In the nineties, I moved between New York and San Francisco and rededicated myself to writing, lecturing, radio commentary, and even teaching. Popular culture has occupied me more than ever in my capacity as a popular journalist, whether on public radio or the masthead of *Elle* magazine. My field of vision has become more generous. I find myself more willing to accept difference, not just in a theoretical argument but in the countless minor negotiations of daily life in the culture industry. I sincerely believe that the people who read GLQ: *A Journal of Lesbian and Gay Studies* (the academic journal where I have edited film and video reviews) and the people who mob the Sundance Film Festival (where I serve on the selection committee) have something to say to each other. I truly believe that my friends in Mexico City, New York, Columbus, London, and San Francisco have as many commonalities as differences.

At the same time, the striking echoes that show up in today's cultural debates like misplaced detritus of long-past disputes and discoveries have restimulated my desire to reexamine the past. What was uncovered in the world of feminism and film in the seventies, and what was buried? I'm convinced that the texts, events, players, and films of this earlier time can now be differently constructed by nineties' eyes, and I find myself encouraged by the newly insurgent unorthodoxies of a new generation of junior faculty, graduate students, and even the undergraduates that I sometimes teach. In part, the new irreverence is a product of changing academic styles owing a debt to cultural studies and postmodernism. But I think it's equally a legacy of the riot grrrl revolution and its willingness to reclaim some of the terrain that feminism lost in the eighties and early nineties. May film, then, learn from music how to stake out brand-new terrain boldly while gaining, not losing, audience. Negotiations over representation and spectator position can now be reopened with vigor, just as the boundaries can be pushed wider past the limit of the text and its analysis, pushing on to the necessary historical work waiting in the wings and perhaps even the empirical studies that could carry today's theory so much further along than mere glosses on established theoretical positions.

There's a serious need for such reconsiderations. Feminist cultural work has hit an impasse in the nineties, as has a great deal of feminist political work in general. What sprang up in the seventies and was institutionalized in the eighties has been stagnating in the nineties, its vigor bypassed by queer culture, on the one hand, multiculturalism on the other, and cultural studies in general. In countless conversations, a shared malaise has surfaced. Feminist film work has been bypassed by newer intellectual land grabs, paralyzed by the dead ends of its own development, sidelined when it's desperately in need of renovation and revival. (Even the AIDS quilt, after all, gets media attention and financial support that the feminist reclaiming of quilts back in the seventies could never have dared to imagine.) It is my intention that this volume expose enough unexplored routes and forgotten byways of feminist film history, as originally explored by myself and others, that new explorations by a new generation might perhaps jumpstart a feminist film culture, revitalized and retrofit for nineties uses. Also, as the veterans of these experiments and struggles age, it's more important than ever to acknowledge their contributions and valorize the nerve and will that made their interventions possible. Many of the early pioneers are today demoralized or cut off from the film world entirely, yet it's thanks to them that the feminist film world of today—in Hollywood, independent production, or the academy—has been made possible.

In reconstructing my memories and formulating my recollections of this past through which I've lived, there's been a temptation to see every moment as a zeitgeist in the making and to give the impression that my every movement was magically touched by an elixir of historical importance. In truth, any number of women who lived through these times could spin out entirely different narratives in which they appear as central players. And we'd all be right. They were exciting times.

That's part of the reason. In truth, though, I suspect that I blundered into historical moments less regularly than I had the nerve to insist that the events that I was experiencing were in themselves, well, momentous. Everyone can play this game, and everyone should. We'd benefit by the contribution of disparate narratives that could explain a great deal about historical process and about how individual lives intersect with historical movements, both subjectively and materially. The film world could use more histories of the sort that the literary world has always inspired, just as feminism will benefit from more personal narratives of the kind that have long chronicled the Beat movement and the New Left.

Consider these pages, then, an opportunity to revisit a past that's recent enough to be remembered and long gone enough to be memorable. I offer up my own writings and ramblings through the world of feminism and film with the idea that there's something of value here. Though I'd like to think that my original essays can stand the test of time, more pertinently I believe they'll gain much in clarity and implication from their location in this web of personal reflection and tales of origin. Equally important is my wish that the link between the personal and the public, between the woman and her text, be acknowledged. For it is only if such links are rearticulated and reenlisted as a necessary mode of cultural production that feminist writing can reclaim the high ground at a time of increasingly professionalized, parochial, self-absorbed, and deracinated writing.

Prologue.

I Found It

at the

Movies

In 1972, I was having a bit of a career crisis. Today, I'd call it the postgraduation blues, but back then it had already been going on for quite a while and I was sure my whole future was going down the tubes. I'd become disillusioned with poetry and literary analysis almost immediately upon arrival at Yale College, where I'd enrolled after dropping out of Simmons College in a 1968-inspired rebellion. Years later, I realized I'd been accepted at Yale the year that Kingman Brewster became president and expanded their admissions standards to include a wider range of students. Poet, dropout, free spirit, I fit the new profile.

Once at Yale, however, my enthusiasm for the written word encountered considerable challenges. Foremost was the challenge of occupying any physical or creative space at all in a male enclave not entirely happy with its change of status (we were the first class of women to darken the undergraduate college's doors). My adjustment was further complicated by the level of competitive cynicism in the literary circles and the poetry circle's maddening binarism of demure poetesses and macho wannabes. I dropped my Harold Bloom seminar after one session, repelled by his hand-wringing and wailing over which edition of Blake we had to be sure to buy. In Mark Strand's poetry workshop, a long-haired blonde debutante wrote poems about Montego Bay and other places she'd been with Daddy, while Strand himself hung out with my coke-dealer roommate

Steve, whose room in our "commune" he'd borrow as a pad to which he'd bring girls.

My ambitions for myself as a poet quickly diminished. As a girl poet, I was a formalist with very haute standards of poetic style, but in lifestyle I was much more aligned with the boys who declaimed talking-blues verse while zipping up their flies. I was caught in a DMZ between those who cared above all where the line would break and those who didn't care in the least, to use a poetic metaphor both literally and symbolically. It was all too much for me to negotiate.

I never wrote another line of poetry after my first year at Yale, but I took refuge in the archaeology department with Michael Coe and learned photography from my friend Warner Wada. I got involved in politics and demonstrations, went to the rally for the Black Panther trial with Jean Genet speaking in their support, and got tear-gassed by the New Haven police. I trekked down to Yucatan with my boyfriend Allen Turner, rented a hut on a lagoon near Tulum, and ate conch and smoked fish tacos, then photographed transitional cave carvings in Loltun Cave, living in a hammock strung between a stalagmite and a stalactite and watching thousands of bats fly by us at dusk. I went to Palenque, took magic mushrooms, descended inside the pyramid on a full-moon night, and fell under the spell of a guide who swore the Mayan carvings represented UFOS piloted by the ancients, thus explaining their mysterious disappearance as a galactic displacement. Back in New Haven, we lived in our undergraduate version of a commune on a street that ended at a Long Island Sound rocky beach, where we regularly gathered mussels to supplement our meager food budget.

The plan was to enroll in graduate school and fulfill my new ambition of becoming a Meso-American archaeologist—until, that is, my beloved archaeology professor invited me to his country house for a weekend. He and I drank vermouth in the study; his wife, Sophie, who I knew had trained as an archaeologist as well, baked bread and carved up pork chops in the kitchen. Even though he generously and sincerely urged me onward, his archaeologist wife never seemed to leave the kitchen. I couldn't reconcile the gender gap in my favor, couldn't figure out how I could be both an archaeologist and a woman, couldn't even articulate the contradiction for a decade or so, but once again I retreated. I switched my allegiances, forgot about graduate school, bought a camera, and began haunting darkrooms and back alleys with Warner.

My artistic formation was typical of the time for women trying to break out of the mold in prefeminist postadolescence: one summer as an artist's model; several years of hitchhiking around the country, in between

8

which I managed to graduate from college; a lot of time spent reading the fiction of Jack Kerouac and Henry Miller, the poetry of Elizabeth Bishop and W. H. Auden and Charles Olson, formalism vying with hedonism for the upper hand; days spent prowling galleries, soaking up the influences of Vito Acconci, Lee Friedlander, Emmet Gowin, and the other golden boys of the day. Woman as muse was still the operative role. (Luckily for the future of my soul, I was too much of a nerd and a rebel to qualify for any such boy-genius service, despite my penchant for thrift shop hats and forties dresses.) My women friends in art school complained that they couldn't get the professors to pay attention to them. You're not going to become artists, they were told back then, you're just going to have babies.

In my case, as fate would have it, I'd also spent my last semester selling popcorn at the Yale Film Society to pay my rent, screening films at home on a "liberated" projector. I was hooked on movies. Warner was the film society treasurer. By the time I talked him into following graduation with a year in Boston, we had two 16mm projectors between us. We spent the summer of 1972 booking titles, selling tickets, projecting films, hauling bags of free popcorn, and dressing in film-specific period costume as the proud founders and directors of the Woods Hole Community Film Society. Warner drew the posters, I wrote the copy. We negotiated the rental of the Community Hall on Main Street next to the drawbridge ($10 a night or 5 percent of the gross) and drummed up partners with local contacts and automobiles.

We showed mostly Hollywood and European art film classics, repertory style, a different show every night, weekends only. *Touch of Evil, Sansho the Bailiff, Singing in the Rain,* all typical art movie taste of the day. We staged the world premiere of our friend Sally Cruikshank's *Fun on Mars* animation to a soldout house of enthusiasts. We thought we were making history. At the very least, we were acting out the classic "Hey, kids, let's put on a show" story. We had loyal audiences and strategic friendships (anyone who owned a car or truck was eligible, with special status reserved for sailboats).

Life was in the making. Sexual adventuring was part of the game, the common denominator in all these activities, a natural accompaniment to dancing, traveling, drugs, movies, fantasies. For years afterward, I was convinced that "travel" was just a euphemism for "sex," and that this explained the universal enthusiasm for seeing the world. In those years, movies were the sexiest medium, and one's own connection to them — even the relatively remote attachment of putting them up on the screen — conferred a certain aura. Life and theater were, if not interchangeable, at least codependent; fact and fancy could comingle promiscuously without any danger. My big catch was a guy in charge of conducting lab experiments with lobsters; it didn't last long, but for a few days we all ate well. I was working hard at being what was quaintly called in those days a nonconformist, and settled into some combination of post-Beat, quasi-hippie-chick.

Decades later, I've still never quite outgrown my fondness for film exhibition, the magic of announcing an event and then witnessing the mass belief of hundreds of people, lined up outside, ready and willing to pay money to participate. Or the satisfaction of repaying their faith with inspiration, revelation, with the catalyst of movie visions. It didn't make me Bill Graham, but it's kept me in the public sector for years. You could actually change people's lives. Or, at least, think so.

When my friend Warner Wada decided to leave at the end of the summer to study photography at the School of the Art Institute of Chicago, I decided to follow friendship and darkroom access. Why Chicago? We talked each other into it. We read the school's catalogue together, thrilled that Chicago had blues, jazz, and country-western bars, beguiled above all by its twenty-four-hour Mexican restaurants. And lofts, cheap and easy to find in a city that at that time hadn't yet caught on to the idea. I was fed up with the East Coast anyway, tired of New England pretentions, and eager to go rumbling across the Midwest to stake out new territory like some latter-day pioneer. The summer of 1972, then, marked an end to my coming-of-age years. I would leave the East Coast behind, and with it the landscape of my adolescent discoveries, drugs, escapades, to explore the heartland of the country, a place I associated with authenticity.

The following piece traces my adolescent relationship to the movies, predating the angst of 1972 but definitely informing it. I was asked by Lisa Kennedy, then editor of the *Village Voice*'s film section, to contribute something to a special section on sixties movies. With the idea of this book already percolating in my brain, I was eager to revisit my own formation. These musings show quite explicitly what will be implicit in so many of the pieces that follow: from the start, my engagement with film was a social engagement. I wasn't one of those film buffs who sat up bleary-eyed watching late-late-night television and memorizing old Joan Crawford dialogue. Nor was I one of those college nerds who pored over *Variety* every week (though I do that now), able to recognize tech signatures the minute a film's screen credits began to roll. Instead, I was more likely to be sitting in a crowd in the dark, holding my breath in anticipation like the most believing of laypeople or else jumping up to fix the focus.

Film spectatorship for me was a state of life before it was ever a theoretical category. It's that continuum between film as object and film as experience that I seek to keep alive, and that I acknowledge unashamedly here at the very outset. I once characterized a critic of my acquaintance by saying that his view of cinema was like that of a wine connoisseur who'd never seen a vineyard. I was making a statement of despair, not admiration. Film, and today video, remain for me living media that continually redefine their position vis-à-vis audience, medium, critic, fan.[1]

1.

Film in the

Sixties

(1991)

The sixties were the last of the preretro decades, the last time in which it was still possible to live in the moment without worrying that it was actually somebody else's reappropriated moment. The sixties were fundamentally themselves: people lived not only in an absolute sense of present, but in an equally absolute sense of living out a historic present, the "we are making history" approach to contemporaneity.

It was also the last decade in which it was possible to discover the movies, not merely as a medium, but as a primer in how to live, how to love, how to think or smoke or lie. It was in the sixties (and the early seventies as well, because everyone knows that the decades never divide neatly across the cusp anyway) that a whole generation discovered the power of films. There was the sheer force of the medium as newly explored in the American avant-garde. There was the reclaiming of the underbelly of the industry itself, as in the "auteurist" rediscovery of classic Hollywood, the valorization of B movies and the legitimation of Roger Corman. And there was the discovery of a brave new world via what were then called (and still are, by the Academy) "foreign films," meaning the Angry Young Men of Britain, the French New Wave, the Czech products of the Prague Spring, or the scandalous Swedish films that had brought down the censorship barriers once and for all (we thought). Take your pick: it was all about art and meaning, and all about sex. Accept the following musings, then, as my recollection of life in the movies, and vice versa, sixties-style.

The decade started inauspiciously. I was in the seventh grade in 1960 when I walked to the neighborhood movie theater with a classmate, unwarned and unaccompanied, to see *Psycho*. We spent much of the film with our coats over our heads. I didn't take a shower for the next eight years. The experience initiated my lifelong affection for baths and my lifelong aversion to horror movies. It's commonly said that cinema was never the same after *Psycho*, but, girl-child on the verge of puberty, neither was I.

My real relationship to movies started in my high school English class. To understand the context fully, keep in mind that English teachers in that period were consumed by a fearful paranoia regarding film and television. In the popular version of history, Khrushchev banged his shoe at the UN and threatened capitalism with impending extinction in the famous statement of confidence: "We will bury you" (today we know he got the sentence right, but the pronouns wrong). The cold war between book learning and image watching was equally heated, even if carried out in the less flamboyant forums of educational classrooms and halls of higher learning. Throughout the United States, teachers of English literature quaked before their students' new viewing habits. They denounced television as a pernicious influence on young minds and cursed movies as mindless entertainment seducing a generation away from the morally uplifting rigors of reading.

In Annette Busse's class at Brookline High School, however, films were recommended alongside books, and we were expected to improve ourselves by paying attention to both. In adolescent circles in those days, a knowledge of European films was as necessary a badge of sophistication as the ability to quote Jean-Paul Sartre, Thomas Pynchon, or Jack Kerouac. But where to see them? Not public television, that's for sure. Our English class was once trucked over to the headquarters of this new place called WGBH-TV to be the test audience for a program on poet Robert Frost, but we left with our noses in the air, contemptuous of the insipid, low-brow approach to poetry as well as to teenagers. Instead, we frequented the commercial "art" houses that were the mainstays of filmgoing in Boston in the sixties. These theaters were so crucial and inspired such fandom in their patrons all over the United States at that time that Todd McCarthy and Charles Flynn even dedicated a book, *Kings of the Bs,* to Chicago's Clark Theatre (1948–70), paraphrasing as testimonial a line from Edgar G. Ulmer: "It wasn't just a theatre. . . . It was a way of life."

In Boston, film devotion meant chronic attendance at movie theaters like the Brattle, where townies eavesdropped on Harvard boys explaining Bergman films to their dates, or the Charles Street Cinema, where audiences sat shivering in coats and scarves through pre-global-warming New England winters to watch sadistic double bills like *Breathless* and *Les Enfants du Paradis.* The double bills were sadistic not just by virtue of length or climate: one that I still recall paired *Dr. Strangelove* with *One Potato Two Potato,* the two films linked only because the first ended with a madman riding a bomb out of a plane, while the second opened with a bomber in the air buzzing a man and child down on the ground. At the Exeter Theatre, programming philosophy was even quirkier: only English films were shown, as though that were the only universe that mattered. It was a constant diet of *Darling, The Loneliness of the Long-Distance Runner,* and *Morgan!*

Such exposure was good training, of course, not just because Boston was always an anglophile town but because Swinging London was the essence of hip in post-1963 America. In the summer of 1965, when I was sent to stay with my father's family in St. Louis as a belated sixteenth birthday gift, I managed to effect a change from high school egghead to the sort of smooth sophisticate eligible for double dates and riverboat rides, simply because I wore a tennis sweater, spoke in my usual Boston accent, and could effortlessly interpret Richard Lester's *The Knack, and How to Get It,* a briefly emblematic film that had just brought Rita Tushingham to Missouri as the very embodiment of cool. Its director was already famous for putting the Beatles on film the year before. However, its title could just as easily have referred to our motivations for flocking to movies like this. The next year would bring *Blow-Up,* the movie that sent college boys all over the United States shopping for Nikons and for girls who'd take their clothes off in front of one. Could it be any plainer? If you went to British films, you'd learn the slang, the mores, what was euphemistically called the "knack." If you couldn't actually get laid by going to the right movie theater, you could at least learn how other people did. And you'd also, incidentally, notice that there was a new way of cutting film and setting up the camera and creating characters.

As the counterculture heated up, the hip films began to show up in different ways. Two incidents from 1966–67 stand out in my memory. The first was made memorable not by personal experience (my date fell asleep) but historical import: it was 1966, and the Institute of Contemporary Art in Boston was presenting a Warhol "happening" with Nico and the Velvet Underground and a projection of *Chelsea Girls* on multiple screens. We all felt hipper than thou, determined to have the coolest reaction, so I still remember my dismay at overhearing some of the New York camp followers recommending a party . . . in Brookline, the place where my parents had moved, the town I'd just escaped in order to come to "happenings" like this.

The second incident is prominent because it involved a memorable loss, that of my favorite jacket. I was climbing the iron fence surrounding the dormitories of Simmons College to evade curfew when my duffle coat snagged and ripped. My friends and I were on our way to the midnight show (one of the first ever) of "underground" films at a local movie house, where I got my first glimpse of Kenneth Anger's *Scorpio Rising*. We were ecstatic, not particularly because of the sexual politics (homosexuality didn't interest me yet) but because of the color and the music. We were becoming art school brats and discovering that irony was a very modern emotion, yet we weren't so far advanced in years from the songs that Anger was eulogizing and we already knew (from films, if not life) that motorcycles were cool. After all, we already had boyfriends who rode them. The fact that a film like this could only be seen at midnight was taken as further proof of its significance.

Other films were too hot even for movie theaters, and they had to be tracked down at college campuses, progressive churches, or rented halls. It was at a Boston University sit-in that I first saw Robert Nelson's *O Dem Watermelons*. Hard as it may be to imagine for anyone who's ever seen this froth of a film, it was received as a "radical" film that denounced racism, and got hundreds of students (yes, mostly White) singing along in solidarity. Hard to believe, but typical of the times. It was at a new college named Goddard, where we'd hitchhiked to visit our friend Turtle, where a friend and I entered a dining hall packed with students watching Tony Richardson's *The Loved One*, the film that based its advertising campaign on the slogan of having "something to offend everyone." Everyone there laughed, secure in the knowledge that *we* weren't the people the campaign targeted, *we* weren't the puritans who could be offended, *we* were cool.

The bravura of youth combined with the grandiosity of the times: we were convinced that there'd never been anyone like us before, and that the world would never be the same again. Coattailing onto the civil rights movement, we were determined to blast Amerika out of the McCarthy period, small-town provincialism, and cold war lockstep — and into a brave new future. (Remember, back then it was the *Republicans* who couldn't win presidential elections.) The foreign films and the new kind of American films helped a whole generation believe that self-invention was not only a possibility but a certainty.

In the free will versus predestination sweepstakes, all the bets were on free will and the movies were a means to an end. Sometimes, though, they threw a wrench in the works. After all, gender did not yet figure into the picture. I remember walking through Harvard Square after seeing *Une femme est une femme*, despondent and existentially depressed, confessing to a friend over cappuccino in a Cambridge coffeehouse that now I was convinced that I would never be a "real" woman. And though it's true that I never did grow up to be Anna Karina, or anybody else French, I was saved by the times. My friend Ruth Kaplan invited me over to hear someone named Betty Friedan speak to her mother's friends about a new idea regarding women; we sat in the kitchen and watched the working wives react angrily. Another friend lent me someone's circulating copy of Simone de Beauvoir. The women's movement came along in the nick of time to rescue me from enforced femininity.

It seemed, in those days, that we lived our lives in the movies, and vice versa. Everyone was movie-mad, and if they weren't, they just weren't worth knowing. My friend Glenn still remembers the first time he saw *Breathless* and watched, transfixed, as Jean-Paul Belmondo passed a poster of Humphrey Bogart and improvised a Bogie imitation. What a thing to do! It was revelatory, getting this new take on American culture from the French, and I bet he used it on the next girl he approached. My friend Lourdes remembers seeing *Weekend* at the Claremont Theatre, then braving the consequent trauma of returning home over the L.A. freeways. My friend Joan will never forget crowding into the basement of some church in Harvard Square in 1968 to see *The Battle of Algiers*. She was so swept away by the crowd, the solidarity speeches, and — especially — the film's scenes of women smuggling bombs for the independence struggle, that she took off for Algeria as soon as she could. But she arrived post-independence, and found the women's organizations shut down by fundamentalism.

Film was like that. It led you to places you wouldn't otherwise go, whether in your own city, your own mind, or another country altogether. It's my friend Debby, New York City brat that she was, who has multiple memories of films gone awry. One night she went to MOMA to see a particularly vicious Chabrol film: the fight onscreen in the opening minutes was echoed by a simultaneous fistfight in the audience and she was so freaked out by the sleazy Chabrolian mood that, afraid to ride the subway home alone, she had to stay at a friend's. Still in high school, she went to a Rockefeller University auditorium for a Jonas Mekas screening; the projectionist didn't know how to focus the film, the audience balked, and Mekas, enraged, took the stage to reprimand his public, paraphrasing Khrushchev while pointing to Debby and pal: "Their generation will bury you!" Finally, when she and her friend Daryl went to France, she remembers journeying all the way to the town of Nevers—only to realize, shocked, that *Hiroshima Mon Amour* hadn't really been shot there.

As for me, I went to Europe for the first time the summer after I dropped out of college, fully equipped with a student charter flight ticket, a backpack, and a head full of visions from all the movies I'd ever seen. But I ended up ignoring the movie theaters for the streets. I never even got to any Italian films, unless you count the screening in a small town in northern Greece of reels 2, 4, and 6 of Fellini's *Satyricon*. No, the closest I got to the movies was a black-and-white television in a public square in Florence. I was one pair of eyes in that Italian crowd of thousands that watched, transfixed, as a U.S. astronaut landed on the moon.

The time was 1969 and, with one "small step," the sixties would be over. The movies continued, of course, but they were different. They are no longer quite the transformative experience they used to be. American films came of age, Italian films declined, Sweden eventually gave way to Japan as the epitome of cool, and the gender and race politics that the "counterculture" had neglected finally got center stage. I came of age as well. I went back to college and, inspired by a stint selling popcorn at the college film society, I turned my passion into a profession, with all the pros and cons that turn implies. I don't get epiphanies at the movies much these days. Nor, I suspect, do the astronauts on the moon. But I still maintain my tie to the cinema, not just as a subject of analysis or a repository of codes and genres, but as a way to live, a place to connect, a passion worth fighting over. The sixties are long gone, but the heritage, the memories, and the movies linger on.

Prologue.

Hippie Chick

in the

Art World

I n the fall of 1972, I found myself sharing a makeshift loft with my
friend Warner and a whole community of would-be art boys on one
half of the sixth floor of a downtown industrial building in Chicago. The other half was rented by an Indian incense factory, which
one day caught fire and would have burned down the whole place, had
we not interceded and fetched the firemen, running the two blocks to the
firehouse to get them. We became hometown heroes to our landlord and
fellow tenants, but nearly blew our cover: it was the very beginning of Chicago's loft era, living there was illegal, and we were pretending it was just
our working studio. Lacking the carpentry skills of my roommates, I set
up camp, literally, in a parachute that I pitched like a circus tent around a
wooden column in the middle of the space. It was hung inside with flowered cloths, had bed and pillows on the floor and an overall decor that
drew its inspiration half from my idea of a New Orleans bordello, half
from the better-known aesthetic of the seventies crash pad.

The whole loft was fantastical: we invented it much as we were inventing our lives. There were dinner parties by candlelight, which were served
on the Oriental-carpet-covered floor of the freight elevator as we took
turns pulling the manually powered ropes that hauled us up and down in
our vertical imitation of a cruise line. We had shining copper radiators,
transformed by purloined paint from the metallic paint company that did

business upstairs but conveniently stored its paints in the basement, thus accessing a fortune in pigment to be splashed luxuriously over the antiquated delivery system of our inadequate hand-shoveled coal furnace (no heat on weekends or evenings). The school's graduate division would use our loft for its periodic student bashes, thereby allowing us to meet our rent payments and hold onto the place, which in the process witnessed performances by most of Chicago's blues legends in the two years of our residence.

Between alternating jobs as a bicycle messenger, bookstore clerk, and ad agency secretary, I began to work nights running the box office for the Film Center then getting underway at the Art Institute. It was an auspicious moment, precisely when the first round of National Endowment for the Arts grants started to create the regional film centers that, twenty years down the road, became a whole alternative network of film and video exhibition. The reason for the start of subsidized exhibition has long been forgotten. At that time, the art cinemas that had long provided European film and auteurist retros for a cineaste public were fast disappearing, as their dedicated and independent managers proved no match for the profits that would flow to property owners who converted their houses to pornography. How ironic that the freedoms won by late-sixties censorship victories in the courts and by lifestyle shifts coincided to produce an unintended result: the loss of choice in the marketplace of the silver screen as the commercial engine of porn usurped the traditional place of art. The NEA's start-up of nonprofit screens was a crucial intervention that maintained a place for quality work in those dark years when theatrical releases were unimaginable for an independent filmmaker.

Once Warner and I recovered from our disappointment at not being able to create our own film society at the school, we lost no time in signing onto the new game in town, run by a woman named Camille Cook, who had just received one of the first NEA grants to start up the Film Center. She had run an experimental film series at the local museum and soon enlisted our help in this new venture. I sold tickets and typed programs, Warner staffed the projection booth, and finally Camille got a grant from the Illinois Arts Council and hired me on as her full-time assistant. There I received an amazing apprenticeship, on-the-job training of the highest order, reading every film magazine that came into the office and meeting every filmmaker. I owe Camille my start in this profession. On weekends, I'd sneak into the darkrooms and print my images of Chicago's industrial netherlands explored daytimes on my bike, or flash photos of my friends' nightlife, explored the rest of the time. It was a limbo time in photography, halfway between the Diane Arbus of the past and the Nan

Goldin of the future, addictive and seductive but lacking the excitement that movies held in the seventies.

Somehow my youthful combination of lifestyle and real estate made me the ideal candidate to host the school's party for Carolee Schneemann, the filmmaker who was coming to the Art Institute to show her work that winter, and I was duly approached and eagerly agreed. Schneemann had recently sailed back from years in Europe with Anthony McCall, then her young lover, in tow; now she was coming to town with her legendary film, *Fuses*. The event was my introduction to Chicago art society—and to radical feminism, early seventies style.

No sooner had the screening begun than the tension in the Art Institute of Chicago's 400-seat auditorium became palpable. This was no small, cozy "womyn's" screening. This was a big event, promoted and antici- pated, claiming one woman's sexuality up there on the big screen. Is there any way to convey the sense of risk and courage that accompanied those early screenings, back when scarcely any films by women had been seen, received, or apprehended as such? Consciousness-raising groups had pro- liferated all over Chicago, women's liberation had already exploded. And now there stood Carolee Schneemann, survivor of years of patronizing by the avant-garde boys' club, heir to a new era: she was about to be savaged by the girls.

There was trouble before the screening even finished. One audience member assailed Carolee over why a *man* was projecting, instead of a sis- ter. To this day, Warner remembers that Carolee stood up for him: he's the projectionist here, she answered, and he's *good*. Then, her defense over and the vibes in the house audibly worsening, Carolee locked herself into the projection booth with Warner, the film, and a bottle of vodka, await- ing the fury to come. (She once confessed to me that things got so bad later in the decade that she began using the cover of darkness to sneak out of her own screenings, on hands and knees, while the show was still in progress and the audience verbally hostile.)

The lights came up and the accusations began. Think back to the years prior to the feminist reclamation of pornography. The only models for open female sexuality in the early seventies were the boyfuck orgies of hippie culture, the Living Theatre gangbang model, the porn movies to which all cool girls had to accompany their boyfriends, and the great crossover film of the time, *Emmanuelle* (my favorite for the scene in which Emmanuelle's pants are cut back to shorts by the sexy archaeologist, but still, that's not saying much for the world of sexual politics). Despite the absence of sex-positive images, there was plenty of renegotiation going on at a theoretical level. Two years before, in 1970, Shulamith Firestone published *The Dialectics of Sex* and Anne Koedt published "The Myth of the Vaginal Orgasm" in Leslie B. Tanner's landmark anthology, *Voices from Women's Liberation.* Old tropes were being debunked but not yet reclaimed or remystified. Penetration, needless to say, was up for debate as a politically correct sexual practice (still is, today, in the Dworkin universe) and heterosexuality itself was a bit on the defensive. Intercourse was believed by some to enforce, automatically, a position of subservience for women.

That night, the sex cops were out in force and were outraged by what was, after all, a "hippie" movie, celebrating sex as Dionysian elixir, a luxurious connection back to nature and the pantheism of sensuality. I still remember the attack on poor Carolee for giving head to her by-then exboyfriend up there on the screen. The practice was ruled subservient and antifeminist. A woman, any woman, performing a blowjob, bigger than life, on film yet, was *not* acceptable. (Back then, issues of consent were not paramount; at least Schneemann would have scored a passing grade on that one.) The fact that Carolee was simultaneously "actor" and director was lost on a crowd not notable for its grasp of issues of representation — a crowd still, to this day, not noted for any ability to distinguish between filmic acts of representation and the enactment of practices offscreen. Never mind that the film had been shot with an old hand-wound Bolex, which meant that she'd had to jump up *every thirty seconds* to wind the damn thing, in between stage managing the sex and enacting it!

In retrospect, the event was probably an early public expression, at least in part, of the developing hetero-lesbian splits within the women's movements of the time, but I'm afraid I was too much of a novice to notice such things. I did learn what a Stalinist show trial must have felt like, though I didn't yet know its name.

What I do remember is that there was a definite artist-audience split. Back at the loft afterward, the artists bonded with Carolee over her rejection by a philistine public, signing on to a typical seventies artistic vanguardism that still rears its ugly head in the art world of the nineties. Not that they didn't have a point. It was old-fashioned political correctness, of course, back when the word was an in-house joke and movements tried to police themselves for ideological excess as well as deficiency. Neither an artist nor a radical feminist, I was curious about both sides of the debate, unclear as to sources for these positions, eager to figure it out in between playing hostess.

What had most outraged me was the censorious puritanism of the film audience, particularly given the bohemianism still valorized in my own circles and enacted in my own life. That same winter, my loftmates and I threw a famous party, the February Fete-a-Tete, which attracted hundreds of revelers, from drag queens to art collectors to members of the Joffrey Ballet, and where the refreshments had included LSD punch and a tank of nitrous oxide. Everyone brought food or drugs. The invitations, after all, had specified "Ruby sez: bring something to put in someone else's mouth." We'd had caviar and cognac; people had taken the assignment seriously. I met Gunner Piotter, my future boyfriend, there. I was on door duty when he arrived in skintight silver lamé and a red velvet cape. In my capacity as operator of the building's old wrought iron elevator (which is to say that it was my shift at the time), I descended through the layers of color created by our installing blue, red, and yellow lightbulbs on every floor; I was dressed all in white with rhinestones and bluebirds pasted onto my suit, my shoes painted pink, and a wreath of silk roses in my hair. This was not a girl who was going to sign on to repression, whatever the ideological imperative. I was having way too much fun.

Looking back on this period, life was a constant feast ready for the taking. In my messenger days, I'd warmed up at the Jazz Record Mart, where Jim and Howard would feed me coffee laced with scotch and teach me the ropes. I knew every jazz and blues bar in town: the tacky West Side joint with a dog leash across the door; the Jazz Showcase, where you could sit at the bar and hear Sonny Rollins; the Quiet Knight, where I'd pay homage to Betty Carter. I knew the Polish clubs with two-accordion bands and bottles of vodka on the tables and the after-hours hillbilly bars where customers came to drink when the other places closed. And those weren't the only shows in town. Our loft was located in the hub of the seventies gay bar scene, a golden triangle formed by the Bistro, the Gold Coast, and the Baton. I once went in semi drag disguise to the Gold Coast with my male pals, just to check out its S/M scene. For entertainment, Warner and Jim would sometimes take the pickup truck and a six-pack into the parking lot on a summer evening to watch the drag queens get dressed and made up, a free show visible through the open backstage door. Disco, leather, and drag, all within two minutes of our front door. And PQ's, one of the early gender-bending bars, just another block down.

The objections of the Art Institute's radical feminist audience had little relevance for this scene. To borrow a phrase that a friend coined years later for a different occasion: there were Party girls and there were party girls. Looking back today at the radical feminist ideology of the seventies can be a humbling experience. It's hard to remember the rules. Why was it, again, that we weren't supposed to shave our legs? (I once asked the writer and activist Ann Snitow to remind me. She said it was because women and men were supposed to be alike, so women shouldn't have to work so hard to make themselves artificially smooth just to distinguish themselves from the male gender. Uh-huh. Also, hair was very sexualized then: men grew theirs long to be attractive, so did women; men grew beards, and women bearded their legs. Or something like that. Mediterranean cultures knew hair was sexy: that's why women left the hair on their legs to drive men wild, or at least we thought so. That's why we didn't shave under our arms, either.) By the mid-eighties, I'd forgotten these formerly convincing arguments. Passing by a shop that did waxing one day with my then-girlfriend, we whimsically decided to go in and put an end, for no apparent reason, to a decade of ideological attachment.

Meanwhile, I was learning the history of the so-called New American Cinema in Chicago. What was at stake was sex, on the one hand, and art, on the other. I saw the audience attack on *Fuses* as a denial of the role of the artist (destined to be a recurring theme, culturally speaking, in the politics of the next two decades). Carolee Schneemann, then and now, was perfectly capable of defending herself. I remember some kind of talk about film and artistic expression, nature and culture, what today Schneemann calls "a counter-thrust against the mythic": something about the wellspring of female power, declared years before Camille Paglia got her reputation for saying things like that.

The next year, when I helped organize the city's first women's film festival, I was determined to validate Schneemann and her work. My allies would strategize over double bourbons about how we were going to get our tastes to prevail in the nefarious politics of collective decision making. Weeks of deal brokering later, a place for *Fuses* was indeed secured.

I would see Carolee Schneemann several times after that initial encounter, most immediately a few months later, when I journeyed to Buffalo, New York, for a conference on women and film. By then she was integrating performance into her film screenings. Receiving to her horror an early-morning slot for her show, she arrived in the chemistry-lecture auditorium in her pyjamas and proceeded to lie, dozing, on the demo table beneath the screen, the mark of the auteur rendered as literal figuration, the filmmaker's body blocking the projection beam to cast its silhouette, a concrete presence superimposed over the ephemeral images. She was a welcome antidote to the dour conference proceedings unwinding in the midst of a deserted state university campus during semester break.

Schneemann's relationship with Anthony McCall broke up soon after her beloved cat Kitsch died and she began to travel with "Kitsch's Last Meal." In 1975, she presented her most legendary performance, "Interior Scroll," in which she read aloud from a long text that she pulled slowly out of her vagina. The text that she read contained a harsh critique of her own work by a "male structuralist filmmaker" who had damned her with faint praise: "we are fond of you / you are charming / but don't ask us / to look at your films / we cannot / there are certain films / we cannot look at / the personal clutter / the persistence of feelings / the hand-touch sensibility / the diaristic indulgence / the painterly mess / the dense gestalt / the primitive techniques."[1] (Years later, Schneemann confided to me that although the remarks were attributed to a fictional male voice in her piece, in reality, they were taken from Annette Michelson's explanation of why she wouldn't watch her films.) Schneemann insisted on keeping her body at the center of her work, whatever the cost, which inevitably was great, given the inhospitable moment she was physically, literally, occupying. By the mid-seventies, she was able to write about the earlier period, "I felt quite alone in my insistence on the integrity of my own sexuality and creativity."[2]

By now, Carolee Schneemann has had a major career as a video and performance artist, outlasting the relevance of all the male filmmakers who disparaged her and marginalized her work during their formalist heyday. Her influence is particularly strong on today's generation of women performance artists who, in reclaiming sexuality and the body as fit stages from which to address an audience, have also reclaimed Schneemann as a contemporary way ahead of her time. She's enjoying her acceptance today in the "magic dyke" world and its renegotiated terrain of female sexuality. In the fall of 1996, the New Museum of Contemporary Art in New York City presented the first museum retrospective of her work as a filmmaker, painter, and performance and installation artist, "Up to and Including Her Limits." It was in this same period that Schneemann was diagnosed with breast cancer, a diagnosis which she has taken on with the same spirit of courage and resistance that has so long characterized her work. Not only has she fought back with alternative therapies, but she has used the breast cancer as the basis for immensely powerful installation and video pieces.

In the fall of 1992, nearly twenty years after her first showing there, Schneemann returned to Chicago to show *Fuses* again, this time to a packed house of attentive and admiring fans at the Randolph Street Gallery. She had just finished regaling the audience with tales of how hard it had been to borrow Bolexes from Stan Brakhage, Stan Vanderbeek, and Ken Jacobs back those many years ago, recalling how reluctant they'd been to place their "tools" in the hands of a woman. It was then that a middle-aged man, probably a veteran New American Cinema camp follower, asked, "What about Stan Brakhage?" This was too much past-life immersion for Schneemann, who refused to answer, begging instead for another question. This one came from a young woman of the nineties, puzzled by the question: "Who was he?" The laughter that followed set history straight.

The following piece on *Fuses* represents my first published writing on film and is excerpted from a much longer piece in the Films by Women/ Chicago '74 catalogue, "The Personal Film," that described independent women's cinema. It's significant to me for two reasons: first, because it exposes my primal recognition of the conflict between art and politics and, second, because it's my first championing of the virtues of independent cinema in the cultural marketplace. A paradigmatic, if sketchy, debut.

2.

Carolee

Schneemann's

Fuses

(1974)

For some reason, this film is treated as a curiosity instead of a classic and has never really received the recognition that by now should be old hat. Several very complicated taboos work against it. Artistic distance, for one. It's an old tradition that the artist must keep a proper distance from her art or compromise its validity; though the events of the sixties dented this theory, it still endures and militates against *Fuses*. For the filmmaker had the nerve, brilliance, or bad taste (depending on your point of view) to star herself in this exploration of sexuality, her camera stationed in front of the bed while she and her lover, James Tenney, made love. It's an artistic risk, to be sure, and the mark of its success is the film's power of enchantment.

Because *Fuses* uses a vocabulary of images shared by pornography, that whole Pandora's box of moral-artistic fever has also come to plague the film. In fact, Schneemann's film and pornography are fundamentally opposite. Pornography is an anti-emotional medium, in content and intent, and its lack of emotion renders it ineffective for women. Its absence of sensuality is so contrary to female eroticism that pornography becomes, in fact, antisexual. Schneemann's film, by contrast, is devastatingly erotic, transcending the surfaces of sex to communicate its true spirit, its meaning as an activity for herself and, quite accurately, for women in general. Significantly, Schneemann conceives the film as shot through the eyes of her cat—the impassive observer whose view of human sexuality is free of voyeurism and ignorant of morality. In her attempt to reproduce the whole visual and tactile experience of lovemaking as a subjective phenomenon, Schneemann spent some three years marking on the film, baking it in the oven, even hanging it out the window during rainstorms on the off chance it might be struck by lightning. Much as human beings carry the physical traces of their experiences, so this film testifies to what it has been through and communicates the spirit of its maker. The red heat baked into the emulsion suffuses the film, a concrete emblem of erotic power.

Carolee Schneemann has made another film, *Plumb Line;* organized intermedia events (in the late sixties) that were multisensory explorations of human relations; and has written a book, *Parts of a Body House.* She lives in New York with her seventeen-year-old cat; she is a constant reminder of the excitement of the creative process and of the joy and pain attached to being a woman and an artist.

Prologue.

Angst and Joy

on the Women's

Film Festival

Circuit

Today, when women routinely produce films — not only "personal" works but documentaries and fiction as well, both short and feature-length, in great quantity (though always with the inequity of scale imposed by the film industry's resistance to any real incorporation of women at the top of the hierarchy: director, executive producer, studio head) — it's an effort to recall that once, not so terribly long ago, there was nothing at all routine about women setting out to make or exhibit films.

Back then, organizing a women's film festival was first and foremost a research project. Such festivals weren't a "ghetto" for women's film, to which individual women or their distributors could decide whether or not to submit their work, calculating market odds to determine if a booking would help or harm mainstream prospects. Instead, they were the only chance, like those signs for gas before crossing the desert — in this case, emerging from a century-long desert. Far from the marketplace, cabals of programmers were volunteering time and energy and literally rescuing films from a life on the shelf: they were dusting off the cans to show women's work for the first time in months, years, decades, *ever*. Women wrote one another around the world, passing on tips of filmmakers rediscovered or long-lost prints reclaimed. The festivals were a secular worshiper's mystical occasion. No wonder an air of expectation and momentum hung over them.

At the same time, they were politically instrumental in their very essence. The new Project on the Status and Education of Women of the Association of American Colleges issued *Women and Film: A Resource Handbook* in 1972, explaining:

> Concern for the education of women is growing across the country. Institutions are increasingly using a variety of materials to focus on this issue. The medium of film is rapidly becoming one of the most common methods. In fact, during the past several years there has been an increasing interest on campus in films about women. Film festivals about women are becoming commonplace. Increasingly, Women's Studies courses, as well as courses in history and the social sciences, are using films to study and to demonstrate a wide variety of issues — the history of the women's movement, the socialization of women and men, sex-role stereotypes, the physical and mental health of both sexes, etc.[1]

The first big women's film festivals in North America were held in New York City (1972) and Toronto (1973). Instant success made for an immediate trend. Here was the public face of feminism. Here was proof positive that women were capable of something big, had made great films, and then — due to sheer sexist injustice — had been denied recognition, relegated instead to obscurity, early retirement, and the withdrawal of backing. The festivals had a shared rhetoric that carried the message of the day. Often the statements were collectively written, reflecting the organizational style of the festivals themselves. Everything was dead serious: there was a point to be made. These festivals weren't being presented only for the fun of it. They had a mission.

Special issues of magazines began to be published focusing on the "women's film" phenomenon. One of the best was the 1972 issue of *Take One,* a now-defunct Canadian film magazine of considerable influence in its time. Kay Armatage (today a programmer for the Toronto International Film Festival and a professor) and Phyllis Platt were the coeditors. In addition to the kind of historical recuperation that was de rigueur, they sought out a variety of opinions, however transgressive, from older as well as younger generations. Anita Loos wrote them a note wishing them luck, but admitting: "Throughout my career, women have done me much more dirt than men. I just find them tiresome, if not vicious. So I don't think you'll find me any help for your project."[2] And Shirley Clarke, interviewed by Susan Rice, was even less encouraging:

> I have yet to receive a piece of women's lib literature. So does [*sic*] Viva. So does every woman I know who has really done anything.

I mean, the movement seems to be made up of people who, for the most part, haven't done anything. You can cop a career any way you want. It's a valid thing, I suppose, copping a career. Now everything they say I totally agree with. But their style and manner is boring and unattractive. . . . That's some kind of snobbism, but I cringe to think of identifying with them. . . . The chauvinism of a Women's Film Festival is so unbearable. I mean, you're talking about jealousy. Here are these poor chicks. . . . I really don't know what they expect to accomplish. I'm not sure that pulling all these films together makes any statement but a sour grapes one.[3]

Yes, it was a different time then, with significant intergenerational hostilities. For a younger generation just emerging from a sixties countercultural framework, women's film festivals were experimental laboratories, producing a new feminist cinematic consciousness while simultaneously putting into practice the political commitment behind the activity. Every planning process was inevitably a political process as well. Debates took place on everything from programming choices to day care accommodations to ticket pricing. Every decision was ideologically charged. Here, for instance, is the *Handbook* suggestion for establishing parameters:

Film festivals focusing on women are being held on many campuses across the country—from New York to Minnesota to California. Although there are many and diverse reasons for holding such a festival, it might be helpful to consider some of the following questions in organizing a festival of films concerning women: What are the goals of the festival? What are the criteria for selecting films? Will the festival revolve around a central theme? . . . What audiences do you wish to attract—18–22-year-old students, continuing education students, graduate students, faculty, administrators, secretaries, other staff, women/men, community members, minority members, high school students and teachers, etc.?[4]

No lack of questions. Today, of course, there's no lack of recognition of just how much times have changed and mutated, far away from the assumed activism of this period. Such rhetoric today would be unthinkable in the context of a program of films. Yet the groups planning the women's film festivals were hardly party formations: they were broad coalitions, mixing contradictory communities and constituencies in a volatile combination. There was lots of disagreement and a bit of consensus, along with inevitable coups, resignations, and takeovers. That was the tenor of the times.

For an instant replay of the festival mind-set, there's no quicker access than the catalogues published to accompany the screenings. Festival committees were full of missionary zeal, situating their exhibition projects with unerring precision within the context of the larger feminist organizing project that they were eager to join, sharing their intentions via the printed page with their friends and enemies, local audiences, and international colleagues. Happily, these texts are still available, making a convincing case for difference between our moment today and the provisional ideological moment occupied by these festivals. Some flashbacks, then, to the early seventies:

> Thematically and technically, simple and personal styles mark a trend towards the humanizing of the camera eye. Close friends, relatives, and admired acquaintances of the filmmaker often become the characters of the films, and besides acknowledging the mechanics of film production, these films show us that filmmaking is a human process. The relationships between the people working on the film and the people on the screen are neither mysterious, objectifying, nor hierarchical.[5]

Or:

> Times have changed. The meaning of the women's film has changed too; it has come to reflect a new assumption — that the films that articulate the experiences of women with the greatest fidelity and clarity are those films made by women. In consequence, a newly engendered consciousness of women's art prompts us to examine our roots. . . . We are finally able to view women who transcend the restricted model that a male establishment deemed "feminine." The characterization of women in these films comments on conventional values and norms by negating, reversing and transforming the stereotypical portraits of women.[6]

And:

> Many of the films we considered, and some we selected, have won prizes in this or that competition, including Cannes. Being unimpressed with the competitive mentality, this was never a criteria [sic] for selection, and we have excluded mentioning such in the programme notes. We assume every woman and man seeing these films to be capable of forming their own opinion.[7]

Plus:

> The questions this kind of event should raise cannot be confined to a mere enumeration of women's achievements together with a plea

for greater opportunities within the film industry. The central issues centre around how far women directors have presented a critique of their position in society, or alternatively how far they have merely reflected dominant ideology.[8]

And finally:

> This [video] is a new medium with women working towards evolving a new style and aesthetics without having to surmount the traditions and style of a male-dominated medium such as film. Video is being used as a vehicle for social change — using it as a feed-back tool for consciousness-raising groups, women with marriage and family problems. Imagine taping your family's evening meal and watching it the night after. . . . Get access!! You can make your own television!![9]

Everyone was mad to have a women's film festival in their city, too. Philadelphia, Washington, Iowa City, and others followed. But Chicago? Events may have been cheaper to stage then, but grants and philanthropy were less developed, and money wasn't easy to come by. I was just settling into my work at the Film Center of the School of the Art Institute, where I'd now been working for nearly a year. My relationship to feminism was still marginal. I had tried going to one of the women's consciousness-raising groups formed by art students at the school, but I didn't land a good group (or perhaps they didn't land a good me). I couldn't get with the program and lasted only one meeting. Intent on expanding my horizons, though, I was reading everything I could find and meeting everyone I could manage, but film won out over feminism as my priority.

I was a curator-in-the-making who would never have presumed to stage a women's film festival if not for a fortuitous phone call from the *Chicago Tribune*'s film critic, Gene Siskel, just back from two weeks of Army Reserve duty in Washington, D.C. While there, he'd checked out a women's film festival and was staggered by what he saw: a scene in Mireille Dansereau's *Dream Life* that showed a teenage pickup scene from the girl's point of view instead of the boy's. Bowled over by the difference a woman behind the camera could make, he'd filed a column for the *Tribune* announcing that "it gave me an appetite for more films conceived and shot from the female point of view. Not because they necessarily would be better, but because they would be different." Then he filed a second column in which he called for a women's film festival in Chicago. He phoned the two friends he thought could make it happen — me and Patricia Erens, then a grad student at Northwestern and a member of the Film Center's advisory committee — and suggested we organize a women's film festival. I remember telling him, "Oh no, we can't do it alone, we'll have to form a collective."

So we did. The first meeting was held at the *Tribune* on December 6, 1973. Gene Siskel was there. "I tried to lead a discussion and was lucky to escape with my chauvinism in one piece," he later wrote. "The women seized control."

So began months of ecstasies and nightmares of the sort that characterized most women's festivals in that period. Patricia and I went to work with Laura Mulvey (who was in Chicago for the programming phase, bringing expertise fresh from the Edinburgh women's film event), Julia Lesage (then an assistant professor at the University of Illinois at Chicago), Virginia Wright Wexman (also at the University of Illinois at Chicago, where she's now a full professor), and a whole pseudo-collective of local women of varying skills and abilities. This uncontrollably anarchic group was nominally directed by lone coordinator Laurel Ross, who valiantly tried to hold the whole thing together in our donated office in the face of constant rifts and conflicting demands. The *Tribune,* faithful to Siskel's promise, lent its full support to the event: not just an office in the newspaper's faux-Gothic downtown bastion, but a real budget, Laurel's salary, the services of its art department, and free ads daily for the duration of the festival.

What to show? Certain mandates were so clear as to be virtually formulaic. Though organizing structures were anarchic and political positions communicated mostly by osmosis, there was an extraordinary degree of consistency among the women's film festivals; there had to be old films by previously unknown women directors, the avant-garde represented alongside documentary and Hollywood or art film narratives, local filmmakers and video-makers showcased, contemporary figures brought to town to speak about their films, and panels or workshops organized to involve the public. Yet the results did not go uncriticized, even though the model has stuck for years. Consider, for example, the complaint by my friend Joan Braderman (at that time, a graduate student at New York University studying with Annette Michelson, who was then film editor of *Artforum*):

> despite the festival's contribution to that rediscovery of creative female models, it might well have been presented without that misguided desire to assign a "female" sensibility to works which are absolutely disparate since they emerge from different economic and artistic contexts. It might also have been conducted according to what we've learned about male structures out of that political necessity—without that same damned (male) authority structure.

Exuberant as we may have been to see films day after day that were made by members of our sex, I assure you that it boggles the mind to see a film by Maya Deren and a film by Lotte Reiniger and a film by the women of San Francisco Newsreel, all in one sitting. . . . but since normal theatrical screening conditions involve the showing of a feature and a short, so did our women's festival. It failed to make any gestures to critical discrimination or even historical differentiation.[10]

Whatever the politics of the organizing or the rhetoric of the program books, the festivals were always rigorously inclusive ("anticensorship," as we would say today) at the level of programming: virtually anything made by a woman could be included and, in the early days, was. The desire for variety and eclecticism overwhelmed any impulse to discriminate at the level of ideology. Shirley Clarke, for example, had her career revived by the women's festival circuit despite her scorn for its goals and methods. Similarly, Stephanie Rothman's films, originally produced in the guise of "exploitation" movies, found a new audience and unforeseen critical approval in the new festival context. Cormanesque in their rock-bottom budgets and soft-core plots, Rothman films like *Terminal Island* were wonderful displays of female power run amuck; despite the guys-get-down tone of the genre, she managed to insert enough signature elements of subversive pleasure or aesthetic spin to please the film festival audiences that never caught them at the drive-in. The charge of creating an unprecedented space for women's cinema in both the imagination and the movie palace led to this philosophy of inclusion; it was only later, with academic careers at stake, that aesthetic lines of demarcation would be drawn and enforced.

Political lines were murky and ill-defined, despite all the rhetoric, at the time of these early festivals. Anyway, films could be significant for lots of different reasons, especially when assuming heterogeneous audiences and using a major urban newspaper to attract them. With the *Tribune*'s help, our outreach went beyond anything we could have imagined, for better and worse. We were being funded not by the paper's editorial side (despite Siskel's instigation) but by its marketing department, which, in a wonderful display of what has always made capitalism strong, saw us as its chance to change the paper's stodgy Republican image and attract a new generation of readers, scoring a potential upset in the city's eternal circulation wars. Their ranks, though, comprised lots of very old-fashioned newspaper men. Not the most natural constituency, let alone collaborators, for a women's film festival. Determined that we hold our own, I took to smoking cigars at meetings with them and downing shots at the Billy Goat, the legendary newspaperman's bar located under Michigan Avenue, alongside the *Sun-Times* and *Tribune* buildings. Meanwhile, the publicity office sent squads of us out to radio and TV talk shows to plug the event. Virginia Wright Wexman was nervous about her ability to articulate the festival's complex details on her assigned talk show; she prepared extensively so she'd have facts and figures at her command if stage fright set in. When the on-air light flashed, though, the previously affable host turned to her and announced: "I bet I can guess your age and weight on the first try." Her shock paralyzed her effectively for the rest of the show. So much for mainstream promotion!

Films held significance for us for lots of different reasons. Sometimes their significance couldn't even be foretold until the audience was given a chance to react. So it was with the Films by Women/Chicago '74 festival and its inclusion of the early Leni Riefenstahl classic, *The Blue Light*. We didn't want to show a "Nazi" film, certainly didn't want to offer any support to Nazism. Yet we were cognizant of the irony that made Riefenstahl probably the best-known and most critically recognized of all the women filmmakers we were showcasing. And we wanted to see for ourselves what all the fuss was about: in 1974, there were few university film departments, and the independent exhibition sector was in the early stages of construction. In point of fact, none of us had ever *seen* most of the films we were presenting.

We felt Riefenstahl was an interesting case, to see and discuss, and never saw ourselves as presenting any species of "role model" movies anyway — though, in truth, *The Blue Light*'s fascination with Riefenstahl herself as a wild mountain girl scaling high peaks actually fit rather well the amazon fantasies of the seventies. All the women's film festivals were showing her work, right alongside other historical figures such as Olga Preobrajenskaia, the early Soviet director who had documented women's lives at the start of Communism. (We had programmed her *Peasant Women of Ryazin,* which Gene Siskel came to my loft to see — on my old 16mm projector that survived Woods Hole duty to facilitate this press screening — and to praise the next day in the *Tribune* in a review that packed the house for a forty-seven-year-old black-and-white silent film.) If there was a problem with the inclusion of a Riefenstahl film under this vast umbrella of worldwide women's cinema, we didn't know it — yet. So much for naïveté.

Momentous decisions are sometimes made by accident. A case in point was the festival's invitation to Leni Riefenstahl to come to Chicago in person for the screening of her film. Tom Luddy (then head of the Pacific Film Archive and one of the directors of the new Telluride Film Festival) was bringing Riefenstahl over from Germany to attend the Colorado event; he called my boss Camille Cook to offer a Chicago stop. Tom was probably looking for someone to share the financial burden of her transatlantic ticket; this was nothing new, for the Film Center had shared programs with the PFA before, and Tom was famous for hustling up cosponsors for his shows. Alas, the invitation to Riefenstahl changed what had been a matter of inclusion into a perception of honor.

All hell broke loose. The festival committee itself split internally. Wexman recalls with horror the incendiary meeting at which she experienced the novelty of having the insult "bourgeois" hurled at her. Other groups of women in the city, previously uninvolved with the festival, made demands and threatened pickets. Finally, the decision was taken out of our hands: Riefenstahl, concerned as ever to keep her hands "clean," avoided participation in any event auguring trouble; she canceled. The screening went on as scheduled, drawing a handful of pickets and the biggest sellout crowds of the entire festival.

In the end, the invitation to Riefenstahl attracted a kind of national attention that the festival itself never did, despite its local success and an audience of 10,000 in two weeks (thanks in large part to the labor-intensive, grassroots promotion that augmented the *Tribune* clout). The following winter, Susan Sontag penned her thoughts on the aesthetics of fascism in "Leni Riefenstahl and Fascism," a review of Riefenstahl's new photo book *The Last of the Nuba* for *The New York Review of Books*.[11] In the midst of her discussion of Riefenstahl's rehabilitation, Sontag wrote: "Feminists would feel a pang at having to sacrifice the one woman who made films that everybody acknowledges to be first-rate."

In a letter to the editor disputing Sontag, Adrienne Rich discussed the Chicago festival's invitation to Riefenstahl.[12] Rich denied that feminists were now supporting Riefenstahl, citing instead Leontine Sagan and Nelly Kaplan as the kind of "anti-authoritarian" filmmakers preferred by the women's movement. She characterized our festival as one "organized by both feminists and non-feminist film-makers and critics" and contended that "the invitation was withdrawn when members of the Chicago women's movement threatened to picket her." Summarizing women's movement principles of egalitarianism, Rich poignantly referenced Nazism with the careful wording of someone who recognized the dangers of trashing other women along with the greater dangers of supporting any remnant of fascism: "It is impossible not to recognize and mourn the pressures that drive token women to compromise their sisters and to serve misogynist and anti-human values." Naturally, Sontag had to reply—with a text predictably longer than Rich's letter. Here's the central point: "But my alleged misrepresentation of what takes place at specialized film festivals is not what most vexes Rich. Her main charge is that I have further let down the good cause by not exploring the feminist implications of my subject . . . namely, the roots of fascism in 'patriarchal values.' . . . Applied to a particular historical subject, the feminist passion yields conclusions which, however true, are extremely general. Like all capital moral truths, feminism is a bit simple-minded. That is its power and, as the language of Rich's letter shows, that is its limitation."[13]

Sontag was replying both to Rich's critique of her Riefenstahl essay and her comments on her previous piece, "The Third World of Women." In part, this was a battle of the stars: Sontag and Rich, darlings of (different) literary worlds who had gone very separate ways, battling over elitism and accessibility, selling out and caving in, political cowardice versus political correctness.

Just as our little festival turned out to have been a pawn in a much more complicated chess game, however, I was already busy organizing a screening of Riefenstahl's *Triumph of the Will* at the Film Center. It was my professional reaction to the curious crowds that had responded to the controversy, typically, with a desire to see the evidence — and had then been disappointed in their efforts to find something fascist in the seemingly innocent *Blue Light*. Debating with them endlessly on that hot summer night on the steps of the museum, I promised myself that I'd show them the goods and let them make up their own minds from the film and the program notes I'd decided to write. The article that follows was based on those original program notes and was commissioned by Patricia Erens, my collaborator on the festival, for her early anthology of feminist film criticism, *Sexual Stratagems*.

Looking at this article today from a considerably different perspective, I am struck less by my prescient wisdom than by a blast of innocence. It was written at a time when I was still firmly enmeshed in the politics of the avant-garde and was convinced that aesthetic forms were themselves politically complicit. Of course, lots of us thought that way back then, whether we were feminists, structuralists, Maoists, or "activists" of any other stripe. Today, I feel differently. Forms are more hybrid, aesthetics less clearly defined, politics itself an increasingly confusing realm that abandons old categories of left and right, or democracy and fascism, for new categories like fundamentalism, feudalism, xenophobia, nationalism, and globalization.

Yet I think this piece is still very relevant. A nineties *Vanity Fair* profile of Leni Riefenstahl, for example, resurrected so uncritically the veneration of a mystique that was begun back in the seventies that it proved yet again the need for an ongoing interrogation of the workings of fascism and its curious position of fascination within our collective cultural psyche. On the occasion of her ninety-fifth birthday in 1997, Riefenstahl took time out from her scuba diving to hold a show of her photographs in a Hamburg gallery, the first one-person show of her photographs in postwar Germany. Predictably, the show's opening elicited the same still-unresolved issues surrounding art and politics, her relationship to the Third Reich, and the meaning of contemporary interest in her work. I hope my own youthful attempt to come to grips with such issues can help to catalyze an analysis necessary to understand as well our own era's forms of encroaching fascism.

3.

Leni Riefenstahl:

The Deceptive

Myth

(1979)

The films of Leni Riefenstahl have never been accorded a full analysis due both to the myths and emotionalism surrounding her best-known works (their political subject and mode of production) and to the charismatic but contradictory persona of their maker herself. Predictable passions dominate the discourse, with criticism generally concentrated in only a few areas of overworked relevance (as detailed below), skirting the very contemporary implications of Riefenstahl's films and career for cinema and more specifically feminism today. In fact, as this piece would suggest, the lesson of Riefenstahl demands a reexamination of the nature of romanticism and its entire legacy of mystic illusionism, a rethinking of the function of myth, and an analysis of the roles open to women living under patriarchy.

There are a few firm facts in the Riefenstahl legend. She is known to have begun her career as a dancer and actor, working first with Max Reinhardt and then with Dr. Arnold Fanck, as the starring actress-athlete in the popular German genre of mountain films that he developed. Her first and last completed works, *The Blue Light* in 1932 and *Tiefland* in 1954, were both romantic fictions celebrating the nobility of the savage (a wild mountain girl or shepherd) over tainted civilization. The intervening films, which form the basis for claims both of her genius and her fascism, were all documentaries made under the aegis of the Third Reich: *Victory of Faith* in 1933, *Day of Freedom* in 1936, *Triumph of the Will* in 1936, and *Olympia* in 1938 (the infamous *Berchtesgaden over Salzburg,* a 1938 home movie of Hitler's mountain retreat, is sometimes credited to her but currently disputed). Her much discussed but never realized projects were similarly divided: *Penthesilea* was to have been a film of Kleist's play about the Amazon queen, while *Black Cargo* was intended as an exposé of the African slave trade (never completed, it evolved into a book of photographs, *The Last of the Nuba*).

Riefenstahl's position in film history's pantheon has been secured by her two masterpieces, *Triumph of the Will* and *Olympia.* Though the latter has been wholly redeemed by aestheticians from fascist charges, it is to *Triumph* that we must look for the focus of most criticism. Two issues have been of primary importance: first, the decision as to whether *Triumph* is properly documentary or propaganda, with defenders choosing the first term and detractors the second; next, a logical extension of this, whether it is possible or correct to separate art and politics. The answers have been as various and quixotic as world events.

Just after World War II, *Triumph* was rather universally attacked and screenings well nigh impossible. Siegfried Kracauer dominated the critical forum to the extent that the Museum of Modern Art prefaced its print with a written apologia. Later, however, as the cold war altered international alliances and as history by virtue of the passage of time became depersonalized, the film's artistic brilliance began to be posited as a counterbalance to its ideology. Furthermore, with the increased publicity granted America's own racism in the early sixties, the victor's moral self-righteousness abated and the art-qua-art position gained in currency. With the late sixties, however, came an increased sophistication about cinema's inherently political functions; combined with the radicalization of filmmakers like Godard and the radical critiques of commercial cinema by Marxist critics, this attitude led the swing of the pendulum back toward condemnation. Today's emphasis on the ideology of form has led to a more far-reaching critique, as in Susan Sontag's promulgation of a Nazi aesthetic underscoring all of Riefenstahl's films and photographs. This sort of approach has the advantage of overpowering facts that previously stocked the arsenal of Riefenstahl's supporters, namely the emphasis on Black athlete Jesse Owens in the allegedly fascist *Olympia,* the participation of leftist critic Béla Balázs in *The Blue Light,* the latter-day devotion to the documentation of African tribal peoples. Unfortunately, by subordinating all such facts to its formal indictment, this theory falls into the Kracauerian trap of inverting cause and effect, so that aesthetics — and not economic determinants or political strategies — become the "cause" of Nazism, a patently absurd notion.

None of the traditional critical positions have ever broken away from a reliance on the quicksand-foundation of the historical "facts" of Riefenstahl's productions: whether her recorded chronology was the real one, whether the Nazi Party funded *Triumph* and/or *Olympia* (an admirable concern with modes of production that the same critics seldom, alas, apply to American films). Recent evidence has shown that both films were bankrolled by the Reich, as were the shorter documentaries, and that *Triumph*'s agenda wasn't true to fact. None of these investigations, though, really clinch the debate over documentary versus propaganda implied by their statistics. Riefenstahl herself has always seen the debate in these very terms, basing her self-defense on *Triumph*'s being a mere record, that is, an apolitical historical document, and has seen a refutation of the charges of Hitler's staging the rally as key to her argument.

However, current theories of documentary ironically displace these lines of thinking. In keeping with an awareness that no camera ever captures the "truth," documentary has increased its emphasis on spirit instead. The American documentary, for instance, owes its paternity to Robert Flaherty, whose acclaimed documentaries were often faked rituals restaged for the camera by native participants who had to be Flaherty-trained in the practice of extinct customs. Parades, rallies, spectacles have traditionally been staged with an eye to public effect, a device exploited by sixties radicals whose flashy politics took full advantage of media hype, giving birth to events that had a "reality" only in the media. The act of filming, the act of editing, both manipulate and distort "reality" onscreen as well as off-frame. Camera as creator of reality is an accepted notion.

Thus Riefenstahl is well within the standards of the new documentary (or, for that matter, "new journalism") in capturing the true spirit of the Nuremberg rally regardless of chronology or staging considerations. Certainly Hitler staged the rally as the ideal mythic event to popularize his brand of Germany's mythology, but he probably would have done so without the filming, changing only his angles. And Riefenstahl photographed his event with a fidelity to this spirit, her cameras and editing reflecting its mythic stature and romantic dynamics, making *Triumph* in this sense a documentary for its communication of the truth about its subject, beliefs, and ideals, all on the subject's own terms.

Since *Triumph of the Will* incorporates the best and worst aspects of Riefenstahl, and remains her most controversial film, it is the best test of any theories about her. Having surveyed these past issues and attitudes, it is possible to move beyond their cinematic and historic specificity to an issue of more immediate relevance. It is easy to identify its beginnings in annexing national/popular culture to its own ideology under less overt guises. An analysis of *Triumph*'s incorporation of the tenets of romanticism provides the basic training to understand the ideological nature of cinema in our society today; the following analysis is indebted to Robert Rosenblum's *Modern Painting and the Northern Romantic Tradition* for its insights into the identification and interpretation of Romanticism in painting.

I set about, therefore, seeking a thread, a theme, a style, in the realm of legend and fantasy, something that might allow me to give free reign to my juvenile sense of romanticism and beautiful images. — Leni Riefenstahl, 1965

Even the most horrible scenes that we must show must convey the nobility of beauty, because it is simply unadulterated nature. — Leni Riefenstahl, ca. 1939

From its initial operatic imageless overture, *Triumph of the Will* is ingeniously filmed and edited to recapitulate the entire corpus of German legend, beauty, and history in terms of its national Romantic style. Over the leitmotif of ancient Nuremberg is imposed the reflection of a plane, bearing Hitler through the clouds for a euphoric descent into the crowds below, firmly identifying Hitler with a Faust-turned-Archangel access to a state of natural grace. Such a deification is common for Romantic portraiture, for after the breakdown of monolithic Christianity and the system of art it supported, the modes of sacred representation became secularized and applied instead to heads of state (particularly after the French Revolution, which made them convincing as architects of a new cosmology) or to landscapes representing an ideal of untrammeled beauty. In landscapes, the inclusion of medieval or Gothic buildings helped to emphasize the atemporality of the scene as well as established a material connection between the artist's idealization and its perceived concretization in a past that, though lost, was still open to revival. Riefenstahl, by picturing the beatific Fuehrer emerging from the natural universe, neatly dovetails two accepted representations into a single mythology of limitless power incarnated in Hitler. The quiet mood of Nuremberg, hushed in anticipation, has a visionary quality not unlike Friedrich's *Meadow at Griefswald*.

Like that "new Jerusalem," Nuremberg had always been considered a spiritual center (and home of Dürer, Hitler's concept of the archetypal German artist). It was for this spiritual significance, rather than any strategic importance, that Nuremberg was bombed so heavily in World War II. Riefenstahl's depiction of the opening, and hence psychologically crucial, scene incorporates the modern factories of the present as a backdrop for the ancient stone buildings, creating a world order where the past harnesses the future, a primordial order reimposed on contemporary chaos, in sum a hierarchy that Hitler — seen as outside and above it — can dominate and direct.

The thirst for order led the Romantics to "fearful symmetry," the imposition of an archaic and artificial structure onto the universe of the work, translated into *Triumph* as the massing of crowds and the geometric precision of the spectacle. The creation of such a self-contained world order was symptomatic of the Romantics' rejection of existing man-made hierarchies. In their paintings, this rejection is translated into a close-up hypnotic intensity of portraiture that removes its subject from the despised hierarchy and places that subject instead in an imagined domain removed from societal intervention. Riefenstahl adheres to this model, framing individuals in isolation, against the sky or a background thrown out of focus, so removed from any time-space continuum that might disrupt the mythic realm hereby constructed. Most noteworthy in *Triumph* is the angle of vision and lighting of the key individuals shot from below to increase their stature, lit from behind to illuminate their otherworldly nature. Artists like Ruge had concentrated on devising images of total purity out of a desire to reconstitute the world from scratch. So did Hitler, in horrifyingly literal racist terms. So did Riefenstahl, in terms of her cinematic language. Isolating singular visual elements (the Reich eagle, heraldic standards, torches, bonfires, billowing cloth), she orchestrated these units into a single all-encompassing universe.

The absence of any middle ground in her style — where all is either the individual or the masses, close three-quarters profile or infinite panorama — is similarly prefigured in the Romantics, where that polarity underlined the struggle of the individual to decipher the cosmos. Here, the polarity functions as a distributor of power, with those singled out for representation in the halo-lit close-up the priestlike bearers of extrahuman power, and those seen only as specks in the masses the vessels made to receive this benediction and carry it toward a concrete realization.

The depiction of the crowd raises another fascinating aspect of early German Romantic painting utilized by Riefenstahl in *Triumph*. Beginning with Friedrich, there was a marked emphasis on mysterious "faceless beings" whose anonymous presence encouraged viewer empathy within the construct of the painting. Led to identify with the enigmatic personage(s), the viewer shares the admiration for the spectacle that constitutes the painting's central subject. By means of this empathetic device, then, the viewer of the work of art is led to exchange the role of third-person audience for that of first-person participant. Hence the traditional passivity of the viewer leads to complicity in the work. A similar device motivates *Triumph*. Whereas the audience for Friedrich's painting was conceived to be the solitary viewer and so depicted within the work, the audience for cinema is quite plural and so pictured in grandiose terms as the huge crowds within the film. The angled shots that were used to magnify the stature of the speakers serve the dual function of leading the audience to identify with their ground-level point of view and therefore with the masses there listening. It's no wonder that the film entrances, for the theater audience in this way becomes its reflection, the rally crowd, swept up in the visual pageantry and urged on by Windt's brilliant orchestration of the *Horst Wessel* and *Die Meistersinger* to join in hailing Hitler with the rest.

Thus were the principles of Romanticism subjugated to the Nazi mythology by means of specifically Romantic pictorial devices. As for parallels in cinema itself, the points of relevance run from antecedents in Soviet montage or German expressionism all the way up to the present, where the practice of equating style with ideology can best be put to the test. For if the hypnotic manipulation of the audience, encouraging identification with the distorted characters within the world of the film and manipulating that identification for ideologically potent ends, is cinema of latent fascism, then just such a cinema dominates our screens today. The conclusion is not far-fetched. There is a great deal of evidence to support the contention, as the Metz- and Lacan-influenced critics have demonstrated. Arguing against the hypnotic seduction of a passive audience by an illusionist cinema, we may posit a new radical cinema of deconstruction, dedicated to demythologizing the film process and reintegrating intellectual responses, so that the audience's active participation and full-aware distanciation become requisite to the viewing/understanding of a film. Admittedly, a cinema wholly given over to such a genre would displease a large potential audience; nevertheless, it is a necessary and imminent component in any development of a modern counter-cinema, and the logical conclusion reached by pursuing *Triumph*'s "fascist aesthetics" to the end. The sins of Riefenstahl in the realm of aesthetics are equally the sins of Hollywood, Moscow, China, India, Egypt, Europe—of everywhere in the world where the notion of representing reality is the basis for cinema and the aim of controlling audience response is the foundation of ideology.

And so Riefenstahl cannot be dismissed into history after all, but remains in the forefront of pressing cinematic concerns. In more ways than one.

It must be admitted that a great many women directors present no critique whatsoever of their position within society and seem to subscribe totally to the myth and rhetoric of the dominant. . . . —Festival handout, The Women's Event: Edinburgh International Film Festival

So began a cycle of women's film festivals and so began the consideration of the Riefenstahl problem that continues to plague feminists. Feminism as a movement has always assumed a leftist position, whether purely Marxist (seeing women's oppression as one aspect of class struggle) or loosely anarchist (its denial of the star system and negation of hierarchical structures). Yet Riefenstahl is a woman filmmaker who is not only not a leftist, but who made films commemorating a political system notable for its fascism, rabid racism, and quintessential sexism as well. Until recently, when Lina Wertmueller arrived on the scene with her misogynist and speciously political films, Leni Riefenstahl held the position as at once the best and most damned woman filmmaker, a thorn in the side of feminism.

Simply seen, perhaps, Riefenstahl could just be condemned and ignored, an error to be expunged by revisionist histories. Or, as in the above statement, she is a woman who failed to deviate from the dominant ideology, which in her case led to tragic conclusions. But one of Riefenstahl's unrealized films, her favorite lifelong project, was *Penthesilea*, Kleist's version of the Amazon queen. Now the Amazon myth is one that has gained widely in popularity with the rise of feminist herstory, a nurturing myth to increase women's strengths, though some warnings have been signaled (notably by Laura Mulvey and Peter Wollen in their film, *Penthesilea, Queen of the Amazons*, for they see the myth as a male fantasy and, as such, a trap that will resist feminist annexation). Riefenstahl herself was a sort of Amazon among the Nazis, the token exceptional woman who was granted "permission" by the patriarchy to be privileged to its power in exchange for adopting its values. For the Nazi values were strength, physical prowess, muscular beauty, raw power, mass force: values traditionally male in their less fascist guises. And Riefenstahl was the simultaneous incarnation of several Romantic types of women: the muse, gracing the Reich's arm with her beauty; the belle dame sans merci, as Fanck's on-screen fantasy; the Amazon, equal to the best of the men. Riefenstahl supplied female values (beauty, humanity, spirituality) with Nazi definitions (the beauty of the ss uniform, the humanity of the master race, the spirituality of Fuehrer-worship).

Amazons would seem incredible to us if they spoke as we do today. Ridiculous, comical—women with male characteristics, without any mythical appearance. These legendary Amazons can be made humanly familiar only through the language of a great poet.—Leni Riefenstahl, ca. 1939

In *Penthesilea*, Riefenstahl seems to have sensed a way of integrating her two filmic interests (the wild mountain girl Junta destroyed by corrupt civilization and the purely male Nazi cosmology) into a self-including synthesis: a Nazi-styled militaristic culture that could admit the contradiction of women, a comprehensive reflection of her own situation. So, upon closer examination: no androgyne, Penthesilea in the vernacular becomes Leni in drag.

Riefenstahl's career thus carries a moral, not only for those who would not make the effort to critique society's dominant ideology, but also for all women who fail to challenge the assumptions of the patriarchy within which we function. Clearly, the mere existence of a woman within a patriarchy's power structure does not belie its pervasive sexism. On the contrary, the complicity of the token woman, whose wholesale adoption of patriarchal standards eliminates any possibility of threat, advances the patriarchy's consolidation of power. So today, women who turn seemingly feminist expertise into corporate careers cannot be seen as "working from within." Instead of building an alternative power base from which to attack patriarchal corruption, such a defection provides the patriarchy with a female front that is, if anything, more effective for its program of unilateral imperialism.

Only by coming to terms with Riefenstahl—with the attacks on her as "Hitler's girlfriend" and the defenses of her as "Goebbel's victim," the shaping influences of Fanck and Balázs—can we understand her significance within the Nazi patriarchal pantheon and avoid repeating her mistakes in the context of our own culture.

Prologue.

Life, Death,

and Tragic

Homecoming

During 1973, my first year at the Film Center, I spent a working vacation in my hometown of Boston. The Film Center
had just received a donation from the film director Joseph H.
Lewis of personal prints of his films, papers, and memora-
bilia, among which was an antiquated wire recorder. The wire recorder
was a transitional technology, invented between the Edisonphone and
the modern tape recorder, involving a reel-to-reel setup that used magnetized wire to record and play back sound. Coincidentally, at about the
same time, the Boston University library had received a donation from
Maya Deren's mother of a collection of her daughter's recently discovered
possessions, which happened to include stacks of Medaglia d'Oro coffee
cans filled with Deren's wire recordings from the forties and fifties.

I spent hours in the B.U. library transferring the fragile wire recordings
to tape cassettes so that their contents would survive. Some contained
ritual music or drumming, repetitive rhythms that went on and on, communicating clearly their power if not their purpose; one consisted entirely
of eerie cat howlings (presumably recorded with Deren's own pair of cats,
which, according to legend, she'd kept in separate pens in her home); one
even featured Deren's appearance on the Dave Garroway show to discuss
Haiti. Garroway had opened the discussion as an entertainment for his
audience but got a lecture in return: "Tell me, Maya, is it true that the sexy

women of Haiti wear their blouses with one shoulder bared?" The tapes remained in the Film Center's archive. Meanwhile, I became fascinated by Deren, by her life and her death, and by her mythic presence as virtually the only woman in the pantheon of the New American Cinema—present at its birth but absent by the time of its maturation, her life cut short by the mysterious powers of voudoun.

That was 1973–74. I left Boston and went back to Chicago and back to work. I was able to have fun and premiere important films. In 1976, when the country was gaga over the bicentennial and screens were full of John Ford retrospectives and celebrations of the Western, I convinced the *Chicago Tribune* to be my partner again and presented Revolutionary Films/Chicago '76, a two-week celebration of films about revolution. By 1977, however, I was ready for a leave of absence from the Film Center. I wanted to travel to Latin America, learn Spanish, recover from years of twelve-hour days of film exhibition, and try to effect a cease-fire with my boss, with whom relations had deteriorated ever since I'd become her co-programmer (and, as I realized years later, ever since the Film Center had grown too large for her to handle and her own self-sufficiency had begun to unravel).

Gunner, by then my boyfriend and constant companion, and I studied at a language institute (wondering if it were really a CIA front operation) in Huehuetenango in the highlands of Guatemala, then traveled through Panama, Ecuador, Peru, and Bolivia, looking up film colleagues with whom I would try to converse in my primitive weeks-old Spanish. At a soiree in Lima, we overheard one guest tell another, "They're probably perfectly intelligent, they just can't speak Spanish," and were mortified. Years later, I would meet these same filmmakers and cinematheque directors at the annual Latin American film festival in Havana and joke, in Spanish, about my earlier pilgrimage.

We retreated to the countryside where, for the Indians as for us, Spanish was a second language. The Shining Path didn't yet rule Peru, military repression hadn't yet decimated the Indians of the Guatemalan highlands, and Ecuador's eastern provinces were just then getting an oil pipeline. We were able to travel from region to region, learning Latin American myths and realities firsthand. My favorite film experience was seeing Akira Kurosawa's Japanese-Soviet coproduction *Derzu Uzala* in a Soviet film festival in a tiny town on the Peruvian coast: I loved it because the protagonist could speak his borrowed language only haltingly, using verbs in the infinitive and converting all tenses to the present, enabling my perfect understanding of the Spanish subtitles. As a means of language acquisition, my trip was of dubious value, but as an initiation into the realities of

Latin American life, both urban and rural, it was invaluable. It was also an important beginning in understanding Latin American cultures and cinemas, which would become part of my life forever.

Back in Chicago, however, we returned to a major catastrophe: the artist Ree Morton, who'd been living in our Palatine Building loft while we were on the road, was lying in a hospital room, deep in a coma, victim of a car crash; she eventually died. While she was still alive, we were loathe to disturb any of her things, so we tiptoed around our home with her paints and clothes all around, superstitiously convinced that to rearrange or pack anything would endanger her survival at a spiritual level. After her death, though, her daughter and friends inherited that grim task and I faced a delayed reentry into Chicago society, which the months-long trip would have made difficult anyway, with a newly pronounced sense of life's fragility and the mysteries of fate. The months in Latin America and Ree's tragic death made the spirit world seem closer than ever before. And timing, predictably, soon proved that there's no such thing as coincidence.

That very week, two women arrived at the Film Center. It was my job to host their visit. They were in Chicago for the first phase of a collective and monumental project: researching Maya Deren's life. Traveling around the country, they were interviewing anyone who'd ever known Deren, including a former member of the Katherine Dunham company who happened to live in Chicago. These women had already been to the Boston University library, listened to my tape transfers, and heard of my trip several years before. Like the women's film festivals, Deren was a shared project, a magnet drawing many of us from the present into the past. The pair of women were VèVè A. Clark and Milicent Hodson, who together with Catrina Neiman and Francine Bailey Price would go on to produce ambitious and encyclopedic volumes of Deren research. Published on an ongoing basis over the years by the Anthology Film Archives with general editor Hollis Melton, *The Legend of Maya Deren* today constitutes the only substantive resource on her life and work.

We talked for hours; I was entranced by their stories of Deren's life and what they were learning. We talked of dance and Haiti, voudoun and power, and the spells people put on one another. Then we talked about the harshness of the avant-garde film world toward women and its condescension toward "Maya," as the boys liked to call her, now that she was gone and they safely held center stage for themselves.

We puzzled over Deren's mysterious death in an alleged apoplectic fit. Years later, after Cherel and Teiji Ito had completed Deren's unfinished documentary film of Haitian voudoun, he too died in an uncanny replay of mysterious forces. His death occurred when he returned to Haiti for the first time in years: he died of an apparent heart attack on August 15, 1982, in Cherel Ito's arms, peacefully, with a smile on his face. Voudoun has continued to interest me, and to intrude into the "rational" events of everyday life. Today I consult a Yoruba priest and a psychic, and find the throwing of shells and reading of signs as crucial as any psychoanalytic or astrological analysis.

Back from Latin America, I was impatient with the aridity of U.S. culture and the sterility of the U.S. avant-garde film scene. I was becoming weary, too, of the male egos that needed to be coddled on the visiting filmmaker circuit that, lacking its own groupies, needed to press its own impressarios (usually women) into filling the role. I was suffering programmer's burnout; it was time to move on from the Film Center. But what to do next? I considered going back to get my Ph.D. in film studies and was encouraged in that path by my friends in academia. I even applied for a summer institute at Northwestern University with the idea that I could test the waters while getting paid a desperately needed stipend; when the professor rejected me as overqualified, I gave up the whole idea of academia. The Chicago *Reader* was looking for a second-string film critic, and Dave Kehr, today's *New York Daily News* film critic who was then on staff there, invited me to begin contributing reviews. I gave notice at the Film Center and began to reinvent my life, this time as a writer, pursuing the same interests from a different angle. The piece that follows is one of those early *Reader* pieces, written as I went about constructing a critical voice in the popular press.

4.

Voodoo Verité:

Maya Deren's

Divine

Horsemen

(1978)

Maya Deren (1917–1961) was a brilliant filmmaker and theorist whose substantial body of films and writings has nevertheless paled beside the even larger legend surrounding her life and death. At the center of the legend is the film, never finished in her lifetime and never seen before this year, that she made in Haiti between 1947 and 1951, of the voudoun dances and ritual ceremonies into which she was initiated. *Divine Horsemen: The Living Gods of Haiti* represents one hour culled from her three years of filming, edited by Deren's former husband and collaborator, Teiji Ito, and his wife, Cherel Ito.

It is a film that conveys, perhaps for the first time, the power and beauty of the voudoun rites free of both the false fantasies of Hollywood and the desensualized distance of ethnographers. It is a picture of voudoun viewed by an artist, as Deren herself was fond of emphasizing, one privileged to conduct a study of emotional and psychological perceptions on a subjective level — a route unavailable to intellectual methodologists. The unprecedented quality of Deren's Haitian footage is no accident, but rather the product of an exceptional life that, in retrospect, seems to have inevitably led her to Haiti on a Guggenheim Fellowship to document the Haitian dance. That project was never completed and Deren made only one more film after 1951; the career of Deren the filmmaker was nearly over, but rumors of Deren the voudoun priestess were just beginning. This is an insider's film, now edited with a more anthropological narration and structure which, though at odds with the original film's rhythm, do no great harm.

When the anthropologist arrives, the gods depart. — Old Haitian proverb

Joseph Campbell quotes the above proverb in his introduction to Maya Deren's painstakingly written ethnographic account of voudoun, *Divine Horsemen,* from which the texts of the film have been drawn. Although she consulted at length with Campbell and Gregory Bateson, Deren was not trained as an anthropologist. It was her interest in dance, ritual, and trance that led her to apply her skills as a filmmaker to the challenge of Haiti. Thereafter, it was her profound modesty and respect for the cultural integrity of the Haitian people that led her to abandon without regret her own artistic project and devote herself instead to "recording the logics of a reality which had forced me . . . to abandon my manipulations." The one-hour film now being distributed easily justifies her devotion, bearing as it does the unmistakable marks of a participatory project. The camera is held close to the steps of the dance, the drawn lines of the ceremony, the beats of the drums.

Maya Deren emigrated to the United States with her parents from the U.S.S.R. in the twenties. She went to college, was trained as a journalist, and became an active socialist. Soon after, she became interested in photography and in dance, touring with the Katherine Dunham company as a writer, photographer, and lover of dance. Her first film, *Meshes of the Afternoon,* was made in 1943 with Alexander Hammid and remains a classic work of the American avant-garde cinema. An early version of psychodrama, the film combines surrealist elements (a mirror, a rose, the mirror broken) with psychological overtones (a woman faced with her doubles, a key turning into a knife) for a narrative of subjective crisis. Deren herself played the woman, who in one scene strides across the elements — sand, water, field — in a single march thanks to the editing process.

Such a mystical stride clearly prepared Deren for the otherworldly steps she would follow in the dance of possession much later. Indeed, *Meshes* is a work very much in keeping with the later interest, emphasizing as it does a trance-like nature struggling to decipher larger mysterious forces inhabiting the objects and bodies of everyday life. Her subsequent films continued to explore space, time, and the nature of form, the possibilities of cinematic manipulation, and the magic of dance.

At the same time that she was pursuing her own interest in altered modes of vision and altered states of consciousness, Deren became a proselytizer for recognition of cinema as an art form, lecturing tirelessly everywhere from Yale University to the Dave Garroway show. Although frequently overlooked in critical appraisals of the initial avant-garde pantheon (Stan Brakhage, Kenneth Anger, Gregory Markopoulos), Deren's pioneering work was crucial in building an atmosphere of respect for the art they would create.

In recent years, major research into Deren's life and work has been carried out by a collective of four women producing The Legend of Maya Deren Project, which is expected to appear in its first installment next year through *Film Culture* magazine. Last year in a Chicago talk, two of the women pointed to one reason Deren might not be more widely acknowledged: ironically, her reputation as a voudoun initiate has fostered a picture of her as a madwoman or witch, a figure not to be taken seriously, a stepmother whom artistic descendants need not feel obliged to credit. The recognition of Deren's importance is one of the aims of the project, which will feature extensive interviews with her collaborators as well as many of her earlier writings.

Myth is the facts of the mind made manifest in a fiction of matter. — Maya Deren

Divine Horsemen opens with a scene of an empty road surrounded by a whited-out landscape, the land giving the impression of an emptied materiality waiting to be filled with its proper meaning. Down the road comes a woman with a basket on her head. We are led down the path to the realm of the voudoun ceremonials. It is a perfect beginning, neither didactic nor abrupt, easing the viewer into the world about to be experienced and warning, through the strange, almost solarized exposure, that outward appearances are no longer the index of reality.

Certainly the footage of a voudoun ritual would excite interest in and of itself, yet the most exceptional aspect of *Divine Horsemen* is the nature of the camerawork. The cinematography immediately gives an impression of subjectivity, handheld in the midst of the dance or peering intimately over the shoulder of the serviteur as he draws a crossroads or other symbol of the loa (god). Many shots are focused on the lower half of the dancers' bodies, catching the movement of their feet and the posture of their legs, looking perhaps for the telltale sign of a left leg rooted to the ground, an early warning of the state of possession. For an audience accustomed to seeing such rituals only in the context of ethnographic films, *Divine Horsemen* may be a shock; for where the ethnographer always intervened as voyeur in the study of filmed cultures, allowing the audience that same

54

distance, Deren took no such position. She witnessed the ceremonies and dances as a full participant, giving her footage an unmediated intimacy that leaves one feeling at times like an interloper.

Included in this edited version are celebrations to many voudoun figures, including Ghede, "the corpse and phallus, god and king," a presence given to manifestations in sunglasses or with a cigarette; Agwe, the "sovereign of the seas," whose ceremony is performed aboard ship; and Legba, the "old man at the gate" and patron of the crossroads at which communication between worlds is set up. Also included are many dances — such as the Congo dance and episodes of the Carnival — and rites to the two different levels of deities, the Rada (or guardian deities) and the Petro (or aggressive deities). Throughout the film, the Itos have interpolated portions of Deren's study to identify what is being seen on the screen. The music has been edited by Teiji Ito (who composed the music to Deren's earlier films) from the recordings originally made by Deren on an early-model wire recorder. The drumbeats cannot be ignored, drawing the viewer into the rhythm and spirit of the dance. Feathers of white hens or black roosters fly; a black goat is castrated, its beard is cut off, and it is sacrificed; conches are sounded; a bull is pursued. The drawings and the rites are amazing, yet the real focus of the film is the dancing, perhaps because here the camerawork is at its most fluid: the frame is daringly composed, the level of vision constantly in flux, plays of shadow and light abound, and the visual record truly aspires to the spiritual experience, as when the agony is clearly visible on the face of the one possessed, the one "mounted" by the divine horseman.

Maya Deren herself experienced the state of possession, became a Mambo (or priestess), and certainly stated her opinion of voudoun in the plainest of terms, writing: "I would say that, as a metaphysical and ritualistic structure Voudoun is a fact, and does exist, and that as such, it incorporates values with which I am in personal agreement, displays an organizational, psychic, and practical skill which I admire, and accomplishes results of which I approve."

When Deren died suddenly in 1961, victim of a strange seizure or apoplectic fit or cerebral hemorrhage (depending on which account you choose to believe), a possible voudoun death was rumored. Why Deren never finished or released the film on which she had spent so much time and into which she had poured such vast energies is a question still unanswered. One plausible suggestion, however, maintains that if Deren indeed became an initiate and priestess, then perhaps she became aware of exactly what she had on film, and decided not to expose those secrets to the uninitiated viewer. Such conjecture certainly adds an irresistible allure to the film, with no possible method of affirming or denying its truth, yet the value of the film in no way depends on any such conjectures. So clearly does *Divine Horsemen* communicate its maker's understanding of and sympathy with the voudoun experience, as well as her knowledge of how best to portray that experience in purely visual terms, that the data and rumors of the history become a minor game.

Rudolph Arnheim, in a remembrance of Maya Deren written in 1962, bemoaned the practicality of the industrialized twentieth century but held out one last straw that this long-lost film has enabled us to grasp: "We are still accessible to a picture language that, half-shrouded in personal meanings, half-revealed by common sensation, can call upon us, distant though the caller may be."

Prologue.

An Iguana,

Some Wolves,

and the

Dawn of Theory

After resigning my post as associate director of the Film Center at the School of the Art Institute of Chicago at the end of 1977, I began sorting out my future. A crystal ball would have come in handy. Instead, two invitations arrived early in 1978 that, in retrospect, changed forever my relationship to feminist film theory.

First, Julia Lesage (*Jump Cut* coeditor and, at that time, still an assistant professor at the University of Illinois Circle Campus), with her characteristically ultrademocratic impulses, asked me (who was neither a filmmaker nor an academic, nor yet a proper critic) to take part in a roundtable discussion on the aesthetics of women's cinema for publication in the *New German Critique*.

Picture the setting. We met in the loft that my partner Gunner and I had created, high above Chicago's near-northwest side. Our home encompassed the top floor of an eight-story structure, the Palatine Building, that became legendary in Chicago in the seventies for the artists living there and the events we staged during our half-decade tenure. My lifelong friend Hollis Sigler, now a well-known painter, lived downstairs in an environment of flamingos and kitsch. My pal Jim was on the sixth floor until he and his girlfriend split up, then it was John and Faith until they too split up (he came out), and then the artist Nancy Bowen, first with one boyfriend, then with another. The painter Janet Cooling lived there, too, and Aigars and Auste, artists of style as much as product, were a few floors down. Kate Horsfield and Lynn Blumenthal had the second floor. On holidays, we would all gather on various floors for extended kinship celebrations, each contributing food or decor according to appropriate talents. On hot summer nights, we'd pile into the back of the pickup truck and swim naked in the Humboldt Park lagoon, right in the heart of Chicago's Puerto Rican barrio, surrounded in the darkness by covert drug dealing and the coupling of couples without a room to call their own.

Our top-floor loft had windows ranged all along its hundred-foot wall that provided wide-open vistas of our three-story Chicago neighborhood and, in the distance, the picturesque skyline of downtown. Gunner and I were particularly known for our rounds of parties. We gave night-long parties that started at midnight and ended at dawn, with breakfast for anyone who lasted; picnic brunches, served al fresco on tablecloths laid directly on the hardwood floors; once even a "sunset salon" that turned disaster to advantage by spotlighting the red-hot glare of the Chicago summer that shined through our west-facing windows and heated up the party, cooled by rum cocktails and canapes. In the winter, the prevailing winds hit the living room windows, leaving only a tiny wood-burning stove or very large parties to keep us warm. Furnishings were thrift-shop eclectic, with a nod to Chicago's dominant ethnicities: wagonwheel sofas, orchids and ferns, guardian angels, posters of Chinese babies, a Thai altar, Catholic saints, Mexican oilcloth, and a resident iguana. Our iguana Inti was a bright green vegetarian housed in his own private gazebo/greenhouse in the kitchen, but with an indulged preference for roaming at will.

It was to the kitchen and its crucial stove, then, that a small band of feminists retreated one weekend in the cold Chicago winter of 1977–78 to share thoughts on women and film. It was a Midwest gathering. Renny Harrigan had driven in from Milwaukee, Michelle Citron down from Grand Rapids, Nancy Vedder-Shults came in from Madison, Judith Mayne and Helen Fehervary from Columbus, and Julia Lesage and Anna Marie Taylor from other Chicago neighborhoods. There were introductions all around; we mostly didn't know each other. The iguana's customary strolls throughout the discussion alarmed some of the guests. Further alarming them was my hospitable effort to keep the day lively by preparing pot after pot of espresso and cream, only belatedly discovering that others didn't share my caffeine habits; as the day progressed, the talk grew increasingly feverish. By the time we stopped for a break before dinner, the majority of the group was verging on collapse. People had to take naps before continuing on to the local womyn-run restaurant, unfortunately notable, as they nearly always were in those days, for the utterly mediocre quality of its cooking. Lacking any better explanation, I came to believe that womyn's restaurants were ruled by an ideology of cooking that apparently held that patriarchy was lodged in spices and had to be rigorously eliminated.

But it wasn't just the coffee that had got us going and worn us out. The excitement of the talk! I vividly remember the sense of whole new worlds to be explored, the mood that transfixed us then in some magic simultaneity of age and Age. There were battles to be fought over ideas and we were ready to enlist in the fight. For me, just leaving a career of film exhibition for the unknown, this incursion into film theory was a journey into my own future. I had never met any of the out-of-towners before, nor had I ever read the *New German Critique,* for that matter. But the encouragement I received for my ideas from them and the rest of this group of women energized me and gave me the confidence to catapult myself into a new arena. (And so it has always been for me: the encouragement of friends, either already known or met in the wake of publication, continues to sustain my participation in the collective discourse of film and feminist/lesbian/queer criticism and theory.)

Our discussion was full of serious assessments and arguments regarding current theoretical practices and positions. Julia Lesage, for instance, extolled Mao but attacked Lacan:

> The use of Lacan in criticism has been really destructive in that it has utilized an essentially patriarchal framework for analyzing patriarchy, and then it says, only now can we look at how patriarchy works on women. . . . When Lacanians associate women with the imaginary but not the symbolic, it's like saying that women are structured from earliest infancy to deal with day-to-day things but they have no "drive" to accede to intellectual life, technology or power—as men do. In the area that concerns us, that's the kind of rationale used to drive women out of the film industry and keep them out, especially, for example, in "technological" roles, like camera person.

Anna Marie Taylor, who had recently quit her position at the University of Chicago because she was fed up with teaching in an elite institution, made some observations that anticipated much later developments in feminist film theory:

> It's important to realize that the Freudian framework that both Mulvey and Johnston use cannot satisfactorily account for the position of female spectators. We sense that women have some kind of different

relationship with what they see, and particularly with women they see on the movie screen. One of the points that the Freudian analysis makes is that the male filmmaker and male spectator fetishize the women as object. But the Freudian analysis doesn't take into account the fact that women spectators (something that Mulvey totally avoids) are also very attracted to these same visual objects. . . . [But] have we as female viewers also been taken in by the way women have been filmed so that our own sexuality and therefore our very intense visual enjoyment regarding female stars is determined in advance elsewhere? This question finds its best response in the fact that a number of feminist filmmakers are attempting to construct alternative images, and to work with even very subtle cinematic effects, such as lighting and color, to decode established cinematic practices in regard to the photographing of women's bodies and their relationship to the space around them.

My own best contribution to the dialogue was my use of dialectic to try to explain the nature of feminist consciousness outside of a psychoanalytic model:

for a woman today, film is a dialectical experience in a way that it never was and never will be for a man under patriarchy. Brecht once described the exile as the ultimate dialectician in that the exile lives the tension of two different cultures. That's precisely the sense in which the woman spectator is an equally inevitable dialectician. . . . As a woman going into the movie theater, you are faced with a context that is coded wholly for your invisibility, and yet, obviously, you are sitting there and bringing along a certain coding from life outside the theater. . . . cinematic codes have structured our absence to such an extent that the only choice allowed to us is to identify either with Marilyn Monroe or with the man behind me hitting the back of my seat with his knees. How does one formulate an understanding of a structure that insists on our absence even in the face of our presence? What is there in a film with which a woman viewer identifies? How can the contradictions be used as a critique? And how do all these factors influence what one makes as a woman filmmaker, or specifically as a feminist filmmaker?

The edited transcript was published in the *New German Critique* "Special Feminist Issue" (no. 13), and was received with due excitement, circulating for a long time in a samizdat afterlife. It was really a seedbed of ideas that were developed and implemented by us and others over the following decade, but the NGC conversation was never reprinted.

My second opportunity for theoretical development came about soon after. My friends Bruce Jenkins and Bill Horrigan were both graduate students in film studies at Northwestern University (and today, curators of film and video at the Walker Art Center and Wexner Center for the Arts, respectively). They'd been my allies in film exhibition, Bill with program notes for the Film Center series, Bruce with companion programs at Northwestern. Now Bruce was soliciting our participation in a panel for the Purdue University film studies conference later that year.

It would be our debut panel, and typical of the ambition of youth out to make their mark, we decided to assail the terminology then in common use. Bruce's plan was to critique the term "structuralist" and show its advantages and disadvantages for the works so considered. Bill would then draw from his dissertation on Sirk, Borsage, and *Screen* magazine to critique the term "melodrama" and show how well or ill it fit. And I would take on the term "feminist" as a descriptive adjective for films made by women, and try to assess its efficacy.

Our canon blasting was a great success. We celebrated by driving out to the Indiana farmlands with fellow Chicagoan and inveterate traveler Patricia Erens to see the laboratory/encampment where studies of alphawolf behavior were then in process. I think back on that visit today, remembering the eerie drive through the moonlit landscape, and figure we made an apt choice to accompany our induction into film academia: to seek out a kindred form of competition and natural selection, not for any strategic or professional goal, but simply to enjoy the howling.

Jump Cut published my talk as an article. By then I was a member of the editorial board and hard at work on the magazine, trudging over to Chuck Kleinhans and Julia Lesage's house every weekend to read manuscripts, write my share of the magazine's notorious letters to contributors asking for inevitable revisions to satisfy our ideological requirements, and carry out the trademark primitive page layouts. Working on *Jump Cut* was a great political education that served me well in the years that followed. It also provided me with an introduction to the world of progressive publishing: we got exchange copies of dozens of journals, from the collectively published Canadian art journal *Fuse* to *Women & Film*, the California-based journal where Chuck and Julia frequently published. I've revised the piece several times in the intervening years and these versions have in turn been reprinted a number of times. This is the most definitive version, even though its later sections skip ahead in time. The finest tribute that the article ever received was the game card that a friend reported drawing in a lesbian version of the Trivial Pursuits game: it called on the player to recite the number and names of categories in my typology of feminist cinema.

5.

In the Name

of Feminist

Film Criticism

(1978–79,

1980, 1991)

Whatever is unnamed, undepicted in images, whatever is omitted from biography, censored in collections of letters, whatever is mis-named as something else, made difficult-to-come-by, whatever is buried in the memory by the collapse of meaning under an inadequate or lying language—this will become not merely unspoken, but unspeakable. — Adrienne Rich [1]

The situation for women working in filmmaking and film criticism today is precarious. Although our work is no longer invisible, and not yet unspeakable, it still goes dangerously unnamed. There is even uncertainty over what name might characterize that intersection of cinema and the women's movement within which we labor, variously called "films by women," "feminist film," "images of women in film," and "women's films." All are vague and problemmatic.

I see the lack of proper name here as symptomatic of a crisis in the ability of feminist film criticism thus far to come to terms with the work at hand, to apply a truly feminist criticism to the body of work already produced by women filmmakers. This crisis points to a real difference between the name "feminist" and the other names that have traditionally been applied to film (that is, "structuralist" for certain avant-garde films or "melodrama" for certain Hollywood films).[2]

"Feminist" is a name that may have only a marginal relation to the film text, describing more persuasively the context of social and political activity from which the work sprang. Such a difference is due, on the one hand, to a feminist recognition of the links tying a film's aesthetics to its modes of production and reception; and, on the other hand, to the particular history of the cinematic field that "feminist" came to designate, a field in which filmmaking-exhibition-criticism-distribution-audience have always been considered inextricably connected.

The History

The great contribution of feminism as a body of thought to culture in our time has been that it has something fairly direct to say, a quality all too rare today. And its equally crucial contribution as a process and style has been women's insistence on conducting the analysis, making the statements, in unsullied terms, in forms not already associated with the media's oppressiveness toward women. It is this freshness of discourse and distrust of traditional modes of articulation that placed feminist cinema in a singular position vis-à-vis both the dominant cinema and the avant-garde in the early seventies.

By "dominant" I mean Hollywood and all its corresponding manifestations in other cultures; but this could also be termed the Cinema of the Fathers. By "avant-garde," I mean the experimental/personal cinema that is positioned by self-inclusion within the art world; but this could also be termed the Cinema of the Sons. Being a business, the Cinema of the Fathers seeks to do only that which has been done before and proved successful. Being an art, the Cinema of the Sons seeks to do only that which has not been done before and so prove itself successful.

Into such a situation, at the start of the seventies, entered a feminist cinema. In place of the Fathers' bankruptcy of both form and content, there was a new and different energy: a cinema of immediacy and positive force now opposed the retreat into violence and the revival of a dead past that had become the dominant cinema's mainstays. In place of the Sons' increasing alienation and isolation, there was an entirely new sense of identification—with other women—and a corresponding commitment to communicate with this now identifiable audience, a commitment that replaced for feminist filmmakers the elusive public ignored and frequently scorned by the male formalist filmmakers. Thus, from the start, its link to an evolving political movement gave feminist cinema a power and direction entirely unprecedented in independent filmmaking, bringing issues of theory/practice, aesthetics/meaning, process/representation into sharp focus.

Because the origin and development of feminist film work are largely unexamined, the following chronology sketches some of the major events of the seventies in North America and Great Britain. Three sorts of information are omitted as beyond the scope of this survey: most European festivals and publications, although some have been extremely significant; the hundreds of films made by women during the decade, beyond the first entry; and the publication in 1969–70 of key feminist writings such as *Sexual Politics, The Dialectic of Sex,* and *Sisterhood Is Powerful,* which must be remembered as the backdrop and theoretical impetus for these film activities.

> 1971: Release of *Growing Up Female, Janie's Janie, Three Lives,* and *The Woman's Film:* first generation of feminist documentaries.
>
> 1972: First New York International Festival of Women's Films and the Women's Event at Edinburgh Film Festival. First issue of *Women & Film* magazine; special issues on women and film in *Take One, Film Library Quarterly,* and *The Velvet Light Trap;* filmography of women directors in *Film Comment.*
>
> 1973: Toronto Women and Film Festival, Washington Women's Film Festival, season of women's cinema at National Film Theatre in London, and Buffalo women's film conference. Marjorie Rosen's *Popcorn Venus* (first book on women in film), and *Notes on Women's Cinema* (first anthology of feminist film theory), edited by Claire Johnston for the British Film Institute.
>
> 1974: Chicago Films by Women Festival. First issue of *Jump Cut.* Two books on images of women in film: Molly Haskell's *From Reverence to Rape* and Joan Mellen's *Women and Their Sexuality in the New Film.*
>
> 1975: Conference of Feminists in the Media, New York and Los Angeles. *Women & Film* ceases publication; *The Work of Dorothy Arzner* (BFI monograph edited by Johnston), and Sharon Smith's *Women Who Make Movies* (guide to women filmmakers).
>
> 1976: Second New York International Festival of Women's Films (smaller, noncollective, less successful than first) and Womanscene, a section of women's films in Toronto's Festival of Festivals (smaller, noncollective, but comparable in choices to 1973).
>
> 1977: First issue of *Camera Obscura* (journal of film theory founded largely by former *Women & Film* members, initially in opposition to it); Karyn Kay and Gerald Peary's *Women and the Cinema* (first anthology of criticism on women and film).
>
> 1978: *Women in Film Noir* (BFI anthology edited by E. Ann Kaplan); special feminist issues of *Quarterly Review* of film studies and *New German Critique;* Brandon French's *On the Verge of Revolt: Women in American Films of the Fifties* (study on images of women).

1979: Alternative Cinema Conference, bringing together over 100 feminists in the media for screenings, caucuses, and strategizing within the left; Feminism and Cinema Event at Edinburgh Film Festival, assessing the decade's filmmaking; Patricia Erens's *Sexual Stratagems: The World of Women in Film* (anthology on women and cinema).

It is immediately apparent from this chronology that the 1972–73 period marked a cultural watershed and that the unity, discovery, energy, and brave, we're-here-to-stay spirit of the early days underwent a definitive shift in 1975. Since then, the field of vision has altered. There is increased specialization, both in the direction of genre studies (like film noir) and film theory (particularly semiotic and psychoanalytic); the start of sectarianism, with women partitioned off into enclaves defined by which conferences are attended or journals subscribed to; increased institutionalization, both of women's studies and cinema studies departments, twin creations of the seventies; a backlash emphasis on "human" liberation, which by making communication with men a priority can leave woman-to-woman feminism looking déclassé.

Overall, there is a growing acceptance of feminist film as an area of study rather than as a sphere of action. And this may pull feminist film work away from its early political commitment, encompassing a wide social setting; away from issues of life that go beyond form; away from the combative (as an analysis of and weapon against patriarchal capitalism) into the merely representational.

The chronology also shows the initial cross-fertilization between the women's movement and the cinema, which took place in the area of practice rather than in written criticism. The films came first. In fact, we find two different currents feeding into film work: one made up of women who were feminists and thereby led to film, the other made up of women already working in film and led therefrom to feminism. It was largely the first group of women who began making the films that were naturally named "feminist," and largely the second group of women, often in university film studies departments, who began holding the film festivals, just as naturally named "women and/in film."[3] Spadework has continued in both directions, creating a new women's cinema and rediscovering the antecedents, with the two currents feeding our film criticism.

The past eight years have reduced some of the perils of which Adrienne Rich speaks. No longer are women "undepicted in images": Bonnie Dawson's *Women's Films in Print* lists over 800 available films by U.S. women alone, most depicting women. No longer are women omitted from all biography, nor are letters always censored. (In this respect, note the ongoing work of the four-woman collective engaged in The Legend of Maya Deren Project to document and demystify the life and work of a major, underacknowledged figure in American independent cinema.) No longer are women's films so hard to come by: the establishment of New Day Films (1972), the Serious Business Company (ca. 1973), and the Iris Films collective (1975) ensures the continuing distribution of films by or about women, although the chances of seeing any independently made features by women in a regular movie theater are still predictably slim (with Jill Godmilow's *Antonia* and Claudia Weill's *Girl Friends* among the few U.S. films to succeed).

Returning to Rich's original warning, however, we reach the end of history's comforts and arrive at our present danger: "Whatever is unnamed ... buried in the memory by the collapse of meaning under an inadequate or lying language — this will become not merely unspoken, but unspeakable." Herein lies the crisis facing feminist film criticism today; for after a decade of film practice and theory, we still lack our proper names. The impact of this lack on the films themselves is of immediate concern.

The Films

One classic film rediscovered through women's film festivals indicates the sort of misnaming prevalent in film history. Leontine Sagan's *Maedchen in Uniform* (Germany, 1931) details the relationship between a student and her teacher in a repressive girls' boarding school. The act of naming is itself a pivotal moment in the narrative.

Toward the end of the film, the schoolgirls gather at a drunken party after the annual school play. Manuela has just starred as a passionate youth and, drunk with punch, still in boy's clothing, she stands to proclaim her happiness and love, naming her teacher Fräulein von Bernburg as the woman she loves. Before this episode, the lesbian substructure of the school and the clearly shared knowledge of that substructure have been emphasized; the school laundress even points to the prevalence of the Fräulein's initials embroidered on the girls' regulation chemises as evidence of the adulation of her adolescent admirers. This eroticism was not in the closet. But only when Manuela stands and names that passion is she punished, locked up in solitary — for her speech, not for her actions.

Such is the power of a name and the valor of naming. It is ironic that the inscription of the power of naming within the film has not forestalled its own continuous misnaming within film history, which has championed its antifascism while masking the lesbian origins of that resistance. The problem is even more acute in dealing with contemporary films, where the lack of an adequate language has contributed to the invisibility of key aspects of our film culture — an invisibility advantageous to the existing film tradition. Monique Wittig writes:

> The women say, unhappy one, men have expelled you from the world of symbols and yet they have given you names . . . their authority to accord names . . . goes back so far that the origin of language itself may be considered an act of authority emanating from those who dominate . . . they have attached a particular word to an object or a fact and thereby consider themselves to have appropriated it. . . . The women say, the language you speak poisons your glottis tongue palate lips. They say, the language you speak is made up of words that are killing you . . . the language you speak is made up of signs that rightly speaking designate what men have appropriated. Whatever they have not laid hands on . . . does not appear in the language you speak. This is apparent precisely in the intervals that your masters have not been able to fill with their words . . . this can be found in the gaps, in all that which is not a continuation of their discourse, in the zero.[4]

The act of misnaming functions not as an error but as a strategy of the patriarchy. The lack of proper names facilitates derogatory name-calling; the failure to assign meaningful names to contemporary feminist film eases the acquisition of misnomers. Two key films of the seventies reveal this process and the disenfranchisement we suffer as a result.

Chantal Akerman's *Jeanne Dielman* (1975) is a chronicle of three days in the life of a Brussels housewife, a widow and mother who is also a prostitute. It is the first film to scrutinize housework in a language appropriate to the activity itself, showing a woman's activities in the home in real time to communicate the alienation of women in the nuclear family under European postwar economic conditions. More than three hours in length and nearly devoid of dialogue, the film charts Jeanne Dielman's breakdown via a minute observation of her performance of household routines, at first methodical and unvarying, later increasingly disarranged, until by film's end she permanently disrupts the patriarchal order by murdering her third client. The film was scripted, directed, photographed, and edited by women with a consciously feminist sensibility.

The aesthetic repercussions of such a sensibility are evident throughout the film. For example, the choice of camera angle is unusually low. In interviews, Akerman explained that the camera was positioned at her own height; because she is quite short, the entire perspective of the film is different from what we are used to seeing, as shot by male cinematographers.

The perspective of every frame thus reveals a female ordering of that space, prompting a reconsideration of point of view that I had felt before only in a few works shot by children (which expose the power of tall adults in every shot) and in the films by Japanese director Yasujiro Ozu (where the low angle has been much discussed by Western critics as an entry into the "oriental" detachment of someone seated on a tatami mat, observing).

Akerman's decision to employ only medium and long shots also stems from a feminist critique: the decision to free her character from the exploitation of a zoom lens and to grant her an integrity of private space usually denied in close-ups, thereby also freeing the audience from the insensitivity of a camera barreling in to magnify a woman's emotional crisis. Similarly, the activities of shopping, cooking, and cleaning the house are presented without ellipses, making visible the extent of time previously omitted from cinematic depictions. Thus, the film is a profoundly feminist work in theme, style, and representation; yet it has been critically received in language devoted to sanctifying aesthetics stripped of political consequence.

Shortly after *Jeanne Dielman*'s premiere at the Cannes film festival, European critics extolled the cinematic as "hyperrealist" in homage both to the realist film (and literary) tradition and to the superrealist movement in painting. Two problems arise with such a name: first, the tradition of cinematic realism has never included women in its alleged veracity; second, the comparison with superrealist painters obscures the contradiction between their illusionism and Akerman's anti-illusionism. Another name applied to *Jeanne Dielman* was "ethnographic," in keeping with the film's insistence on real-time presentation and nonelliptical editing. Again, the name negates a basic aspect by referring to a cinema of clinical observation, aimed at "objectivity" and noninvolvement, detached rather than engaged. The film's warm texture and Akerman's committed sympathies (the woman's gestures were borrowed from her own mother and aunt) make the name inappropriate.

The critical reception of the film in the *Soho Weekly News* by three different reviewers points up the confusion engendered by linguistic inadequacy.[5] Jonas Mekas questioned: "Why did she have to ruin the film by making the woman a prostitute and introduce a murder at the end, why did she commercialize it?" Later, praising most of the film as a successor to *Greed* (1923–25), Mekas contended that the heroine's silence was more "revolutionary" than the murder, making a case for the film's artistic merit as separate from its social context and moving the work into the area of existentialism at the expense of its feminism. A second reviewer, Amy Taubin, considered the film "theatrical," and, while commending the subjectivity of the camerawork and editing, she attacked the character of Jeanne: "Are we to generalize from Jeanne to the oppression of many women through their subjugation to activity which offers them no range of creative choice? If so, Jeanne Dielman's pathology mitigates against our willingness to generalize." By holding a reformist position (that is, Jeanne should vary her menu, change her wardrobe) in relation to a revolutionary character (that is, a murderer), Taubin was forced into a reading of the film limited by notions of realism that she, as an avant-garde film critic, ordinarily should have tried to avoid: her review split the film along the lines of form/content, annexing the aesthetics as "the real importance" and rejecting the character of Jeanne as a pathological woman. Again we find a notion of pure art set up in opposition to a feminism seemingly restricted to positive role models.

Finally, Annette Michelson wrote a protest to Mekas that defended the film for "the sense of renewal it has brought both to a narrative mode and the inscription *within it* of feminist energies" (my italics). Yes, but at what cost? Here the effect of inadequate naming is precisely spelled out: the feminist energies are being spent to create work quickly absorbed into mainstream modes of art that renew themselves at our expense. Already, the renaissance of the "new narrative" is underway in film circles with nary a glance back at filmmakers like Akerman or Yvonne Rainer, who first incurred the wrath of the academy by reintroducing characters, emotions, and narratives into their films.

The critical response to Rainer's films, especially *Film about a Woman Who . . .* (1974), adds further instances of naming malpractice. Much of the criticism has been in the area of formal textual analysis, concentrating on the "postmodernist" structures, "Brechtian" distancing, or cinematic deconstruction of the works. Continuing the tactic of detoxifying films via a divide-and-conquer criticism, critic Brian Henderson analyzed the central section in *Film about a Woman Who . . .* according to a semiological model, detailing the five channels of communication used to present textual information.[6] The analysis was exhaustive on the level of technique but completely ignored the actual meaning of the information (Rainer's "emotional accretions"), the words themselves, and the visualization (a man and a woman on a stark bed/table). At the opposite extreme, a *Feminist Art Journal* editorial condemned Rainer as a modernist, "the epitome of the alienated artist," and discounted her film work as regressive for feminists, evidently because of its formal strategies.[7]

Rainer's films deal with the relations between the sexes and the interaction of life and art within a framework combining autobiography and fiction. Whatever the intent of Rainer's filmmaking in political terms, the work stands as a clear product of a feminist cultural milieu. The films deal explicitly with woman as victim and the burden of patriarchal mythology; they offer a critique of emotion, reworking melodrama for women today, and even provide an elegy to the lost innocence of defined male/female roles (*Kristina Talking Pictures*, 1976). The structure of the themes gives priority to the issues over easy identification with the "characters" and involves the audience in an active analysis of emotional process.

Yet little of the criticism has managed to reconcile an appreciation for the formal elements with an understanding of the feminist effect. Carol Wikarska, in a short review for *Women & Film*, could only paraphrase Rainer's own descriptions in a stab at *Film about a Woman Who . . .* seen in purely art world terms.[8] More critically, the feminist-defined film journal *Camera Obscura* concentrated its first issue on Rainer but fell into a similar quandary. Though an interview with Rainer was included, the editors felt obliged to critique the films in the existing semiological vocabulary, taking its feminist value for granted without confronting the points of contradiction within that methodology. The lack of vocabulary once again frustrates a complete consideration of the work.

Lest the similarity of these misnamings merely suggest critical blindness rather than a more deliberate tactic, an ironic reversal is posed by the response to Anne Severson's *Near the Big Chakra* (1972). Silent and in color, the film shows a series of thirty-six women's cunts photographed in unblinking close-up, some still and some moving, with no explanations or gratuitous presentation. Formally, the film fits into the category of "structuralist" cinema: a straightforward listing of parts, no narrative, requisite attention to a predetermined and simplified structure, and fixed camera position (as defined by the namer, P. Adams Sitney). Yet Severson's image is so powerfully unco-optable that, to my knowledge, her film has never been called "structuralist," nor—with retrospective revisionism—have her earlier films been so named. Evidently, any subject matter that could make a man vomit (as happened at a London screening in 1973) is too much for the critical category, even though it was founded on the "irrelevance" of the visual images. Thus, a name can be withheld by the critical establishment if its application alone won't make the film fit the category.

"Whatever they have laid hands on . . . does not appear in the language you speak," writes Monique Wittig. Here is the problem: not so much that certain names are used, but that other names are *not*—and therefore the qualities they describe are lost. Where patriarchal language holds sway, the silences, the characteristics that are unnamed, frequently hold the greatest potential strength. In Chantal Akerman's work, what is most valuable for us is her decoding of oppressive cinematic conventions and her invention of new codes of nonvoyeuristic vision; yet these contributions go unnamed. In Yvonne Rainer's work, the issue is not one of this or that role model for feminists, not whether her women characters are too weak or too victimized or too individualistic. Rather, we can value precisely her refusal to pander (visually and emotionally), her frustration of audience expectation of spectacle (physical or psychic), and her complete reworking of traditional forms of melodrama and elegy to include modern feminist culture. Yet these elements, of greatest value to us, are not accorded critical priority.

The effect of not-naming is censorship, whether caused by the imperialism of the patriarchal language or the underdevelopment of a feminist language. We need to begin analyzing our own films, but first it is necessary to learn to speak in our own name. The recent history of feminist film criticism indicates the urgency of that need.

Feminist Film Criticism: In Two Voices

There have been two types of feminist film criticism, motivated by different geographic and ideological contexts, each speaking in a different voice.[9] According to Gilles Deleuze: "History of philosophy has an obvious, repressive function in philosophy: it is philosophy's very own Oedipus. All the same, you won't dare speak your own name as long as you have not read this and that, and that on this, and this on that. . . . To say something in one's own name is very strange."[10]

Speaking in one's own name versus speaking in the name of history is a familiar problem to anyone who has ever pursued a course of study, become involved in an established discipline, and then tried to speak out of personal experience or nonprofessional/nonacademic knowledge, without suddenly feeling quite schizophrenic. Obviously it is a schizophrenia especially familiar to feminists. The distinction between one's own voice and the voice of history is a handy one by which to distinguish the two types of feminist film criticism. At least initially, these two types could be characterized as either American or British: the one, American, seen as sociological or subjective, often a speaking out in one's own voice; the other, British, seen as methodological or more objective, often speaking in the voice of history. (The work of the past few years has blurred the original nationalist base of the categories: for example, the Parisian perspective of the California-based *Camera Obscura*.)

The originally American, so-called sociological, approach is exemplified by early *Women & Film* articles and much of the catalogue writing from festivals of that same period. The emphasis on legitimizing women's own reactions and making women's contributions visible resulted in a tendency toward reviews, getting information out, a tendency to offer testimony as theory. Although the journal was fruitful in this terrain, the weakness of the approach became the limits of its introspection, the boundaries established by the lack of a coherent methodology for moving out beyond the self. An example of this approach is Barbara Halpern Martineau's very eccentric, subjective, and illuminating analyses of the films of Nelly Kaplan and Agnes Varda.[11] A dismaying example of the decadent strain of this approach is Joan Mellen's mid-seventies book *Big Bad Wolves,* which offers personal interpretations of male characters and actors in a move to shift attention to the reformist arena of "human liberation."

The originally British, so-called theoretical approach is exemplified by the book *Notes on Women's Cinema* edited by Claire Johnston, by articles in *Screen,* and by the initial issues of *Camera Obscura* (which, like the British writing, defers to the French authorities). Committed to using some of the most advanced tools of critical analysis, such as semiology and psychoanalysis, this approach has tried to come to terms with *how* films mean — to move beyond regarding the image to analyzing the structure, codes, the general subtext of the works. The approach has been fruitful for its findings regarding signification, but its weakness has been a suppression of the personal and a seeming belief in the neutrality of the analytic tools. The critic's feminist voice has often been muted by this methodocracy.

Two of the most important products of this approach are pieces by Laura Mulvey and Claire Johnston.[12] Johnston critiques the image of woman in male cinema and finds her to be a signifier, not of woman, but of the absent phallus, a signifier of an absence rather than any presence. Similarly, Mulvey analyzes the nature of the cinematic spectator and finds evidence — in cinematic voyeurism and in the nature of the camera look — of the exclusively male spectator as a production assumption.

Another way of characterizing these two approaches would be to identify the American (sociological, or in one's own voice) as fundamentally phenomenological, and the British (theoretical, or the voice of history) as fundamentally analytical. The texts of Johnston and Mulvey taken together, for example, pose a monumental absence that is unduly pessimistic. The misplaced pessimism stems from their overvaluation of the production aspect of cinema, a misassumption that cinematic values are irrevocably embedded at the level of production and, once there, remain pernicious and inviolable. Woman is absent on the screen *and* she is absent in the audience, their analysis argues.

And yet here a bit of phenomenology would be helpful, a moment of speaking in one's own voice and wondering at the source in such a landscape of absence. As a woman sitting in the dark, watching that film made by and for men, with drag queens on the screen, what is my experience? Don't I in fact interact with that text and that context, with a conspicuous absence of passivity? For a woman's experiencing of culture under patriarchy is dialectical in a way that a man's can never be: our experience is like that of the exile, whom Brecht once singled out as the ultimate dialectician for that daily working out of cultural oppositions within a single body. It is crucial to emphasize here the possibility for texts to be transformed at the level of reception and not to fall into a trap of condescension toward our own developed powers as active producers of meaning.

The differences implicit in these two attitudes lead to quite different positions and strategies, as the following selection of quotations helps to point up. When interviewed regarding the reason for choosing her specific critical tools (auteurist, structuralist, psychoanalytic), Claire Johnston replied: "As far as I'm concerned, it's a question of what is theoretically correct; these new theoretical developments cannot be ignored, just as feminists cannot ignore Marx or Freud, because they represent crucial scientific developments."[13] In contrast to this vision of science as ideologically neutral would be the reiteration by such theoreticians as Audre Lorde, Adrienne Rich, and Mary Daly: "You have to be constantly critiquing even the tools you use to explore and define what it is to be female."[14]

In the same interview with Johnston, Pam Cook elaborated their aim: "Women are fixed in ideology in a particular way, which is definable in terms of the patriarchal system. I think we see our first need as primarily to define that place — the place that women are fixed in." In marked contrast to such a sphere of activity, the *Womanifesto* of the 1975 New York Conference of Feminists in the Media states: "We do not accept the existing power structure and we are committed to changing it by the content and structure of our images and by the ways we relate to each other in our work and with our audience."[15] In her own article, Laura Mulvey identified the advantage of psychoanalytic critiques as "their ability to advance our understanding of the status quo," a limited and modest claim; yet she herself went beyond such a goal in making (with Peter Wollen) *The Riddles of the Sphinx* (1976), a film that in its refusal of patriarchal codes and feminist concerns represents in fact a Part 2 of her original theory.[16]

I have termed the British approach pessimistic, a quality that may be perceived by supporters as realistic or by detractors as colonized. I have termed the American approach optimistic, a quality that may be viewed by supporters as radical or by detractors as unrealistic, utopian. It is not surprising, however, that such a dualism of critical approach has evolved. In *Woman's Consciousness, Man's World,* Sheila Rowbotham points out: "There is a long inchoate period during which the struggle between the language of experience and the language of theory becomes a kind of agony."[17] It is a problem common to an oppressed people at the point of formulating a new language with which to name that oppression, for the history of oppression has prevented the development of any unified language among its subjects. It is crucial for those of us working in the area of feminist film criticism to mend this rift, confront the agony, and begin developing a synthesis of maximally effective critical practices. Without names, our work remains anonymous, insecure, our continued visibility questionable.

Anticlimax: The Names

Without new names, we run the danger of losing title to films that we sorely need. By stretching the name "feminist" beyond all reasonable elasticity, we contribute to its ultimate impoverishment. At the same time, so many films have been partitioned off to established traditions, with the implication that these other names contradict or forestall any application of the name feminist to the works so annexed, that the domain of feminist cinema is fast becoming limited to that work concerned only with feminism as explicit subject matter. Feminist, if it is to make a comeback from the loss of meaning caused by its all-encompassing overuse, requires new legions of names to preserve for us the inner strengths, the not-yet-visible qualities of these films still lacking in definition.

Because this need is so very urgent, I here offer an experimental glossary of names as an aid to initiating a new stage of feminist criticism. These names are not likely to be an immediate hit. First, it's all well and good to call for new names to appear in the night sky like so many constellations, but it's quite another thing to invent them and commit them to paper. Second, there's the inevitable contradiction of complaining about names and then committing more naming acts. Third, there's the danger that, however unwieldy, these new names might be taken as formulas to be applied willy-nilly to every hapless film that comes our way. The point, after all, is not to set up new power institutions (feminist banks, feminist popes, feminist names), but rather to open the mind to new descriptive possibilities of nonpatriarchal, noncapitalist imaginings.

Validative. One of feminist filmmaking's greatest contributions is the body of films about women's lives, political struggles, organizing, and so on. These films have been vaguely classified under the cinema verité banner, where they reside in decidedly mixed company. Because they function as a validation and legitimation of women's culture and individual lives, the name "validative" would be a better choice. It has the added advantage of aligning the work with products of oppressed peoples (with the filmmaker as insider), whereas the cinema verité label represents the oppressors, who make films as superior outsiders documenting alien, implicitly inferior cultures, often from a position of condescension.

The feminist films of the early seventies were validative, and validative films continue to be an important component of feminist filmmaking. They may be ethnographic, documenting the evolution of women's lives and issues (as in *We're Alive*, 1975, a portrait and analysis of women in prison) or archaeological, uncovering women's hidden past (as in *Union Maids*, 1977, with its recovery of women's role in the labor movement, or Sylvia Morales's *Chicana*, 1978, the first film history of the Mexican American woman's struggle). The form is well established, yet the constantly evolving issues require new films, such as *We Will Not Be Beaten* (1981), a film on domestic violence culled from videotaped interviews with women. By employing the name validative in place of cinema verité, we can combat the patriarchal annexation of the woman filmmaker as one of the boys, that is, a professional who is not *of* the culture being filmed. It is a unifying name aimed at conserving strength.

Correspondence. An entirely different name is necessary for more avant-garde films, like those of Yvonne Rainer, Chantal Akerman, Helke Sander, and Laura Mulvey and Peter Wollen. Looking to literary history, we find a concern with the role played by letters ("personal" discourse) as a sustaining mode for women's writing during times of literary repression.

The publication of historical letters by famous and ordinary women has been a major component of the feminist publishing renaissance, just as the longstanding denigration of the genre as not "real" writing (that is, not certified by either a publishing house or monetary exchange) has been an additional goad for the creation of feminist alternatives to the literary establishment. A cinema of "correspondence" is a fitting homage to this tradition of introspective missives sent out into the world.

Equally relevant is the other definition of correspondence as "mutual response, the answering of things to each other," or, to take Swedenborg's literal Doctrine of Correspondence as an example, the tenet that "every natural object symbolizes or corresponds to some spiritual fact or principle which is, as it were, its archetype."[18] Films of correspondence, then, would be those investigating correspondences: between emotion and objectivity, narrative and deconstruction, art and ideology. Thus, *Jeanne Dielman* is a film of correspondence in its exploration of the bonds between housework and madness, prostitution and heterosexuality, epic and dramatic temporality.

What distinguishes such films of correspondence from formally similar films by male avant-garde filmmakers is their inclusion of the author within the text. *Film about a Woman Who . . .* corresponds to very clear experiences and emotional concerns in Rainer's life, and *Jeanne Dielman* draws on the gestures of the women in Akerman's family, whereas Michael Snow's *Rameau's Nephew* (1974) uses the form to suppress the author's presence. (Of course, there is a tradition of "diary" movies by men as well as women, but, significantly, the presence of Jonas Mekas in most of his diary films, like that of Godard in *Numero Deux,* is of the filmmaker rather than the "man" outside that professional role.) Similarly, Helke Sander in *The All-Round Reduced Personality — Redupers* (1977) revises the ironic, distanced narration of modernist German cinema to include the filmmaker in a shared first-person plural with her characters, unlike her compatriot Alexander Kluge, who always remains external and superior to his characters.

It is this resolute correspondence between form and content, to put it bluntly, that distinguishes the films of correspondence. Such films are essential to the development of new structures and forms for the creation and communication of feminist works and values; more experimental than validative, they are laying the groundwork of a feminist cinematic vocabulary.

Reconstructive. Several recent films suggest another name, located midway between the two described above, and dealing directly with issues of form posed by the political and emotional concerns of the work.

One such film is Sally Potter's *Thriller* (1979), a feminist murder mystery related as a first-person inquiry by the victim. Mimi, the seamstress of Puccini's *La Bohème,* investigates the cause of her death and the manner of her life, uncovering in the process the contradictions hidden by the bourgeois male artist. Michelle Citron's *Daughter Rite* (1978) probes relations between women in the family, using dramatic jump-cut sequences to critique cinema verité and optical printing to reexamine home movies, that North American index to domestic history.

Both *Thriller* and *Daughter Rite* are reconstructive in their rebuilding of other forms, whether grand opera or soap opera, according to feminist specifications. At the same time, both Potter and Citron reconstruct some basic cinematic styles (psychodrama, documentary) to create new feminist forms, in harmony with the desires of the audience as well as the theoretical concerns of the filmmakers. By reconstructing forms in a constructive manner, these films build bridges between the needs of women and the goals of art.

Medusan. Humor should not be overlooked as a weapon of great power. Comedy requires further cultivation for its revolutionary potential as a deflator of the patriarchal order and an extraordinary leveler and re-inventor of dramatic structure. An acknowledgment of the subversive power of humor, the name "Medusan" is taken from Hélène Cixous's "The Laugh of the Medusa," in which she celebrates the potential of feminist texts "to blow up the law, to break up the 'truth' with laughter."[19] Cixous's contention that when women confront the figure of Medusa she will be laughing is a rejoinder to Freud's posing the "Medusa's Head" as an incarnation of male castration fears. For Cixous, women are having the last laugh. And, to be sure, all the films in this camp deal with combinations of humor and sexuality.

Vera Chytilova's *Daisies* (1966) was one of the first films by a woman to move in the direction of anarchic sexuality, though its disruptive humor was received largely as slapstick at the time. Nelly Kaplan's two films, *A Very Curious Girl* (1971) and *Nea* (1976), also offer an explosive humor coupled with sexuality to discomfort patriarchal society (even though her fondness for "happy" endings that restore order has discomfited many feminist critics). Jan Oxenberg's *A Comedy in Six Unnatural Acts* (1975) is an excellent example of a Medusan film, attacking not just men or sexism but the heterosexually defined stereotypes of lesbianism; its success has been demonstrated by its raucous cult reception and, more pointedly, by its tendency to polarize a mixed audience along the lines not of class but of sexual preference. It is disruptive of homophobic complacency with a force never approached by analytical films or those defensive of lesbianism.

Another highly Medusan film is Jacques Rivette's *Celine and Julie Go Boating* (1974). This may be somewhat curious, as it is directed by a man, but production credits indicate a total collaboration with the four actresses and coscenarists. In the movie, Celine and Julie enter each other's lives by magic and books, joined in a unity of farce; once they are together, each proceeds to demolish the other's ties to men (an employer, a childhood lover) by using humor, laughing in the face of male fantasies and expectations and thus "spoiling" the relationships with a fungus of parody. The film has been criticized as silly, for Juliet Berto and Dominique Labourier do laugh constantly—at the other characters, themselves, the audience, acting itself—yet their laughter ultimately proves their finest arsenal, enabling them to rescue the plot's girl-child from a darkly imminent Henry Jamesian destruction simply through a laughing refusal to obey its allegedly binding rules. Again, *Celine and Julie* has consistently divided its audience according to whom it threatens: it has become a cult feminist movie even as the male critical establishment (except for Rivette fan Jonathan Rosenbaum) has denounced the film as silly, belabored, and too obvious.

Corrective Realism. As mentioned earlier, the tradition of realism in the cinema has never done well by women. Indeed, extolling realism to women is rather like praising the criminal to the victim, so thoroughly have women been falsified under its banner. A feminist feature cinema, generally representational, is now developing, with a regular cast of actresses, a story line, aimed at a wide audience and an acceptance of many cinematic conventions. The women making these films, however, are so thoroughly transforming the characterizations and the narrative workings of traditional realism that they have created a new feminist cinema of "corrective realism."

Thus, in Margarethe von Trotta's *The Second Awakening of Christa Klages* (1977), it is the women's actions that advance the narrative; bonding between women functions to save, not to paralyze or trap the characters; running away brings Christa freedom, while holding ground brings her male lover only death. The film has outrageously inventive character details, an attention to the minutiae of daily life, an endorsement of emotion and intuitive ties, and an infectious humor. Marta Meszaros's *Women* (1978) presents a profound reworking of socialist realism in its depiction of the friendship between two women in a Hungarian work hostel. The alternating close-ups and medium shots become a means of social critique, while the more traditional portrayal of the growing intimacy between the two women insistently places emotional concerns at the center of the film. Both films successfully adapt an existing cinematic tradition to feminist purposes, going far beyond a simple "positive role model" in their establishment of a feminist cinematic environment within which to envision female protagonists and their activities.

These, then, are a few of the naming possibilities. However, it is not only the feminist films that demand new names, but also (for clarity) the films being made by men about women.

Projectile. One name resurrected from the fifties by seventies criticism via Molly Haskell's recoining was the "woman's film," the matinee melodramas that, cleared of pejorative connotations, were refit for relevance to women's cinematic concerns today. Wishful thinking. The name was Hollywood's and there it stays, demonstrated by the new "woman's films" that are pushing actual women's films off the screen, out into the dark.

These are male fantasies of women: men's projections of themselves and their fears onto female characters. The name "projectile" identifies these films' true nature and gives an added awareness of the destructive impact of male illusions in the female audience. It is time the bluff was called on the touted authenticity of these works, which pose as objective while remaining entirely subjective in their conception and execution.

The clearest justification for this name can be found in director Paul Mazursky's description of his *An Unmarried Woman* (1978):

> I don't know if this is a woman's movie or not. I don't know what that means anymore. I wanted to get inside a woman's head. I've felt that all the pictures I've done, I've done with men. I put myself inside a man's head, using myself a lot. I wanted this time to think like a woman. That's one of the reasons there was so much rewriting. . . . There were many things the women I cast in the film . . . wouldn't say. They'd tell me why, and I'd say, "Well, what would you say? and I'd let them say that. I used a real therapist; I wanted a woman, and I had to change what she said based on what she is. In other words, the only thing I could have done was to get a woman to help me write it. I thought about that for a while, but in the end I think it worked out.[20]

Films such as this one (and *The Turning Point, Pretty Baby, Luna,* and so on, ad infinitum) are aimed fatally at us; they deserve to be named projectile.

Certainly the names offered here do not cover all possibilities, nor can every film be fit neatly into one category. But I hope their relative usefulness or failings will prompt a continuation of the process by others. The urgency of the naming task cannot be overstated.

Warning Signs: A Postscript (1979)

We are now in a period of normalization, a time that can offer feminists complacency as a mask for co-optation. Scanning the horizon for signs of backlash and propaganda, the storm clouds within feminist film criticism are gathering most clearly over issues of form. It has become a truism to call for new forms. Over and over, we have heard the sacred vows: you can't put new revolutionary subjects/messages into reactionary forms; new forms, a new antipatriarchal film language for feminist cinema, must be developed. Although certainly true to an extent, form remains only one element of the work. And the valorization of form above and independent of other criteria has begun to create its own problems.

There is the misconception that form, unlike subject matter, is inviolate and can somehow encase the meaning in protective armor. But form is as co-optable as other elements. An analysis by critic Julianne Burton of the cinema novo movement in Brazil raised this exact point by demonstrating how the Brazilian state film apparatus took over the forms and styles of cinema novo and stripped them of their ideological significance as one means of disarming the movement.[21] If we make a fetish of the long take, the unmediated shot, and so on as feminist per se, then we will shortly be at a loss over how to evaluate the facsimiles proliferating in the wake of such a definition.

Furthermore, the reliance on form as the ultimate gauge of a film's worth sets up an inevitable hierarchy that places reconstructive films or films of correspondence at the top of a pyramid, leaving corrective realist or validative approaches among the baser elements. This itself is a complex problem. First, such a view reproduces the notion of history as "progress" and supposes that forms, like technology, grow cumulatively better and better; some believe in that sort of linear quality, but I don't. Second, criticism by Christine Gledhill (of film) and Myra Love (of literature) has questioned the naturalness of the Brechtian, postmodernist, deconstructive model as a feminist strategy, pointing out the real drawbacks of its endemic authoritarianism and ambiguity.[22] Third, our very reasons for supporting such work must at least be examined honestly. Carolyn Heilbrun's point should be heeded: "Critics, and particularly academics, are understandably prone to admire and overvalue the carefully construed, almost puzzle-like novel [read *film*], not only for its profundities, but because it provides them, in explication, with their livelihood."[23] Just as a generosity of criticism can provide the strongest support for feminist filmmakers, so acceptance of a variety of filmic strategies can provide the vigor needed by the feminist audience.

For we must look to the filmmaker and viewer for a way out of this aesthetic cul-de-sac. Aesthetics are not eternally embedded in a work like a penny in a cube of Lucite. They are dependent on and subject to the work's reception. The formal values of a film cannot be considered in isolation, cut off from the thematic correspondents within the text and from the social determinants without. Reception by viewers as well as by critics is key to any film's meaning. As my chronology indicates, feminist cinema arose out of a need not only on the part of the filmmakers and writers, but on the part of the women they knew to be their audience. Today we must constantly check feminist film work to gauge how alive this thread of connection still is, how communicable its feminist values are.

We are in a time of transition now, when we still have the luxury of enjoying feminist work on its makers' own terms, without having to sift the sands paranoically for impostors. But this transitional period is running out: as the cultural lag catches up, the dominant and avant-garde cinema may begin to incorporate feminist success before we recognize what we've lost. The emphasis on form makes that incorporation easier.

Burton ended her presentation with a call for the inscription of modes of production within the body of Third World film criticism. Therein lies a clue. Feminism has always emphasized process; now it's time that this process of production and reception be inscribed within the critical text. How was the film made? With what intention? With what kind of crew? With what relationship to the subject? How was it produced? Who is distributing it? Where is it being shown? For what audience is it constructed? How is it available? How is it being received? There is no need to establish a tyranny of the productive sphere over a film's definition, nor to authorize only immediately popular films, but it will prove helpful in the difficult times ahead of us to keep this bottom line of method and context in mind, to avoid painting ourselves into a corner.

Formal devices are progressive only if they are employed with a goal beyond aesthetics alone. Here, finally, is the end of the line. Feminist film criticism cannot solve problems still undefined in the sphere of feminist thought and activity at large. We all are continually borrowing from and adding to each other's ideas, energies, insights, across disciplines. We also need to develop lines of communication across the boundaries of race, class, and sexuality. In Cuba, I heard a presentation by Alfredo Guevara, founder and director of the Cuban Film Institute. He explained its efforts to educate the Cuban audience to the tricks of the cinema, to demystify the technology, to give the viewers the means with which to defend themselves against cinematic hypnosis, to challenge the dominant ideology of world cinema, to create a new liberated generation of viewers. I will never forget his next words: "We do not claim to have created this audience already, nor do we think it is a task only of cinema." The crisis of naming requires more than an etymologist to solve it.

Yet Another Postscript (1991)

Writing in the seventies, with no crystal ball at hand, I could not have foreseen how changed a landscape would welcome this essay back into print. Now, in the first decade of the post–cold war, of the total militarization of American life, of worldwide recession, the end of Communism and Socialism as viable alternatives, the rollback of civil rights and reproductive rights, the evolution of a quasi-fascist form of capitalism, and the emergence of a repressive apparatus directed explicitly at representation (photography and film, in particular, though the art world as a whole is under siege), this essay shines for me today brightly but innocently, a clarion call from another era.

This is not to say that its lessons have gone out of date, that its insights are not still relevant, nor its terminologies obsolete. Not at all. But they are insufficient. Within the world of feminist film, three shifts of direction since this essay's first appearance are particularly striking.

First, narrative has assumed precedence over documentary as the favored medium for women filmmakers and video artists. In part, this turn to fiction has been necessitated by changes in economics and funding patterns (the politically motivated withdrawal of the National Endowment for the Humanities monies that funded the early ambitious documentaries, the increased costs of shooting in film at the ratio demanded by the seventies working methods, and the development of investment models for film production by independent director-producers). In equal part, however, it was probably a response to the very real pressures brought to bear on filmmakers who took on the burden of uplifting the gender: fiction allows more leeway, sits more easily with the auteurist style demanded by the age, and offers more freedom from collective expectations. Also, the short film has lost ground to the feature in terms of prestige, with many filmmakers trying hard to make the transition. Though numerous films are still made in the short format (particularly by women of color), the market that once sustained that arena is diminished.

Second, the whiteness that is so pronounced a characteristic of this text thankfully has been eradicated by the important works produced in the United States throughout the eighties and nineties by women of color. A filmography and videography of considerable length would be required to do justice to the subject; any such list would certainly have to include the independent works of Martina Attille, Camille Billops, Shu-Lea Cheang, Ayoka Chenzira, Christine Choy, Julie Dash, Zeinabu Davis, Leslie Harris, Indu Krishnan, Daresha Kyi, Alile Sharon Larkin, Tracey Moffat, Sylvia Morales, Emiko Omori, Midi Onodera, Ngozi A. Onwurah, Michelle Parkerson, Pratibha Parmar, Lourdes Portillo, Demetria Royals, Kathe Sandler, Jacqueline Shearer, Valerie Soe, Renee Tajima, Rea Tajiri, Pam Tom, Janice Tanaka, Trinh T. Minh-ha, and dozens more.

The genre choices and narrative strategies are wildly divergent, as would be expected from such a broad movement of what's increasingly (and inadequately) seen as "multiculturalism" in a female chord. But already — to take just one example — in the lyrical revivalism of Julie Dash's first feature, *Daughters of the Dust,* there are dream glimpses of a future of a different color, in which aesthetic decisions follow a different history. Further, the arrival of a critical film theory advanced by women of color has begun to parallel the evolution of the films and videotapes: writers like Jacqueline Bobo, Rosa Linda Fregoso, Coco Fusco, bell hooks, Lisa Jones, Valerie Smith, and Michelle Wallace are redefining the field, moving easily outside the parameters of official haute theory within which so many texts are restricted and from which so many actual films and videotapes are excluded. They are looking, sometimes for the first time, at the aesthetic foundations of these new works and, just as important, critiquing productions from the brothers (Spike Lee, Luis Valdez), whose films are filling the commercial screens still empty of women.

Third, and perhaps most obvious, is the degree to which the shape and structure of feminist film criticism has moved decisively into the academy since the original writing of this piece—and as a result, how much further it has moved away from the women making films and videos today. No longer are festivals and non-university-based conferences likely to be cited in an imaginary timeline of significances. No longer do diverse sectors of the women's "community" meet in fractious dialogue in a common space occasioned by a film screening. The very word has changed: the operative noun is *theory,* not criticism, not history, not women's studies.

One positive development within academia is the sudden explosion of queer studies, with the annual gay and lesbian studies conference besieged by papers on films and videos and popular culture (the most recent event even included a reconsideration of Dusty Springfield). Most exciting here is the common cause made by critics, activists, academics, filmmakers, and video artists, not yet separated by the conflicting allegiances and career paths that will undoubtedly set in later. Even in the established bedrock of film studies, established scholars like Judith Mayne and Teresa de Lauretis have moved increasingly into the development of a lesbian theory for film analysis and viewing, while other scholars like Sue-Ellen Case and Martha Gever challenge the heterosexual biases of mainstream feminist theory. In film and video, artists like Sheila McLaughlin, Cecilia Dougherty, Sadie Benning, Jane Cottis and Kaucyila Brooke, and Julie Zando (and Onodera, Parkerson, and Parmar mentioned above) are inventing new vernaculars for the future. Others are continuing the example they've already set (Ulrike Ottinger, for instance) or preparing to have their work reflect a changed status (the newly out Yvonne Rainer).

The field has changed a great deal, and with any luck, it will change even more. For these are urgent times that we face. It's already clear that the old categories and ways of thinking will not work well enough for us. Hopefully the decade of the nineties will bring exciting breakthroughs from new generations forged in struggles against increasing oppression, but speaking also from the power and authority and sense of self that the work of the seventies and eighties has made possible. Now, for the first time, we have communities constituted that can speak in (their own) tongues. We don't all speak the same language, but translation is still possible.

Of course, the diversity of the field depends on the ability to move forward against today's strong current of racism. Relations between the races are the worst I've seen in my lifetime, with segregation, both exclusionary and chosen, increasingly the major form of social organization. Like the rest of society, this field must come to terms with racism, up to and well beyond the element of curriculum inclusion, so that full participation can ensure the field's renewal, heterogeneity, and value. Like patients on the couch, we need the Talking Cure. Like patients rising up to leave the session, we need action, too. If the field of feminist film studies, encompassing video and including theory alongside practice, can transcend the status quo, build on its foundation, and move forward, then the worst of times could be the best of times — soon.

Prologue.

O Brave

New World

Havana in 1978? The very idea smacked of a kind of pilgrimage to a Shangri-La, an illusion suddenly made manifest. It was still a time of dictatorships in Latin America, and Havana had become the great crossroads where Latin Americans met each other and where the rest of the world came still to pay homage to the great socialist experiment fomenting revolution under the nose of the United States. Havana was a mecca for Latin American intellectuals, freedom fighters, political exiles, European fellow travelers, and anyone curious enough to brave the trip. I had never been New Left enough (or macho enough) to join one of the Venceremos brigades that defiantly broke the blockade to work on sugarcane harvests or build houses. Suddenly, though, an alternative route materialized.

Tricontinental, the company that at that time distributed virtually all Latin American films in the United States to a network of solidarity committees, activist organizations, and university Latin American curricula, decided to organize a special trip to the Cuban Film Institute (ICAIC) to educate North American journalists and critics about Cuban film firsthand. I had programmed lots of Tricontinental's films at the Film Center. Now that I'd left there, I had time on my hands and, with my Latin American travel still fresh, I had a deep desire to witness the phenomenon of Cuba. My new friend Joan Braderman talked me into coming along as her roommate.

Back then, it was impossible to fly directly from the United States to Havana. The U.S. embargo had been fiercely enforced by the Nixon administration, the Carter-era thaw was just beginning, and U.S. law still prohibited direct contact in any form, especially a Cuban plane landing on "our" soil. (Still true today, by the way.) My parents, filled with images of the Cuban Missile Crisis and press coverage of Castro as the devil incarnate, worried that Cuba wouldn't let me back out; I reminded my lifelong-Republican father that the problem instead was whether the U.S. government would let me back in without harrassment or prosecution. Just before leaving, I met with a Cuban friend in Chicago, Nereida Garcia, to get letters and photos to deliver to her grandmother and aunt, whom she hadn't seen since leaving the island for the United States with her family eight years before. I packed their names and address, promising to visit them, deliver the package, and bring back reports.

Our Chicago group, which included my *Jump Cut* compatriot Julia Lesage, was scheduled to fly via Toronto. There we received an impromptu orientation from Canadian filmmaker Vivienne Leebosch, whose documentary about the lives of Cuban women, *Buenos Días, Compañeras*, had recently been finished. She kept us awake late into the night with her remarkable story of a legendary Cuban director, Sara Gomez, whose family she visited whenever she traveled to the island. Her name was new to us. Vivienne explained that Sarita, as she'd been called, was the only Black woman director in the entire Cuban film industry and the only Cuban woman ever to have made a feature film, *One Way or Another* (*De Cierta Manera*), which was nearly finished at the time of her sudden and unexpected death in 1974. The postproduction was nearly complete, but her 16mm negative had been damaged by Cuba's 35mm labs, delaying its completion by several years. The film supposedly was ready for release now, and she urged us to ask about it.

First, however, we asked her all about Sara. Vivienne had gone to Cuba with the idea of making a documentary in collaboration with Sara on the situation of Cuban women and had already contacted her to make arrangements. Alas, by the time Vivienne arrived, Sara had died. Her family took Vivienne's arrival as a kind of sign and welcomed her nonetheless, teaching her the ropes of working in Cuba and providing her all kinds of protection, including the benefits of Santería, the syncretic Yoruba-Catholic religion that Sara's mother practiced. (Her mother's status as a *santera* was ignored by the many Western critics who later faulted the film for a condemnation of Santería, when it was actually one sect only, the machismo-dominated *abacua,* that Sara targeted in her film. Sara herself was a lifelong devotee of Santería, which in Cuba has always had a reputation for inclusivity and incorporated women and gay men as figures of authority.)

It was from Vivienne that we heard the first, and for me still the definitive, version of Sara's death. It goes like this: Sara's daughter was critically ill in the hospital and Sara, in the final stages of postproduction, was distraught. The doctors told her that her daughter would live if she survived that night, but that if she were going to succumb to the illness, it would be that night that she would die. Sara herself suffered from asthma, as do a vast number of Cubans and other Caribbean islanders. Sara's family believed that she made a deal with the Santería gods that night: take me, let my daughter live. By dawn, Sara was dead from an acute asthmatic attack and her daughter was out of danger.

We were an odd little ship of fools there in Cuba, a group of U.S. fellow travelers with an interest in film and some version of progressive politics to bind us until other interests would tear us asunder. Peter Biskind and Elizabeth Hess (of *Seven Days* and *Heresies* allegiance at the time), Judy Stone (journalist, I. F. Stone's sister, authority on B. Traven), Marti Wilson (then running a social service agency in the Bay Area and organizing the African Film Society), Rob Baker (film editor of the now-defunct *Soho Weekly News*), Michele Russell (then a member of the triumphant Black political movement in Detroit), Julianne Burton (a professor at U.C.-Santa Cruz and editor of *Jump Cut*'s special Cuban film sections), Cheryll Greene (then an editor at *Essence*), and Joan and Julia and *Jump Cut*'s John Hess, among others. And I, of course, deep in professional limbo and trying to figure out just who I was.

We arrived in Cuba variously full of New Left expectations, feminist suspicions, gay agendas, and impossibly lofty ideals mingling with hard-headed journalistic inquisitiveness. We'd leave no stone unturned, no film unseen, no byway unexplored. A trio of us even made a pilgrimage to the tiny apartment home of Sara's parents and her daughter to hear their stories. (Times have changed, of course: today, they all live in France.)

We watched films day and night, met with Cuba's best-known directors and actors and technicians, ate at legendary restaurants like the Floridita and the Bodeguita del Medio, visited the Hemingway museum, and swam at Veradero Beach in front of the Du Pont mansion that had once ruled its shore in elite isolation. We grazed the fields of attractions that served, before us and long after, as de rigeur stops for first-time gringo visitors. We wandered the streets at all hours and stayed up half the night talking with our new Cuban friends. We drank mojitos and daiquiris and Cuba Libres until the early hours of the morning.

One night, a few of us out prowling the city stumbled upon an old, decommissioned prop plane sitting in the middle of an empty lot with airfield stairs leading up to it. Inside, we found a strange scene: all the airline seats in place, lights out, drinks served on fold-down trays, and a bunch of Cuban "passengers" necking in the darkness. Something about lack of private space. We had a drink and left, walked the Malecon seawall the rest of the night. Joan and I kept talking through our culture shock, trying to assimilate as quickly as possible cross-cultural experiences that happened without a script, without preparation, sometimes even without language, but never without euphoria.

Our daily seminars immersed us in the history and current debates of Cuban cinema. It was clear to me that Sara's example had continued to haunt Cuban cinema long after her physical departure. Her mentor, the late Tomás Gutiérrez Alea (known as Titon), was the most famous of all Cuban directors; yet a decade later, he would go on to break with his own style to make *Hasta Cierto Punto* (*Up to a Certain Point*) and explicitly invoke Sara's method of mixing documentary and fiction together to represent the life of ordinary Cuban workers and the conflicts dogging women in particular. Rigoberto Lopez, who became known for his documentaries on African struggles and Cuba's military involvement, had been an assistant to Sara on the film. Even in the late eighties, Sara was enough of a cause célèbre for the Center for Cuban Studies in New York to mount an exhibition of her early documentaries.

Years later, back in Toronto on a visit, I met someone at my friend Helga Stephenson's house who turned out to be central to the narrative of Sara's life. Helga had lived in Havana for several years and this houseguest turned out to be her great friend, Chino, a Cuban who still lives on the island, works as a restaurateur, and deserves an oral history of his own. Chino treated me to tales of growing up with his mother's best friend's daughter—one Sara Gomez Yera—in the provinces in the forties, then moving with her to Havana to study and make their fortune in the artistic ferment of their generation. They were inseparable pals—except for the time Chino spent as a prisoner in the notorious UMAP (Military Units for the Aid of Production) camps for the "reeducation" of homosexuals in the mid-sixties—until her death; he is as close to her family today as when they all lived in Havana.

Back in 1978, a trip to Cuba was not to be taken lightly, nor did the experience sit lightly on our shoulders. The ten days in Havana were transformative. To be sure, people reacted in different ways: one by having an affair with a Cuban critic, another by drawing up petitions calling for the chain-smoking Cubans to enforce smoke-free rooms. Charges of ethnocentrism, classism, racism, sexism flew wildly. Yet the usual vituperative nature of left events in that era was muted by the profound effect on us of the Cuban political example and the nature of the society that we saw, or thought we saw, all around us.

We talked to people who seemed to be living history. One night, Julianne Burton and I sat for hours around a table with less than half a dozen other Cubans and Americans listening to Julio Garcia Espinosa, then head of the cultural ministry that oversaw film as well as cabarets. Something about the discussion triggered his curiosity: instead of ending the session late that night, he invited us all downstairs to a screening room and showed us a film that he'd recently finished but hadn't yet decided whether to release (he never did). His title, *Son o no son,* used Shakespeare's "To be or not to be" to pun off the Cuban musical form, the *son,* in a bilingual joke. The film opened with Garcia Espinosa's addressing a crisis in Latin American film: Why, after nearly two decades of development, had nobody yet produced a Latin American musical? The film struck me as a brilliant consideration of art, audience, popular culture, and genre. I was so inspired by that evening that scenes of the never-released film live on in my head today even though I never saw it again. I still dream of reviving it.

Other meetings yielded other sets of knowledge and moments of pleasure. In the "Filmmakers in Angola" session, for example, assistant director Norma Martinez described going to Angola with a theater troupe in 1976 to perform at the front for the Cuban troops, then volunteering to go back to work on the Cuban film, *Angola, Victory of Hope.* She was charismatic and articulate and turned out to be pivotal when we finally convinced the ICAIC brass to allow a meeting between U.S. and Cuban women. Stiff and formal, it finally was galvanized into a true exchange of views when Pastor Vega, one of the Cuban men who insisted on attending, intervened with remarks about feminine nature that managed to infuriate and therefore unify all of us. Eventually we were able to bypass formality and have a real exchange of views and develop friendships. For a cross-cultural, multiracial group of women, it was a significant achievement.

By the end of the stay, we were all instant experts on Cuban film, society, gender issues, international politics, and anything else we could get our hands on. It was a bonding experience: Marti and Joan and I have remained friends for years, across miles of separation, different relationships, and divorces, but always with a shared sense of historic mission that, for one month in 1978, centered around a little island and its example. Many of us would go back and write about the experience, while others would live it—in some totally unexpected fashion. I returned to Chicago and gave my friend Nereida her family's greetings. (I had indeed tracked them down and met briefly with them in the lobby of the fifties Mafia-built Habana Riviera.) In a mirror image of the Toronto orientation, we sat up for hours talking about Cuba in a marathon debriefing. Among other things, I told her of our clumsy attempts to find out about gay life in Havana. She proceeded to fill me in on the scene in detail, where people hung out, which theaters and cafés, and of course, La Coppelia, the outdoor ice cream parlor immortalized by Titon in *Strawberry and Chocolate*. I was amused at our ignorance and dashed off a postcard to Rob Baker in the spirit of sharing that the trip had engendered.

I never heard back from him, so imagine my horror when the next *Soho News* arrived in my mailbox with a surprise: the message from my postcard, word for word, appended to the end of Rob's article, with my name prominently displayed and Nereida not only named but outed, avant la lettre. That's how I lost my innocence about journalistic practice, discovered the difference between "off" and "on" the record, and stumbled into the limits of camaraderie when tested by careerism.

That trip to Cuba would haunt my life for years to come, and is part of it still. *One Way or Another* remains one of the few films from the Third World, certainly by a woman of color, to receive attention in feminist film circles. It figures in several books and anthologies of the early eighties, where scholars who'd discovered it in U.S. or British release frequently misunderstood its race politics and misinterpreted its view of Santería. I knew enough people involved with Santería to view it differently, and my experience of seeing the film for the first time in Havana, surrounded by Sara's colleagues and family, forever marked my sense of its wisdom and power.

My tendency to see the film in a political context was reinforced by a project I undertook a few summers later, when I organized a community film exhibition series of Latin American film with Nereida and a group of Puerto Rican neighbors and friends with ties to the Puerto Rican independence struggle. It was a hot summer, just before or after (memory isn't always infallible) the Puerto Rican nationalist group FALN was busted in the suburbs of Chicago. Around the same time, the Puerto Rican nationalists who had been held in prison for decades for their daring armed attack on Congress were released, and a group of us raced to a rally at a neighborhood church to hear the legendary Lolita Lebron speak.

Our group decided to present the films in another church near Humboldt Park: it was cheap, it was located in the middle of the barrio, and it was run by elderly progressives whose Communist credentials were apparent from the USSR happy peasant posters on the walls and the Soviet projectors in the booth. The church's caretaker was proud of its solidarity work: "Last winter, we had a meeting here of Iranian militants. For days, they met and talked and argued. They ate here and slept here. Five months later, boom, a revolution in Iran." Well, fine. But when we tried to publicize the film series, Cine del Pueblo, by handing out flyers in the neighborhood, we were met with deep suspicion. If a movie wasn't showing in a movie theater, it turned out, then the show must be a ploy or a trap, either religious or political. We were met with distrust and had to work hard to develop an audience for films for which we mistakenly thought that the *gente* would have a natural taste.

After reviewing the film in the Chicago *Reader,* I decided to expand my article into a longer essay. So I happily accepted an invitation from Patricia Erens, who was going through a stormy divorce, to spend a few final days at the summer house she was about to lose. We held a sort of two-woman writing retreat. I hauled out my IBM Selectric typewriter, state of the art for the time, and produced the following piece, but I never did publish it. However, I continued to lecture on *One Way or Another* throughout the eighties and rediscovered a use for it in documentary film classes in the nineties, where its mix of documentary and fiction and its wonderfully multivocal narration provide a useful precedent to the docufiction mixes of the current decade.

6.

One Way or Another: Sara Gomez and the Cuban Experience (1978)

The Filmmaker

Sara. Already a legend in Cuba and abroad. One of the first women to train at ICAIC, beginning after Stokely Carmichael's visit to the island. The first woman to direct a feature film in Cuba. The first feature director to shoot in 16mm. The first Cuban director to die before the film's completion. Dead at the age of thirty-one, struck down by an asthma attack in the final stage of the film's production, which was completed in her stead by Tomás Gutiérrez Alea (Titon), who dedicated his *Last Supper* to the memory of Sara Gomez.

In Cuba, I heard enough stories about Sara to fill in some of the facts of her life. How she originally went to Havana as a pianist (six years of piano, no less, at the Conservatory of Havana) and then switched to journalism, working on the youth paper *Mella* and the Sunday supplement, *Holy Domingo*. At the university, she worked with the folklore/ethnography unit and dedicated herself to the study of traditional cultural practices. Then she entered the bastion of White patriarchal privilege: she went to ICAIC, the Cuban Film Institute, to learn filmmaking and to fuse that medium with her journalistic and artistic interests. She started out as an assistant editor and assistant director.

Legend has it that Sara was influenced by the Black Power movement in the United States and by Stokely Carmichael's visit to Cuba. She was the first Cuban to wear an Afro, causing a sensation. Her first husband and father of her child was a "blanco," or White Cuban, who after her death tried to reclaim his daughter by telling her she was White; no, "Soy negra," said the girl and refused to leave her grandparents' house. Sara's companion at the time of her death, Germinal Hernández, was an Afro-Cuban like herself, but one who came from the class of *marginales* and upon whom the character of Mario supposedly was based. He was the sound recordist on the film and was still at ICAIC in 1978.

ICAIC was reportedly divided for and against Sara: supposedly, Santiago Alvarez, dean of the Cuban documentary, hated her; but she also had friends, and was protected within ICAIC by Titon himself. Between 1964 and 1973, she directed ten documentary shorts, a number of which were extraordinary pieces that clearly anticipated her final achievement. Today they read as blueprints for *De Cierta Manera,* early runs at the same material in an entirely documentary idiom, fascinating for their sophisticated relationship to the contemporary problems of Cuban life. Gutiérrez Alea described the immediacy of her personality that led to her ability to sell her ideas within ICAIC and to forge relationships with her film subjects. He described her working process as "a fiery chaos" that produced unique views of Cuban society.

The Tradition

One Way or Another (made in Cuba in 1974, released in the United States in autumn 1978) is the most original film to come out of Cuba since Gutiérrez Alea's *Memories of Underdevelopment,* with which it is likely to be compared for its utterly frank appraisal of the difficulties besetting individuals trying to live in a new revolutionary society. The film is at once entirely typical of, and very different from, the Cuban film tradition.

Cuban cinema has been widely, and rightly, acclaimed for its ability to invent new formal strategies, most notably the breakdown of documentary and fiction distinctions to arrive at an integrated style capable at once of unmasking the realism of traditional narrative and the verisimilitude of documentary. Past approaches have included such devices as restaging historical events according to a demystified contemporary perspective (e.g., *Bay of Pigs*), allowing actual newsreel footage to impinge upon the narrative and thus challenge the naturalness of its fictions (e.g., *Memories of Underdevelopment*), counterpointing the visual flow with a song that encourages an analysis of its representation (e.g., *Lucia,* part 3), juxtaposing styles indicative of differing ideological structures (e.g., *The*

Other Francisco), and utilizing flashbacks to open up the closed world of the film's own moment (e.g., the films of Manuel Octavio Gomez). Sara Gomez uses virtually all of these techniques, yet both formally and thematically she pushes past existing boundaries to create a film that is far more than the sum of its parts.

One instance of this new terrain is the extent to which she has integrated documentary and fictive modes of representation. Although the two had been integrated before, the documentary passages most often functioned in other films as a reality check on the narrative without actually dislodging the narrative dominance. *One Way or Another,* however, can be seen as an instance of actually pushing narrative into a subordinate relation to the documentary elements. The actors, for example, were popular stars in Cuban film and television, yet they were made to surrender part of their professional privilege through having their actual names (Mario and Yolanda) assigned to their "characters." Not only do they inhabit otherwise anonymous cinema-verité-looking street scenes — a popular technique — but they also must interact with nonactors playing out their own lives in intimate, improvised scenes. Gomez used psychodrama methods to build the unified, equitable level of interaction apparent within the film.

Another instance of her radical expansion of Cuban formal innovation is her insistence on shooting in 16mm, a rarity in the 35mm industry. Traditionally, the use of 35mm had granted the documentary segments a "look" equally weighted with the larger narrative whole. Instead, Gomez has kept her fiction rigorously within the aesthetic realm of her documentary subject. The unintimidating nature of the portable 16mm equipment has effected a spontaneity and trust on the part of those real-life protagonists, while lending a necessary roughness to the depictions of the three scripted characters. The clear consciousness motivating this strategy is spelled out in the film's opening credits, which announce it as "a film about real people, and some fictitious ones." Gomez has tipped the balance of the scales, successfully playing out a fiction on the stage of daily life, an unprecedented achievement even for the resourceful Cuban cinema.

There is another instance of Gomez's departure from previous Cuban cinematic practice that occurs not in these realms of form or methodology, but surprisingly enough in the area of theme. When most Americans think about the Cuban Revolution, they are likely to focus on the dilemma of the intellectual or the bourgeoisie in adjusting to a society no longer stratified in their favor. Thus the popularity in the United States of a film like *Memories of Underdevelopment.* We tend to assume that, because the lower classes are the beneficiaries of a revolution, their adaptation to the revolutionary society must be automatic. Not so. The Cubans know the enormous problems attending the integration of all sectors of society into the ways of the revolution—but *One Way or Another* is the first film to communicate to us the magnitude of that struggle. Returning to the example of *Memories of Underdevelopment,* it is clear that Gomez has turned that film upside down to examine the experience of the "marginal" class, the class of which she herself was a product.

One Way or Another critiques machismo, class and race discrimination, and people's dogged resistance to change. Specifically, Gomez has focused her attention on the *marginales,* those people who, prior to the 1959 revolution, lived on the very margin of society—as the unemployed, beggars, illiterates, prostitutes, or criminals—and who now, after the revolution, still cling tenaciously to old patterns of defensive behavior that no longer work to their advantage. Areas of concern include the unstable family structure, inertia, daily violence, and male chauvinism. At no point does Gomez resort to rhetoric, allegory, or abstract solutions. She is concerned with real people and individual growth, with the process of confronting contradictions rather than the status of formulas. These are people and themes barely glimpsed in Cuban cinema prior to 1974.

The Story

Yolanda, Mario, and Humberto are the three "fictitious ones" in the story. Yolanda is a young, city-bred schoolteacher of middle-class background who has divorced her husband because of his opposition to her independent career. She has come to teach in Miraflores, a model housing development constructed on the site of Las Yaguas (a notorious Havana slum) in 1962 by volunteer brigades composed of the residents. There she meets Mario, a young worker born and raised in Las Yaguas now struggling to overcome his past as a macho punk and act on the new advantages offered him by the revolution, to which he had long remained indifferent out of his commitment to loafing, love affairs, and the *abacua* sect of voudoun. His pal, Humberto, is an incorrigible macho and slackard whose ruse concerning a week's unscheduled absence from the factory provides the film's dramatic structure.

The film opens in the midst of a factory council meeting convened to hear the evidence concerning Humberto's behavior. As Humberto testifies that his mother has been critically ill and coworkers speak either for or against leniency, a man tries to leave the meeting. It is Mario. But he is stopped by the chairman (his own father) and other workers, and explodes with fury over the lie: in fact, Humberto was "shacked up" with a new girlfriend across the island. An upbeat musical refrain sweeps us outdoors as the crash of a wrecking ball reduces an old building to rubble, clearing the air for a montage of street scenes containing glimpses of Yolanda at work. Over this montage, the credits appear. This precredit sequence, like the title of a Bresson film, is a flash-forward to remove the suspense of the ending. That done, the film is free to move at leisure through its examination of the causes.

Yolanda and Mario are both situated by the film very much within the sphere of the workplace, where each faces a different problem regarding his or her responsibility to revolutionary principles. Yolanda, raised in Havana, has trouble adjusting to Miraflores; the behavior patterns of the population have survived the change in material conditions and reflect still the nature of "marginalism." She has difficulty restraining her temper in meetings with the mothers of her delinquent students, whom she wants to counsel about their failure. One mother has eleven children, another beats her son, both are husbandless. Yolanda feels despair over the persistence of such lifestyles after fifteen years of revolution. She is criticized by her coworkers for lack of sympathy and feels, in turn, unsupported and isolated.

Mario has been "saved" by the revolution from following in Humberto's footsteps, yet internally he still has not absorbed a truly revolutionary way of thinking. He still internalizes the old street codes that demand loyalty to oneself and one's friends above social responsibility. Mario must decide what to do about Humberto's lie. Humberto is a slacker and example of the unintegrated personality, unrepentant and not even trying. Yolanda at first seems the representative of the revolutionary woman, but her class and race attitudes are subtly critiqued. Mario is somewhere in between the self-anointed fervor of Yolanda and the backward pride of Humberto, and therefore he becomes the dynamic focus of the film. Essentially a drifter up to this point, he feels pressured by Yolanda's example to make a decisive step. He says he is "scared shitless."

The story of Yolanda and Mario is informed by the wider historical analysis of the frequent sociological sections in which the film's docufictive narrative gives way to a straightforward, scientific-style investigation of the culture's history, replete with maps, old footage, and an omniscient narrator. These sections provide a background on the creation of the marginal population through the slave trade, Spanish colonial adventures, and the pre-1959 breeding ground of corruption and neocolonialism. One target of this analysis is the *abacua* sect, a secret voudoun society that Gomez condemns for its misogyny and male chauvinism. The narrator provides statistics on the current *marginal* sector and provides a view of its persistence.

On a more private level, Yolanda and Mario struggle over issues of machismo within their relationship. Their differences are emphasized whenever their friends appear, magnifying issues of race and class. Their spectacular fights provide equally universal views of male-female hostilities and misunderstandings. The film refuses to wrap up loose ends in a deceptively simple resolution. At the close, Yolanda and Mario are still arguing, out in the street, flanked by the buildings housing the students; he's still troubled by his action against Humberto. A group of workers at the factory debate the case of Humberto after the film repeats the scene of confrontation a second time. These workers present an audience surrogate within the film, and their debate thus becomes an encouragement to viewers to involve themselves in uncovering solutions — to be found not in the movie house, but, as Brecht once urged, in the lives of the audience. The fluid editing and offhand termination of the film reinforce this response. Indeed, the film's release in Cuba set off debates in the communities of *marginales,* with individuals in bars, streets, and factories continuing the arguments over the rightness of Mario's action that had begun among the characters of the film.

One Way or Another

The phrase "one way or another" is not simply an English stand-in for a Spanish idiom but rather conveys a meaningful, modest definition of the revolutionary process that characterizes Cuban society, a process based on dialectical thinking and pragmatic actions, free of frozen dogma, endlessly reinventive. It is also a phrase expressive of the film's structure, which attempts to communicate certain observations by hook or by crook, in one way or another. A close look at three such one way/or another oppositions can clarify the film's dynamics.

Behaviorist versus Materialist. The film's juxtaposition of sociological and dramatic materials reveals two very different discourses on the problems at hand. The narrator consistently provides the analysis that we would expect from a Marxist-Leninist thinker: change the material conditions of these people and their problems will be solved; build new houses so people can live new lives. The problem, as Gomez was acutely aware, is the time lag: a house can be built faster than a person can change (thus the recurring symbol of the wrecking ball). The film insists on contradicting one voice with another, including both the theoretical course of action and the living individuals stuck in this moment of development.

For despite the narrator's quite correct explanations of cause, *One Way or Another* insists on showing effect: a group of people still stuck with old ways, learned more than twenty years earlier and preserved into a new era, fomenting self-destructive behavior that is no longer a reaction to oppression.

The film's editing underscores this perception. One narrated sequence coolly lists the problems of the *marginales,* while its last shot is replaced by a close-up of a sign reading CDR (Committee for the Defense of the Revolution, literally a neighborhood block organization) and a man's voice crying out "Let's get to work." The scene then turns into a view of a street-cleaning day, with many of the film's characters sweeping, painting, and tidying Miraflores to the tune of a rousing, joyous song. The carefree spirit of the people, momentarily tamed to the task of a community action, immediately modifies the harsh view of them recited by the narrator.

Another sequence similarly mitigates the verbal position with visual evidence. Yolanda has complained that the revolution isn't offering enough opportunities for girls, which is why they are continuing in backward life patterns. Her statement is made in close-up, facing the camera, addressing us directly. The camera pulls back to resituate her within a teacher's meeting, where an authoritative woman rebuts the charge, insisting that there are plenty of opportunities for girls. As she speaks, however, we watch various scenes of a woman dancing and carousing in the streets, finally being slapped around by her man. Again, the force of the materialist argument (that opportunities have been created for the girls, that they get a good education) is tempered by a display of "incorrect" behavior. The attitudes of the women have survived the material changes, which suggest that a new look be paid to behavioral factors. Gomez seems to believe in the truth of the narrator's words — as far as they go — but also sees the need to look further, and with more understanding, to use the resistant sectors of society as a clue to new strategies. Everywhere visitors to Cuba journey, they hear the one statement that's heard as well throughout the film: the process of change is still ongoing, the revolution isn't over yet.

Woman versus Macho. This central conflict is manifested on a multitude of levels in the film, whether between characters, between shots, or through the narrator. It is a factor in virtually every interaction between the film's characters. It is no coincidence this film is made by a woman.

When Yolanda visits the mother of her student Lazaro, she hears a pathetic tale of an unstable, violent home life. The mother has not seen the father of the boy "since 1962," the last man she lived with was a drunkard who beat her and who now provides support money but lives elsewhere, and she herself beats the boy for his delinquent behavior even though she swears "he's my right arm." Gomez cuts from her whining testimony to a shot of four machos playing dominoes. The connection is unmistakable: Humberto boasting of his new "broad" could easily be the same man who left her in 1962, for the unprincipled moral code of the macho male produces exactly this type of societal consequence. The woman, victimized, perpetuates the cycle of violence in her home, raising a son prone to continue the pattern into another generation.

One of the domino players is Mario, whom Yolanda finally takes to task for his machismo in a comic scene set in their bedroom. She impersonates his cocky walk and jive bravado, contrasting it to the quiet sincerity he projects in bed with her. It's a finely tuned critique of the common contradiction between the "private" and "public" man. Taking the point a step further, Yolanda and Mario discuss the qualities each likes most about the other. She readily volunteers her affections, while he, as a male unaccustomed to expressing emotion or giving support, is at a loss for words. It's a simple scene that needn't be overemphasized, but its humor is effective.

Another complex sequence of images and conversations raises another issue in the treatment of women: infantilization. Yolanda has been kept late at school to be criticized by her coworkers for her handling of the mothers. Fed up with the attacks, she complains, "I don't like being treated like a child." There is a cut to Mario, furiously waiting for her outside a movie theater way past starting time, and having a fit of anger when she finally arrives. His male pride has been offended; he won't let a woman make him wait one hour. Yolanda storms out of the lobby and down a street; when he catches up, she fumes, "Don't treat me like a child." At this crucial moment, his old friend Guillermo, a singer, happens down the street; the film cuts to a scene of him singing. Next to Guillermo is his wife, smiling shyly and hiding from the camera behind her child. The identification of women with children, both positively and negatively, is yet another dilemma, particularly for Yolanda as a schoolteacher.

The crisis for Mario, of course, occurs when his old male code of honor is challenged by his revolutionary responsibility. After he has made the "right" decision by calling Humberto's bluff in the public meeting, he feels terrible and complains that he's behaved "like a woman." He defensively argues that he's "no *maricon*" (a derogatory term for homosexual); in his mind there are only two kinds of men: *macho* or *maricon*. Only gradually does he begin to admit the possibility of a new middle ground.

It would be incorrect to imply that the film centers on a critique of sexism. Though Gomez targets machismo clearly and unflinchingly, she often merges her views of antisexism with class and race analyses, a combination that yields a more complex perspective on the character of Yolanda. For example, there is one scene set in a restaurant lavatory where Yolanda chats with her friend Migdalia, out together on a double date. Rather than illustrating a positive bond between the two women, however, their conversation exposes Migdalia's lingering racism and class snobbery as she chastises Yolanda for dating "a man with a gold tooth." This attitude in no way protects her, however, from mistreatment at the hands of her boyfriend Joe, who easily bonds with Mario on the basis of male privilege. As if emphasizing her point about the relationship between racism and sexism, Gomez closes the scene with a long static shot of Migdalia, alone by the seawall, with only the dark night around her. It's an evocative image of isolation, making a point far more complicated than the easier examples of female solidarity in U.S. women's films of the time.

This same conflict between gender identification (among women) and class alienation (between women) is repeated later in the film in a scene between Yolanda and Lazaro's mother, who has gone down on her knees to beg Yolanda to help her son. Gomez shows us Yolanda's eyes, upset and panicked, torn between identification with the plight of this woman and a need to separate herself from such a fate. In the scene with Mercedes, the mother of eleven, Yolanda's class bias obviates any sympathy and the two quarrel over the teacher's paternalistic reprimand. *One Way or Another* makes clear how complex are the dilemmas of class/race/sex bias for a Black woman of Sara Gomez's background.

Abacua versus Santería. Some viewers have expressed concern that Sara Gomez is attacking voudoun, an important part of the Afro-Cuban heritage, with her critique of *abacua*. This is a misinterpretation that, I believe, can be rectified by examining women and their relation to machismo. *Abacua* is a particular voudoun sect, which, as the film makes clear, has its basis in male chauvinism (no women are admitted) and a myth of female betrayal (similar to our Eve/Lilith onus) to justify the exclusion. The documentary footage of the *abacua* rites shows their threatening air of secrecy: a dancer wears a dark hooded mask; a goat is castrated and killed; the overall impression is negative.

Were this the only portrayal of voudoun in the film, its critics would have a point. However, Gomez shows a very clear alternative to *abacua* in the person of Mario's mother, a sympathetic figure who practices sympathetic magic: Santería. Santería, unlike *abacua,* is an open and participatory form of voudoun, practiced by many Cubans today, particularly in Gomez's environment. There is a corresponding scene of the Santería rites that is brightly lit and positively presented: whole families participate; women are dressed in white and seen in active roles; a goat is present but not killed.

It is tempting to see the two kinds of voudoun as representative of male and female power, the one aggressive and violent, the other receptive and social. However, it is more likely that Gomez is critiquing the *abacua* sect for other reasons: for its male chauvinism as antisocial aberration and for its reputed history of involvement in murders. Santería, being nonhierarchical and open, is a form of benign voudoun more easily amenable to socialism. (Though the Cuban government officially frowns on the practice, there's widespread unofficial participation — and a persistent legend that, when Fidel Castro came down from the mountains at the moment of the triumph of the revolution, he was wearing Santería amulets around his neck.)

In Progress

It is said that one of founder Alfredo Guevara's earliest injunctions to the directors at ICAIC was that they should never, in their films, make the process of revolution look easier than it really was. In its concern with the difficulties of that process, *One Way or Another* communicates the typically Cuban struggle over the reconciliation of oppositions. At film's end, neither Yolanda nor Mario has arrived at a state of redemption (so popular in U.S. and European films), neither in their work nor in their relationship. She still faces the need for a support network for herself in Miraflores, while he still faces a final severing of the old support network that held him back.

They are still fighting in the final shot, even as the buildings through which they walk continue their processing from rubble into new edifices. Guillermo's song of change throws an air of optimism over the scene's ambiguity as its words urge Mario to leave his old ways, his old world of hypocrisy and its street milieu (although the print's poor subtitles may mislead the viewer into thinking it is Yolanda he is being urged to give up). Mario has already set out on the route that will lead him from the bad example of Humberto to the promising model of Guillermo. Yolanda, with persistence and integrity, still refuses to compromise.

"Sara was not approaching these themes 'intellectually' but as an authentic interest. There was no paternalism or superficiality to her, which is why we find such an authentic reality in the film, a tenderness and love for the people and the issues." Tomás Gutiérrez Alea's words on Sara Gomez lead back to the woman behind the film, to the experience that led to such a formally and thematically integrated work. Indeed, the film bears witness to the possibility of making a film that in no way condescends to its subjects.

And that's not all he had to say. "Sara was an exceptional person, with an extraordinary capacity for communication and spontaneous interaction. She planned a lot, there was a script as a starting point, but the film as we see it developed through the production — she was constantly solving problems during the shooting. . . . As a result, you find beautiful fresh unimpoverished things in the film: it was left to the editing to give coherence to a very rough improvisational shooting. . . . Sara was doubly oppressed, as a Black and as a woman, so she was very much moved on the question of how sexism and racism could be dealt with after the revolution. So it is not surprising that she, a woman, undertook the problem of machismo or was interested in the secret societies, where the macho elements are so well established."

One Way or Another could prove a most fruitful influence on American cinema, initiating as it does an approach to documentary without mere mimicry, to fiction without dishonesty, and in both, an estimation of its characters and audience that is free of condescension, full of respect. As the debate lingers over the relationship between radical form and radical content, and over the relevance of the avant-garde to the political, participants in such debates would do well to consider the example of Sara Gomez's work. Particularly for feminist filmmakers and critics today, *One Way or Another* demonstrates how successfully ideological and artistic strategies can be consolidated when the filmmaker is at one with her subjects and when the heart of a project isn't sacrificed to false notions of audience demands.

Prologue.

A Woman's

Declaration

of Secession

from the

Avant-Garde

During the seventies, I began to develop an antipathy to some of the prevailing wisdom in the independent film world. Experience had made me reconsider my earlier affiliation with the New American Cinema. I was, actually, fed up.

Part of my reaction had to do with an overdose of Stan Brakhage, who throughout that decade performed in large lecture halls at the School of the Art Institute of Chicago, delivering the history of cinema as a succession of Great Men wrestling with genius. As more and more feminist consciousness penetrated my spirit and I became more formed as a critic, I was less and less impressed by such a cosmology, or by the prescriptive nature of a worldview that always seemed to see the present in terms of its ability to reflect the image of the Master himself in its aesthetic choices. I'd also begun to notice that this narcissistic preoccupation with the past and its traces in the present was making for a singularly uninteresting filmic practice, fossilized into the structural formalism (cinema's version of minimalism) of the preceding decade and incapable of reinventing itself. It was, actually, the beginning of the end for avant-garde film as an inspiring or living practice.

In addition to my misgivings about the avant-garde on the aesthetic front, once the arena became sexual politics my discomfort turned to outright mutiny. The role played by women in the films of the avant-garde was, to quote Martha Coolidge's film title of a few years later, not a pretty picture. It wasn't only leftie politicos that thought a woman's place was on her back: these avant-garde artists, whose politics were often closer to royalist than anything else, thought the same (or, in their case, on her back and on camera). Imagine the seventies: a chosen circle of guys elevated as gods for their cutting-edge work, the deification of structuralism as the only genuine way to make films, a total absence of women filmmakers in any pantheon, and a determinedly uncritical attitude toward representations of women on celluloid. It was the reign of Tony Conrad, Paul Sharits, Michael Snow, and a coterie of male compatriots anointed by the troika of powerbrokers: Jonas Mekas, P. Adams Sitney, and Annette Michelson. It is impossible to overemphasize the extent to which power back then was consolidated in their hands. A ridiculous situation, really, that took many good writers and filmmakers out of the field entirely, exiled by the force of orthodoxy that prevailed.

In that atmosphere, "feminist" film was regarded as a vulgar, unsophisticated, political project, not fit company for the Great Artists. But times were starting to change. Thanks in part to women's film festivals, in part to the arrival of new cinematic theories, and in part to the welcome decentering of authority that split up the centralized rule, the reign of "structuralism" eventually collapsed, making way for a prolonged interregnum that has continued to this day, as competing theories and hierarchies jostle for position.

I wasn't alone in my responses to cinematic representation in those years, as the representation of the female body in a post-Godardian filmic universe was beginning to be hotly debated. Laura Mulvey had published "Visual Pleasure and Narrative Cinema" in *Screen* that autumn, moving on forever from her former status as bookstore clerk to eminent feminist theorist. She and her then-husband Peter Wollen had made *Penthesilea* two years before (our loft was the alternative rain-date location for the garden scene), inspired by the equipment availability and student labor at Northwestern University, and were well on their way to *Riddles of the Sphinx*. Now, at Peter and Laura's urging, Gunner and I decided to attend the 1976 Edinburgh Film Festival special event, The International Forum on Avant-Garde Film, the catalogue copy for which explicitly evoked both *Penthesilea* and Peter's seminal essay on "The Two Avant-Gardes" that had appeared in *Studio International* almost simultaneously with Laura's publication in *Screen*.

Mulvey and Wollen had a big influence on the Edinburgh festival and conference in the seventies, while it was under the direction of Lynda Myles, who balanced the high-theory concerns of her *Screen* friends with an attention to avant-garde films and to the new auteurism of American directors like Brian De Palma (with a tribute this same year), Roger Corman's New World products, and Martin Scorsese, whose *Taxi Driver* came to Edinburgh straight from its Palme d'Or victory at Cannes. Once in Edinburgh, everyone hung out in the same shabby guest lounge up on the second floor of the festival's old headquarters, the Film House in Randolph Crescent, drinking and arguing, complaining about the Scottish cuisine, and making unlikely friends across genre lines.

At Edinburgh that year, I first met Jackie Reynal and her companion Sid Geffen and saw Jackie's film *Deux Fois,* encountered the embattled editors of *Screen,* and began to learn about British film politics (a long study that would occupy me for years). Sid Geffen was one of a series of men who made a huge difference in film history through their exhibition choices in New York City. Geffen, who ran the Bleeker Street Cinema in the crucial years of the late seventies and early eighties, along with Amos Vogel and Fabiano Canosa, significantly effected the course of film history. So did the Museum of Modern Art's Adrienne Mancia, Larry Kardish, and Mary Lea Bandy; so did the Film Forum's Karen Cooper. It's the festivals that get all the attention, but others deserve more serious and sustained recognition.

I made the acquaintance of a young performance artist there by the name of Sally Potter, who was living in a London squat at the time and came because she was thinking about starting to make films, having already secured a name for herself with some famous London alternative theatrical presentations (unnamed, because the term "performance art" hadn't yet been invented, but already chronicled and celebrated in an influential *Studio International* issue). It was at Edinburgh, too, that I heard Peter Gidal recite his pledge never to show a woman's body in one of his films again, because he'd realized the impossibility of doing so without inherent objectification and subjugation, presumably in terms of both production and reception. Everything would be different henceforth. Sure.

It was at that same conference that I became friends with Yvonne Rainer. I'd already heard her, at one of the conferences staged by the Center for Twentieth-Century Studies in Milwaukee (the in-spot of the seventies), intellectually cornered and trying to defend herself against "accusations" of some kind of prescribed feminism from the emergent *Camera Obscura* crowd; she was an artist and at that time in her life was stubbornly confessing her lack of affiliation with any such movement.

Like Gidal, though for different reasons, Rainer was at that time reevaluating her approach to the body as she completed her transition from celebrated modern dancer to filmmaker. After so many years as the fetishized object of the public's gaze, Rainer was particularly attuned to the dynamic. She knew a thing or two about self-representation. Unlike Schneemann's exuberant dives into the soup of sexualized representation, Rainer was ill at ease with cinema's circulation of female bodies and had begun to wonder if any redemption of such images were possible.

I wondered much the same as I went through my own transition, beginning to move my sexual-object choice from male to female. Such a shift did nothing to endear to me the prevailing cinematic traditions. I was eager to pursue new ideas, whether theoretical or cinematic, on the representation of sexual practices and gender realignments. JoAnn Elam (the filmmaker who made *Rape,* an early classic of feminist avant-garde agitprop, itself a rare category) was at that time running the N.A.M.E. Gallery film group, then in the process of becoming the Chicago Filmmakers organization. She'd formed a board, I'd joined it to help out, and she and I decided to curate a women's film series together. There'd been quite a stir around the film debut of a New York woman who was part of the *Fox* collective (*Fox* was the hot conceptual-theoretical journal of the moment). Intrigued, we decided to show her film, which is how I came to see Lizzie Borden's now-forgotten first film, *Re-grouping.* It, too, had premiered with controversy at Edinburgh in 1976, where its screening had been accompanied by film and art critic Regina Cornwell's public reading of a statement denouncing the film, with a text sent over by the New York women's group that constituted the film's subject. After seeing the film, Elam was so outraged that she wrote Borden a letter telling her that she thought the film would have been more accurately titled *Bad Faith;* Borden wrote back, agreeing. Debates over female representation were raging — puritanism at one extreme, exploitation at the other — and every new film was grist for the mill. In this case, the controversy was focused on Borden's responsibility to her subjects and the question of whether she could be accused of defrauding them aesthetically by dint of the use she made of their bodies and voices in the final product.

It was at this moment that Joanna Freuh, then a local freelance writer and curator, read my pieces in the Chicago *Reader* and asked me to contribute to a special feminist issue of the *New Art Examiner* that she was editing. This piece, one of the first theoretical articles I published, became my manifesto of separation from the New American Cinema. Not that I inspired any immediate conscriptions. Indeed, Yvonne Rainer immediately sent me a letter requesting her removal from the company in which I'd placed her: "I absolutely do not accept being associated with Ti-Grace's absolutist dichotomy of sex and freedom. My films are not a call to the barricades of (hetero) sexual renunciation. If they work at all they support a life lived with struggle, if not outright contradiction, and contradictions consciously questioned more often than outright rejected."

A few hours after handing my article over to the *New Art Examiner,* I hopped in a car with friends to drive across the country from Chicago to Upstate New York for the Alternative Cinema Conference, an event in 1979 that had far-reaching effects in the alternative media world for many years. Typical of the times, the majority of people in attendance described themselves either as "cultural workers" or "media activists," two terms that I have yet to decipher to my satisfaction, but that revealed a widespread unwillingness to identify as academics or artists or, for that matter, as professionals at all. The higher ground was politics, so culture and media had to be converted into subordinated adjectives modifying the "real" world of work and activism.

At the conference itself, the excitement of hundreds of like-thinking people coming together on the Bard College campus was dampened by the immediately apprehended difficulties and contradictions of such a gathering. The gay and lesbian caucus event, for example, was in conflict with the Third World caucus event. Small matter? No, major crisis. Hours of negotiation led to compromise and a cathartic plenary: Chicana filmmaker Sylvia Morales managed to unify and electrify the crowd by declaring "I have loved men, and I have loved women" at the start of her speech. And so it went. Political agendas were recalculated, race politics reprioritized, questions of sexuality taken more seriously than ever before. Identity politics were strong, but fragmentation was setting in — my own most of all. What categories did I belong to, what affiliations could I claim? At one plenary, the late Peter Adair asked everyone who was gay to stand up. Lots of us did, as ripples of discovery and surprise moved through the crowd.

Behind the scenes, organizing committees struggled over the language of manifestos. I met my lifelong friend Lillian Jimenez there for the first time. She still remembers the struggles over using the word "racism" in a Third World statement. I remember being part of the socialist feminist organizing group, seeking some unity across categories with Joan Braderman and Marti Wilson, strengthening the ties established the year before when we'd all been in Cuba together and using our platform of friendship to mediate the ideological tensions. On the cusp of the seventies turning to the eighties, the Alternative Cinema Conference was an uncanny avatar of the decade to come, its issues and crises — political correctness, multiculturalism, gay/lesbian identities — and, yes, in moments, even its leaps forward.

Soon after I returned from the conference, my "Sex and Cinema" piece hit the stands. From the perspective of the nineties, it may seem archaic. I'm not so sure, though, that its central concerns regarding sex and representation have yet been exhausted or laid to rest. Looking back, I still find its youthful passion endearing, its anger rousing, and its certainty impressive, if no longer entirely as convincing.

7.

Sex

and

Cinema

(1979)

The notion of a more personal, poetic, experimental cinema is not without some promise. At this moment, however, it is difficult to determine whether poetry or pornography is the ultimate destination of the new filmmakers. — Andrew Sarris, *Show*, 1964

Works of art are above obscenity and pornography, or, more correctly, beyond what the police understand as obscenity and pornography. Art exists on a higher spiritual, aesthetic, and moral plane. — Jonas Mekas, *Village Voice*, 1964

I have constantly found a remarkable belief that in what is currently called the "underground" film, the primary concern is with sex. The problem is that sexuality has long been a controversial topic in our Western societies. . . . As a matter of fact, it is typical of the sexual element in the independent cinema that it is never seen as unusual. Rejection of sexual and personal subjects in film is symptomatic of the confined and immature mind. — Stephen Dwoskin, *Film Is*, 1975

Feminists are on the fence, at the moment, on the issue of sex. But I do not know any feminist worthy of the name who, if forced to choose between freedom and sex, would choose sex. She'd choose freedom every time. . . . By no stretch of the imagination is the Women's Movement a movement for sexual liberation. — Ti-Grace Atkinson, *Majority Report*, 1977

The terrain of sexuality and art is a vast one, nearly global in scale. An attempt will be made to confine the boundaries of this article to that art known as the New American Cinema, the art cinema that was sparked in the forties, developed through the fifties, came into its own in the sixties, and has been alternately growing and static throughout the seventies. The major question to be considered is what effect this cinema's early birthright of sexuality has had on its practitioners, particularly women, in the era of women's liberation (and, also pertinent, gay rights).

The reputation of independent cinema as the "other," the outsider or interloper that in its purity challenges the values of a corrupt society and its cinema, has always derived part of its strength from its attack on that society's puritanism. The breaking of sexual taboos, the Baudelairian transcendence of false morality, has been an aspect of the New American Cinema championed by Mekas and others for decades.

Kenneth Anger's first 16mm film, made on a weekend when his parents were away, was an S/M fantasy of an invasion and exquisite defilement by a score of sailors. His subsequent films have continued his themes of homosexual rituals, violence, orgies of eroticism or magic, and sublimated representations of the same sexual concerns. Gregory Markopoulos, one of the most important figures of the early New American Cinema, secured his position with a number of films portraying an inverted troubled homosexuality or fantasy scenes of idyllic youths enacted within, and inspired by, Grecian mythic tradition. The arrival on the scene of filmmakers like Jack Smith, Ken Jacobs, and Andy Warhol signaled a switch in tone from reverence to camp. The transvestites of *Flaming Creatures* and *Blonde Cobra,* like the drag queens and other underground denizens of Warhol's works, were a slap in the face to America's antiquated fifties moral code.

Not all the early independent filmmakers were gay, and not all onscreen activity was unisex. One of the earliest practices of the independent filmmaker, though one probably more prevalent in popular mythology than in fact, was the convenient casting of girlfriend (or, later, boyfriend) as star. Mitch Tuckman, in a recent *Film Comment,* referred to this sixties practice as marking a time when "any guy who could get his girlfriend to undress was halfway to becoming a filmmaker." Granted, most of these "filmmakers" never got more than halfway. Still, the tradition was common enough to provide fodder for parody in George Kuchar's early and hilarious *Hold Me While I'm Naked,* which chronicled the malaise of just such an underground filmmaker who can't get any action himself.

Other filmmakers whose careers have spanned many facets of cinema art have also trained their lenses on sexuality at some moment. Various films by Stan Brakhage, for example, dealt explicitly with sexual fantasy, masturbation, or intercourse (*Flesh of Morning, Lovemaking, Sexual Meditation*). Diary films as a genre were particularly prone to this subject, as evidenced by the work of Andrew Noren. Ken Jacobs no less wrote of *Say Nothing:* "The rape continues until we have only an unhappy girl before us . . . unhappy, but not broken; there's a surprisingly hard core of self-respect to her, a trueness to her emotions that Andrew can't budge. Brooding and haunting without her cover, she is at last, because recognizable, profoundly loveable."

Clues like this Jacobs description, however, were largely ignored in the sixties and early seventies rush to embrace sexual liberation as a revolutionary force. The early union between the New American Cinema and sexuality as a cinematic subject perfectly suited the mood of the culture, prompting an enormous popularity for what became viewed as "underground films." Particularly on the West Coast, erotic films artfully executed could enjoy the best of both worlds: Scott Bartlett's *Lovemaking,* James Broughton's *The Bed,* Ed Emschwiller's studies of women, all found success. Meanwhile, in his "Movie Journal" columns in the *Village Voice,* Jonas Mekas (who, together with P. Adams Sitney and Barbara Rubin, defied the censors and ministers of culture in Belgium to break the censorship codes with *Flaming Creatures*) now began to deplore the abandonment of avant-garde cinema by fickle "sensation seekers" just looking for sex. Where would it all end? And when would women enter the debate?

Cut to the start of the feminist movement. Enter women fed up with the exploitation of hedonism, the misogyny of the left, the use of women's bodies to sell everything from the antiwar movement to "underground" movies. Cut, also, to the arrival of a new film criticism attuned to the power structures of cinema, the hierarchy of the filmmaker-to-subject relationship, the corrupt nature of the cinematic spectacle. The two concerns formed a powerful alliance. The use of women in films became suspect, the exhibition of sexuality even more so. My concern, proceeding ever so leisurely through this history, is to examine how the intervention of this critical and ideological reassessment has affected the films being made today, by male filmmakers, but more acutely, by women.

Most male filmmakers have felt the cultural pressure to eschew blatantly sexist behavior, which has rendered some changes in their subject matter. For instance, Andrew Noren had to be defended against a sex-maniac reputation after the first of his *Exquisite Corpse* series; now, the latest section avoids the explicit, no longer bending women to his will, the traces of body parts still remaining but subsumed into a more wholly abstract sense of eroticism. Paul Sharits, similarly, kept audience attention during his early structuralist *Peace Mandala/End War* by titillating with frames of a couple in the midst of intercourse, an image that of course was supposed to be subordinate to the formal strategies of the film; today, Sharits sticks to the abstract. Broughton has turned his physical examinations entirely toward the male model. Many of the old guard are no longer making films, while the new generation is generally more cautious or differently attuned: politics and purely formal considerations occupy more attention than sensuality. Of course, this is a selective filmography that leaves out the exceptions (like Hollis Frampton, whose latest film intercuts a stripper with a fish). In addition, the filmmakers may have quite different explanations for their development. Still, it is the necessary complement to what follows.

A landmark for the start of any discussion of women and cinematic sexuality is Carolee Schneemann's *Fuses*. An early performance artist, stager of happenings, and one of the first creators of body art, Schneemann made *Fuses* in 1967. Turning the tables on the boys, she succeeded in controlling her own lovemaking image — by filming herself and her lover in bed. An attempt to make an erotic film that was not pornographic, as well as to give an equal voice to women's eroticism, *Fuses* was an important work. As feminist criticism has progressed, however, some women have begun to feel that such a counterthrust does not substantially alter the problem, and that even control of one's own image does not necessarily influence the perception of its nudity or sexual meaning.

Indeed, jumping ahead twelve years to the Suzan Pitt animated film *Asparagus* provides a startling contrast to *Fuses* and an index to changes in attitude during the intervening time. Again there is a desire to present the act of heterosexuality on screen, but this time there are significant reservations. The face of the cartoon heroine (who represents *an* if not *the* artist) is concealed by a mask, which when removed reveals a face absent of all details except the eyes; and her suggestive actions, signifying first a hand job and then a blow job, are performed on a giant stalk of asparagus. Thus, *Asparagus* portrays the sex act only while specifying the anonymity of the woman and the removal of the phallus entirely from any corporeal connection with a man — thereby ensuring the woman's utter independence even within the sex act. And this is the cartoon world, where a certain immunity would already prevail over its realistic counterparts.

The furor over one film in 1976 further illuminates the current sensitivity surrounding the depiction of women's sexuality in cinema. Lizzie Borden's first film, *Re-grouping,* was the study of a women's consciousness-raising group that she had begun to film, only to run into disagreements, abandon the collaboration, but salvage the project. Mixing the group sessions with street footage of the women and scenes of lesbian lovemaking (often with participants resembling but in fact not being these same women), Borden confronted the whole issue of cinematic voyeurism straight on by making a film that is unabashedly voyeuristic as hell. The women retaliated by vehemently attacking Borden's abdication of feminist principles of process, complete with a statement read at screenings. Probably the film's most damning scene was one of two women making love, matched to a sound track of a third woman describing how disgusting she found making love with a woman to be.

Other filmmakers have tried, rather more conscientiously, to find solutions to the problem of woman's representation on the screen. Bette Gordon's latest film, *Exchanges,* conducts experiments on how a woman may be viewed on film with an attention that is direct and involving without being at all degrading. Several Chicago women have worked with the problem in their own way. Barbara Scharres, for example, no longer felt comfortable with the portrayal of her own body as an erotic emblem within her films, so her recent *Northern Light* relies much more on abstracted textures, shadows, even sheets as the traces of the often absent body; the soundtrack of loon calls supplements the evocation of the imagery. Jean Sousa, on the other hand, continues to display herself as lover within her films but has attempted to undercut the force of the depiction (though with only mild success) by directing a confrontatory gaze at the audience through binoculars at the close of *What Am I Doing Here.*

Several films by European women recently shown in Chicago bring other perspectives to bear on this same dilemma. In Chantal Akerman's *Jeanne Dielman,* sex is present only as prostitution, which in itself becomes so unbearable that the heroine murders her third and final client. In Akerman's subsequent film, *Meetings with Anna,* the central character tries sex with two different men, but both instances end in coitus interruptus; meanwhile, she confides to her mother her infatuation with another woman (who, however, remains an offscreen ideal). In Helke Sander's *The All-Round Reduced Personality — Redupers* there is a strikingly telling moment that hinges on sexual assumptions. The woman (played by Sander) has gone for a drink with a man after an art opening, only to find herself aggressively embraced in a hallway clutch on the way back home. Then, there's a cut. Schooled in the traditional narrative use of such ellipses, the viewer is likely to expect a follow-up of the two in bed. But instead, there's a cut to the woman alone out in the street, vomiting into a gutter. It is one of the most devastating comments on contemporary mating games anyone has dared to put on film. A review of most contemporary films by women, in fact, is likely to find the only really optimistic views of sexuality in the lesbian films of such figures as Jan Oxenberg or Barbara Hammer. Otherwise, an impasse over the whole issue of sexuality seems to prevail.

The filmmaker whose films are perhaps most central to this entire debate, and who herself is quite clear on the matter, is Yvonne Rainer. One of the most important filmmakers of this decade, Rainer has consistently refused to pander to any audience expectation of spectacle, sentimentality, or easy character identification. She has reworked even such resistant modes as melodrama and elegy to find new ways of making an art adequately informed by the consciousness describing a modern urban woman, living in a time when easy solutions are no longer possible. In her *Film about a Woman Who* . . . , there is an elegant sequence entitled "An Emotional Accretion in 48 Steps" that posits a man and woman lying atop a symbolic bed/table as various modes of narration (voice-over, intertitles, subtitles) detail the emotional tug-of-war transpiring between the two, as it transpires between so many men and women of our time.

Much later in the film, a woman has a sexual fantasy that involves being undressed by the couple she is visiting. The fantasy is literalized on screen in dreamlike slow motion and silent solemnity; as in the 48-step section, the establishing medium shot is followed by close details. As the undressing is completed, however, Rainer shifts to a view of her own face, plastered over with printed excerpts from Angela Davis's love letters to George Jackson that had so inflamed the media. It is a crucial reminder of the way society uses women's emotions to undermine them, how not even the strongest are immune from the barbs of sexuality with which our culture's social codes encircle us as provision against any betrayal.

It would seem that the Angela Davis text offers sufficient warning to the viewer regarding the erotic fantasy just preceding it. However, Rainer soon had second thoughts. Viewing the film at the 1976 Edinburgh Film Festival, on the same program with Jean-Luc Godard's *Numero Deux* (to which she objected for its graphic, unpleasant use of sexuality), she decided that the strategy didn't work. At that point, she vowed in conversations that she would never again show a woman naked in one of her films, nor any explicit sexuality. She had become convinced that no matter what techniques surrounded that depiction, no matter what contradictions were embedded in the presentation, nothing could ever recoup the image of a woman's body or sexuality bared.

Sure enough, in her subsequent *Kristina Talking Pictures,* there is a very different replay of that earlier bed/table theme. This time, there is a shot of Rainer herself and her brother seated in bed, facing the camera; his chest is bare, but she is prudently garbed in a glittery halter top (the prescribed costume for her circus character). The image of the two is not unlike the puritan bed scenes of Hayes Act Hollywood, when even husband and wife retired to separate twin beds, but the motivation is different. Then, it was a paternalistic attempt to protect the idealized purity of every American husband's wife and children. Now, it is a direct act of self-defense inspired in women filmmakers and viewers by years of cinematic assault.

One subject of *Kristina Talking Pictures* is the breakdown of simple relations between the sexes. And if that breakdown is indeed epidemic, if heterosexuality cannot be freed of the taint of unequal power relations even in its cinematic guise, then it is to women's advantage as makers or viewers of film to avoid its literalization. Yvonne Rainer is now at work on her fourth feature film, which will have neither nudity nor sex.

Thus this article, which took as its starting point the contract between avant-garde cinema and sexuality, has concluded with the vehement rejection of that contract by women working in cinema today. The words of Ti-Grace Atkinson echo still in the darkened rooms where the works of avant-garde cinema still are seen.

Prologue.

Love's Labor

Lost

If sex on-screen was seeming problematic, no such fate afflicted sex off-screen. On the first day that I went to work at the Film Center, I noticed a woman named Marjorie Keller sitting a few desks away from me. She was busy organizing Stan Brakhage's class and clandestinely pursuing her own cinematic and political activities. She lived with Saul Levine, a filmmaker who is now a part of 8mm history but then was merely a graduate student at the School of the Art Institute (though he already looked way older than his years, a Talmudic scholar born into the wrong time and place). Margie and I were instant friends, discovering already overlapping interests and acquaintances, equally seized with the excitements of film, youth, politics, and adventure.

We all became a gang, together with our friend Diego Cortez and the other art school orphans in search of opportunities to act out. In 1973, she and Saul staged a heretical Passover seder at which the exodus of Jews from Egypt was recast as an early SDS action long before the official Liberation Haggadah was invented; we all cared more for food than ceremony anyway. And the food was great, because Margie was already a fabulous cook: for a rebel-girl of that era, she was remarkably versed in the female arts, well-trained by her mother in the social graces.

Once Gunner and I decided to spend a long weekend escorting Margie from Chicago to Lockport, New York, for her mother's fiftieth birthday party. The problem was that Margie was the only one who could drive, yet the timetable required nonstop driving there and back. When she discovered I held a valid driver's license despite swearing off driving years before, she insisted I share the time on the steering wheel, taking me out in rush-hour Chicago traffic to gauge my ability and boost my confidence. So drive I did, white-knuckled much of the way, and we arrived in record time. The party was a hit. Our friend Jimmy De Sana (the photographer who died in 1990) came up from New York City and took flash-photos of everyone sitting around the pool and lawn in the full sun; after dark, Margie's brood of nieces and nephews set off sparklers and squealed at the sight.

One day of family life was enough for all of us. Gunner departed for the big city, Margie and I set off by car for Chicago. Armed with a pornographic novel we'd found to keep us awake on the road, we took turns reading out loud to each other ("jazz me, jazz me, she cried") to the consternation of the male hitchhikers we occasionally collected and stashed in the back seat. *On the Road* was still a dominant cultural influence (even Sheila Rowbotham had opened her first book with a reference to it), so maybe we were just inventing a girl-version. Or something.

Life continued along magically in our version of Chicago until Margie decided to leave town, to move to New York to enroll in the Cinema Studies program at NYU and make films herself instead of just enabling other people to make and show them. We had a big send-off at The Bakery, a haute-fashionable restaurant of the era that didn't know what to do with the strange crowd of artists carousing in the midst of the usual suits.

I remember clearly the winter weekend when everything in my world shifted on its axis. That weekend, I was out of town at a film conference and Margie was in town, visiting with us at the loft. She and Saul were on the rocks and she'd already begun other dalliances back in New York: she was in the mood for experimentation and everything was up for grabs. The early seventies were very much a continuation of the late sixties, as people tend to forget, and Gunner and I were no exception: we had an "open" relationship, and that weekend it opened further. When I returned on Sunday, she'd prepared a multicourse feast with a centerpiece of rabbit roasted in cider (years before *Fatal Attraction* made the killing of such an animal suspect). The cause for celebration turned out to be the real surprise: she and Gunner had slept together in my absence.

The surprise for me, though, was my reaction: I realized that the jealousy that swamped me was not over her sleeping with *him* but over his sleeping with *her*. It seemed silly, suddenly, for her to sleep alone, so I suggested we all three sleep together. Just another random event in the sexual history of the early seventies. Not.

Once in bed, the physical reality of being sexually intimate with a woman for the first time caught up with my spontaneous decision, and I held on for dear life. And the feeling was mutual — or whatever variation of "mutual" might be devised for a feeling shared three ways round, because Gunner, Margie, and I fell into a profoundly satisfying ménage à trois that lasted for several years, until the world shifted on its axis once again. The two of us kicked Gunner out of bed and charted new territory on our own (selfishly, though I still lived with him, I simply didn't want to share her anymore). That's the moment from which I date my own beginnings as a lesbian.

In what would turn out eventually, for me, to be a transitional period, Margie and I acted out a variety of scenarios of self-discovery, for better and for worse. I remember going to hear Gato Barbieri in New York, walking home through the streets of Soho, still deserted in the early seventies, to her walk-up apartment on Forsyth Street, falling into each other's arms to the tunes of Brazilian sensuality. I remember breakfasts at Moishe's deli and tea at The Cupping Room, our amusement at running into New York film denizens who, stopping to chat, had not the slightest inkling of what we were up to, why we sat there so flushed and contented.

On the other hand, I'd be lying if I didn't remember as well the terrible rows over our increasingly different attachments to men: mine was fast diminishing while hers was as strong as ever. Once I picked up a Swiss soundman at a New York Film Festival party stacked with enough stars to thrill any name-dropper: Mick in one corner, Bianca in another, showgirls passing around trays of food while Jack Nicholson and his pals chatted on the stairs. When we couldn't get into his friend's room at the Chelsea Hotel, I brought him home to (her) bed, spitefully announcing that I'd brought him to make her happy. Other nights I drank myself into oblivion on bourbon in midtown hotels, dialing her number over and over and over, fruitlessly, while she left the phone off the hook and spent the night with her boyfriend instead.

Eventually, the differences grew too great. I resented her permanent relationship with my male rival, while she was indifferent to my escalating desires. To our sexual differences were added our emerging aesthetic enmities: as I developed into a critic, she resented my turning on the avant-garde tradition that she more than ever venerated and that I was increasingly attacking as masculinist. She, by contrast, was researching her dissertation on Brakhage, Cocteau, and Joseph Cornell. The more attracted to lesbianism I became, the more heterosexual she wanted to be. I was the one who was changing, and changing the rules. We finally ended our long affair of the heart (and, not at all incidentally, the body), stayed friends for a while, met for dinner occasionally, feebly attempted to preserve some echo of our earlier intimacy. She even gave me her prized copy of that great classic of lesbian prehistory, Djuna Barnes's *The Ladies' Almanack*. But we had grown too far apart—and we never found the words to bridge the distance that remained after our touching ended. The last time I saw Margie was at her wedding party, celebrating her marriage to her long-time partner, P. Adams Sitney. Chantal Akerman and Carolee Schneemann, both wedding guests, were snapping photos. Afterward, I heard that she'd given birth to twin daughters.

Three years later, Margie was dead, collapsed on the floor of her parents' home, victim of some terrible and inexplicable medical accident. I was devastated by the news and brooded for weeks. I felt as if part of my past had been stolen away from me through the deadly actions of fate. I desperately tried to make sense of our intimacy, our distance, our silences, but ended only by mourning in secret this woman to whom I could no longer stake any claim. To this day, I'm haunted by our failure to discuss our past and reconcile our differences, for it's to our beginnings together that I owe so much of my present identity.

The piece that follows was written for the premiere of her film *Misconception* in Chicago. I had seen the film on her editing table in Kingston, where she taught at the University of Rhode Island and where she'd invited me to speak at a regional conference of the National Women's Studies Association. It was during one of the platonic periods that we periodically enforced to try to change our worsening dynamics, but the sexual tension was ever present as we rose at 5 A.M. to drive through the darkness to her editing room. She wanted me to see the almost completed evidence of her big leap forward into full-length lyrical documentary, an attempt to push avant-garde principles onto an expanded terrain. She knew I had brought affection and interest but little enthusiasm to her avant-garde Super-8mm projects, but thought I'd feel differently about this one. Sure enough, I loved *Misconception* and instantly wanted to champion it. For once, in our professional skins, we were in sync.

I invited her to my class at the School of the Art Institute, where the film won a great response while we playfully bantered back and forth about feminism, gender relations, and our different stances. I cornered her: wasn't she really saying that, cozy as it was to hang out in the kitchen with the girls, she'd really rather be in the den with the boys, even knowing she could attract their attention only marginally, if that? Yes, she insisted, she still preferred the company of the boys. My students thought they were witnessing an ideological debate. But they were only partly right. Margie and I knew what actually was at stake, but at least we had a sense of humor about it by then. I still believe that *Misconception* is a significant film, one that's been underrecognized precisely because of Margie's reluctance, typical within the avant-garde at that time, to situate herself within any feminist lineage. Rereading the piece today, I still agree with its points. But I can't help but read it, retrospectively, as a poignant effort at reconciling on the page the contradictions that were experienced without any such reconciliation in our lives.

8.

Misconception:

Laboring under

No Illusions

(1978)

As its punning title implies, *Misconception* is a film devoted to re-examining our patriarchal society's mythologies about the experience of childbirth. Because of her own history as an avant-garde filmmaker (this is her nineteenth film), Marjorie Keller does not conduct this reexamination in any clinical or polemical fashion. Rather, she concentrates on the visual and aural essences of the mother's experience, in an effort to critique the contradictions between male theories of what childbirth ought to be and the persistent phenomenon of women's alienated labor. The film's successful fusion of artistic and political feminist elements is an encouraging example of the vitality possible when an artist works with equal measures of sensitivity for her subject and skill in her medium.

Misconception is composed of six parts that together chronicle the experience of one woman (Keller's sister-in-law) and her husband during the course of her natural childbirth. The filmmaker has gathered several sorts of documentary footage and organized them into a roughly chronological progression of preparation, birth, and aftermath. Mother, father, and firstborn child sit around the house and out on the lawn; they bathe in a stream and in a bathtub. With the filmmaker participating, they discuss theories of childbirth while a bulldozer tears down a house next door. The family paints a room of their house to while away the time, all the while timing the labor pains that punctuate the film and seem to last for days. The child plays under a table and down the stairs. The intensely painful drama of labor and the sudden delivery of the new baby are followed by the afterbirth of calm and congratulations.

Though the chronology parallels the flow of events, the filmmaker has disordered this strict temporality to more closely approximate the subjective experience. Some scenes reappear as flashbacks, some figure as anticipation or prophecy, and some assume a more transcendent force, stretching out symbolically beyond the literal sphere of the film into the extrafilmic space of the audience's consciousness. This structure lends the film a pacing and rhythm that have less to do with traditional cinema verité documentary or film journalism than with the pacing and rhythm of poetry (perhaps a poem by H. D. or Charles Olson), which in its fragmentation of consciousness can capture more than any strictly literal representation could offer.

The film communicates the precision and care with which it has been assembled (the editing took three years) and thereby suggests the weight with which we can interpret its sounds, images, and often witty counterpoints. Perfectly acceptable as mere documentary data (i.e., evidence of a physical event), the imagery and soundtrack frequently overstep this boundary to assume the aspect of metaphor. For example, a conversational statement — "then the baby was born" — is connected to a screen image of the child; absorbed in play, the child suddenly pops out from under a table, as if a participant in some primitive tribe's coming-of-age ritual. Shots of a bulldozer bent on destruction are contrasted with shots of labor and birth, similarly suggesting a range of associations: the different roles of men and women in our culture, with men as builders and destroyers of property and women as procreators of life; the domain of women from which men are no longer excluded (childbirth) versus the domain of men from which women are still excluded (the construction industry standing in for the world of commerce in general); the brutality of the construction work related, in turn, to the brutality of forceps delivery, imposed centuries ago by men eager to build a power base to displace midwives.

In one section of the film, the husband quotes various doctors' theories on childbirth methods while the mother speaks out of knowledge of her own experience and body. Differences in perceptions of childbirth, between the woman's primary experience and the well-meaning husband's secondary experience, could probably use even more investigation and clarification.

The sense of intimacy and sympathy that the film reveals has been emphasized by the filmmaker's choice to shoot in synchronous-sound Super-8, an experimental, low-budget system that utilizes very unobtrusive equipment yet permits a great deal of editing control. The film's qualities of color, texture, and image parallel those of a home movie, the market for which Super-8 was developed, and reinforce the atmosphere of trust. In turn, the clear-cut editing of images in the film (splices bisect the screen in places) and the sophisticated layering of sounds and dialogue clearly illustrate the craft behind Keller's chosen presentation.

With the rise of feminist politics in the United States, there has emerged, over the past few years, a new genre of films about women's bodies, the right to physical self-determination, and the relations between women and the medical profession. Unlike *Misconception,* most of these films tend to be pragmatic (e.g., the instructive genius of *Self Health* or the acute analysis of *Chicago Maternity Center Story*). A pertinent argument for Keller's approach, which brings the genre into the sphere of avant-garde filmmaking, is suggested by the words of Adrienne Rich in her analysis of motherhood, *Of Woman Born:* "In the 19th century, the possibility of eliminating pain and travail created a new kind of prison for women — the prison of unconsciousness, of numbed sensations, of amnesia, and complete passivity. Women could choose anaesthesia. . . . But the avoidance of pain — psychic or physical — is a dangerous mechanism, which can cause us to lose touch not just with our painful sensations but with our selves."

It is precisely this blocked consciousness that Keller's film seeks to restore. Her kinesthetic handling of images works at freeing our sensations from numbness, just as the layered soundtrack employs words and syllables and "unintelligible" cries to communicate the meanings that amnesia has forgot.

Thankfully, Keller sidesteps the sentimentality that has repeatedly plagued the birth process on film — there is no earth mother here giving birth like an overripe fruit popping out of an Agnes Varda movie. Likewise absent is the overclinical approach, which has often worked to the disadvantage or debasement of the subject in film, much as women can feel debased by male doctors' emphasis on antisepticizing the female body. Instead, Keller's film places priority on the individual woman's subjective experience, even to that white-hot, ice-cold physical trauma that goes by the name of pain. The Adrienne Rich book quoted above goes on to fault the Lamaze natural-childbirth method for substituting distraction for the mother's centered concentration, and to fault Letelier for annexing the mother's power to the doctor; interestingly, the material in this film tends to support both views through its depiction of the husband's and doctor's roles in the delivery.

Misconception is an important addition to the body of films made by women working toward a new feminist consciousness, particularly for its work on creating a new language with which to articulate that experience. Equally valuable is the film's contribution to the avant-garde tradition of the lyrical or diaristic film, a genre overloaded with male filmmakers' subjective romanticizations of the women in their lives. That Keller has situated herself within this world of avant-garde filmmaking bodes well for a renewed vitality in that floundering tradition.

Prologue.

Cows

and Hero-

Worship

Notice how Yvonne Rainer seems to enter into most everything I wrote in this period? Aha. You'll also note that she'll soon vanish completely. Each can be explained. In the case of the former, my attention can best be justified by the central position that Rainer held in the seventies for anyone fascinated by the intersection of art and politics in a feminist key. The major issues of the day could be argued through her works, which in turn were quickly responding to the shifting debates in the art and film sectors. I make no apologies for paying close attention. In the case of the latter, my sudden ceasefire on the Rainer front would be dictated by my joining the New York State Council on the Arts, where I was no longer free to write about her work (though I would get the compensation of funding it instead). But that's getting ahead of the story. Just be advised that this essay appears at this point in my history precisely because it remains frozen in time, midway through the Rainer oeuvre.

At the time of writing my definitive consideration of Yvonne Rainer's opus, I was friends with her. We had met in Edinburgh in 1976. Our bond of friendship resulted specifically from our shared reaction to enduring so many words in such close quarters for so many days: we were seized with a desire to see nature, or more specifically in her case, cows. She, her niece Ruth, Gunner, and I rented a car and toured the Scottish Highlands together when the conference ended. I remember my amusement at hearing the stentorian Rainer voice, so familiar from the soundtracks of her films, reading out loud from travel guides as roadway entertainment. The experience gave me an unfortunate belief that meeting one's idols could be a pleasurable pursuit, but eventually I realized that Rainer was the exception to the rule of (more frequent) disappointment.

She was about to leave for Berlin to spend a year there on a D.A.A.D. fellowship (then a cold war strategy to alleviate West Berlin's isolation and attract international artistic talent there), and was both anticipatory and nervous, wondering what effect the stay would have on her work. Three cinematic effects, in the end: her own film, *Journeys from Berlin/1971;* her film clip's inclusion, as homage, in Helke Sander's later *The All-Round Reduced Personality — Redupers* and her fanciful appearance in Ulrike Ottinger's *Madame X,* in which she played an American avant-garde artist on roller skates.

I first wrote about Rainer's work in 1976 for *Chrysalis,* a "magazine of women's culture" published for several years in the seventies by the Woman's Building in Los Angeles and edited by a collective of four women (two couples) that included the feminist art critic Arlene Raven. My friends Kate Horsfield and the late Lynn Blumenthal had spent a summer teaching video at the Woman's Building and made the introductions that resulted in this invitation. A consideration of Rainer's early films, the essay was commissioned for *Chrysalis* before the magazine had even been launched and appeared in the second issue (1977). Other journals that were active in the same period were *Heresies,* where Rainer's champion and fellow traveler Lucy Lippard was a collective member and made sure that an appreciation of her work was included, and the *Women's Art Journal,* where Rainer's films had just been attacked. In *Women & Film,* which tried to be very inclusive, Chuck Kleinhans had written on Rainer's *Lives of Performers.* Given the context, my essay argued for an appreciation of Rainer's work by what had come to be known as "cultural feminists," who were wont to dismiss it on grounds of intellectualism, opacity, and, probably, elitism.

Now, cultural feminists were more typically found at womyn's music concerts or practicing how to use specula than at film conferences. Their objections to works like Rainer's were part of a more generalized hostility to all intellectual work that was, by their definition, tainted by patriarchal modes of thought, analysis, and expression. Anything that wasn't instantly accessible to the hypothetical woman-in-the-street was suspect. It was an enforced egalitarianism that probably owed as much to that notorious patriarch Mao as to any imagined foremothers, but it was the dominant style that had survived the New Left model of collective organization and decision making to become the consciousness-raising model that deemed every woman an expert. Tricky business. On the one hand, the strategy was a rational response to women's extreme disempowerment and low sense of self-worth in those days; on the other hand, it tended to have a disastrous leveling effect on many types of knowledge pursuit and institution building.

I expanded and considerably revised my Rainer article for the Walker Art Center for a series of monographs on independent film, largely drawn from the consecrated ranks of the avant-garde. I was savoring what would turn out to be my last days in Chicago, with my economic struggles momentarily eased by a Critic's Fellowship from the National Endowment for the Arts for the huge sum of $5,000, the most money I'd ever seen. (This was, of course, before Hilton Kramer's attacks prompted the NEA brass to banish the category from its guidelines.)

Half-paralyzed by my decidedly exaggerated notion of how definitive a monograph ought to be, I seemed to forestall endlessly the completion of the piece, working on it through much of 1979 and 1980. I lectured on Rainer, too, whenever the chance arose. The essay was published in the Walker's monograph series and eventually got a second life in a volume of Rainer's collected scripts. But first I got a chance to speak about Rainer in a context where her work made absolute sense: the "Feminar" at Northwestern University.

As anyone who has ever seen issue 5 of the short-lived Northwestern film journal *Film Reader* will know, 1980 was the year of the Lolita Racklin Rodgers Memorial Conference on Feminist Film Criticism, organized by the feminist graduate students in the university's film department (including, among others, Jane Gaines, Rusty Herzog, Lisa Lewis, Gina Marchetti, and Ellen Seiter, all of whom had studied with Chuck Kleinhans and Michelle Citron, both relatively new to the faculty but already a significant influence).

Women came from near and far: Joan Braderman flew in from New York and slept on my couch, using the visit for advice on her romantic impasse; Claire Aguilar, then a UCLA student, drove all the way from Los Angeles to present her paper on "Feminine Space in Five Hollywood Films," and remembers how Barbara Hammer licked her hand in homage after her presentation. Sharon Russell, now at Indiana State University, gave a paper on "The Image of the Witch in Contemporary Film" that predated Susan Faludi by years in its assessment of the antifeminist backlash in Hollywood. Andrea Weiss was there, too. Martha Gever drove with a carload of dykes from Rochester. Gail Seneca and Lucy Arbuthnot were giving a paper they'd written together on lesbian investment in outré Hollywood heterosexual films and actresses. And there were lots of friends who came, half in support and half out of curiosity. Some worked in video, but most had no professional connection to film at all. Yet the conference worked for them: academic enough to be stimulating, but not so rarified that they felt shut out due to ignorance.

Presentations were divided between analysis of Hollywood and the avant-garde or independent sectors. *Mildred Pierce* graced the poster, and paper-doll costumes from the movie covered the conference T-shirts. Yet it wasn't all Hollywood or classics, by any means: it was there that Julia Lesage convened a group of women to talk about pornography, a controversial discussion that found its way into a future issue of *Jump Cut.*

The Feminar was positioned midway between a women's film festival and a conference, clearly showing its antecedents and complex allegiances (both the Edinburgh Conference on Feminism and Film and the Alternative Cinema Conference had taken place the year before). Committed to bringing state-of-the-art feminist film theory to a broader audience, it mixed the political with the academic, and committed itself to "nonhierarchical" ways of doing that, including the injunction to speakers not to use specialized language. The "Feminar Position Paper" distributed to participants took pains to state: "We don't believe in any single correct approach to feminist film criticism." And it went so far as to suggest an experimental format for conference interaction: "The discussion model which we would like everyone to use, called 'snowballing,' consists of a chain in which each speaker is responsible for calling on the next person who is to be given the floor. We feel that this will encourage audience participation and facilitate discussion in a non-hierarchical way." In a sense, the conference was struggling to have its cake and eat it, too, signing on to the high-theory enterprise that would be so crucial to so many people's academic careers and tenure appointments throughout the eighties while trying to hold onto an ideal of nonacademic connection that was fast disappearing from under its feet.

The Feminar was refreshingly self-conscious about its own procedures; inevitably, that resulted in a certain deconstructing of the actual event while it was underway. Still, the numbers of women who attended that event and were profoundly affected by it are legion: Ithaca College professor Patricia Zimmerman recalls it as a sort of trial by fire, a turning point in her maturation as a feminist film professional. It was the last U.S. conference on feminist film issues for many years that was this inclusive. Indeed, it remains the last of the seventies events, the end instead of the beginning of a lineage, reminding us of struggles worth having, contradictions still dormant, passions still appealing.

9.

The Films

of Yvonne

Rainer

(1976/1981)

T he start of a new decade is an auspicious moment at which to survey Yvonne Rainer's work in cinema over the past eight years. Rainer had begun the seventies as an established and celebrated performer, a dancer/choreographer credited with the wholesale reinvention of dance within a modernist lexicon. Now she has begun the eighties as an established filmmaker, a key force in the re-invention of narrative, thereby contributing to the course of avant-garde cinema through this past decade. Of her dance work, it was said that she worked at "tearing away the facade of artificiality" and suggested that "no one who has ever been exposed to her work can again succumb to theatrical illusion with quite the same innocence."[1] The same might be said of her work in cinema, where this theme of innocence forever lost has been a constant thread, linking Rainer's frustration of narrative continuity with her jabs at character identification and her landmining of emotional terrains. Initially conceived within the context of the performance world, Rainer's films have grown in complexity and assurance, reaching a climax of synthesis in her fourth and latest film, *Journeys from Berlin/1971*. In titling the film with that particular date, Rainer has provided a clue to the necessary starting point for any examination of her filmmaking career. As arbitrary as the choice of any particular date will inevitably appear, the year 1971 is, nevertheless, a persuasive index to Rainer's development.

In retrospect, 1971 is a crucial year for a number of reasons pertinent to Rainer as dancer, filmmaker, woman, and traveler. It marks the ten-year point in Rainer's career as a dancer, which formally began with her performance of "Three Satie Spoons" at the Living Theatre in 1961. Her work in dance was characterized by a hostility to artifice, an insistence on granting the everyday movement of the ordinary body the status of dance, a concentration on pure movement unencumbered by metaphor, a will to make the body stand for nothing but itself. During the days of the Judson Church performances, a complaint often leveled at Rainer and company was: Why are they so dead set on being themselves? When reviewing the history of dance in this period in a recent lecture at the Walker Art Center, Rainer commented on the similarity between this dance emphasis and the parallel art world commitment to "unadorned, uninflected, sculptural objects," but admitted that bodies in space could never attain the level of abstraction that a painting or sculpture could. It is precisely this limitation of the body that, transferred to film, became Rainer's greatest strength.

Rainer made the move from dance to film for a number of reasons. Struggling with her attraction/repulsion to authority, Rainer had disbanded her own company and formed a new collective group under the name of the Grand Union. The collective was calculated to maximize improvisation, decentralize decision making, combat the dance world's notorious star system, and democratize its processes. Doubtless its formation was intended to solve Rainer's dilemma of 1969: "The weight and ascendancy of my own authority have come to oppress me."[2] Yet, once formed, the company's very anarchy came to exercise its own form of oppression on the now-incipient director: "There was no way of my getting back in control. . . . When there's no boss, there are new problems."[3] Such individualist anarchy was no doubt an attractive model for Rainer, judging by an exercise sheet distributed at a dance workshop she conducted at roughly the same period, which includes in its exhaustive list of possibilities the seductive #18: "Do anything you want (at your own risk)."

Certainly the new situation quickly became riskiest for Rainer, who found the old oppression of authority replaced by a new, more equitable one: competition. "It wasn't the right atmosphere for me," she recently acknowledged.[4] The way out appeared in the unlikely form of a travel grant awarded to Rainer by the Experiments in Art and Technology. Under its auspices, she spent the beginning of 1971 in India, where the impact of the music and theater events that the still-minimalist-inclined New Yorker attended took root, tapping into the desire for character and narrative that had already begun to appear in her performance work. In the future, this brief India sojourn would have a major effect on the shape of Rainer's creativity. Its immediate effect, though, was a culture-shock negative: "I went into a deep funk, was flooded with contemptuous feelings toward my culture and my place therein, entertained fantasies of giving up my profession because I no longer had anything meaningful to say. . . ."[5] As these feelings of contempt and inadequacy were played out during the low days of 1971, Rainer presented a new performance.

"Grand Union Dreams," perhaps the pivotal work in moving her concerns wholly out of performance into film, was presented on May 16, 1971. Autonomous, it was the last of its kind (after May, all performance work was linked to the film meant to incorporate it). It was also the first of her performance pieces to emphasize individual characters and fictional plot strategies, showing the Indian influence. At the same time, however, the masquerade of "Grand Union Dreams" as performance belied the fact that it was already the seed of a film. The film would be *Lives of Performers,* in which both rehearsals for and audience response to the performance would play a part.

Rainer's own writings from the summer of 1971 (in Vancouver) make it clear that film as future was already forming in her mind.[6] She writes of her dissatisfaction with mixed media (the bits of film she had used as backdrop in her performances before) and of her determination either to stop making films or to do it right. Her plans revolved around her antagonism to voyeurism as a cinematic component and her attraction to the theme of human relationships. In a letter published after the premiere of *Lives of Performers,* in fact, she stresses that the need to deal more specifically with emotion was a prime motivation behind her move from dance to film.[7]

In 1971, film must have looked like an art in its ascendancy. The Anthology Film Archives had opened its doors just before the New Year, with an energy that could not have failed to impress the inflated art world spirit of the time. A key year for avant-garde cinema, 1971 witnessed the release of a score of works that by now constitute its orthodoxy (such as Michael Snow's *La Region Centrale,* George Landow's *Remedial Reading Comprehension,* and the first half of Hollis Frampton's *Hapex Legomena*). There could hardly have been a body of work, though, more foreign to most of Rainer's intentions: the avoidance of emotion, psychology, even character, a purity of expression and damn the consequences, an emphasis on the materiality of the film screen/frame/grain/splice/flicker/camera, an antipathy to narrative and cinematic representation. Except for some of the Frampton work (like *Critical Mass* and *Poetic Justice,* which appealed to Rainer), there was quite a line of demarcation between the dominant avant-garde direction and the sort of emotional and procedural investigations that Rainer was pursuing. Probably more pertinent influences lay elsewhere. "Martha Graham and Jean-Luc Godard were as responsible for my leaving the circus as anybody."[8] The first influenced her dance, the second her films. Though Rainer's work takes up some of the same issues raised by Godard, particularly regarding the autonomy of the director and the inviolability of the audience within the system of cinema, her point of view is quite different.

An accounting of Rainer's development in film (particularly her attention to issues of sexuality, power, and emotion) cannot bypass the emergence of a vital women's movement in this same period.[9] Rainer had always been "political." Her father was an anarchist whose politics were a persuasive influence that colored her childhood. Her own performances during the time of the antiwar movement were aimed variously against the Vietnam War, flag jingoism, and the invasion of Cambodia. By 1971, though, the war was coming to an end, flags would soon be a bitter reminder packed away, and the unified counterculture audience was splintering. A new politics was growing in its wake, developed alongside the recognition that "the personal was the political" and extended to the same themes now occupying Rainer: the power politics of interpersonal relations, male-female dichotomies, the ambiguity of power, and, in terms of media, a critique of dominant modes of production and representation. In the performance "Inner Appearances," Rainer worked through and reworked the implications of having either a man or a woman perform the primary activity that constituted the piece (vacuuming the performance space), weighing the audience response that seemed to adjust meaning according to gender. In the performances, and even more so in the scripts of the new films, Rainer began to present material clearly attuned to the feminist culture then coming of age.

Simon and Schuster published, in 1971, the screenplay to G. W. Pabst's classic *Pandora's Box (Lulu)*, which would become the closing coda to *Lives of Performers*, which Rainer subtitled parenthetically "a melodrama." This film, essentially a series of exercises coming to terms with a series of problems, lays out the basic terms upon which Rainer would proceed in her three succeeding films. Here, however, she is still dogged by the world of performance. The disarrayed scrapbook of stills and script instructions littered across the frame at the film's beginning reveal a cartoonish figure at frame left. It is a cutout photo of Rainer herself, suspended in space apart from the clustered groups of dancers in the other photographs, with a handwritten comic-strip balloon labeling her "director." However ambivalently, she has again taken up that role.

The title evidences what is to come. The performances of the preceding years had often been rehearsals for themselves, enacted on stage before an audience; the film offers, in place of such a rehearsal of a performance, rather a performance of a rehearsal. Rainer plays off that deception on the soundtrack, as the characters' voices challenge the illusory spontaneity of her dialogue with: "Yvonne, were you reading those questions?" Her response introduces the problem of directorial authority (which cinema can so smoothly mask). The title also questions the autonomy of art from daily life, by mixing modes in its very phrasing (of the "lives" as "melodrama") and by keeping the performers' names and seeming identities as the data for the characters as well. If the performer could not be separated from the performance, nor the performance (with its "ordinary" movement) from daily life, then how to sort the dancer from the dance? Thus rehearsal time was now screen time, the private now public, and emotion—so long off-limits for ascetic modernists—now itself a form of melodrama, expressed via a vocabulary of cliché and banality in place of drama. The unity of the film derives from its constant themes of artifice and deception, as variously manifested in dance or film, product or process, story or image, male or female, art or life. The "melodrama" of daily life and artistic process is still very much with Rainer, and with us.

The film's first sequence presents a quotation from the "Walk, She Said" performance world: a rehearsal space, with the bodies moving but the sound, at least initially, removed. The voice of the director does intercede, after much exploration by both camera and performers, leading to the second, discursive section. Here, a cast of voices appears to improvise reminiscences off the photographs of past performances laid out before our eyes. The voices continually interrogate both the material and the director who has assembled it, quarreling over past history and present process. When Rainer objects to a particularly overromantic remembrance with a "Bullshit," she is admonished, "Oh come on, Yvonne, get with it," followed on the soundtrack by a burst of canned laughter (that was actually canned live at a previous performance). As this section winds to its conclusion, a particularly crucial exchange is included. There is an objection to Rainer's inclusion of the words of Jung, which she tries to defend self-deprecatingly: "Well, you know, Shirley, that I have always had a weakness for the sweeping revelations of great men." They constitute a form of authority already being questioned throughout the film, leading to an audience reception of this line as entirely comic. It is, furthermore, an indictment of those who, as Shirley contends, exhibit "a tone of self-congratulation or complacency" common to one who "has had a revelation and is laying it out," a response that might have been familiar to many an audience member at the mythopoetic or structural film screenings of the time.

Scenes of purportedly fictive narratives constitute a third section, with a soundtrack constantly shifting from instruction to reaction, prediction to afterthought. Variation is the operative word. Intertitles frequently supply motivation to the ambiguous representations on screen. The camera runs through (as though provisionally) visual approaches to the woman's and man's body. When one woman speaks, face-front to the audience, it is another woman's voice that summarizes for us what she might be saying. Corrections and contradictions abound.

If the sense (and dread) of women's interchangeability surfaces throughout this third section of the film, then its central sequence acknowledges the possibility and examines the consequences.[10] It is an intertitle that gets the ball rolling. "I remember that movie. It's about all these small betrayals, isn't it?" Valda proceeds to run through the variants of a triangle composed of one man, woman #1, and woman #2, as all three onscreen enact a primitive choreography entitled "Story." The possibilities are legion, the visual enactment crushingly skeletal, until Shirley is permitted the film's first sync-sound line in order to interrupt: "Which woman is the director most sympathetic to?" Valda guesses that it might be woman #1, but wagers that might be only because she appeared first. Such is, indeed, the nature of perception and of cinematic power politics. (And not just in film. Perhaps the man stays with #1 simply because she appeared first.) As Rainer becomes increasingly concerned with the politics of visual representation, such "screen tests" become increasingly crucial.

As the narrative devices of the third section continue, time passes, if only fictively: "One week later." The scene seems suddenly to compose itself into the familiar outlines of an age-old story, as Valda opens the letter from The Other Woman and begins to read, revealing that the familiarity was an error. Valda herself is The Other Woman (if, as Rainer suggests, that means simply the one who appears second), and this letter, far away from Hollywood convention, has a new message. Complaining of the two little boxes "he" has stuck both of them into, the writer goes on to reject her half of that false equation and, handing over the reins to power, wishes Valda good luck: "I just wanted to tell you that I like you and I wish you'd take him away from me right now." The letter is a transitional document, carrying as it does a new perspective on an old pattern, as though "sisterhood" at that time carried all the burden of a feminist consciousness focused on older, still oppressive behavior. Women could empathize with each other, but could find no way out of the old roles. Tradition still prevailed, standing despite its cracks—a paradox that the balance of the film reflects.

The narrative takes the shape of a series of tableaux, varying the shots and the characters in an effort to gauge the variables of viewer response in a reasonably controlled manner. Just as Fernando is about to leave in search of cigarettes, though, Rainer shifts modes to present "Valda's solo," which in actuality was filmed at a Whitney Museum performance, a fact that supplies the elegance of parquet floors and the purity of museum-white walls in contrast to the rougher environs of the preceding action. The solo is similarly high in the register of expression. Dressed in a black evening gown, traced by a handheld spotlight, Valda Setterfield moves between the classicism of the Cunningham style (in whose company she was a dancer) and the exaggerated expressionism of Nazimova in the silent film *Salome,* which, according to Rainer, inspired her choreography here. The performance is a Greek vase in the midst of an industrial age. The shadow etched on the wall becomes a throwback to another age of cinema as well, a simple shadow play keyed to our imagination. She freezes into certain positions, providing a pun on "silhouette" as the shadow mimics the black paper cutouts that long ago served as portraits. Her audience is unimpressed: "he has seen it a hundred times" and despite the claim to difference, "it looks the same to him." It is a judgment that cuts in two directions, both as a critique of male insensitivity and of the arch-subtlety of minimalist work.

As the film winds to a close, Rainer pulls no punches. Indeed, the intertitle that appears in the midst of this fourth section (which again quotes from the "Walk, She Said" rehearsals) charts the course of much of her work since and refocuses our attention in this one: "Emotional relationships are relationships of desire, tainted by coercion and constraint. . . ." The performers are moving about their central prop, a box, inevitably calling to mind the "little boxes" alluded to in the letter from one woman to the other. Though Valda is now in functional overalls, the shadow of the black evening dress is still upon her. Valda and Fernando are in the box together; by the end of the intertitle's warning, she is outside the box, apart from all four other characters inside. By the scene's conclusion, all have emerged, yet the specter of the box remains in the background, with its symbolism intact.

Lives of Performers concludes with the performance of the end of a life: the sequence of stills, reenacted, from Pabst's *Lulu,* terminating with the death of Lulu at the hands of Jack the Ripper. During the course of that film, the sexual power of the femme fatale becomes transformed, first into the powerless sexuality of the prostitute and last into the terminal victimization of murder. In a technique that would be explored further in *Film about a Woman Who . . . ,* the characters are made to simulate photographs by holding stasis for periods of time, lending an edge of tension and artificiality to an otherwise straightforward scene and punning visually off the word "still" used in the movie biz. In a stagy replica of the 1928 melodrama, the four characters get to exhibit extremes of emotion never displayed in the preceding footage. Lest the viewer, however, thereby assume that the emotions themselves were not in evidence (albeit devoid of the matching acting style), Rainer slyly matches the last three minutes of the "stills" to the Rolling Stones song, "No Expectations," token of yet another affair of the heart gone wrong. What might, then, have been a swan song to a lost era becomes instead a reminder to what extent the present conceals the past, intact within it. The theme of woman as victim is one Rainer has just begun to consider.

If *Lives of Performers* is a compendium of possibilities, then *Film about a Woman Who . . .* is their fruition. Again in black and white, again photographed by Babette Mangolte, this film pushes even further Rainer's initial thoughts on representation, narrative, sexual relationships, and the politics of personal power manipulations. The effect of feminist thinking becomes even clearer in this work, especially as reflected in hindsight by Rainer's own remarks (in 1973) on the attraction of film over dance: that because "rage, terror, desire, conflict et al." were not unique to her experience in the way that her body had always been, now she "could feel much more connected to my audience, and that gives me great comfort."[11] It was during this period, in fact, that a whole new audience was opening up for the work of women filmmakers, and an equally new context for their work. No longer was it sufficient to bring the brunt of film history to bear upon each individual work; new values were at stake. What Rainer was up to, after all, was the reinvention of melodrama as a genre, accented for the contemporary psyche: "This is the poetically licensed story of a woman who finds it difficult to reconcile certain external facts with her image of her own perfection. It is also the same woman's story if we say she can't reconcile these facts with her image of her own deformity. . . . Not that it's a matter of victims and oppressors. She simply can't find alternatives to being inside with her fear or standing in the rain with her self-contempt."

Contradiction is the basic grammar of *Film about a Woman Who . . .* , dialectic its movement, cliché frequently its vocabulary. As always, the title is a significant indicator, for the various characters on the soundtrack are identified only as "he" and "she," while the screen offers us the actions and words of a cast of characters we can match up or discount at will. From the opening scene, Rainer plays upon audience expectation of filmic tradition and foils its fulfillment. Even as the credits are rolling, the soundtrack sets us up with violent thunder, the cinematic code for horror movie suspense or emotional revelation, in sardonic counterpoint to the list of names onscreen. When an image does appear, it initiates a further dupe of preconditioned senses: expecting to find the film up there, we find instead another audience watching their own show, which appears to consist of slides on a screen, judging from the light flashing with the light-dark rhythm of the carousel apparatus (just as ours, at this moment, must be reflecting the 24-frame-a-second rhythm of the sound-film projector). Continuing the hall of mirrors, Rainer transforms our screen into theirs, which is filled with a second level of images: snapshots and slides of a life heretofore unidentified. Lest the viewer try for the easy way out, and identify with the onscreen audience, the image switches to another locus altogether: a moving sound-and-image ocean, the archetypal movie set. The switch signals, as well, Rainer's own successful crossover from dance to the vocabulary of cinema. Though *Lives of Performers* may have been more self-reflective, it is *Film about a Woman Who . . .* that exhibits the assurance of a director dealing with known materials.

The effect can be seen, for example, in Rainer's new points about the cinema-to-audience relationship. The soundtrack, as always, concentrates on charged reminiscences dealing with self-image, intimacy, sexuality, and human interaction as performance, until interrupted by an intertitle: "Social interactions seem to be mostly about seduction." Like most of Rainer's wry statements of "fact," this one reverberates at several levels. In terms of the narrative, it offers a missing piece to assemble the fragmented characters on view. In terms of the audience, it sets up a conduit carrying the narrative directly into play with our own experiences. And last, it offers a coded comment on cinema itself. If "social interactions" stand as well for the "movies" that depict them, then a shift in the locus of "seduction" from the sphere of the bedrooms illuminated on the screen to the sphere of the viewers couched in darkness would suggest a seduction of the audience by the filmmaker through the medium of the text, the film itself. "Who is the victim here?" is asked. The question echoes the point made earlier (in *Lives of Performers*) about woman #1 versus woman #2. Now, Rainer has collapsed the distance separating character from viewer, removing our protective spectatorship through her intertitle's direct recognition of our in-process manipulation. The hypnotism of cinema and the concurrent need to free the audience from its enthrallment to the cinematic apparatus were both hot topics of discussion in theoretical circles at the time of this film; yet Rainer is able to construct an object lesson far more persuasive than any text by fusing the moment of our realization with that of our participation in the very system we come to identify.

As a woman filmmaker, Rainer is particularly aware of the function that women's victimization has served within the narrative structure. If the death of Louise Brooks in *Pandora's Box* provided a fitting climax for the previous film, then the death of Janet Leigh at the start of *Psycho* offers an even more fitting middle to this one. As before, Rainer is playing with the notion of "stills" by using, this time, actual stills frozen out of an earlier film's footage and now, rehydrated, incorporated into her own film text for a different purpose: no longer a murder, the stills this time around are an autopsy. The stills detail the famous 45-second sequence in which Marion Crane (Janet Leigh) is stabbed to death in the shower. The scene provoked a furor of attention, not so much for its since-recognized brilliance of editing as for its violation of a treasured principle of the suspense genre: that is, that the "star" is guaranteed survival through to the end of the picture, both because of the studio's financial investment and the audience's emotional investment. Hitchcock's transgression in killing off the high-salaried idol so early in the film paid off in shock value at the time, while Rainer's quotation of the famed sequence redefines its significance. In fixing on a moment that, historically, marks an undermining of narrative convention by Hollywood's own hand, Rainer manages to annex the traditional movie making to her own enterprise, a feat of re-vision that makes film history supportive of her own terms.

The feat is not an idle one; woman's fate is inextricably caught up in the balance, as the choice of the *Psycho* material should indicate. "An Emotional Accretion in 48 Steps," the tour de force central section of the film, employs a range of narrative strategies to elucidate a particular, albeit typical, male-female interaction. Rainer avoids any one stylistic choice, overturning every possible variation of presentation in the effort to dissect the subjective emotions of an affair going awry. Settling on a single mode of communication would have placed the film within a prevailing convention, as Rainer lists them: "the *acting* of the narrative film, the *inter-titles* of the silent movie, the *sub-titles* and *dubbing* of the foreign-language film, the *voice-over* of the documentary and the *flash-back* and *face-front-to-camera* delivery of Godard." [12]

The *Psycho* stills in the middle of *Film about a Woman Who . . .* numbered forty; Rainer's psychic stills in "Emotional Accretion" number forty-eight. The disjunctions between sound and image, between text and voice-over, correspond to the alienation separating "he" and "she," to the contradictions between how "she" feels and how "she" acts. At points, she seems to be dubbing her own behavior, substituting the authentic gestures with conciliatory translations. The movie remembered for all its "small betrayals" in *Lives of Performers* has been consolidated into one crucial moment in which the woman asks the man to hold her. "Somehow she had betrayed herself," reads step 46. It seems she hadn't really wanted to be held: "She had wanted to bash his fucking face in."

The section dedicated to the emotional accretions presents a story in rather the same sense that the choreographed "Story" did in the earlier film. Its coherent narrative may well be a precis for the film's overall fragmentation of narrative causality, while its climax in emotional resolution points to the central theme, indeed the genre definition, of the film as a whole. To be sure, the ellipsis of time, the flat nonemotive voice, nonnaturalistic stagy movement, verbal cliché, tableaux vivants, and unidentified pronouns, all combine to engage the spectator in the shaping of the film. At the same time, however, it is evident that these techniques precipitate a complete abstraction of the narrative. The only constant left to the film, finally, is emotion itself. It is the narrative structures of *Film about a Woman Who . . .* that advance the emotions instead of the usual model of emotion advancing a superimposed plot. In preserving the customary elements while inverting their relationship, Rainer has created a meeting ground for the sort of formal and psychological concerns that, prior to her work, were frequently dismissed as mutually exclusive. In so doing, Rainer has arrived at a redefinition of melodrama for our times.

One of the major contributions of feminism to the arts has been an insistence on the inclusion of emotion as a primary value. For women, whose emotions and instincts have so long been denied as fraudulent or unrepresentative, the revival of emotion as a proper subject of artistic concern is a crucial issue. In the area of film, the revival and legitimization of the "woman's film" genre, previously despised as matinee weepies worthy of extinction, is significant. Simone de Beauvoir, in an argument pointed at annexing Stendhal to the feminist cause, once cited his upholding of the life of the heart as the worthy equal of the life of physical adventure. Molly Haskell has applied that standard to the screen, suggesting that the very qualities that provoked denigration in the past (i.e., the emphasis on emotion and sentiment) were proto-feminist values.[13] Melodrama and, by extension, soap opera deal in the drama of emotional involvement, substituting the risks of emotional commitment for the risks of physical danger. A provisional set of elements can be identified as intrinsic to the "woman's film" melodramas, indeed, so implicit as to require a feminist attention. Such a set includes the presence of a woman at the center of the film; a domestic setting, usually the site of domestic conflict; an ellipsis of time to allow for the development of emotion, always central to the drama; extreme verbalization, which replaces physical action as the means of communication for the now interior movement; and finally, the woman's ultimate decision to release her emotions.[14]

Though Haskell's work has been concerned primarily with analyzing this pattern as found in Hollywood films of a particular period, it can be traced as well throughout *Film about a Woman Who . . .* (and other Rainer films). In such a context, the very aspects of the films that appear most offensive to traditional movie making and so scrupulously modernist in source (the use of texts, one-room staging, lack of physical activity, atemporality) may be viewed as the most natural, indeed requisite, characteristics of traditional melodrama. In turn, Rainer's fidelity to such a wide range of melodramatic conventions throws into sharp relief her flagrant departure from its codes in her handling of narrative and audience expectation. Retaining the still valid emphases of the genre, Rainer has reshaped them to fit specifically contemporary concerns — a formal complexity to match overwrought sensibility. *Lives of Performers,* despite its titular claim to being a "melodrama," was too much of a roman à clef to allow for that wider interpretation. It took Rainer until the next work, *Film about a Woman Who . . . ,* to develop the mechanisms by which the materials of autobiography could be successfully combined with those of fictional and documentary materials to form a unified, personal text.

When I woke up he expounded his ideas about education. Victimized once more victimized once more victimized once more . . . No, it wasn't a breeze. — Yvonne Rainer [15]

Though excised from the text before the final filming, this passage points directly at one of the central themes of *Film about a Woman Who . . .* (and much of Rainer's other work as well). If women seemed to be victims of relational triangles or the machinations of art in Rainer's first film, then now the more pernicious mechanisms of society enter into the picture. For example, a long scene detailing one woman's sexual fantasy transpires within a theatrical, uninflected space, in which she is undressed by a couple ministering to her needs. Slowed down and prolonged, the scene bears witness to her disrobing via sculptural camerawork that accents the dreamlike quality. Yet, lest the viewer fall for this vision of sexuality self-controlled and removed from society, Rainer follows with herself in pasties: not the literal pasties of a striptease, but rather the pasted-on bits of newspaper which, originally a public testament, now adorn Rainer's own face. These patches of newsprint carry the words of Angela Davis to George Jackson, letters of affection that were used by the press to undermine and negate Davis's political work and strength.

Thus is Rainer able to convey to what extent women are still victimized through the exercise of emotional rights or powers. Furthermore, the closing performance in the film (pas de deux with ball) is choreo-graphed in accordance with twenty poses derived from photographs and drawings of Isadora Duncan. In citing these two legendary women, Davis and Duncan, from the worlds of politics and dance, Rainer is making the first step toward an identification with other women (apart from film stars) that would lead, eventually, to her very different handling of iden-tification and distanciation in *Journeys from Berlin/1971.* First, the notion of victim would have to be broadened through the strategies of *Kristina Talking Pictures,* the film that also initiates Rainer's first extended use of color (alternating at this point still with black and white).

Kristina Talking Pictures opens with the same theme of emotional risk established in its predecessor, but eventually moves to a broader con-sideration of more global, less individual, crisis. At the film's center is one Kristina (actually, several, as the character is represented by various women), a lady lion tamer from near Budapest who comes to New York to become a choreographer, and one Raoul, her seaman love who leaves her at the film's beginning, only to return to join the dance and leave once more. The image of the lady lion tamer is a charged one, crying out to us immediately on the level of metaphor: the lady in a cage, the woman in danger, Daniella in the lion's den. She's the supreme embodiment of the paradox of the public persona: invulnerability endangered. Her scanty, sequined costume reinforces the paradox. Allegedly symbolic of her skill, power, and mastery of the elements at hand (presumably the lions), the costume yet produces an effect of exposure, vulnerability, a body prone to danger. The paradox is that of femininity itself. And whence the danger? Following her introductory cast of characters, a get-acquainted section featuring lion-taming footage and Christina stand-ins from the circus past, Rainer presents a scene that explicates the lion tamer myth as yet another performance, with the circus now taking the place of the dance world in her first film.

The scene is actually a remake of a similar scene in *Lives of Performers,* in which a roving handheld camera focused on a woman in what seemed to be her bedroom, moved across her bed onto the floor, surveying a sheet of paper with a quotation about "cliché," charted her body and eventually the body of the nearby man, and concluded with her resolution of ambiva-lence: "she starts to leave, then changes her mind, and rejoins him." By the time of *Kristina Talking Pictures,* Rainer has a different scene in mind.

Kristina and the camera both roam the bedroom, their points of inter-section allowing us a view of her movements. Otherwise, we are free to explore the room, clearly seventies Soho, at leisure. Again, there is a sheet of paper lying on the floor, but it's a letter this time instead of a critique, an embodiment of cliché rather than a treatise on the subject. Also in the room, prominently visible to us for its iconic significance, is a green-glittered costume lying atop the radiator. Kristina misses both. After brushing her teeth, getting dressed, packing her bag, hailing a taxi for LaGuardia Airport, yelling "Stop" — only then does Kristina rush back into the room for her costume, notice the letter, and collapse on the bed. "To hell with it," she says (or rather, doesn't say, for little of the film is sound-synced and voices bear no necessary relevance to the faces occupying the same screen time). The letter is by now an obligatory object for a Rainer film (compare The Other Woman's letter to Valda with Angela Davis's letter to George Jackson). This one from Raoul, with the usual narrative omniscience of movie letters, says that he's left her, to please forgive him, and so on. The reaction shot of Kristina, shot from above, finds her lying on the bed with the sequined costume in place atop her street clothes, like a body laid out for a wake gone wrong.

This crucial scene, like Kristina's body, is layered with meaning. The emotional content of the letter and her reaction immediately supply a corrective to any notions of the lion tamer as invincible. Though Kristina has tamed the wild beasts, her conquest of the physical world cannot help her escape a woman's fate of emotional risk. The lesson posed by the Beauty and the Beast fable is an enduring one: danger may be disguised as a lion but will be revealed as a man. Thus, Rainer incorporates the metaphor of the circus into her continuing preoccupation with the contradictions between the public and private persona, particularly as that split afflicts the woman artist.

By privileging the emotional struggles of Kristina over her animal-training skills as a sphere of investigation, Rainer is recommitting her work to the territory of melodrama as cited above for the centrality of emotion as authentic experience. That point was underlined sardonically in the last film by the choice of "the 48 steps" in conjunction with a quotation from Psycho, as though Rainer were pointedly challenging Hitchcock's prioritization of physical suspense and skill, in films like his 39 Steps, with her own drama of emotional accretions that required a full nine steps more to reach its goal: "The sensitive intellectual or artist agonizing over the nature of his existence in the face of world poverty, over-population, pollution, and the depletion of natural resources . . . But when it comes to women all he can think about is tits and ass." The formal disjunctions of image, text, continuity, framing, all lend a textural codification to the disjunctions between the private and public politics of daily life. The tone may be ironic, but the contradictions are ever present. Moving between memory and history, sexuality and world politics, Rainer assiduously removes all mock-naturalistic cues, flattening the acting, disinflecting the voices, even blocking any escape hatch into history or nostalgia by conflating past with present and background with foreground. Ironically, one character opts out with "Oh, let's forget about it and go to the movies," as though there could be at least a film-within-a-film immune from ideology.

"The Return of Raoul" is announced on plain lined yellow paper, its arrival onscreen accompanied by a silent-movie musical flourish. In a sense, the scene is reminiscent of a very different boy-remeets-girl scene in an equally different film, Josef Von Sternberg's *Shanghai Express*. Meeting up with Shanghai Lily again, Doc recounts his adventures and physical exploits of the intervening years to an unimpressed Lily, who responds only "Sounds like a lonely life, Doc," a judgment from which he does not dissent. Thus, Shanghai Lily succeeds in imposing the standards of the "woman's film" (emotional richness) upon the material of the male action script, devaluing his acts of valor on the basis of their emotionally barren nature.

Though Rainer does not affix any hierarchy to the testimonies that she has Kristina and Raoul present, the polarity is clearly etched. Kristina (enacted by Rainer herself) and Raoul (her brother Ivan) sit together in bed in an asexual intimacy reminiscent of the Hayes Act movie bedrooms of the fifties. Strange pillow talk, though: Raoul speaks texts on the mechanics of crude oil carriers (based on Noel Mostert's *Supership*); Kristina speaks texts on the mating habits of lions. The obvious phallic significance of the supertanker, gliding silently across the screen, reinforces a sense of its male world of mechanization; Kristina, despite her lion taming, concerns herself with the domestic sphere of her beasts' sexuality and procreation. The scene is played straight by the two actors, with stiff, elocution class delivery, but is broken up in the editing by words that skip and circle back on themselves, by gestures that command instant replays and looped repetitions, by camera movements that abandon the characters entirely to climb the walls, spying out the pictures there. This long, difficult scene stands at the heart of the film, epitomizing as it does a duality of focus: the emotional battlefield of alienated affections between men and women, on the one hand, and the worldwide battlefield of past and future holocaust, on the other.

The pictures on the wall offer one key to this duality. "Talking pictures," they are enigmatic souvenirs of different times and places. One seems to be of a circus, some emblem of Kristina's past. Others speak of war, ration lines, interrogation, slaughtered bodies piled up in anonymity. There is a profound feeling of alienation and loss that suffuses more than sexuality, encompassing history and infecting the present. Just as Rainer has superimposed the story of the Budapestian upon the '76 Soho milieu, and the persona of the lion tamer upon that of the dancer/filmmaker, so has she layered the politics of the seventies with the moral crisis of the Third Reich. There's a broader focus in terms of character as well. Unlike the first two films, which concentrate almost exclusively on the high-art banter of Soho liaisons, there are other personae here, ranging from James Cagney to an old bag lady with a German accent who's invited in off the stoop (to talk about menstruation, Marlon Brando, and the anxieties of sexuality).

In the background of many scenes, shadowy figures move about in shades of gray performing an ongoing nightmare of human suffering. Their presence sparks memories of concentration camps that are reinforced by key remarks in conversation, such as the analysis of a Yiddish joke that dominates a dinner party. As the need for a Yiddish-accented punchline is questioned, the scene begins to shift registers like so many Berlitz accents: clothing switches from shot to shot; voices change in midsentence from one speaker to another; remarks begun in one location conclude in another; cuts move from color to black and white; the scene becomes a continuity nightmare, at once challenging the illusionism of "realistic" mise-en-scène and defying the audience to catch the punchline without the "accent" of traditional cinematic codes. "The theater has gone out of it," the jokester concludes.

In fact, it is no longer a simple world in any realm. Raoul's bedtime conversation laid out our alienation from the earth itself, as represented by the creation of monster supertankers that destroyed the life of one sailor and may destroy all life on the planet in the event of accident. The old models of behavior and belief don't hold. If women no longer want to fill the roles previously imposed, well, men no longer have much left in the way of traditional roles to fill. Raoul laments the passing of the sailor's life (quoting at one point from Melville in despair) and its degeneration into the sterile world of the modern tanker, which no one would dream of calling "she." That world of glamor and adventure, the life of the seaman, is no more. Raoul can no longer be a sailor, nor Kristina a lion tamer. If simple roles are nowhere to be found, neither is simple representation. The camerawork reinforces the breakdown, splitting both Kristina and Raoul with the frame line, isolating portions of their bodies, mismatching one's face with another's voice. Just as the old ways of living are dead, so are the old forms, in politics, literature, dance, film. Our ways of perceiving and our modes of illusion are equally dead.

Death, in fact, is a frequent theme in the film. At one point, Kristina breaks up a roomful of chairs, tossing them into the air and crashing them to the ground in a dreamlike slow-motion explosion of grief as the sound-track relates, "Max, I heard you died." As the memory of Max unfolds, we realize that the mourning is not for Max alone but for an entire way of life that has passed on as surely as he (Cocteau, Chinese rugs, "soigné young men who spoke of axiology"), as well as for Kristina's own past (the chairs, after all, are the lion tamer's tools of trade). A voice recalls, "Mama, I heard you died last night" and makes reference, at another point, to a daughter's death. Throughout, ever present, is the reference to the death of the six million in a Germany past our memory, muted by time but still speaking in pictures on the wall or texts that issue unexpectedly, ventriloquist-like, from characters' mouths. Most chillingly, near the end of the film, when its most elegant personage (Valda) consults her arm for Kristina's telephone number, it is with newly learned horror that we perceive the concentration camp tatoo inked onto her forearm, and with newly felt relief that the seven digits become a Bell-Tel joke. In the specter of ecodeath raised by the supertankers, death is a less humorous threat, lurking almost unimaginably in the shadow of *Supership* disaster, where the plankton are merely the first of us to go.

If this summary begins to resemble a dirge, rightly so. *Film about a Woman Who . . .* might have lent the final touches to the reworking of melodrama first begun in the autobiographical researches of *Lives of Performers,* but *Kristina Talking Pictures* presents another genre altogether. Consider Kinsley writing on Burns in the *Oxford English Dictionary:* "The poet descends from . . . the dramatic domain of song, into the subjective and reflective one of elegy."

Melodrama was *melos* (song) plus drama. In prerelease references, the title of the film was described initially as "An Opera" and then as "For a Novella," finally on screen becoming *Kristina Talking Pictures.* "We think there is a sure road. But that would be the road of death," spoke the Jungian text in "Grand Union Dreams" and Rainer's first film. Elegy is prompted by death, at least insofar as death touches and is incorporated into the spirit of the filmmaker (or, as above, the poet). In *Kristina Talking Pictures,* it may be said, melodrama met elegy and was consumed.

The film is an elegy, not only for the characters delineated above, but also for periods, roles, styles, forms, solutions (even Final Solutions) that have passed on. In the earlier works, the references to death were specific and individualized (Lulu, *Psycho*). Here, the deaths are broadened, the blow encompassing more victims, just as the character of Kristina now encompasses more performers. References that before were cinematic here are historical.

Yet the personal has not been forsaken. Elegy permits, indeed demands, a probing into one's own life and feelings, easily suiting Rainer's own penchant for including the details of her life in her fictions. When Kristina gripes "I'm fucking around in more ways than one," we can find her sentence in Rainer's own journals. When the line of figures files hands-up through the SoHo streets, a precedent is visible in Rainer's own performance in the same streets at the time of the invasion of Cambodia. Such references proliferate throughout the film. More than the previous works, however, this film insists on pushing past the circle of private lives and loves into the wider arena of public action, concentrating our gaze on the points of intersection between the two, and laying the foundations for the more intensive mining of this same intersection in *Journeys from Berlin/1971*.

Kristina Talking Pictures, moreover, may be seen as elegy even at the fundamental level of form. The title itself harkens back to an antiquated moment in movie making, that era in which film "progressed" from the golden age of silent film to the much heralded future of synchronized sound. Rainer turns her back on any such notion of "progress" by ignoring even that future in her desynchronized sound-image combinations throughout the film. Though there has been much talk, this year particularly, about just where the medium of film went "wrong" in its development since the days of so-called primitive cinema, and how avant-garde film practice might present a remedy to a misguidedly narrow path of technological orchestration, Rainer herself does not seem to be calling for any return to basics. Rather, by pursuing the logic of disjunctions and refusing to pander to our voyeurism, she has pushed the classic forms to the very point of disintegration, that is, death. In this film, in particular, she has made a frontal attack on the intelligibility of narrative, pushed dysfunction past the point of illustration, defeated temporality with simultaneity of tense and ellipsis of action, and beat illusionism on its own ground.

The tone of elegy, despite the implication of mourning, need not be a somber one; there is nothing dirge-like about *Kristina Talking Pictures*. In a program note to her "North East Passing of 1968," Rainer cited a definition of "to pass" as "to undergo, live during, discharge from the body . . . undergo transition . . . come to an end, die, depart, go by, move onward."[16] The various elements of the film are neatly marshaled under these definitions: to undergo World War II; to live during an era of impending annihilation; to discharge blood, as in the old woman's menstrual memories; to undergo transition from lion tamer to dancer (or sailor to supertanker); to come to an end (as a film) or die (as a person) or move onward (as a form). Committed, as always, to her future work,

Rainer ends the film with the words "to go on." Form, as workable entity or possible ideal, no longer holds. By coming to terms with the death of the old forms and passing through our ritual of nostalgic grief, *Kristina Talking Pictures* prepares us for the future and, incidentally, for Rainer's next film. If it seems less accessible, less immediately pleasing, than the other films, it is precisely because of its determination to take a step forward in the evolution of new film languages and inflections. If its theme, as I have suggested, is one of elegy, then it is above all an elegy in the spirit of one who believes in resurrection.

Rainer, indeed, is here moving toward an acceptance of polarities, a move beyond the either/or confrontation of contradiction that toned the earlier work. Kristina's departure from the circus suggests her affinity with another cinematic figure, Leni Peickert (in Alexander Kluge's *Artistes under the Big Top*), who tried to transform the circus from an arena of physical expertise into a carnival of the imagination, but in vain. If Peickert's dedication to the circus clearly paralleled Kluge's own in terms of cinema, surely Kristina is a similar stand-in for Rainer, the circus itself a metaphor of the theatrical illusion she rejected. But how, then, to break with that need for the utopia of the circus, that clear enactment of ideal fantasies intermixed with fears and hopes? In the "Grand Union Dreams" performance, Rainer divided her cast into heroes and mortals, thereby allowing our daily life its failure to be mythic. By the time of *Kristina Talking Pictures,* however, a détente has been achieved. The introductory narration defends the characters to come: "For after all . . . they are . . . in a sense . . . if nothing else . . . nothing less than heroes." If we are not in the circus, we are nonetheless performers. If we do not walk the high wire, we nevertheless survive.

Rainer could have ended the film on its blackboard lesson, bearing the "faint and cold" words from Samuel Beckett's *The End.* Instead, she follows his story of despair with Valda's reading of a very different letter from the one that opened the film, this one a letter full of pain, longing, love, and above all, consolation. It is only then, after this text has been spoken, that the camera can return to the hopeful last three words that close the film: "to go on." The camera pans from the blackboard to the white wall (a black-and-white case?). The screen goes white. The texts have been exhausted, the forms cracked open. *Kristina Talking Pictures* has passed on, leaving the task of transformation to *Journeys from Berlin/1971.*

I was pretty happy doing the lion act for a while. But I'm afraid Emma Goldman and Virginia Woolf ruined me for the circus. Dominating brute beasts . . . how can that compare to what they did? — Yvonne Rainer, *Kristina Talking Pictures*

Feminism, anarchism. The swaying of public opinion, the organizing of popular action. Two women, furthermore, whose private and public lives were fused as one and entered into the log of history as a unity. How to justify her own taming of the wild beasts of creativity and imagination with what they did? That's the question posed by Kristina and answered, at last, by Rainer in the next film, *Journeys from Berlin/1971.*

Building on and diverging from the researches of the past works, this film is Rainer's culminating deep-sea dive into the wreck of the psyche and the violence of history. If *Kristina Talking Pictures* can be compared to an elegy as phrased by a resurrectionist, then *Journeys from Berlin/1971* must be the consequential next step, the phoenix arisen from the ashes. The spirit is uncannily akin to that discerned by John Berger in his critique of Soviet artist Ernst Neizvestny, whose sculpture treats some of the same subjects (the body as metaphor, the contradictions of the political being, the responsibility of the individual) that have concerned Rainer: "It would be wrong to conclude that [he] is obsessed by death. I spoke of a polarity. Death for him is a starting point rather than an end. It is from death that he measures, instead of toward it."[17] The analogy may be applied to Rainer's latest film thematically and stylistically, for here she has reshaped both her past material and her formal trajectory. She has transgressed the provincial boundaries of Soho's art world mentality geographically and artistically, as evidenced in her Berlin locus and in her new use of rolling titles to communicate certain information free of ambiguity. *Journeys from Berlin/1971* is without a doubt the most ambitious, most risk-taking work of Rainer's cinematic career so far.

The film is constructed out of a variety of filmic and literary materials. Its two major sections involve a psychoanalysis session, which occupies much of the screen time, and a kitchen conversation about political violence, which resembles a radio drama that we hear but never visually witness. The dysfunction between the public and the private, always a central focus of Rainer's work, here is made wider and more explicit through the counterpoint set up between the analysis session and the conversation about terrorism: the one an excavation of innermost fantasies and emotional traumas within an impersonal space, the other a debate of pressing social issues enacted as tabletop repartee. The counterpoint weaves in and out of that tricky terrain wherein the individual psyche connects to the historical body politic.

The motif of the psychoanalysis session dominates the film visually and metaphorically. Certainly some of its strength derives from the inspired casting of Annette Michelson as the patient. Her physical presence, age, stature, and sheer acting ability must have determined Michelson as Rainer's choice, but there is also a hidden irony. Writing about *Lives of Performers,* Michelson had astutely characterized its discourse as "that idiom of somewhat manic autoanalysis which characterizes life and love in a therapeutically oriented culture . . . there is really one single mode of intellectual discourse . . . that of psychoanalysis."[18]

Rainer has cast Michelson into precisely the arena that Michelson herself had first detected as the subtext of Rainer's work. And yet, perversely, Rainer has removed the sign that once prompted the diagnosis: the analytic language. Michelson's character often speaks in non sequiturs, shifting sense and direction in a blink of the eye, traversing her subject in a stream-of-consciousness flow, sounding at times as though an editor has been hacking away at her words in some nonexistent postproduction phase of the film; but no, she is simply speaking, as Rainer puts it, "in tongues." The sync-sound strategy shifts attention away from the film's construction and onto its constructed: the patient and her text. With the emphasis on printed texts, subtitles, and visual addenda stripped away, the psychoanalysis session portion of the film invests meaning in the soundtrack more intensely than any previous Rainer work, using that intensity in turn to reinvest layers of meaning into the comparatively static image.

The mere use of a psychoanalysis session, of course, is redolent with formal implications. Given Rainer's standing interest in narrative, the psychoanalytic monologue inevitably becomes a model of narrative possibility. Roy Schafer, in a paper analyzing the psychoanalysis patient's history as a kind of narrative, has established a persuasive correspondence between the two. He sees the patient's testimony as "a series of tellings and retellings in the terms of self and others and the events in which they have played a role." As to the structure of these tellings, and apropos of the film under consideration, Schafer observes: "The telling of that history is achieved in a circular fashion, the present questioning and informing the past and vice versa," in other words, an approach identical to Rainer's own handling of temporality. In conclusion, Schafer explicitly identifies "transference and resistance . . . as narrative structures," in which "the analysand shows and tells, shows by telling and tells by showing, as in 'acting out.' The analysand is a certain kind of unreliable narrator."[19] The device of the psychoanalysis session in *Journeys from Berlin/1971* thus integrates with precision Rainer's dedication to narrative experiment and her attachment to mediated autobiography. The two are joined in that most intimate of performances, psychoanalysis, which, like dance and the circus, battles still with illusion and theatricality. Schafer's critique centers on aspects of oral history and physical presentation, but the nature of cinema suggests a further extension: into the area of representation.

Throughout the footage of the psychoanalysis session, Rainer has slyly positioned her camera behind the back of the therapist in a reference to that prevailing film theory that sees the entire filmic enterprise as a voyeuristic endeavor. If all films pander to the voyeurism of the audience, then Rainer at least underlines the institutionalization of the peeping by assigning her audience the place of society's other privileged voyeur, the psychiatrist. Lest the viewer become comfortable in that role, however, Rainer pulls the rug out from under such a system of identification by recasting her doctor at unpredictable intervals. Whether a function of transference, resistance, or directorial design, the doctor appears variously as a woman, a bearded man, and a nine-year-old boy who barks. The visual perspective shifts in accordance with the hierarchy of power, the specially built, wedge-shaped set tilting our line of vision down on the patient as the man, up as the boy, or, with the possibility of equality, as the woman. There are interruptions. The patient's monologues are mixed with readings from Rainer's own adolescent journals, altering the scene's chronology. Obscene phone calls disturb the air of security. A rug literally is rolled out in the background, a space peopled by a shadowy cast of characters not unlike the extras moving through *Kristina Talking Pictures*. Sometimes they form a silent chorus, other times a proper crew.

This is no realistic psychoanalysis session, which, after all, is simply a new way of getting to the bottom of the private-public split underlying art making in general. Its counterpart, its alter ego perhaps, is the other part of the film: the tabletop conversation between two Soho types (played by the voices of Amy Taubin and Vito Acconci) idly talking politics while preparing dinner. Their conversation offers an initial connection between the two segments:

> He: Did you ever read Emma Goldman on political violence?
> She: No. I have a collection of her essays, but all I've read is her autobiography.

These two characters embody the contradictory, self-absorbed view of political violence held by a fair share of artists and other mortals of the U.S. cultural establishment. Their vision of past anarchists is idealized and therefore prone to excessive criticism. They debate a succession of points, bolstering their positions (and our knowledge) by reading aloud, not only from Goldman but also from accounts of women nihilists fighting against the czar and from writings by Ulrike Meinhof. Their voices animate a host of historical figures: Angelica Balabanoff, Olga Liubatovich, Elizaveta Kovalskaia, Vera Figner, Vera Zasulich. The models are both defended and attacked.

Rainer does not restrict our view to the studio-like space enclosing the psychoanalytic session. Much of the voice-over accompanies shots out train windows or through the windows of various flats and lofts of Berlin, New York, London. Film as a window on the world? a train of thought? Other tracking shots reveal a mantelpiece in perpetual displacement and rearrangement, cluttered with objects culled from the patient's narrative. Bread, knives, shells, steaming pasta, all appear at one time or another to break the spell of the soundtrack, provide comic relief, or literalize with cutting irony a number of seemingly serious philosophical points. The irreality of the shifting sequence parallels the patient's own leaps of logic.

Other interpolated footage is more systematic. Rainer includes two symbolic sets of aerial footage, one circular and one linear. The first shows Stonehenge, mute mysterious witness to prehistory, interpreted sardonically as standing for "flight, romantic agony, futility of effort, history as impenetrable." The second, man-made, is the Berlin Wall. Not one unified structure at all, but a series of barriers laid end to end across rural and urban landscapes, dividing the natural terrain with political rigor. The circle of stones is an analogue for the psychoanalytic session, that circling and probing of essential mysteries removed from time, space, and social context. The wall dividing East and West, in turn, is an analogue for the march of history as embodied in the terrorist debate and, more graphically, in the rolling titles detailing the history of state repression in Germany. The mantelpiece and the train tracks shuttle us visually back and forth between these symbolic terrains. The counterpoint moves closer and closer to resolution as the film progresses. The human psyche must somehow relate to the social body politic. Psychoanalysis must be made to acknowledge history. Berlin becomes, for Rainer, their meeting ground.

The combination of psychological and political reflections is an explosive one. How easy to go wrong, linking suicide and violence together, to equate political action with neurosis. It is to Rainer's credit that no such wrong step is taken. A corrupted psychoanalytic practice becomes the state's method for making (helping) its individuals adapt, while political violence becomes the individual's attempt to make the state change. Rainer sifts through the two with infinite care.

If the word "suicide" is repeatedly blipped off the soundtrack record of Michelson's speech, perhaps that is another sign that Rainer has moved beyond the Jungian notions of death that inflected her earlier work. One scene does stand out from the rest of the psychoanalysis session, though, offering the key to some of the film's innermost meanings. The scene opens with a bucket of water being thrown across the frame in slow motion, just after the patient has raged that "my cunt is not a castrated cock" in a rejection of fashionable Lacanian film theory. While the phone rings, the therapist rapidly shifts from woman to little boy and back again. Meanwhile, a rowboat has appeared; in it, the patient, wearing Slinky glasses. It's a radical displacement, landing us in an unexpected homage halfway between Tallulah Bankhead in *Lifeboat* and Maya Deren in *Meshes of the Afternoon*. A ship of fools? The boat of life? The strange glasses call to mind the similarly odd headgear of Deren in *Meshes,* which she wears precisely at the moment of traversing the universe with a knife directed ultimately at her own sleeping body: "What I meant when I planned that four-stride sequence was that you have to come a long way—from the very beginning of time—to kill yourself, like the first life emerging from the primeval waters." [20]

What Deren made explicit here takes a different shape. The texts surrounding the boating interlude deal with the dilemma of woman's existence. While a crank telephone caller bemoans the distance between this untried soul and the brave movie women who always fought the good fight, the patient realizes, "it isn't as though I haven't been through pain." She is recalling her surgery, though the obscene phone calls stand for the other, less physically direct kinds of pain inflicted on women far more often. The patient takes out a comb and fixes her hair. When she tries to brush off her clothes, the sound of birds beating their wings in attempted flight fill the soundtrack. She is still, after all, a woman: combing her hair, virtuously maintaining the shape of her vulnerability (which is horrifyingly acted out, at scene's end, by a dummy auto crash).

In a sense, then, *Journeys from Berlin/1971* does not break from the refitted "woman's film" genre of its predecessors. In fact, it rather fits one type: "[Molly] Haskell identifies a category of 'affliction' which particularizes in certain films the genre's general tendency to center on the suffering of its female characters. The 'affliction' films make this tendency manifest in their portrayal of woman as middle-class, female, Job." [21] Woman is indeed at the center of this film, both in the person of the patient and that of the historical anarchists and nihilists. On one level, the film seems to be acknowledging woman's location as a member of an oppressed class. Women needn't look elsewhere for victims to liberate. Woman as the victim has always been a figure in Rainer's cinema—and yet, here there's a change. Is the personal the political? Is the political merely the personal? Is the personal always political? Surely there's a difference between this woman, talking to her analyst, and Ulrike Meinhof, in prison. A difference, surely, between the power struggles of patient/analyst (or woman/man) and class struggle. A sure difference between the politics of art making and the global politics of nations and peoples. Rainer is aiming for a more rigorous demarcation of the political, omitting none of the complexities to simplify her route. Contradictions are not swept under the rug. The motivations of revolutionaries are examined as intently as those of noncombatants. Nothing is automatic, simple, taken for granted.

Journeys from Berlin/1971 was begun when Rainer was living in West Berlin on a D.A.A.D. grant. It was a chaotic time in the Federal Republic. The woman whose apartment Rainer had rented was forced, by the *Berufsverbot* (blacklist), to leave the country to find work. The degree of repression attending everyday life for West Germans rarely finds its way into the subject matter of the celebrated New German Cinema, but as an outsider Rainer apparently found it hard to ignore the spirit of her locus of production. She has credited Sebastian Cobler's *Law, Order, and Politics in West Germany* with providing her a veritable dossier on the history of state repression, and its historical antecedents to the terrorist actions used often as its justification. The dossier of facts and figures found its way into this film as the rolling titles that Rainer has affixed to the start and finish. Crucially, the need to accommodate such new material led to a marked shift in style.

Journeys from Berlin/1971 is the least self-reflective of her four films. Though traces of her penchant for formal exercises, or ambiguity for its own pleasure, do remain (in the form of the characters pacing in front of an ornate church, or the recorder lesson, or the boy with a dog and an invention), they are no longer emphasized. Though she is still concerned with codes of power, no longer is power a question only of visual manipulation or cinematic theory. Though her own power was a source of considerable preoccupation in *Lives of Performers,* by now it is the powerlessness of others that bears scrutiny. When Rainer stands in for the patient in a last, videotaped monologue, she is no longer the go-between, the one who must wear another's words (like the Davis texts) to qualify. Tearfully facing the camera, half tourist and half daughter, she recounts her shock at seeing a film of lost Berlin, the city before the war. Rainer has dared to enter into the zones of ambiguity, breaking with the avant-garde codes that long dictated allegiance to an infinite play of meanings, and show her willingness to fix meanings within the delicate balance of contradictions.

"A new style in art evolves—if it is not artificially stimulated—to meet the problem of treating new content born of social change."[22] Though a style might appear unrestrictive and ever open, its very unity of form and (older) content mitigates against any new material. To continue with Berger's analysis: "The further new content then demands a further new style. But this new style does not necessarily render the former one obsolete . . . its initial opposition may start a process which leads to the liberation of the former style from its latter-day formalism . . . [leading to] more complex expression in a liberated version of the former style."[23] Such a process certainly seems to be operative in Rainer's expansion of her former strategies for *Journeys from Berlin/1971*. She has sacrificed neither grace nor substance in her broadening of permissible styles (for example, the inclusion of fixed roles, like "patient" and "therapist"). She has worked through a number of minimalist concerns, solving the formal problems and, by now, exhausting the aesthetic pleasures. Melodrama has reached its most naked mirror in the authorized confessional of psychoanalysis. Even the battle of the sexes has been displaced from center stage, to be replaced by a woman struggling, perhaps, with the same eternal issues, but now confronting directly the woman in the form of the therapist and the woman in the form of the mother to whom the videotape of Rainer is addressed. The Soho pundits and the dance world bodies are still very much present, but no longer are they the heart of the matter. The exercise of compassion and the acceptance of personal responsibility shape a demand for (not obviation of) condemnation. A last statement, a clear drawing of the lines, is a necessary finale.

Were the film to end on the psychoanalysis session, or within the unsettled debate on the ethics of political violence, it could remain on too individual a plane. Were it to end on the recorder lesson in the comfortable apartment, it could end without struggle. Or it could end on the videotape confession, in which case the soul of the artist would provide the classical finish. But, no. The rolling titles bear the weight of history, transporting its traces past our vision. It is precisely the uncompromising end title, quoting the sinister words of H. Herold, head of the Federal Criminal Investigation Bureau, which confirms the target of Rainer's new trajectory. It is an uncompromisingly political ending, one that places *Journeys from Berlin/1971* into unambivalent, courageous focus.

The political deliberations that characterized Rainer's thinking throughout the making of *Journeys from Berlin/1971* have not ceased with its completion. In private correspondence with me recently, Rainer laid out the thoughts that form the core of the film and must inflect any interpretation of it, as of her work in general. With her permission, then, I let Yvonne Rainer have the last word:

> It is only when the patient stops believing in the absoluteness of her powerlessness in relation to others — men and women — that she can confront her suicide attempt. The feelings of powerlessness have been manifested in her projections and evasions, or "resistance." The signification of the therapist can be extended to include the power of the parent, of authority, of the state, of men. But in each case, one's

personal, actual power is available, to however limited a degree, and must be confronted, or acknowledged, in some fashion. The patient takes responsibility for her own destructiveness — and stops struggling with the shrink. She assumes responsibility for her own life. This is truly the sphere of Psychoanalysis — and the personal. What one does here would not be appropriate or possible in an extermination camp.

It is obviously not the same case — to maintain the values of the oppressive culture when other options are open, as in a relationship with a reliable shrink (or lover, or friend), or to maintain them when no other options are open. I don't mean to underestimate the limits of the psychiatric ideal in our own culture where notions of freedom and self-determination everywhere obfuscate the needs of minorities, middle-aged women, the aged, and problems of illness, labor, and pleasure. The issue of personal autonomy in the extermination camp, or prison, and in the streets of the democracy is more a difference in degree than substance. Thus the patient's situation can be seen as analogous to Meinhof's. The former, in her limited personal sphere, has taken her first faltering steps out of her condition of powerlessness. Meinhof, on the other hand, has died a victim, never having figured out where her real power ended or her imagined powerlessness began. Her real power ended at the hands of the police, the "state apparatus." She could have anticipated that from the beginning and weighed possible gains in the balance. Her imagined powerlessness began in her womanhood, and was greater than she ever knew. Or so I suspect.

The personal and the political are not synonymous. They overlap and intertwine. And one must struggle constantly to assess one's power, or lack of it, in every sphere of one's life. This is all very general. Approaching from a somewhat different angle: I find it necessary to question the relationship of my personal frustrations to my social criticism. When am I justified in explaining the former in terms of the latter? Social criticism may not be disqualified by personal interest, but then neither do social formations always account for my private frustrations.

Prologue.

Knokke-Heist

and the Fury

That Was

Edinburgh

T he Knokke-Heist EXPMNTL Film Festival announced its vanguardism defiantly with its disavowal of vowels. By the seventies, it was legendary in avant-garde film circles. This was, after
all, the festival at which Jack Smith's *Flaming Creatures* was
busted and Jonas Mekas barricaded in the projection booth in one of
the American avant-garde's most famous censorship battles. It was where
the young bloods of the New American Cinema got their start, creating
shocks and making reputations. Now, after years of inactivity, the festival was taking place again. The year 1974 didn't exactly mark a high-water
point for experimental film; in fact, this would turn out to be the last such
festival. But it was the chance for our generation to participate in a grand
tradition, a sort of state-funded *salon de refusés* (underwritten by the
Belgian government and its cinematheque's big-hearted director, Jacques
Ledoux), so off I went with Gunner and a gang of our School of the Art
Institute of Chicago filmmaker friends.

The festival was held on the cold North Sea coast of Belgium in December between Christmas and New Year's Day, a time of year otherwise
favored for professional usefulness only by academic conferences like that
of the Modern Language Association. The festival screenings were held in
a theater that was part of a glittering casino complex. Between films, we'd
mingle with an older generation of gamblers who were as oblivious to the

attractions of our particular compulsions as we were to theirs. Between cups of coffee, we'd pocket the spoons with "Knokke-Heist" engraved on the handles. And we'd escape whenever we could, ducking outside for bouts of Belgian winter air, tours of espalliered trees, and endless meals of mussels and frites at the cheapest places we could find.

I was pleased when the director Nelly Kaplan showed up one afternoon, a forbidden figure from the kingdom of narrative (tsk tsk, so commercial) visiting the cloistered monks of the avant-garde. What was even more delightful was her invitation to Gunner and me to take New Year's dinner with her and her producer companion Claude Makovski, to be shared while we were in Paris for a few hours awaiting our vacation train to Barcelona and Lisbon.

I had met Nelly Kaplan for the first time when she came to Chicago for our women's film festival a few months before with *A Very Curious Girl*, already a classic of the women's festival circuit; she would later go on to make *Nea*, one of the first feminist pro-pornography statements, a wonderfully heretical film, far ahead of its time and too soon forgotten. It deserves revival today. Kaplan was unconcerned with avant-garde purity, and she was fun.

Hers was an invitation to enter history and myth; not just dietary sustenance, but a sort of holy communion with a tradition I much preferred to the North Sea shrine. Kaplan had known the Surrealists. She had studied with the legendary French director Abel Gance when she arrived in Paris from Argentina, a glamorous young *porteña* determined to make films, who got her start with a documentary portrait of Gance himself. To get to her house, one had to enter the magical arcade on the Champs Elysées with neon-edged balconies, ride the elevator to the top floor, ring a doorbell labeled "penthouse" for admittance, and then cross the roof to the even more magical two-story cottage perched in the center (one floor for her, one for Claude, a modern liaison). There were mannequins and piles of *objets,* stories to be told, pistachio rice à la Gide to be consumed, and a ring given her by Gide himself to be admired. Oh, and cognac so smooth and powerful that we floated all the way to our Barcelona holiday.

Back at Knokke-Heist, the actual future of the avant-garde turned out to belong not to the mediocre "structuralist" films that occupied so much of the screen time — not even the festival's hit, *Line Describing a Cone* by Anthony McCall (Carolee Schneemann's former paramour), which fashioned the projection beam into both image and structure — but to the films, never shown there at all, by an unrecognized interloper. On the steps of the casino, ducking out of some interminable structuralist opus, I met an adorable gamine who was lounging there. No, her films hadn't been accepted into the festival, but she'd come up from Brussels anyway to see what was favored. Her name was Chantal Akerman and she was all of twenty-four years old. European friends told me that her work was incredibly interesting (this was around the time of *Je tu il elle*), more significant in its newness than the end-of-the-line work that screened before our eyes, unwittingly advertising structuralism's bankruptcy.

Perhaps it was inevitable, then, that when *Jeanne Dielman* hit the film world in 1975–76 with all the grandeur of a new paradigm being wheeled onstage, it came to Edinburgh not as part of the "International Forum on the Avant-Garde" (though Chantal was listed there) but as an offering by the concurrent "Psychoanalysis and Cinema" program, excluded once again from the formalist perfection of the fraternity.

The reaction? I was dazed, possessed, virtually levitated by the film, and I invited Chantal Akerman to come to Chicago and premiere her film at the Film Center (on November 19, 1976), eager for everyone to see it. I became fascinated by the woman as well as the work. She was still young enough to make an improbable auteur, even though she was already scripting her next film (*Les Rendezvous d'Anna*) and soliciting advice on how to cast the role of the mother. She eventually cast Lea Massari, but at the time she was also considering Sophia Loren for another project. As our houseguest, she occupied the Palatine loft's guestroom, the same parachute that I had used as my tent downtown, and found it acceptable.

So much so, in fact, that she phoned her friend Marilyn to join her. We found this quite dramatic—a pal who would fly all the way from Belgium for a few days—and thought it must be a case of *l'amour fou*. It clearly was, but the impact was slightly lessened by learning that Marilyn's father's job with the airlines let her fly almost free, and that their relationship was at least partially a business one (this was Marilyn Watelet, who went on to produce most of Akerman's films). They constantly whispered to each other in French and giggled uncontrollably. We finally made our friend Sharon come over, instructing her to conceal her fluent knowledge of their language and assigning her to eavesdrop for clues to their secret amusements, but all she ever caught them talking about was *us*. Otherwise, Chantal was the perfect houseguest, even cooking us scrambled eggs one morning in what I imagined to be a European style of slow cooking, so slow in fact that I supposed I'd stumbled upon the secret of *Jeanne Dielman*'s pacing, or that she didn't know how to cook, until I tasted how delicious they were.

Downstairs at the Palatine Building, my neighbors Kate Horsfield and Lynn Blumenthal were starting up the Video Data Bank by recording interviews with artists, particularly women. Why not do Chantal? Hesitantly but dutifully, we trooped off to the Data Bank office one Sunday morning for me to interview Chantal in front of the portapak camera. We talked for twenty-five minutes about *Jeanne Dielman,* her intentions, my perceptions, the film's reception, by which time the tape had run out. Somehow there was no tape stock readily available to continue. Anyway, we were both worn out from the unfamiliar effort, and I was sure the interview was a disaster. Today, in limited release in virtually unedited form, the videotape is a priceless time capsule equally full of self-importance and self-deprecation, all earnest and passionate.

Jeanne Dielman was the crucial film of its period, at a time of crucial texts: the era of Monique Wittig and the late Audre Lorde, Mary Daly and Susan Griffin, Adrienne Rich and the late Dorothy Dinnerstein (whose 1976 classic *The Mermaid and the Minotaur* has gone from being the bible of the late seventies to going out of print). The women's film festivals may have failed to mount a convincing argument on behalf of a new feminist film aesthetic, but now Akerman seemed to have accomplished the task single-handedly. We felt we needed a new vocabulary to talk about the film, and set to work educating ourselves to deserve it. In Chicago, we even had a study group on *Jeanne Dielman* for a while. Our emotional investment in the film can't be overstated. I still have folders filled with notes, pages and pages of ideas that never found their way into print: my favorite was the piece that Anna Marie Taylor and I planned to write together, applying Althusser's notion of the "epic" and the "chronicle" to explain its timing and structure. I saw the film over and over, lectured on *Jeanne Dielman* and Akerman's other films at film conferences and screenings. It was an all-consuming passion for several years, sustaining me with a vision of what kind of film could come about by combining feminist theory, avant-garde practice, and daily life (in this case, that of Akerman's mother, whom she used for her model of a woman trapped in a lifetime of daily domestic routine).

All my work on Akerman came to a head in 1979, when I was invited to speak at Edinburgh's Feminism and Film conference, organized by the same four women (Angela Martin, Laura Mulvey, Lynda Myles, and the late Claire Johnston) who had delivered Edinburgh's women's festival five years before. My friend Laura Mulvey would deliver the opening address, expanding on "Feminism and the Avant-Garde," which she'd published in *Framework* that spring. Then the conference would be structured as two debates between pairs of speakers (Pam Cook and I in one session, Claire Johnston and Christine Gledhill in the other), framed by panels on journals (*m/f, Jump Cut, Camera Obscura, frauen und film*) and British feminist filmmaking (Sally Potter, Jan Worth, Sue Clayton, and others), all of which would transpire in the mornings, followed by small-group discussions.

My invitation had been prompted by the publication of the first version of my "Naming" piece in *Jump Cut*. I was invited to expand my article's conclusions as well as to speak on Sara Gomez's *One Way or Another,* but that plan had to be changed when the print never arrived. Fortunately, all my speaking in that period (still, to a great extent) was impromptu. I was constantly scribbling notes in airplanes on my way to engagements, or waking up at dawn on the day of my presentation, daring myself with the threat of total humiliation to win the prize of spontaneous, responsive speech. It was my magic trick: I could always pull the rabbit out of the hat, as long as I was willing to risk coming up empty-handed.

We agreed that I would do a presentation on Akerman instead, which I could easily manage after months of total immersion in discussions and lectures. *Meetings with Anna* had recently been released — I'd already praised it in the Chicago *Reader* — and *Je tu il elle* had by now been widely seen. Laura Mulvey had published an interview with Akerman in the London weekly *Time Out* that spring. The London-based *Feminist Review,* then in its first year, published my BFI pal Angela Martin's monumental "dossier" on Akerman. At the same time, Akerman's relation to her films and her public was changing with her expanded fame. Questioned by Angie about *Je tu il elle,* Akerman confessed, "I can't stand seeing myself doing those things in the film." And then, too, there was a rumor that Babette Mangolte, her cinematographer for *Jeanne Dielman,* had been removed from *Anna* at the demand of the production company, Gaumont — something about taking too much time to set up her signature shots — and that Chantal hadn't stuck up for her. After expanding my original "Naming" essay (to include what would become its "Warning Signs: A Postscript" section), I decided to do my own assessment of Akerman's trajectory in the years before and after her Chicago visit.

The conference itself intervened in my plans. I realized that Pam Cook, whom I'd never met but whom I'd already attacked for her work with Claire Johnston in my "Naming" article, had been paired with me in the expectation that we would come, if not to blows, at least to public disagreements. Instead, she and I were equally horrified at such a prospect: we met, adored each other, and reworked our talks to insist on our theoretical complementarity, to some people's disappointment. I remember that Pam called for a "heterogeneity" of discourse, a term taken up by the conference, and thus separated herself from the orthodoxy that Johnston had been so bent on enforcing. She faulted the creation of a "metadiscourse" as counterproductive and sought an approach to modernity that didn't enforce a false choice between what was popular and what was avant-garde. Rather, Cook cautioned against ignoring "subjectivity" in any search for a "women's discourse" located in cinema.

If her talk frustrated expectations, however, mine provoked scorn, anger, and actual outbursts, particularly by my chronic public adversaries of that era, the *Camera Obscura* editors, with whom I seemed to be engaged in some public dispute at virtually every event that we attended together, then and for years to come. We had a long history. They were already vexed with me for my timeline in the "Naming" article that revealed that *Camera Obscura* had started life as the result of infighting at *Women & Film* magazine; unable to take it over, they'd left and started their own to oppose its soft, inclusive approach to feminist cinema.

Though they contended that I'd misrepresented the history, I eventually located their original letter to the San Francisco women's paper, *Plexus,* signed by Janet Bergstrom, Sandy Flitterman, Liz Lyon, and Connie Penley, in which they criticized *Women & Film* and announced that they were quitting it to start their own journal "which fits better our conception of a feminist activity." The rivalry hastened the end of *Women & Film,* which had been a much more politically progressive and inclusive publication. *Camera Obscura,* on the other hand, restricted itself in the early days to its own endorsed theoretical positions. In enemy camps, they were dubbed the Obscurettes for their efforts. The filmmaker Jan Oxenberg once amused a whole table by explaining to a woman who'd innocently asked about it: "Oh, *Camera Obscura* is a very important scholarly journal published by a feminist collective of four women in which they translate and publish the theoretical writings of . . . their French boyfriends." (She wasn't wrong, though in later years the journal came into its own as a place for women's film scholarship.)

My talk started by summarizing points about aesthetics and politics, then charted Akerman's movement of lesbianism offscreen between her first and third features. I termed this her move "from hypoglycemia to anorexia nervosa" in homage both to the prominent food scenes in Akerman's work and the prominent psychoanalytic proclivities of so many of her admirers. I ended by expressing concern that her work was becoming less radical and more aestheticized as her budget increased.

I had spent two years by then celebrating Akerman's work everywhere on earth I'd had the chance: I naïvely thought that in this setting a more critical debate would be possible, where misgivings or questions could be raised. But I didn't stop there. Having taken on Akerman's own work, I decided to take on the work of those writing about her. Here's exactly what I said next, quoted verbatim from my archaic handwritten text: "It is fascinating to look at what has gone un-named in the film theory built upon Akerman's work. We find an extreme mystification of the artist, an emphasis on her avant-garde strategies at the expense of others, a reluctance to confront the issues of sexuality in any straightforwardly honest way, and a complete silence regarding how directly Akerman has moved away from her early connection to women's-movement concerns and processes toward a system of representation coded specifically to cinema itself as its major referent."

And that wasn't the end of my talk. It was what I said next that *really* caused the trouble — but to understand why, you need to understand the conference's structures of authority. First, debate had been mandated to follow the formal presentations strictly: any issues or questions not raised by the speaker could not be addressed from the floor in the discussion period that followed. Second, all conference participants had been assigned to one of several groups, according to which format we adjourned after the plenaries for intensive small-group discussion. This structure was a noble attempt to hold on to the ideal of intimate talk within a large public event. But there was a catch: there were a few men in attendance (less than a dozen among 100+ women) and the conference organizers had carefully assigned a man to each of the discussion groups. A number of women made strenuous objections to this arrangement and ultimately set up a women-only discussion group. This quickly became the largest discussion group of all, even though a hastily drawn regulation prohibited our changing between it and our assigned group: we were supposed to choose (though I didn't, preferring to be a scofflaw and move at will between the two, comparing the sanctioned and stigmatized discourses).

In fact, the best discussions I heard at the conference took place within that charmed circle of the women-only discussion group. My favorite was one filmmaker's memorable statement that echoed in my brain for years afterward: "I want to learn to make films that will be infinitely pleasurable for women and profoundly threatening to men." I would think of those words in the ensuing years, especially at those moments when *Born in Flames, Question of Silence,* and *Thelma and Louise* were attacked and defended. I'd smile to myself, thinking of her ambition realized by these other directors.

Full of loyalty to this affinity group and cognizant of the rule that would prohibit its concerns from ever surfacing in the main sessions, I decided to close my talk with a direct address to the conference's organizational dynamic. Here's how its rhetoric went, again quoting from my archival slips of paper:

> I love the Edinburgh festival. I have the greatest respect for many of the women running it. But I must raise the question of how women have been put on the defensive here: we've been forced to sort our-

selves out according to our degree of "separation," when in fact the men are a tiny minority who, by their very presence, have succeeded in fragmenting the women. Not wanting to make a fuss, we've gone along with the estrangement from other women. Whereas in fact we could have kept our group dynamics (modeled, after all, on women's consciousness-raising groups), by simply placing them all together in a "men's" discussion group and going on our way. My experience in the all-women's group was my best here: not a "lesbian" discussion at all, but simply the most political debates I've yet had.

Well, all hell broke loose, over my bad manners if not my substance. "I can't believe she's saying this," gasped one of the *Camera Obscura* editors to her neighbor. I immediately made a lot of enemies, and a lot of new friends as well — for this conference, so fractured and fractious, was actually one of the very last events to permit the mingling of women from all sectors of film activity. Filmmakers, distribution collectives, journalists, scholars, festival committee members, film editors and composers, even would-be filmmakers had come from all over Europe. The festival roster identified women as "technician" or "student" as well as "theorist," as simply "interested in women and film" or, in one case, even "filmmaker, unemployed."

Daniela Trastulli was there scouting films for a women's film festival in Florence, Italy, with a number of women from Milan. A corps of women from Cinemien, the well-funded Dutch distribution collective, had come from Amsterdam. Mandy Merck and Helen MacKintosh came to report for *Time Out,* writing a piece subsequently titled "Rendezvous D'Edinburgh." Also there from the U.K. were Lindsay Cooper, Elizabeth Cowie, Rose English, Sylvia Harvey, Tina Keane, Caroline Sheldon, Carolyn Spry, Jo Spence, the conference organizers and speakers, and too many more to name. Lesley Stern, who'd traveled all the way from Australia, would eventually write the report for *Screen* (and warn me, ahead of time, of her negative view of the "*Jump Cut* position"). From Germany, there were Hildegard Westbeld, who at that time had just started Chaos Film to distribute women's films, Helge Heberle, representing *frauen und film,* and several others. From the United States came Teresa de Lauretis, Bette Gordon, Karyn Kay, Michelle Citron, and dozens more. (Even today, I find new names.) All of us had very different aesthetic, political, and theoretical positions. Also from the U.K. came a younger generation of filmmakers, composers, and others with an economic critique, complaining about the registration fees and the lack of subsidy for those without economic clout or institutional posts.

There were many conflicting dynamics at the festival, some in open contradiction with others, but few were acknowledged or discussed. The *Time Out* report summarized the debates as follows:

> Neither the varying theoretical perspectives nor the films them-
> selves went undisputed. Indeed "heterogeneity" became the watch-
> word of the week, as successive arguments over the place of "theory
> and practice," formal experiment and accessibility, filmmaking, film
> watching and film criticism were enthusiastically (if not vehemently)
> aired. . . . Conspicuous by their absence (again, perhaps not surpris-
> ingly) were cinema verité works and campaign films. The realism
> and didacticism of such approaches, like the straightforward narra-
> tives and identification figures of Hollywood, have gradually been
> eroded in feminist work (regrettably leaving the questions of acces-
> sibility and audience still unanswered).

My own analysis was a bit different at the time, and different yet today. Most prominent back then was the excitement (which actually unified the various crowds) over the two new films premiered there, fresh from their respective labs on both sides of the Atlantic: Michelle Citron's *Daughter Rite* and Sally Potter's *Thriller*. We'd never seen anything like either of them before, and women were wild with excitement over their demonstrated integration of feminist analysis into highly sophisticated cinematic form. Rigorous films like Jan Worth's *Taking a Part* (about prostitution) and Sue Clayton and Jonathan Curling's epic *Song of the Shirt* (about seamstresses) further advanced the sense of a new feminist cinema in formation.

If the films were the points of unification, however, theoretical and critical approaches to cinema constituted the points of division. A crude labeling of the two opposing forces would yield "theoreticism" versus "anti-intellectualism," or perhaps Lacanians versus empiricists, but such labels would tell only part of the tale. Many of the women there subscribed to neither camp: instead, they saw themselves, particularly the Europeans, as part of a global women's movement that offered numerous positions vis-à-vis film, in the practical world of distribution, exhibition, publication, even industrial production, as well as in the symbolic world of theory. (The Italians, for instance, would go on to develop psychoanalytic approaches in a pre-Oedipal direction very different from the Mulvey-Johnston Lacanian model, eventually explored in a conference at New York University in 1984, Italian and American Directions: Women's Film Theory and Practice, and its resulting volume, *Off Screen: Women & Film in Italy*, edited by Giuliana Bruno and Maria Nadotti, an anthology that includes a piece by Giulia "Bundi" Alberti, who was at Edinburgh

'79. I met Bundi years later at a women's film festival in Florence, where I discovered that she'd given up film to become a stained-glass maker.)

Employing or discarding labels, however, cannot obscure the fact that there was indeed a deeply rooted division within the Edinburgh conference. My realization today, looking back at the event, its participants, and my own notes and statements, is that the division was most fundamentally sexual in nature, though never acknowledged as such to my knowledge. A significant percentage of the women at Edinburgh were lesbian, many of us then just forming attachments to women for the first time. We were full of our newfound sexuality, thrilled to be meeting up with others of our kind across all kinds of borders, energized by the films and discussions, and flirting like mad (indeed, a roll call of future relationships could easily be derived from the guest list, my own included). For some of us, then, the conference was an eroticized zone.

Most of the time, though, it was a battle zone in which we occupied a particularly schizophrenic position. Though we were increasingly powerful and plentiful, running key feminist film organizations, making films, and reporting on the scene, the emergent feminist theory that held the high ground was determinedly heterosexual and heterosexist, relegating us to a second-class position of symbolic marginality. Sally Potter's *Thriller* explicitly addressed this split in its climactic scene—which *Time Out* termed "chilling"—of Mimi reading *Tel Quel* for theoretical enlightenment, oblivious to the other woman's being carried offstage by the men. Nevertheless, gay-straight splits within feminist communities were as much a reality in 1979 as before or after, unless you exempt our current postmodern stance of pseudoidentification, bordering on appropriation as everyone rushes to declare herself "queer." Only since the late eighties has work by Sue-Ellen Case, Judith Mayne, Teresa de Lauretis, and younger scholars like Rhona Berenstein, Cynthia Fuchs, Judith Halberstam, Chris Straayer, and Patricia White begun to address directly and explicitly the longstanding homophobia of orthodox feminist film theory.

At the end of the conference, a half dozen of the U.S. participants, including both lesbians and heterosexuals, decided to hold a "women's party" in our shared flat, and invited all the women at the conference. Is it surprising that a convincing chart of "theoretical" differences could be drawn by tallying those who did or didn't attend? Or that "women's" had become a code word for both "separatist" and "lesbian," incurring contamination by association? Or that those who did come to that party abandoned debate and stayed late to dance, get drunk, act out? I went to bed alone. I woke up the next morning with an auburn-haired Scottish lassie in bed with me: she swore she'd just got up drunk in the night and stumbled back into the wrong bedroom, unaware, but the story quickly made the rounds, as fitting an emblem as any other of one Edinburgh Spirit of '79.

The contradictions of Edinburgh, however, cannot be contained even in this recuperative retelling of its themes, events, dynamics. It was a landmark event that ultimately was about process rather than product. No consensus was ever reached. *Daughter Rite* and *Thriller* entered a new canon as feminist films that could both inspire emotion and support theory making. Numerous other films were forgotten. The conference ended and we scattered around the world again, friendships and relationships and antagonisms set in motion for the decade to come.

I went down to London to meet Laura Mulvey and then off to spend a few days in the country with her, her young son Chad, and her mother. Drinking her mother's dandelion wine, we enjoyed a laugh over how astonished the conference participants would have been to witness us abandon our theoretical antagonisms, lay down the swords, and return to the refuge of our affectionate friendship.

For Claire Johnston, the immediate aftermath gave little hint of the nightmare to come. She was a central figure throughout the seventies, actively publishing, collecting essays, organizing events. Her alliance with her partner Paul Willeman, on the one hand, and with her collaborators Pam Cook and Laura Mulvey, on the other, had made her indispensable to the creation and evolution of feminist film theory. But she was also a destructive force, a theory terrorist who enforced *Screen* discipline (where she served on the board) in the field at large by strategies of attack, taking no prisoners, steadfastly uninterested in any theoretical or political coexistence. Pluralism was a dirty word. There was only one true way: hers.

At the conference, we'd all been astonished and taken off guard by her suddenly denouncing "theoreticism" (without ever admitting her own role in creating that very beast). Typically, she maximized her effect: she was the only one to pass out copies of her speech. Combined with the nature of the text (which urged a move away from textual analysis to a more active engagement with cinema's social relations), her speech acquired the status of a Politburo announcement, complete with theoretical spin-masters intent on deciphering the new line.

Several years earlier, a strange event had befallen Johnston. She was driving alone back to London from an Edinburgh conference (on psychoanalysis, if memory serves) when she had a terrible automobile accident: her car spun out of control, flipped over and went off the road, leaving her trapped for hours, pinned behind the wheel with the full weight of her volumes of Lacan piled, literally and symbolically, onto her head. Fortunately, she was rescued in time.

Worse fates, however, awaited her around the next curve. Johnston came from a family with a history of mental illness, and as she aged, she turned clinically paranoid with a combative edge. The intense theoretical aggression against enemies that had been her intellectual style escalated into physical aggression against former allies in London. She turned violent and members of her inner circle actually had to take precautions for their own safety. In the end, though, it was herself that she chose to destroy. In 1987, Claire Johnston committed suicide. And an era died with her. I can't help but believe, despite the genetic marker in her family, that her demise had something to do as well with the agony of living under the Thatcher regime and watching feminist filmmaking run out of steam along with the erosion of her theoretical base. Though she reengaged with Irish cinema, she was no longer central to debates that increasingly recentered on theorists and filmmakers of color, whose energies took center stage in the U.K. in the eighties.

I never did publish any report on the Edinburgh conference of 1979, though I presented my version at a Society for Cinema Studies panel organized by my friend Ruth Perlmutter. My own work on Chantal Akerman continued fitfully into the early eighties even though her films remained unavailable in the United States outside of the occasional museum or festival screening. When the Film Forum finally gave *Jeanne Dielman* a theatrical run in 1983, eight years after its Belgian release, the *Village Voice* dedicated its cover to Akerman. Chantal's face beamed out, framed between Jim Hoberman's rave review of *Jeanne Dielman* and my essay that follows. Thanks to the *Voice* hype and the record box office that followed, a young entrepreneur named Lloyd Cohen was able to convince investors to back him as Akerman's U.S. distributor, finally ensuring access to her work.

Akerman and I crossed paths again in 1997 for a public discussion at the Film Arts Foundation in San Francisco. She was in an unusually buoyant mood and regaled the audience with tales I'd never heard before concerning how she got her start in film: she'd arrived in New York after a few months in Israel with no money and got a job working as the ticket seller for a gay porn theater, only to discover that guilt-ridden closeted customers would just toss money at her without waiting for the change as they dashed in for a lunchtime fix. She cut a deal with the ticket taker and for a few weeks managed to amass a substantial sum. Then the manager caught on to what they were doing, fired her, and installed his girlfriend in the lucrative job instead.

With the proceeds, Akerman was able to shoot *Hotel Monterey,* the film that first made her reputation as a film prodigy. She had a similar story concerning her return to Paris, when she came upon a box of 35mm black-and-white film in an editing suite that a friend was using. The purloined footage became her first feature film, *Je tu il elle.* Petty larceny had launched a great career. The young hopefuls in the audience that evening looked suitably inspired.

10.

Designing

Desire:

Chantal

Akerman

(1983)

C hantal Akerman is a cause célèbre, an enfant terrible, a filmmaker's filmmaker. Her films routinely play commercial runs
in Paris, get distributed in England, get broadcast on television in West Germany. The thirty-two-year-old Belgian has
made five feature films and an equal number of shorts that have played
at film festivals and been toasted in retrospectives internationally. And
in the United States? Not a single Akerman film in distribution. And in
New York City? Until this week, none of her films has shown in any form
but a one-night stand. Why did Julie Christie tell me, in an interview this
autumn, that whenever she plays the what-films-would-you-take-on-a-
desert-island game with friends, *Jeanne Dielman* is on her list? And why
did Peter Handke confess, when his *Left-Handed Woman* premiered at
Cannes, that his major influence had been Akerman? Chantal Akerman is
one of the most important European directors of our (post-sixties) generation. Not only are her films handily brilliant, but they're profoundly
feminist as well, in form as well as subject matter. It's about time New
Yorkers got to find out, firsthand, just what all the fuss is about.

Akerman's work can be suggested through its themes. The exercise and
repression of sexuality. Systems of desire. The nature of voyeurism. Ex-
plosions of repression. Hunger and appetite. Woman's isolation. Woman's
exclusion from language. Housework. The maintenance of order. Mother-

daughter bonds. Mother-son ties. The relation of woman to woman, and of woman to man. Travel.

Outlining themes, however, even in such an epigrammatic fashion, is misleading. Akerman's films aren't really "about" any subject so much as they're about cinema itself. In her greatest work, the meditation on cinema is matched to a thematic investigation worthy of its endeavors; in even her slightest films, the purely cinematic flourishes command attention. The camera, in her early films, never moved. Now, when it does, it is always with a compositional rather than a narrative purpose. The frame is always perfectly composed, often in a classical symmetry. The zoom — hallmark of an exploitative film practice that closes in on pathos and strip-mines private space — is resolutely absent.

Akerman's version of cinema returns to a sort of "filming degree zero" in which shots are held so long that meaning dissolves into play, interest into detachment, detachment back again into involvement. Akerman scorns the realistic speeded-up tempo of movieland, opting instead for the artificiality of real-time pacing. Making meat loaf, making love, making conversation, all occupy their necessary screen time. The style is minimalist, stripped of all distractions, concentrating on the most basic and mysterious component of cinema as a medium: the passage of time. Akerman designs films that interrogate the march of time in the form of narrative, playing with audience desire, thwarting even the most humble expectations, and providing an entirely unprecedented sort of pleasure.

When *Jeanne Dielman* became Akerman's breakthrough film in 1975, it seemed to speak directly to all of us engaged in feminist theory and film criticism. It was a time dominated by Adrienne Rich's influential *Of Woman Born* and a concentration on the nature and tensions of domestic life. In many films, this took the form of documentary scenes, on-camera interviews, history through film clips, or struggle through filmed demos. Akerman started from a different point altogether: the point of gesture. She studied her memories of her own mother and aunt, fashioning a 200-minute film that described three days in the life of a woman, a mother, a once-a-day prostitute. In black-and-white stills, the film looks severe. In its true color, however, the film is downright lush. Delphine Seyrig, as Jeanne Dielman, ensures the pleasure of the three-and-a-half-hour gaze.

Never before has the materiality of woman's time in the home been rendered so viscerally. Never before has the tempo of endless time, repetitively restoring itself, been demarcated so precisely. Prufrock may have had the luxury of measuring out his life in coffee spoons; Jeanne Dielman has the task of measuring hers by washing them. To the extent that we internalize these rituals, learn to count to her rhythm of gestures, come to feel instinctively the precise calibrations of her daily routines — to that extent, we as viewers inherit a sense of drama that lies closer to the bone than any witnessed before in cinema. It is this transformation of the literal into the symbolic and, ultimately, the political, that defines Akerman (no matter what she says, year to year) as a feminist filmmaker. She does what feminist cultural theory has called for: she invents a new language capable of transmitting truths previously unspeakable.

In her modernism of the emotions, Akerman calls to mind a sinister fairy tale. In that story, a couple are magically granted three wishes but fail to secure what they want owing to the form of extreme, unpredictable literalization that the wish granting takes. Akerman deals with the wishes/expectations of the Hollywood-trained spectator in much the same manner. You want a story about murder and prostitution? Okay, you got *Jeanne Dielman*. Precisely because the expectation is sensationalist, there is no sensationalism in the film. Because the desire is voyeuristic, there is no voyeurism. Because the wish is for sex, the sex acts aren't shown (until, briefly, at the end). In place of the connotative trappings of a *Belle de Jour*, Akerman literalizes the situation to give us a view of a woman making coffee, turning lights on and off, shopping, cleaning herself and her house, and gradually, barely perceptibly, imploding under the pressure of a repressed sexuality and a suppressed existence.

Akerman has turned audience expectation inside-out in this fashion throughout her films. *Je tu il elle,* arguably her most radical film, offers the filmmaker herself in a three-part sexual journey. Akerman is astute at psyching out her audience; she detects our assumptions as coolly as a prosecutor detects lies on the witness stand.

If *Jeanne Dielman* plays on a less-than-touching faith in the genre safety of melodrama, it falls to *Je tu il elle* to address the cynically voyeuristic attraction of pornography. A summary would fit the fairy tale well, seemingly satisfying the most explicit desire. Akerman plays around at home, naked, all through the first section, which ends in her writing a letter to an unidentified beloved; she hitchhikes somewhere in the second part, jerking off a friendly truck driver along the road; and, in the third section, she arrives at her goal — her woman lover's apartment — where the two make love for a very long time onscreen. So far so good? Like the fairy tale, though, the film deliberately frustrates complacent desire while satisfying quite other hungers. Akerman may be naked, but the ascetic framing and her utterly noneroticized behavior thwart any sexual pleasure. She may give her trucker a hand job, but the action is offscreen; all we see are talking heads (so to speak) while the sex act takes place literally below the belt, in this case, below the frame line. Finally, the graphic scene of lovemaking occurs with such violence and hungry abandon and lasts for so very long that its excess tends to embarrass or exhaust the voyeuristic gaze.

One of the clearest examples of Akerman's cat-and-mouse game is *Les Rendezvous d'Anna*, a big-budget film produced by the prestigious Gaumont in 1978. Akerman must have seemed commercially compliant by virtue of her casting. Aurore Clement played the central role, with a full-house combination of Lea Massari, Jean-Pierre Cassel, Helmut Griem, and Magali Noel. It is easy to imagine the eager French filmgoer attracted to the roster of matinee idols, expectant in the glow of movie romance. Instead, the arch-professional actors deliver their lines in the style of amateurs, every sex scene ends in coitus interruptus, the hottest moment occurs when Anna gets into bed with her mother to confess love for another woman, and the climax of the film is the closing shot of Anna's face as she listens to this never-glimpsed woman's voice on her answering machine. (Yes, light years before *O Superman!*)

Akerman's newest film, *Toute Une Nuit* exemplifies her fairy tale wish granting on a grand scale. As in the other films, extremes of hunger and appetite, need and excess, too-much and not-enough retrain our senses. Avant-garde filmmaker Anne Severson once made a film of animals running, culled from archive footage, to satisfy her own childhood hunger to see more jungle every time the Hollywood camera returned to Ava Gardner, or some such colonial-abroad star, wiping sweat from her brow. I can imagine Akerman indulging the same hunger for the archetypical movie embrace, that mad dash into (or out of) each other's arms in the cathartic moment of numberless Hollywood or French movies of the thirties. Enter the fairy tale. Akerman stacks her film with these embraces — and virtually nothing else — so that they are totally stripped of psychological definition and narrative meaning. The embraces become, like many of the actions in her films, very nearly existential. They have no meaning beyond their visual literalization. And yet, having given up the expectation of emotional drama, the viewer is rewarded with a semblance of a postmodernist musical in which the tableaux, rhythm of shots, exchanges of looks, even falling of glasses, become a choreographed and scored performance played to the hilt. The film turns itself inside out, embodying a critique of romance and the musical genre all at once.

Akerman adds an extra layer to her metacinema by seeding her films with jokes and references to earlier work. In *Toute Une Nuit*, Akerman's own mother smokes a cigarette as her daughter cries "Mama" on the soundtrack, in a simultaneous invocation of *News from Home* (her earlier film about New York City letters written home to Mom) and *Les Rendezvous d'Anna*'s pillow-talk sequence. In *Les Rendezvous d'Anna*, Anna cannot seem to eat, complaining that she is not hungry or eating too much or too little in a confusion of appetite that parallels her blocked sexuality; the result is a grand form of anorexia nervosa that reverses the early scenes in *Je tu il elle* of an almost hypoglycemic consumption of sugar and Nutella culminating in a sexual frenzy. The films build on each other in the finest auteurist tradition. But *Jeanne Dielman* has the cool self-sufficiency of a certified masterpiece, making it the perfect introduction.

Reached in Brussels this week, Chantal Akerman was buoyant over her New York opening and over the auspicious start of 1983. Why? After the commercial failure of Gaumont's *Rendezvous d'Anna,* Akerman couldn't raise the funds to film I. B. Singer's *The Manor & the Estate.* Her brash move to Los Angeles to raise $25 million for the ambitious project was a catastrophe. Back in Belgium, she didn't make another film until last year's *Toute Une Nuit,* done on less than $60,000 with a cast of virtually every friend she had in Brussels. The four-year silence had ended.

Today, Chantal Akerman is on the verge of a renaissance. She is planning three films for 1983: a television production starring the director, a musical about "love, sex, and commerce," and a third film about which she would divulge nothing. It seems as though Akerman don't need Gaumont no more ("Tell them," she shouted cheerfully by transatlantic telephone, "Gaumont has lots of money but no balls!"). But she still needs a U.S. distributor.

Imagine repertory houses without Fassbinder. Imagine that we never saw Godard. Imagine that the Taviani brothers just couldn't get a theater. Imagine that New Yorker Films hadn't stashed *Les Rendezvous d'Anna* in a closet for four years.

Imagine a distributor for Chantal Akerman. And write them a letter.

Prologue.

Euphoria

Reclaims

History

I t was March 1979. I had just moved into an apartment with my first
full-time woman lover and was full of the joys of coming out and
true (for the moment at least) love. Camped out there amidst piles
of boxes, I pulled out a typewriter, balanced it on some books, and
wrote the first version of what would become my article on *Maedchen in
Uniform*. I was scheduled to deliver it as part of a panel on early German
cinema at the Fourth Annual Purdue Film Conference in a few days. Imagine, then, an author remarkably in tune with her subject. Breathlessly in
tune: the original notes that constituted the conference presentation were
really telegraphed bulletins to a barely imagined audience from a consciousness energetically in the midst of self-formation.

The change had been a long time coming. My sexuality had been in flux
since the early seventies and the ménage-à-trois with Margie Keller and
Gunner had made the universe fair game for sexual fantasy and adventure.
The seventies had a sort of sixties hangover that lasted most of the decade: we were all cool, relationships were "open," we could handle it. Ha.
My explorations of the fair sex took me into uncharted territory, where
my judgment was wildly erratic, passing from friends and colleagues to
other people's students and other colleagues' wives. I remember the comment by my downstairs neighbor Kate Horsfield, who functioned in those
days as my dyke-courtship mentor via an endless series of consultation

sessions in the second-floor kitchen of the Palatine Building: "My god, you're going to bed with women I wouldn't go to lunch with!" Years later, another friend would say: So what, I myself go to bed with women I wouldn't go to lunch with! Life was wildly exciting. It's a wonder I got any work done at all.

I might have defined myself as "bisexual" back then if it hadn't been such a despised category. I really thought I had the best of both worlds: monogamy for the heterosexual side of my sex life, and a world full of interesting women alongside it. Eventually, however, all my thoughts turned to women. Gunner noticed before I did and forced me to confront my changed identity. We agreed to part when circumstance helped us along: as we liked to tell it, we broke up because "we both fell in love with other women."

In truth, it was also because I'd quit my job at the Film Center and found myself with time on my hands ("idle hands do the devil's work" is no idle saying). Nereida crossed my path just as I returned from Cuba born-again, full of Cuban film, culture, and politics, ready to be imprinted. I carried back photographs and reports of her grandmother and aunt in Havana. We talked and talked and went out dancing, then went to bed. Before long, I was moving out of the Palatine Building and my heterosexual life was over for good.

By spring 1979, I found myself taking up residence in a Logan Square apartment hastily sublet from a friend and became busy doing the work of revising what today might be called my subject position. Hardly a unique or unprecedented situation, but each of us always feels so at the time. I was writing like crazy and throwing myself simultaneously into lesbian culture and Cuban exile culture.

Apart from Latin American film, the New German Cinema was the riveting center of attention in seventies film circles, propelled by the new generation of German auteurs as well as by the pioneering academic work of journals like the *New German Critique*. Film exhibition was fostered at a national level by the network of Goethe Institutes, spearheaded by the heroine of that era, Ingrid Scheib-Rothbart at New York's Goethe House, who did much to create the U.S. phenomenon of New German Cinema popularity. I myself was so involved in its exhibition and popularization through my Film Center work that when the late Herr Schultz came to Chicago to establish a Goethe Institute, he invited me to come on board as his cultural officer; it was left to me to explain to him gently that my utter lack of German made me an inappropriate choice.

I had brought Werner Herzog to the Film Center and listened to his egomaniacal ravings. With considerably more interest, I had followed each new Rainer Werner Fassbinder release, thrilled with his fusing of melodrama, camp sensibility, gay subjects, and political engagement. Though Fassbinder had displaced Godard as the wellspring of cultural truths, any serious consideration of the relationship between his sexuality and aesthetics was still a long way off. (When Lynda Myles served as a juror for the Chicago International Film Festival, known worldwide for its posters of wet T-shirt pinup boys, she anticipated a debate over his cinematic style at the jury meeting following the premiere of *Fox and His Friends*. The only woman on the jury, she was amazed when her fellow jurors muttered, "Well, we all know where *he's* at," and then adjourned, most of them heading for the gay baths.) Gender politics and sexual politics were still extremely bifurcated. But the late seventies were also the beginning of a public unified gay/lesbian presence in film: *The Word Is Out* had played theatrically, Jan Oxenberg had made her first films, Barbara Hammer was well on her prolific way, and lesbian feminism was making inroads everywhere.

For me, then, the occasion of a conference panel on early German cinema was an opportunity to try to fuse my old interests with my new, put cinema into play with emerging lesbian feminist history, and put the film scholar in me into closer communication with the lesbian I'd become. As anyone knows who has ever done this kind of work, such times of synchronicity between one's own sexual/political identity and one's professional work, between an individual life and a collective cultural moment, are times of extraordinary power. The ecstasy of such moments fuels both creative work and political action; when the two combine, how much the better.

I wondered how the fairly conservative audience of German film scholars and professors would receive my presentation and was pleased at how interested they proved to be. I credited my theory—that the speaker's confidence and comfort allows an audience to respond in kind—for the absence of any homophobic hostility, though I've since had this little hypothesis sorely tested. My talk grew and grew into piles of notes as I continued to research the period and rethink the film. Through contacts that originated at Edinburgh, I began to correspond with Karola Gramann in Frankfurt: she and Heide Schlüpmann were researching the film and had tracked down Hertha Thiele, the actress who played Manuela. Nothing like major discoveries of living legends to get the blood going. Thanks to them, I eventually got my own photograph of Thiele herself, inscribed to me on the back. They would eventually publish a special lesbian issue of *frauen und film*, which included a "utopian erotic moment" section: their interview with Thiele and articles on *Maedchen* and *Anna und Elizabeth*.

In November 1981, they staged a retrospective of Hertha Thiele's films in Frankfurt. Though we'd never met, it was a time of shared research, contacts, and excitement.

I would finally publish my article in *Jump Cut* as part of the Lesbian Special Section and then put an abridged version into *Radical America,* another of the progressive alternative journals with which *Jump Cut* and my friends and I were aligned. It was a great time for writers, because you could be sure you were being read as the alternative press world nurtured and cross-fertilized both its readers and contributors. The article didn't take its final shape, though, until I received a request from Linda Williams to revise it for a collection she was preparing with Mary Ann Doane and Pat Mellencamp for the American Film Institute's publications series.

There was already antagonism between both Mellencamp and Doane who were associated with the Center for Twentieth-Century Studies at the University of Milwaukee and myself, as a *Jump Cut* associate editor. In the seventies, the Milwaukee conferences, as they were called, were high-status events that conferred prestige on their participants and virtually determined theoretical agendas within the academy. I had spoken at one and stayed away from others, but it was one particular conference that *Jump Cut* took it upon itself to boycott that established a set of hostilities for many years to come.

The Center for Twentieth-Century Studies had announced an invitation-only conference (until then, the roster of speakers was carefully controlled to ensure theoretical coherence, but attendance was always open). The psychoanalytic subject of the conference would have been a red flag for *Jump Cut* in any event, but now the change in structure provided the evidence that *Jump Cut* had been waiting for. Here was plain proof that these theorists were turning their backs on fundamental American democracy, meeting behind closed doors, secretly anointing their hierarchical leaders, and shunning lesser mortals who might disagree with their master plan. A response was required! (As Yiddish grandmothers used to tell their grandchildren, "Who appointed you?" But we were beyond such modesties in our effort to fight the good fight against any hint of elitism.) *Jump Cut* prepared its trademark scorched-earth approach to political differences. We particularly targeted Stephen Heath, by then a prominent British theorist, and Teresa de Lauretis, who was teaching at Milwaukee; they were the conference organizers, with Teresa necessarily doing most of the actual work from her faculty base in Milwaukee.

How did *Jump Cut* respond exactly? We circulated a critique of the conference, announced our refusal to participate, and encouraged a boycott, with partial success and significant national support. We then published a detailed history of the event and critique of the process entitled "The Scalpel beneath the Suture: Report on a Conference Not Attended," written by Chuck Kleinhans, Julia Lesage, and me. We supplemented our criticisms with comments from other academics who'd shunned the event, then filled in the details of what had actually transpired with help from sympathetic moles who'd attended. The whole jousting match became a scandal that kept people talking and established enmities and alliances for some time.

I knew that the new collection into which Linda was inviting me actually was intended to gather together essays presented at the Cinema Histories, Cinema Practices I conference, held at the Asilomar, California, conference center in May 1981 and organized by Pat Mellencamp. It all sounded like more of the old Milwaukee deal to me, with the same small coterie of invited speakers. Linda Williams, however, was an important liaison between warring factions. Based in Chicago, able to combine politics with academics, she managed to have good relations with both the Milwaukee and *Jump Cut* crowds. And she somehow convinced Doane and Mellencamp to augment the collection with essays not only by me but by Christine Gledhill and Judith Mayne, neither of whom had been invited to Asilomar. Thus did the *Re-Visions* anthology, so widely used in curricula, end up taking shape as a much more inclusive collection than its originating event would have suggested.

11.

From Repressive

Tolerance to

Erotic Libera-

tion: *Maedchen*

in Uniform

(1979–1983)

What in God's name does one call this sensibility if it be not love? This extraordinary heightening of all one's impressions; this intensification of sensitiveness; this complete identification of feeling? . . . I was Manuela, as she is Manuela, and everything that has happened to her has in essence, and other circumstances, happened to me. This incredible feeling of sisterhood. — Dorothy Thompson, upon meeting Christa Winsloe [1]

There are moments when one historical period seems to beckon to another, offering the semblance of lessons to be learned or errors to be avoided. Certainly, that is true today for those of us reviewing the fate of progressive political organizations in the Weimar period preceding Adolf Hitler's coming to power in the inflation-torn and authority-hungry Germany of 1933. In particular, the history of women's rights groups and homosexual-emancipation organizations is one that needs to be better known and analyzed. It is a testimony to our ignorance of the period that Leontine Sagan's film *Maedchen in Uniform* (1931) is generally assumed to be an anomaly, a film without a context, or else a metaphor, a coded tale about something else, something other than what appears on screen. If we are to understand *Maedchen in Uniform* fully, then it is important to keep in view the society within which it was made: the celebrated milieu of Berlin *avant la guerre*, the Berlin with dozens of gay and lesbian bars and journals, the Berlin of a social tolerance so widespread that it nearly camouflaged the underlying legal restraints (which were to grow, rapidly, into massive repression). I would stop short of claiming an outlandish Rosetta stone status for the film, no matter how tempting, lest the reader lose faith. Yet, it might be emphasized, *Maedchen in Uniform* is an exemplary work, not only for what it presents to us on the screen but also for the timely issues that its analysis must confront. It is the film revival most central to establishing a history of lesbian cinema.

Maedchen in Uniform was filmed by Leontine Sagan in Germany in 1931, based on the play *Yesterday and Today* by Christa Winsloe (the Baroness von Hatvany) and republished as a novel, *The Child Manuela*, also by Winsloe. The film, like the play, enjoyed a tremendous initial popularity, both in Germany and internationally; yet it has been nearly invisible in the past few decades in the academic study of German cinema. The film has frequently fallen into a seeming limbo between the silent German Expressionist cinema and the notorious products of the Third Reich studios. Despite its remarkable sound quality (praised by Lotte Eisner as the work in which "the prewar German sound film reached its highest level")[2] and in spite of its evocative cinematography (which Kracauer cited as transmitting "the symbolic power of light"),[3] *Maedchen in Uniform* faded from the textbooks, the revival houses, and even eventually from distribution entirely. During the early seventies, however, Sagan's classic was resoundingly redeemed by the cycle of women's film festivals, gathering a solid following and the critical attention it had long lacked. The result, today, is that the film is back in distribution in a beautifully reconstructed print (in contrast to the butchered, mistitled print that made the rounds of the early festivals) and is accorded a secure spot in the history of pre-Reich cinema.

In part, the film's reputation rests upon unusual stylistic components. Sagan's montage-inflected structure manages to break away from the usually stagy and claustrophobic mise-en-scène of early sound films. Her montages, no doubt Soviet-influenced, establish a persuasive counterpoint to the more theatrical scenes and mold them into a cinematic rhythm. Dramatically, her use of a large cast of nonprofessional actresses lends the film a fresh and documentarylike tone, while the performances of the lead actresses won widespread praise.

Sagan was a pioneer in her use of sound, not only as a functional synchronous accompaniment, but also as a thematic element in its own right. However, most important to the film's reputation through the years has been its significance as an antiauthoritarian and prophetically antifascist film. And, to be sure, the film has suitable credentials for such a claim. Any film so opposed to militarism, so anti-Prussian, so much in support of the emotional freedom of women, must be an antifascist film. Furthermore, it was made through the Deutsche Film Gemeinschaft, a cooperative production company specifically organized for this project — and was the first German commercial film to be made collectively. Add to such factors the fact that the film was made on the very eve of Hitler's rise to power, just prior to the annexation of the film industry into Goebbel's cultural program, and the legend of Sagan's proto-subversive movie is secure. In emphasizing the film's progressive stance in relation to the Nazi assumption of power, however, film historians have tended to overlook, minimize, or trivialize the film's central concern with love between women.

Today, we must take issue with the largely unexamined critical assumption that the relations between women in the film are essentially a metaphor for the real power relations of which it treats, that is, the struggle against fascism. I would suggest that *Maedchen in Uniform* is not only antifascist, but also antipatriarchal in its politics. Such a reading need not depend on metaphor, but can be more forcefully demonstrated by a close attention to the film text. As I propose to read it, *Maedchen in Uniform* is a film about sexual repression in the name of social harmony; absent patriarchy and its forms of presence; bonds between women that represent attraction instead of repulsion; and the release of powers that can accompany the identification of a lesbian sexuality. The film is a dual coming-out story: that of Manuela, the adolescent who voices "the love that dares not speak its name" and who, in distinguishing between fantasy and desire, dares to act upon the latter; and that of Fräulein von Bernburg, the teacher who repudiates her own role as an agent of suppression and wins her own freedom by accepting her attraction to another woman. In this reading, the film remains a profoundly antifascist drama, but now its political significance becomes a direct consequence of the film's properly central subject, lesbianism, rather than a covert message wrapped in an attractive but irrelevant metaphor. If *Maedchen in Uniform* is the first truly radical lesbian film, it is also a fairly typical product of late Weimar society, a society in which "homosexuality . . . became a form of fashionable behavior" linked to "the Weimar idea of making a complete break with the staid and bankrupt past of one's parents' generation."[4] As such, it offers a particularly clear example of the interplay between personal and collective politics — and the revolutionary potential inherent in the conjunction of the two.

The film centers on the relationship between two women. Manuela (Hertha Thiele) is a young student newly arrived at a Potsdam boarding school that caters to the daughters of German officers who, in the mid-twenties, are largely impoverished, as is the school itself. With her mother dead, her father unable to look after her, and her aunt guardian icily uncaring, Manuela is left craving affection. Fräulein von Bernburg (Dorothea Wieck) is the school's most adored teacher, champion of a maternalistic humanitarianism opposed to the school's Prussian codes. Harsh, ascetic, militaristic, the boarding school environment is enforced by a totalitarian principal (Emilia Unda) dedicated to toughening up her charges.

Manuela quickly develops a passionate attachment to Fräulein von Bernburg, who simultaneously nourishes and discourages her admirer. Manuela's infatuation is even more intense than the crushes that her fellow students have on the esteemed Bernburg. Furthermore, she carries matters to an unprecedented level by announcing her passion publicly, to all the school. The declaration occurs when Manuela, drunk and in male attire, celebrates her thespian success in the school play by offering the news of her affections as a convivial toast. For such a transgression, Manuela is confined to solitary in the infirmary by the school principal, who forbids students and faculty alike from so much as speaking to her.

The mounting crisis impels Fräulein von Bernburg to confront the principal and challenge her authority, a climax that coincides with the desperate Manuela's own decision to solve the problem by committing suicide. Distraught at having to give up her beloved teacher, Manuela climbs the school's forbidding staircase (a central leitmotif in the film) and is about to throw herself from its uppermost railing when her schoolgirl companions, disobeying the injunction, come to her rescue. Their arrival is paralleled by the rush of Fräulein von Bernburg to the scene, confirming her affection for Manuela and her identification with the students' action. The averting of imminent tragedy is a triumph for the forces of love and community, signaling the coming of a new order. The event seals the fate of the evil principal, who retreats down the hall into the shadows even as Fräulein von Bernburg remains in the light, united through crosscutting with Manuela and the students grouped above her on the staircase.

As should be clear from the summary, the action of *Maedchen in Uniform* transpires entirely within an all-woman environment and, indeed, a thoroughly "feminine" atmosphere. However, the very first establishing shots of the film serve to inform us of the real power of absent patriarchy and remind us that an all-woman school in no way represents a woman-defined space. The montage of visual icons in the first few frames establishes an exterior world of military preparedness, steeples and archways, bugle calls and the marching rhythm of soldiery. And this world of regimentation extends to the neat rows of students who, two by two, file past the gateway into the domain of the school. The link between the exterior authority and the interior order is explicitly visualized only once, but it informs our reading of the entire film (particularly as represented by the emblematic use of offscreen sounds and onscreen symbols, like the staircase).

On her first day of school, Manuela listens to the principal's speech outlining her required duty and identity: "You are all soldiers' daughters and, God willing, you will all be soldiers' mothers." The girls are there to be taught the Prussian values in order that they might transmit the "correct line" to their progeny. They are destined to be the transmitters of a culture, not its inheritors. The learning is not for them as women in their own right, but for their function as reproducers of bodies and ideologies. The extent to which the absent patriarchy (which at no point in the film takes the shape of actual men on screen) dominates the women's world is a theme constantly reiterated by Sagan in her many visualizations of classically Romantic leitmotifs. Barred shadows cross the women's paths, a sternly overbearing staircase encloses their every movement, a frantic montage marshals their steps into a militaristic gait, and even the school songs reinforce the authority of a demanding fatherland with a handful of schoolgirls in its grasp. The film's very title underlines this theme, with its play on the word "uniform," meaning (as a noun) the clothing of a regimented educational/military/professional institution, and (as an adjective) the regulated, all-alike behavior of uniformity dictated by the rules of the patriarchal order.

The ultimate incarnation of the absent but controlling patriarchy is the school principal. Her identity as the "phallic woman" is suggested by her reliance on an ever present cane with which she measures her steps and signals her authority, and by the phallocentric codes of *Kinder, Kirche, Küche,* which she is dedicated to instilling. Her mandates and bearing call to mind a vision of Frederick the Great, to whom she has been compared. Perhaps coincidentally, her jowly face and disassociated affect are equally reminiscent of that other prophetic cinematic persona of demented authority, Dr. Caligari. Like the mad doctor, this principal is accompanied by an obedient assistant, a dark hunchbacked figure who carries out her orders. Unlike Caligari's missions of murder, the principal's agenda is more properly "feminine" in its details of manipulation and reconnaissance. The henchwoman is a warped figure; like the principal shuffling with her cane, the assistant presents an image of womanhood carrying out patriarchal dirty work and physically warped by her complicity. Her hands huddled close to her chest, her eyes pinched and shoulders stooped, the assistant becomes a physical marker of emotional damage. In *The Cabinet of Dr. Caligari,* madness and hypnotism were held responsible for complicity in murder; Sagan is willing to pinpoint a more precise cause in the dogma of an authoritarian ideology. Just as nuns have long provided an easy example of a woman's order subject to entirely male authority (in the form of priest, pope, or God the Father, Son, the heavenly bridegroom), so, too, the institution of the woman's boarding school is shaped to the mold of the militaristic patriarchal society, poured like molten liquid into its empty spaces to keep it whole.

How, then, does the power structure within the school itself function? Specifically, what are the roles assumed by the beloved Fräulein von Bernburg, champion of the emotions, and the hated principal, enforcer of discipline? Traditionally, critical readings of the film have identified Fräulein von Bernburg as a sort of freedom fighter, a humanitarian standing up to the forces of repression, and have targeted the principal much as I have described her, a tyrant ruling over a regime of denial. I would take issue with this romanticized view and trade its simplistic hero-villain dichotomy for a different model, that is, a system of repression based instead on the "good cop, bad cop" pattern, with the principal as the bad cop and Fräulein von Bernburg as the good cop.

To comprehend the logic of such a system in the case of the boarding school, it is necessary to return to the point made earlier in the principal's opening speech. As she made clear, the young women are being bred ("educated") as transmitters of the patriarchal German culture ever present in encoded form within the world of the school. To ensure this training, preserve the young women's "honor," and most effectively carry out their special socialization, it is necessary for society to shape women within an all-female setting; in fact, prior to feminist movements, this was no doubt the primary reason for "separatist" institutions. What, however, is the danger to the patriarchal society presented by such an institution? It is a sexual danger: the threat that the heterosexuality required of these women may, in the cloistered pressure-cooker atmosphere of the boarding school, become derailed into a focus on their own sex. The possibility that heterosexuality on the part of women may become transferred ("warped," as the father might say) into homosexuality presents a powerful threat to a system geared for procreation and the rearing of male offspring. "Gender is not only an identification with one sex; it also entails that sexual desire be directed toward the other sex."[5] The danger of the boarding school is that a concentration on the former entails a corresponding relaxation of the latter. Perhaps it is because the women's boarding school is the Achilles' heel of patriarchy that it figures in so much lesbian literature and cinema.

In *Maedchen in Uniform,* the code name for this sexual threat is "emotionalism." When Fräulein von Bernburg early in the film catches two schoolgirls exchanging a love letter, she confiscates the paper and, to their relief and delight, rips it up without reading a word; smiling but strict, she warns them to desist in the exchange of such letters because they can lead to "emotionalism." Again, later in the film, the student ringleader, Ilse, uses the same expression with the same negative message. She is engaged in declaiming a series of mock toasts during the postplay banquet, all phrased in the language of the school's official ideology, and thus she reprimands Manuela for the acting style of her male impersonation: "Remember, next time, less emotionalism."

In line with the model of repression that I suggest, Fräulein von Bernburg's task as the good cop seems to be to keep emotionalism in check and to make her charges more comfortable in their oppression. She acts as a pressure valve and as the focus of dissident energies in order that the overall systems not be endangered. Fräulein von Bernburg has two guises, then, for coping with the social and sexual schisms. Socially, she polices the heart, that is, the emotional life of her students. As she puts it at one point to Manuela, "You mustn't persuade yourself it isn't nice here." It is her presence in the school's cabinet of power that keeps the girls from rebelling against an order that would otherwise be totally abhorrent. Likewise, it is her presence as a confidante that permits her to discern and block any tentative moves in the direction of revolt, as, for example, when she persuades the headstrong Ilse not to run away from the school. Thus she functions as mediator between the top and bottom of the school hierarchy.

It is made clear, however, that the methods by which Fräulein von Bernburg exercises her functions are sexual. For instance, she succeeds in persuading Ilse to stay by slapping her on the ass and speaking to her seductively. This is her second guise: she capitalizes on the standard form of transference that leads adolescent girls to develop crushes on their teachers. Her positioning of herself as the exclusive object of schoolgirl affection may be seen as a tactic of repressive tolerance carried out in the arena of sexuality. Under the camouflage of her tolerance is the reality of repression. If the girls focus their sexual desires on her — where they can never be realized — then the danger of such desires being refocused on each other (where they could be realized) is averted. The figure of the teacher remains ever more powerful, more attractive, more worthy of adoration, than any mere fellow student. It is, in fact, very nearly a relationship of adoration in the religious sense, with forms of expression that are thoroughly ritualized and contained, as, for example, the evening bedtime scene makes clear.

The scene is set in the dormitory on Manuela's first night in the school. It is filmed with the soft focus and radiant light of a Romantic painting, for example, a Friedrich. The lights are dimmed by Fräulein von Bernburg to make the scene more seductive. All the girls are poised on the edge of their beds, kneeling in identical white gowns, heads upraised to receive the communion of her lips touching their foreheads, which she holds firmly as she administers each ritualistic kiss. This extreme fetishizing of the kiss by the nature of the teacher's gestures and the film's style is emblematic of the unspoken codes of repressive tolerance. The kiss is permitted, to each alike, but it is at once the given and the boundary. Nothing more may be allowed or even suggested, although the tension of that which is withheld suffuses the scene with eroticism and grants the teacher her very power. The kiss is both minimum and maximum, a state of grace and a state of stasis. The entire equilibrium is founded upon this extreme tension, which is snapped when Manuela, overwhelmed by the atmosphere and her feelings, breaks the rules. She throws her arms around Fräulein von Bernburg's body in a tight embrace and receives not a punishment but a kiss — a kiss, not merely on the forehead, but full on the lips.

Of course, the school's system of sexual repression does not crumble from this one transgression; it is much too securely established. Less so is Fräulein von Bernburg, whose situation is a difficult one. It is apparent that the sexual repression she forces on the students she also forces on herself. Yet Manuela causes a surplus of feeling that she cannot control. Sagan carefully presents Fräulein von Bernburg almost entirely in terms of Manuela. The first time she appears in the film, she is looking at the newly arrived Manuela on the stairway. The extent to which she begins to identify her own desires and sensitivities with Manuela's takes the shape of a literal superimposition. When Sagan presents a scene of Manuela as student in Fräulein von Bernburg's classroom, it is the anguish of the conflicted pair that she portrays through an extraordinary dissolve that predates the more widespread (and more pernicious) use of the motif by Ingmar Bergman in *Persona*.[6] In the scene, while struggling vainly to retrieve a memorized passage from a mind gone blank in the beloved teacher's presence, Manuela's vision begins to blur. Fräulein von Bernburg's sight, subjectively rendered, blurs as well, as her face becomes superimposed and fused with Manuela's staring back at her. It is she, as teacher, who breaks the locked gaze, averts her eyes, and reprimands Manuela with a "not prepared again," thus reasserting her authority and utilizing her rank to shield her emotions.

The next meeting of the two takes place in Fräulein von Bernburg's office soon after, where she has called Manuela to give her one of her chemises (in response to an attendant's expressed pity for the young girl's lack of undergarments, due to her lack of a caring mother). By giving Manuela one of her own chemises, she attempts to channel her concern and affection into the quasi-permissible form of a maternal gift that, however, is clearly an erotic token. The conversation that transpires between the two provides further evidence of the code of repressive tolerance exercised toward the student's incipient homosexuality. From the start, it is clear that "emotionalism" rules the encounter, as Fräulein von Bernburg begins by reprimanding Manuela, who has burst into tears at the gift of the chemise: "What an excitable child you are." Manuela confesses that she isn't crying out of unhappiness, and finally is coaxed to explain by the teacher's concern: "Is there a reason you can't confide to me?" It is the loneliness of the nights that plagues her, the moments after the goodnight kiss: "I stare at your door and would like to get up and go to you, but I'm not allowed. . . . I like you so awfully much." She is tortured by the passage of time: "I think of when I get older, and have to leave the school, and you'll kiss other children." Her expression of love, desire, and jealousy is quite explicitly phrased (although, in the older prints of the film, it was largely unsubtitled). Unprepared for such a declaration and unwilling to face the consequences of receiving such information, Fräulein von Bernburg lays down the law: "I think of you, too, Manuela. . . . But you know I can't make exceptions. The others would be jealous."

Her response is telling. She doesn't say that she does not share the girl's feelings of attraction; if anything, she implies that she does. She does not invent a boyfriend to assert a defensive heterosexual identity. She asserts only that she is under obligation to love all the girls equally to maintain her position as object of their affection; therefore, she cannot break that egalitarianism to reciprocate Manuela's passion. The system she must serve — as its token humanitarian — represses her own sexuality as well as that of the students. She is as much the victim as the promulgator of its repression, unlike the principal, whose phallic identity cancels out any homoeroticism. However, despite her struggle to repress her own emotions, Fräulein von Bernburg does act. The gift of the chemise is a turning point: it leads to the crisis of the school play, which is the central moment of the film, the moment that changes its direction from repressive tolerance to erotic liberation, the choice taken by Manuela throughout and by Fräulein von Bernburg, more complexly, at the film's end.

The school play, a favorite device of the boarding school genre, necessitates the pleasurable moment of cross-dressing in male attire. Manuela plays the lead role of Don Carlos in the 1787 play of the same name by Friedrich Schiller, scion of the Sturm und Drang school that brought to culmination the ideals of the Weimar classicism movement led by Schiller and Goethe. (It was Schiller's *Don Carlos* that formed the basis of Verdi's opera in 1867.)

The choice of this play by Sagan and Winsloe to be the play-within-the-film is particularly significant.[7] *Don Carlos* is identified with the youthful Schiller, in that it represents the peak of his early idealistic period (indeed, after it, Schiller went into a period of doubt and reevaluation that kept him from writing plays again for a full decade). Sturm und Drang was a literary movement that presaged German Romanticism in its emphasis on the individual in conflict with a rationalist, unjust order. Both Schiller and Goethe stressed emotional harmony and a community of sympathy as the basic social values to put forward in opposition to the oppressive rationalism of the Enlightenment; *Don Carlos* is considered the very embodiment of that theme.

Based on the life of Don Carlos, son of the Spanish king Philip II, the play counterposes the son's liberal idealism with the brutal tyranny of his father's reign. In the play, Don Carlos forms an alliance with the older and wiser Marquis Posa, who conspires with him to advance a humane order and overthrow the ruler. In Schiller's play, the Marquis, learning that their plans are suspected, saves the prince by drawing all guilt upon himself, consequently suffering execution by the king's decree in order to spare the prince. The play ends tragically, with Don Carlos refusing to relish his fatally bought freedom, showing his true face to the king, and thus suffering a similar death at the hands of the bloodthirsty Inquisition.

Thus far, then, *Don Carlos* would seem the perfect corollary to the film's much-advanced theme of humanitarian idealism counterposed against a fascist reign. In such an interpretation, Manuela would essentially play herself, while the Marquis Posa would represent the Fräulein von Bernburg role and the king would represent the principal. Schiller, like Winsloe/Sagan, thus assumes the mantle of proto-antifascist for his eloquent, romantic opposition to the maddened illogic of absolute order. The principal's invited guests seem prone to this same interpretation, for they cluck disapprovingly over their tea that "Schiller sometimes writes very freely."

However, the subsequent scenes following this admonition, as well as the choice of the scene from *Don Carlos*, suggest the same sort of alternative reading that I have been suggesting for *Maedchen in Uniform* as a whole. The scene immediately following the tea talk is one of the schoolgirls, giddy from a dose of spiked punch, dancing in each others' arms, disobeying the rules, and generally enacting their guardians' worst fears. The scene chosen from *Don Carlos* is not one dealing in political matters, but rather, the rarified scene in which Don Carlos at last wins an audience with the queen and declares his forbidden love to her. Reprimanded for his rashness in compromising them both by coming to see her, Don Carlos tells the queen: "Even if it means death, I shall not go from here: One moment lived in Paradise is not too dearly bought with death." These are the lines spoken by Manuela (as Don Carlos) in the scene we see of the school play. A significant key to the narrative of *Don Carlos* is the fact that the prince's beloved is his father's newly acquired wife: she is, then, his mother, which makes their love forbidden as, in the words of Schiller's play, "the world and nature and the laws of Rome condemn such passions." Sagan clearly annexes this sentiment by choosing the scene in which Don Carlos proclaims his love for Elizabeth, the name both of the Queen Mother and of Fräulein von Bernburg. With Manuela cross-dressed as the passionate suitor (in a performance heralded by all for its remarkable sincerity!), the sequence represents the central theme of forbidden love encoded within the sanctity of German high culture.

Drunk with punch and the euphoria of her success, Manuela decides to extend her role into real life: she rises to deliver an impassioned toast in which she declares her love for Fräulein von Bernburg and announces the gift of her chemise as proof of its reciprocation. She abandons caution to proclaim "I know she likes me." She echoes and reprises Don Carlos in her insistence on sharing the news: "Nothing else matters. . . . I'm not afraid of anything. . . . Yes, everyone should know." In a coming out that is the opposite of Don Carlos's vow of silence, she concludes with a celebratory generosity: "Long live Fräulein von Bernburg, beloved by all."

Despite the school's aura of eroticism, it is this act of pronouncement that constitutes the unpardonable transgression. It is the naming of that which may well be known, this claiming of what is felt by the public speaking of its name, that is expressly forbidden.[8] For her speech, which is witnessed by the dread principal, Manuela is immediately imprisoned, significantly enough within the confines of the infirmary—in a reference to the pseudoscientific view of homosexuality as a species of mental imbalance, a disease, but one that nevertheless can be punished as a crime. Indeed, the first view of Manuela in the hospital traces her position in bed below heavy bars of light emblazoned on the shadowed wall above her head. The immediate wish of the principal is to blot out history, to expunge the traces of the "scandal" and pretend that nothing ever happened. It is a wish that is initially reflected in Manuela's own coming to consciousness, as she emerges from her hangover with the complaint that she cannot remember what has happened or what she has done. So powerful is the taboo that amnesia is the consequence of its transgression.

The public speech, in fact, can be seen as an extremely powerful transgression, one that, unlike the private actions between Manuela and Fräulein von Bernburg, publicly disrupts and subverts the prevailing order of the school. The principal's regime could tolerate the widely acknowledged schoolgirl crushes and libidinous undercurrents as long as they remained marginalized and subservient to the dominant ideology. The homoeroticism had been portrayed graphically ever since the time of Manuela's arrival: Ilse told her how envious other girls were, asking if it were true that "the Golden One" really "kisses you good night, oh god, oh god"; the laundrywoman explained the heart and initials on her school uniform, E.V.B., by laughing that "the girl who wore this dress must have been infatuated with Fräulein Elizabeth von Bernburg, thus the initials"; and pairs of girls were repeatedly shown holding hands, embracing by windows, or passing love notes. An unendorsed de facto eroticism could be contained within the reigning patriarchal order, but a double challenge could not be abided: the challenge of Manuela's public naming of that eroticism and the challenge of Fräulein von Bernburg's material action in presenting the chemise over and above the limits of egalitarianism. For this reason, amnesia was a possibility only for Manuela. Everyone else remembered quite well what had occurred.

Unable to turn back the clock, the principal opts for quarantine: Manuela is sentenced to solitary confinement, as though homosexuality were a communicable disease spread by social contact. As Manuela becomes distraught in the final phase of the film, Fräulein von Bernburg struggles, more consciously than her young student, to come to terms with her sexuality and acknowledge her feelings for her own sex. In her final meeting with Manuela, held clandestinely in defiance of the principal's prohibition, she tries to tell the girl the exact nature of a "crime" she seems unable to understand: "you must be cured . . . of liking me so much." At the same time, she makes a telling complaint about Manuela's speech. She does not reproach Manuela for what she has brought upon herself, as we might expect, but instead says: "What you have done to me, you know." There is more meaning to the statement than the fact of Manuela's speech, which to be sure has damaged Fräulein von Bernburg's standing at the school but yet is not wholly different from countless other private declarations she no doubt has withstood. Rather, Fräulein von Bernburg may well be referring to the terrible inner conflict into which Manuela's speech has thrown her. It is a conflict not unlike that felt by so many in-the-closet homosexuals of both sexes in this country following the opening up of sexual boundaries during the Stonewall eruption and the succeeding gay liberation movement of the late sixties and early seventies. This period carried for many an undesired pressure to identify a previously privatized sexuality (in Fräulein von Bernburg's case, to make that identification not only to others, but to herself as well). From the moment of this reproach, the teacher's struggle to "come out" and emerge from the raging conflict within her becomes the central theme of the film. It is a theme concerned with finding the courage to oppose an unjust authority, a courage shared, finally, by the other students of the school.

Fräulein von Bernburg's inner struggle reaches its peak immediately after this meeting with Manuela, which has concluded badly, with the girl rushing out of the room in desperation and the teacher's race to call her back blocked by the arrival of the principal. In fact, her confrontations with the principal have been escalating ever since the "theatrical" incident. She has begun assuming more radical stances in opposition to the principal's edict. Earlier, arguing over her permissiveness toward Manuela, she had declared: "What you call sin, I call love, which has a thousand forms." She was speaking in general terms of her philosophy of maternal nurturance versus the principal's punitive discipline, but the more explicit meaning of the statement also holds true. Intent on subjugating the teacher to her authority, the principal now threatens her: "I will not permit revolutionary ideas." Fräulein von Bernburg then breaks rank in the only truly decisive way possible, responding: "I resign." Herewith, she makes her choice to reject her role as the good cop and seek a genuine humanitarianism outside the corrupt system of the school, which in turn means seeking also her genuine sexuality as she has come to recognize it.

As the teacher and the principal enact their battle of will and authority, Manuela prepares to throw herself over the stairwell. It is at this point that the film's second superimposition of the faces of Manuela and Fräulein von Bernburg takes place. Again, it is Fräulein von Bernburg who "experiences" the blurred vision and "sees" Manuela's face projected through her own image. This time, however, having made her choice to break with the patriarchal order, she does not avert her gaze or try to separate herself from the vision. Instead, she recognizes this "vision" as a psychic signal of her bond with Manuela.

What does the superimposition mean in this context? The principal had earlier warned the teacher to "dissolve" her contact with Manuela, suggesting the nature of this shot. The blurring of definition and melding of identities has usually had a negative impact when applied to women in cinema. In Ingmar Bergman's *Persona*, for example, the loss of individual identity is the threat that haunts women's intimacy like a destructive specter: getting too close to another woman means losing oneself. In addition, there is always the companion myth of narcissism. The superimposition shots here may also be a tacit recognition by Sagan of the myth of homosexuality as a narcissistic doubling, an attempt to solidify one's identity by the addition of its likeness in another. Rather than balking at the vision, however, Fräulein von Bernburg recognizes the merged faces as a signal of power by combination. She does not read the superimposition as erasure (the patriarchal warning) or negative bonding (the mirror phase prolonged), but rather as a positive depiction of the strength exercised by such a redoubling of energy and identity. She trusts the sign and acts on it. Shouting Manuela's name, she rushes from her office (and the startled principal) to the stairwell, intent on rescuing Manuela, whereupon she discovers that the schoolgirls have arrived ahead of her and saved the day.

There are only these two superimpositions in the entire film, and significantly they are both assigned to Fräulein von Bernburg at times in which Manuela is in distress. It is Fräulein von Bernburg, and the force she has come to represent, who prevails in the film's final scene: the rescued Manuela is cradled by the schoolgirls as the defeated principal, bereft of her authority, slowly retreats down the long, gloomy hall. The darkness of the hall deepens in her wake, her cane taps faintly on the floor, the sound of bells and finally bugles can be heard in the distance. As the bugle calls signify, it is a provisional victory, and yet the patriarchal order has been ruptured within the school by the liberation of eros among the women.

In terms of the interpretation I have been suggesting, as well as the more traditional interpretation of antifascism, the ending of the film is extremely important. Yet the nature of the ending has been frequently obscured in cinema histories. Many reports of the film have cited a supposed "other" ending in which Manuela successfully commits suicide, and some critics have even cited the existence of a "Nazi" suicide ending and an "export" version like this one. Yet as several German sources testify, such was not the case.[9] However, the original play *did* have Manuela kill herself and ended with the principal setting a cover-up in motion at play's end; but this is one of many differences between the play and the film that I will discuss later. In point of fact, the film *Maedchen in Uniform* concludes with an ending of rescue. What does this ending signify? Such an ending confers a unity upon the film's two themes — the widely acknowledged one of anti-authoritarianism as well as the previously ignored one of erotic liberation — and shapes them into a consistent and harmonious whole.

It has frequently been argued that the preferred ending for a proto-Nazi film was suicide, the ultimate abandonment of hope that leads the individual to throw herself or himself into the depth of oblivion or, conversely, into the hands of a superhuman savior. That was the scenario against which a film like *Kuhle Wampe* (by Slatan Dudow with script by Bertolt Brecht) rebelled, by refusing to end on a note of despair and insisting instead on the persistence of faith in the future. So, too, Sagan. Her anti-Nazism is nowhere more apparent than in the ending, which posits not only the maintenance of hope but also the vindication of resistance as a very different "triumph of the will" from Leni Riefenstahl's brand. In Riefenstahl's film of the same period, *The Blue Light* (1934), the heroine (played by Riefenstahl) finally throws herself from a cliff, despairing, isolated from others of her kind, done in by an unsympathetic society. Not so Manuela: the schoolgirls of the boarding school integrate her sensibility into their own consciousness; instead of closing ranks against her, they come to her (and, by extension, their own) rescue. The cliffhanger ending is at once a powerful statement of political resistance, both individual and collective, and a validation of lesbianism as a personal and public right.

The principal earlier condemned Fräulein von Bernburg's feelings and actions as "revolutionary," and so they may indeed be. In a patriarchal society that depends on women for the reward and procreation of its (his) own kind, a break in the link is disastrous: "What would happen if our hypothetical woman not only refused the man to whom she was promised, but asked for a woman instead? If a single refusal were disruptive, a double refusal would be insurrectionary." [10] The ending of the film serves to validate Fräulein von Bernburg's difficult development from humanitarian disciplinarian to a free, stronger, and woman-identified woman. The progression of the scenario depends on her inner struggle and final evolution in response to the catalyst of Manuela's passion. At the film's end, Fräulein von Bernburg stands triumphant with the schoolgirls witnessing the principal's melancholy retreat. She wins this position not by maintaining her power in the hierarchy but by rejecting it, not by tightening the reins of her repression but by casting them down, not by co-option but by refusal. Her place on the staircase at the end may be seen, then, as a reward for her "coming out" and acknowledging her sexuality, just as Manuela's rescue at the end represents a social legitimation of her passion. *Maedchen in Uniform* presents a positive vision of lesbianism that has been largely disregarded for years, a film victim of a subtle, critical homophobia that has insisted on perceiving the literal as the merely metaphoric.

An analysis of the film today clarifies the meaning and can easily annex Sagan's work to our contemporary tradition of lesbian culture. But historical differences nevertheless persist between the perspectives of Sagan making a film cooperatively in Berlin on the eve of the Third Reich and most of us today. Differences are apparent even in the shifts of meaning between Christa Winsloe's original play and its metamorphosis into *Maedchen in Uniform*. Yet most surprising, perhaps, are the similarities that slowly become recognizable upon reexamining both the film and its period similarities, which in some cases are crucial for us to recognize as we proceed into the eighties.

Sagan's movie is in many respects a more radical work of lesbian celebration than Winsloe's play, while at the same time it focuses far more
on the codes of patriarchal power than does the stage production. The
stage play (both the original, *Yesterday and Today,* and the international
version, *Girls in Uniform,* which was widely performed after the film's release) [11] actually fits quite tidily the model of the "lesbian fairy tale" that
Elaine Marks traces to its Sapphic origins in her important essay on lesbian literature:

> Although there is no evidence in Sappho's poems to corroborate
> the notion that she did indeed have a school, religious or secular,
> for young women, the gynaeceum, ruled by the seductive or seduc-
> ing teacher has become, since the eighteenth century, the preferred
> locus for most fictions about women loving women. . . . The younger
> woman, whose point of view usually dominates, is always passion-
> ate and innocent. If, as is usually the case when the author of the
> text is a woman, it is the younger woman who falls in love, the nar-
> rative is structured so as to insist on this love as an awakening. The
> older woman as object of the younger woman's desire is restrained
> and admirable, beautiful and cultivated . . . the exchanges between
> the older and the younger woman are reminiscent of a mother-
> daughter relationship. The mother of the younger woman is either
> dead or in some explicit way inadequate. Her absence is implied in
> the young woman's insistent need for a goodnight kiss. The gynae-
> ceum, particularly when it is represented by a school, also controls
> time. Time limits are set by the school calendar whose inexorable
> end announces the fatal separation, which may involve a death. Tem-
> poral structures reiterate the almost universally accepted notion that
> a schoolgirl crush is but a phase in the emotional development of the
> young woman, something that will pass. The dénouement in these
> lesbian fairy tales is often brought about by a public event during
> which private passions explode. [12]

If the contours of Marks's paradigm bear a striking resemblance to the
film (which in fact was viewed as an adolescent tale far more than a lesbian
one), its elements fit the play even more so. For example, in the play a sub-
plot involves Manuela's pursuit by a diligent, if unwanted, male suitor: her
equestrian instructor, no less. In the play, Fräulein von Bernburg is not
unmotivated in her feelings for the girls: she secretly wants to be the head
of the school herself. She does not resign in the final confrontation with
the principal, but merely tries to increase her power base through the face-
off; and Manuela throws herself out a window before anyone has had the

chance to rescue her. Because the play can end with only Manuela having stepped out of line and dead for her actions, it is far more easily recuperable into the tradition of lesbianism as tragic, powerless, passive, and, in particular, fatal to its adherent. As Marks emphasizes, the "constraints" of the genre signify the "marginal status of lesbians and lesbianism." [13]

Though incorporating the classic elements of the fairy tale in *Maedchen in Uniform,* Sagan goes further. She changes a few areas of the story line and utilizes the visual and editing codes particular to cinema to extend the meaning of the original text.[14] One of the film's strongest features is its success in making palpable the functioning of patriarchal codes despite the absence of any male or militaristic figures. The use of the central staircase is one such case, with a symbolism both visual (its barred railings and threatening abyss) and philosophical (its use by the girls prohibited from using the formal front staircase). The stairwell suggests a confining enclosure, carceral in its grates of iron and shadow, as well as the functional confinement of virtually all the activities of the girls. At one point, the schoolgirls drop an object from the top to test a formula for calculating the time a falling body takes to reach bottom. The staircase is thus both a representation of the prevailing order (and its powers of organization) and a portent of tragedy. The camera frequently views the marching of the girls through the iron forms, further emphasizing their molding into Prussian "women of iron." And, of course, the very first meeting between Manuela and Fräulein von Bernburg occurs on the staircase, their bodies positioned midway between forbidding shadows at screen left and a bright window screen right.

In addition to such visual compositions, Sagan inserts a series of montages that provide a bridge between the fairly theatrical scenes involving the central characters and the documentary-style observations of schoolgirl behavior. The large cast of schoolgirls—all nonprofessional actresses—functions as an alternative discourse to set against the patriarchal regimentation. The students horse around, express homesickness, carry on multiple intrigues with each other, play jokes, dress and undress, and relate to each other in a tone that shifts between childishness and eroticism.[15] At one point, a locker-room scene of bedtime activities is immediately followed by a montage that marshals the disorganized activities into a marching order of mouths in extreme close-up barking orders, feet hurrying to obey, identical lines of students filing past, and so on. The montage ends with a shift to the famous dormitory scene of Fräulein von Bernburg's goodnight kisses, a scene that is itself ambiguous in its resolution of eroticism with regimentation.

Most significant are the montage sequences that frame the encounters between Manuela and Fräulein von Bernburg, and indeed, frame our entire encounter with the film. The montage that opens the film communicates a view of the exterior towers of Potsdam; the old stone putti and a statue that resembles a tiny soldier and the sounds of church bells and bugles portray an atmosphere of patriarchal readiness within which the school building itself is located. Traces of the same montage appear as narrative interruptions at key moments in the evolution of Manuela and Fräulein von Bernburg's relationship. For example, just after Manuela has thrown her arms around the teacher in the goodnight scene, Sagan inserts a rapid cut to the towers and statues. Later, when Fräulein von Bernburg gives the student her chemise, Sagan similarly terminates the scene with a cut to the stone towers and the sound of bells tolling. The montages appear to be cautionary, clues to the audience that emotions between women are never free of the shadow of patriarchal aggression. Their intrusion into the film is an antidote to viewing this all-female space as a "free zone," given the patriarchal society seen to dominate not only in the concrete form of the staircase or principal, but in the equally threatening form of external authority that waits just outside the school gates.

Even at the film's end, when the two women and their student supporters seem most victorious, the ominous sound of the bugles reappears to accompany the principal's retreat. Though Siegfried Kracauer contends that the prominence of the motif at the end of the film proves that "the principle of authority has not been shaken" within the school,[16] I would suggest otherwise: the motif reminds the audience just how provisional the victory is, and just how powerful are the patriarchal forces with which any new order within the school must contend. It is a warning that separation from the dominant order does not automatically grant freedom from its dominance. It should have been a warning to lesbians then living in Germany that the time for strong collective action was upon them, as the forces of fascism gathered outside the windows. Instead, the Third Reich indeed came to power, and most of those responsible for *Maedchen in Uniform* left the country.

Who were they? Little has been written and little known about the women behind this work. Their sexuality has been as thoroughly veiled as the lesbian theme of the film itself. Rumors, anecdotes, and bits of stories form the customary trail of unofficial history. Blanche Wiesen Cook is instructive regarding what *not* to look for. Commenting on *Maedchen in Uniform*, Ann Elisaber Weirach's *The Scorpion*, and other works of this period and genre, Cook warns against accepting the tragic tales of unrequited love and tragic abandonment as autobiographical fictions: "The truth is that these passionate little girls were not always abused and abandoned. They did not commit suicide. They wrote books about passionate little girls, death, and abandonment."[17] Not infrequently, the lives of the authors and their models display a depth and breadth of options not readily visible in their constructed tales. When, that is, their lives are recoverable at all.

Leontine Sagan was born in Austria in 1889 and was married at some point to a doctor from Vienna. She trained as a stage director and actress and worked with such directors as Bernofskey and Max Reinhardt, teaching for a time at Reinhardt's drama school. As an actress, she appeared alongside Salka Viertel in an early production of the Ibsen play *John Gabriel Borkman* and also in a rare production of Franz Blei's *The Wave*. The circumstances of her taking on the direction of *Maedchen in Uniform* are not now available, although she was certainly a popular figure in the Berlin theater scene. She left Germany soon after and went to England, where Alexander Korda sought to capitalize on her success by engaging her to direct *Men of Tomorrow*, a sort of "boys in uniform" film about Oxford; not surprisingly, the success was not repeated. Judging by the published script and cast list for a production of *Maedchen in Uniform*, Sagan also worked in theater in London. The play, retitled *Children in Uniform*, is listed as being "produced by Leontine Sagan" at the Duchess Theatre, London, opening October 7, 1932. Soon after, Sagan left England. She moved to the United States for several years and thence to South Africa, where she cofounded the National Theater. She died in 1974 in Johannesburg. As far as is known, she never made another film.

The two leading actresses of *Maedchen in Uniform*, Hertha Thiele and Dorothea Wieck, starred together in another film shortly afterward. Directed by Frank Wysbar in 1933, *Anna and Elizabeth* returned to the traditional view of intimate attachments between women as debilitating and demonic: Hertha Thiele played a young girl with miraculous powers who drove Dorothea Wieck to attempt suicide because Thiele failed to resurrect her husband! The women are portrayed as having an unnaturally close, almost supernatural, relationship; lesbianism is explicit only as the power of darkness. (Both actresses are still alive today, and much additional material should be forthcoming from Karola Gramann, the *frauen und film* editor who has been interviewing Thiele.)[18]

Christa Winsloe is the best remembered of the *Maedchen in Uniform* women, perhaps simply because her intimates wrote memoirs. Erika Mann, who herself played one of the schoolgirls in the film, remembered Winsloe (the Baroness von Hatvany) in her memoirs of 1939 in a fashion that would please Blanche Cook. Smiling and confident, dressed in white shirt and tie, Christa Winsloe looks out at us from a photograph captioned "once a maedchen in uniform." Erika Mann recalls Christa's life as a "beautiful and amusing society woman" who ran an expensive household in Munich and hosted salons in Budapest and Vienna as the wife of Baron Ludwig Hatvany, a Hungarian writer and "grand seigneur." She made animal sculptures and held exquisite dinner parties, at one of which Mann remembers her announcing her plan to write a play about her own childhood boarding school experiences. Trying to explain the play's phenomenal success, Mann suggests: "How was it? . . . Because Christa Hatvany had guarded in her heart, and now rediscovered, a simple, strong and genuine feeling, and because she could so express it that hundreds of thousands of people [sic] recognized the pain and ecstasy of their own childhood, their own first love, which had, in their own hearts, been overlaid, but never stifled. The poignant feeling of recognition . . ."[19] If Mann holds to the favorite view of lesbianism as a phase through which "hundreds of thousands" of women pass during adolescence, she at least manages to hold out a phrase of reservation regarding the impulse that is yet "never stifled."

Certainly it was never stifled in Christa. Nor in Dorothy Thompson, the U.S. journalist who was married to Sinclair Lewis when, in 1932, at her own ten-day Christmas party, she fell in love with Christa, who was then on the verge of getting a divorce from the baron. Dorothy Thompson's diaries of the time reveal her struggle to name her experience, to try to understand how she can be "happily married, and yet wanting that curious tenderness. That pervading warm tenderness — there are no words for it . . ."[20] When the party guests had left, Dorothy followed Christa to Budapest. In March, the two met in Italy, where they shared a villa at Portofino for several months. Upon leaving the villa, Dorothy brought Christa back to the United States with her. In August, the two women traveled back to Austria together. When apart, they wrote constantly. In early 1934, Sinclair Lewis had to be out of town for several months and Dorothy stayed in New York with Christa. "They were a couple," said their friend John Farrar. "If you asked Dorothy for dinner, you asked Christa too."[21]

After two years, however, relations between the two began to break down, with Dorothy answering one of Christa's letters: "I feel that something between us has broken. . . . I had a strange dream last night. I dreamed I was putting out into a very rough sea in a frail ship, and the crew were all women. I was afraid, and woke up, sweating."[22] By this time, Thompson was persona non grata in Germany, having been expelled on her last trip by Adolf Hitler himself because of an uncomplimentary interview (and, no doubt, her habit of laughing at Bund rallies). Christa couldn't return to her home, so went instead in 1935 to live in southern France. Their continued intimacy was so strong that, in 1940, when the

Nazi occupation of France made it impossible for Christa to withdraw money from her Munich bank, Dorothy began sending her money every month to live on.

Christa Winsloe's life had a sad end, but nothing at all like a Marks fairy tale formula: she was murdered on June 10, 1944, by a common criminal named Lambert, who pretended to be operating as a member of the French resistance. His claim led to ugly speculation that Winsloe had been a Nazi spy and to an old friend's writing Dorothy Thompson at the end of the war (1946) to inform her of the death and beg help in clearing Winsloe's name. The friend explained the rumors by Christa's liaison at the time with a French-Swiss girlfriend, Simone Gentet, who was alleged to be a spy: "Christa once described her as a hysterical, dissolute morphine addict and alcoholic, but she certainly knew nothing of Simone's other activities, should the rumor be true . . . we know with such absolute certainty that Christa was the most violent enemy of National-Socialism and that she would never have made the slightest compromise. On the contrary, we were always worried that the Gestapo would grab her and we still believed this is what happened to her because she had helped many Jewish friends get out of the country."[23] Thus, the author of *Maedchen in Uniform* was killed by a man claiming to be a resistance fighter but whom her friends believed to be a Gestapo agent, an ambiguity that lends to her death the same confusion that continues to surround the relationship between homosexuality and the Nazi era.

As an example of their conflation, Rossellini's *Rome, Open City* established an early tradition of identifying homosexuality with fascism through its narrative of hearty male resistance fighters betrayed by a lesbian morphine addict and her Gestapo lover. Bertolucci continued the tradition by consistently portraying fascists as suffering from sexual repressions or "perversions" in his films (with time out in *The Conformist* for a lesbian resistance fighter in the person of Dominique Sanda, although he did equip her with a male mentor and suggest that her attraction to women was her weakness). Nor have such connections depended on cinema, either Italian or German, for promulgation. The stereotype of Nazi campiness, of ss regalia as S/M toys, of the Gestapo as a leather-boy thrill, of the big bull dyke as concentration camp boss, etcetera, all seem to have a firm hold in our culture's fantasy life and historical mythology—this despite the facts of the Third Reich's large-scale massacre of homosexuals as pollutants of Aryan blood and a stain on the future master race. Hitler apparently agreed with Manuela's boarding school principal in seeing homosexuality and lesbianism as "revolutionary." He didn't hesitate to purge his own ranks, as on the infamous "night of the long knives" of June 1934, when Ernst Rohm (the SA chief of staff and a well-known homosexual) and his followers were murdered to make the SA, as Hitler put it, "a pure and cleanly institution."

Why the Nazis wanted to eliminate homosexuals along with Jews, communists, and various national minorities is a question that seems fairly well answered and understood now in the light of Nazi ideology and the "final solutions" it proposed for the united, fascistic, patriarchal Aryan race. Why gay men or any women should have joined the Nazi Party at all is quite another question. What circumstances led to the existence of a Rohm? What sort of outlook could have lent credence to Christa Winsloe's murder as an act of resistance, or alternatively, as an act of Nazi vengeance? What sort of lesbian community inhabited Berlin during the Weimar Republic and the rise of the Third Reich? What sort of women's movement was there to combat the Nazi ideology of woman's place? What were social and legal attitudes toward homosexuality? Who liked *Maedchen in Uniform,* and why? To answer these questions fully lies outside the possibilities of this article, but to address them at least in part is crucial to our understanding of the film and to our recognizing just how exemplary was Leontine Sagan's combination of personal liberation and collective action.[24]

Germany had a radical women's movement in the early years of the century, beginning with the country's first large rally for women's suffrage in 1894. The movement for women's rights was part of a larger movement for overall reform known as the *Lebensreformbewegung* (the Life Reform Movement), which encompassed groups working on behalf of women and homosexuals as well as youth, natural health, clothing reform, and nudity. There do not seem to have been lesbian political organizations as such, but many lesbians were active in women's suffrage and feminist groups (notably, Anita Augspurg and Lida Gustavs Heymann, who fought for suffrage and opposed World War I as "a men's war fought between men's states"), and many others worked with the Scientific-Humanitarian Committee founded by Magnus Hirschfeld (the key figure in homosexual rights struggles). As early as 1904, Anna Ruling had addressed the Committee at a meeting on the common struggles of women's and homosexuals' rights groups, complaining that women's organizations were "not lifting a finger . . . doing nothing, absolutely nothing" in support of homosexual emancipation.

In 1909, however, a bill was proposed to criminalize lesbianism, which up until then had not been subject to the Paragraph 175 laws against male homosexuality. Seeing the bill as a clear retaliation against the gains of the women's movement, Dr. Helene Stocker (who in 1905 had founded the League for the Protection of Maternity and Sexual Reform) spoke at a meeting held jointly with the Committee to support its petition drive against the proposed bill and to denounce the criminalization of lesbianism as "a grave error." The arguments on behalf of both women and homosexuality were diverse and at times contradictory, with variations in ideology so wide that some elements could be supportive of the new Russian Revolution as a model while other elements drifted into support of National Socialism. Stocker's argument for keeping lesbianism legal rested on the defense of "individual freedom in the most private part of private life — love life;" Hirschfeld rested his arguments on scientific theories of human sexuality/psychology and on a human-rights-type plea for tolerance; other groups based their homosexuality on theories of male supremacy and past models of soldiery and lovers-in-arms, leading to an early Nazi identification; while still other groups initially supportive of sexual freedoms for women, like those in the "sexual hygiene" movement, turned anti-abortionist for racial reasons and ended up merging with the proto-Nazi "racial hygiene" groups.

Varying definitions of private and public life — and private versus public rights — are key to the differences. Hirschfeld, unlike many others, threw all his energies into effecting social education and legal changes (although with a tone of apology and tolerance-begging that's foreign to our styles today). The years of the Weimar Republic witnessed a flowering of women's rights and of struggles for homosexual emancipation, as well as a bursting forth of a large lesbian and gay subculture quartered largely in Berlin. And the sexual theories of the time are fascinating. In 1919, Hirschfeld opened the doors of his Institute of Sexual Science and won substantial support for the theory of "a third sex" that was neither male nor female: he called homosexuals Uranians and based much of his strategy on this notion of a literally alien species.

The move to criminalize lesbianism was dropped with the advent of the Republic and the end of World War I, which had seen women move so totally out of the former spheres as to make such a bill ineffective as a stay-at-home device. Therefore, much of Hirschfeld's Committee's efforts went toward the repeal of Paragraph 175 (prohibiting male homosexual practice). The Coalition for Reform of the Sexual Crime Code (founded in 1925) worked to legalize acts between "consenting adults." The German Communist Party, following the lead established by revolutionary Soviet laws in support of homosexual rights, had a strong presence on the Reichstag committee for penal code reform, which succeeded in recommending for approval the repeal of Paragraph 175. (Unfortunately, its approval came on October 16, 1929, when the crash of the U.S. stock market changed the whole nature of the political scene in Germany, leading to the tabling of the resolution and the quick rise of the Nazi forces.) As anti-Semitism, misogyny, and homophobia grew alongside the move to the right in Germany, Hirschfeld became an ever more popular target. Attacked in 1920, his skull fractured in 1921, fired upon in 1923, attacked verbally by a Nazi delegate to the Reichstag in 1927, he had the dubious honor of seeing the library of his Institute become one of the first victims of book burning on May 10, 1933, just four months after Hitler became chancellor.[25]

The cycle of free expression followed by total persecution experienced by Magnus Hirschfeld was symptomatic of the treatment of the larger gay population and culture he had come to symbolize. Jim Steakley provides a partial answer to the obvious reaction (How could such a thing happen?) when he pinpoints the Weimar contradiction "between personal and collective liberation" — a contradiction manifested in the simultaneous existence of a widespread social tolerance of homosexuality (including the flourishing of gay culture, the growth of bars, and de facto police acquiescence at least in Berlin) alongside repressive laws and the frequent failure of most legal actions on behalf of lesbians and gay men.[26] The history of Berlin's gay male subculture is fairly well known today; according to Steakley, there were some forty gay bars and between one thousand and two thousand prostitutes in the city by 1914, as well as perhaps thirty homosexual journals published during the course of the Weimar years. However, the same "invisibility" that granted lesbians immunity from the criminal laws has also granted the Weimar lesbians a less welcome immunity from the history books.

Recent research has begun to yield materials that can outline for us the contours of the lesbian community that was so lively during the same period, especially in the larger cities of Berlin and Munich. Louise Brooks (who starred as Lulu in G. W. Pabst's *Pandora's Box*, which offered a glimpse of Berlin's decadent ways) has reminisced about the mood of Berlin, recalling for example a lesbian bar, the Maly, where "there was a choice of feminine or collar-and-tie lesbians."[27] Alex de Jonge provides a more embroidered account in a male visitor's description of the Silhouette, which was "one of Berlin's most fashionable night spots." He, too, describes the scene of role-dressed couples on a night out, but makes an important point: "You could see women well known in German literature, society, the theater and politics. . . . There was no suggestion of vice about the place. It was a usual phenomenon in German life."[28] Though the Silhouette admitted men if accompanied by a lesbian regular, other women's bars did not; de Jonge mentions Die Grotte and Entre Nous as two of the "more exclusive" places, about which he therefore can provide no information.

Ilse Kokula has provided one of the most complete accounts of the period in her brief but tantalizing summary, "The Uranian Ladies Often Meet in Patisseries."[29] She expands upon the meaning of Uranian by tracing its root as an epithet for Aphrodite taken to mean "celestial" or spiritual, and she reiterates Hirschfeld's popular theory of a third sex. The estimate of homosexuality in Weimar Berlin is placed at fifty thousand out of a population of two and a half million (although the methodology behind the statistics is not specified). Whereas bars, hotels, and saunas serviced gay men, there were also, more surprisingly, various services for lesbians seeking to meet each other. For example, there were *Vermittlungsbüros*, or agencies that fixed up single lesbians. There were personals columns in which lesbians advertised for partners. One such ad from the period listed the following: "Fräulein, decent, 24 years old, looking for pretty Fräulein as a girlfriend." There were also a number of social clubs for lesbians that met in cafés and *Konditoreien* (patisseries), such as one group of "Israelite" (Jewish) lesbians who met from 4:00 to 6:00 in the afternoon to talk and play chess. Balls were held regularly, run by and for lesbian women. There was a general attitude of self-recognition, with many lesbian couples eager to convince the world how well-adjusted they were and to combat the stereotypes of depravity and tragedy.

From 1918 on, lesbian journals were part of the culture, usually presenting a perspective that was part political and part educational; they had such titles as *Frauenliebe* (Womanlove), *Ledige Frauen* (Unmarried women), and *Die Freundin: Weekly Journal for Ideal Friendship between Women. Die Freundin* was published continuously during 1923–32 by the *Damenklub* (women's club, or bar) Violetta—itself a coded name, as violets were considered a sign of lesbianism at the time. Some of Ilse Kokula's information is evidently derived from firsthand sources, as she is able to comment that many older lesbians still remember the cafés "with great pleasure," and that one such woman, Kati R., remembers that the lesbian balls continued into the fifties and sixties, with as many as two hundred women attending. What emerges, then, is a picture of lesbian life as a widespread phenomenon, surprisingly aboveground and organized around its own publications, clubs, and rituals. This is reflected in virtually none of the films or official histories of the time.

Despite such a spirit of freedom and such an ambience of lesbian permissiveness, at no point, either in its own time or in ours, has *Maedchen in Uniform* been critically (i.e., publicly) discussed as a lesbian text. And yet the histories specify its initial succès de scandale, implying an at least unofficial recognition of the film's true meaning. Why has this meaning been so hidden, so difficult to retrieve? The extent of the obstacles in the path of the gay historian seeking to reinterpret film texts was emphasized by Vito Russo's uncovering of the original New York State censor's notes on the American release of *Maedchen in Uniform*.[30] Almost line for line, scene for scene, the shots and subtitles that I have specified as revolutionary and most fundamentally lesbian were the sections of the film that the censors wanted to cut. Initially condemned, the film was approved by the censors for release in August 1932 only after all evidence of lesbianism had been cut. Their notes were specific; for example, "Reel Four: Eliminate all views of Manuela's face as she looks at Miss Von Bernburg in the classroom." The censors at least understood the power of the superimpositions! But, in a cruel irony of manipulation, contemporary critics reviewed the butchered film positively, using its now antiseptic contents to ridicule all who had been holding the film up as an example of "neuroticism . . . a celluloid *Well of Loneliness.*"

Ever since, most critics have been eager to harness its tale of schoolgirl struggle to an assumed "universal" of humankind's fight against fascism, rather than some perverse championing of inverted emotions. With hindsight, however, we can equally read the film as a celebration of and warning for its most sympathetic audience: the lesbian population in Germany in 1931. Like Manuela and Fräulein von Bernburg, the lesbian community was proud and outspoken, romantic and idealistic, equally opposed to bourgeois morality and outdated models of woman's proper place. The schoolgirls may have been stand-ins for the lesbian women they could grow up to become (if they passed through Erika Mann's famous "phase" intact). If the boarding school was chosen as a literary and cinematic motif because it was more socially acceptable than the grown-up reality, then how ironic that it is all that remains for us. We need more research into our history. We need more information on films of the period that have been almost entirely forgotten, like *Anna and Elizabeth* and *Different from the Others*.[31] We need to heed carefully Blanche Cook's warning not to judge the authors entirely by their texts, lest literary conventions of the time blind us to the unexpected. We need to recognize *Maedchen in Uniform* not only as a beloved fairy tale but also as a powerful expression of its own time — an individual record of a collective aspiration.

Maedchen in Uniform has been extremely influential for other writers and films as well as for lesbian viewers down to the present day. Colette herself wrote the text for the subtitles of the French release print.[32] None other than Hollywood mogul Irving Thalberg was a fan of the film. He quizzed Salka Viertel, as she worked on the screenplay of *Queen Christina*, as to whether she'd seen Sagan's film. "Does not Christina's affection for her lady-in-waiting indicate something like that?" he asked, and urged her "to keep it in mind," because "if handled with taste it would give us very interesting scenes."[33]

Stephen Spender came to New York in February 1982 to speak about "Experiencing the Cinema in Berlin."[34] The film he most vividly remembered was *Maedchen in Uniform,* which he and Christopher Isherwood had gone to see during their 1931–32 residence in Berlin. Spender recalled that they had slipped away from some other event to see what he described as "the most remarkable film we'd ever seen," due in large measure to the "extraordinary impression" made upon them by Hertha Thiele; indeed, he went so far as to describe the film as "full of extraordinary images based on this girl's face."

Of special relevance to us is Spender's description of a Berlin caught up in a cinematic fever inspired by the Soviet films that showed two or three times a week. "Unlike futurist art," said Spender, the Soviet and progressive Weimar films "really did make you think they would change your life." With a certain nostalgia for a time before everyone became "suspicious about photography," Spender pinpointed the importance for him of *Maedchen in Uniform* and the progressive films with which he identified it: "The great thing about photography in this period was that it seemed an expression of freedom." It is only in today's historical considerations that this film and others like it have come to be graded on formal qualities disassociated from any political meaning. Spender's remarks are useful in reminding today's viewers (and scholars) that Sagan was working at a time when "the camera was linked to the idea of a revolution that was still possible."

Like Spender, we can acknowledge what Colette, Thalberg, Viertel, and Garbo all seem to have known: that *Maedchen in Uniform* was a film about women's love for each other. And what Louise Brooks knew: that such love was no rarity in Weimar Berlin. And what Alex de Jonge knew: that it was no vice. And today we can also begin to consider what Jim Steakley knew: that there was a disturbing gap at the time between "personal" and "collective" liberation.

Maedchen in Uniform emerges from such a review of Weimar's lesbian subculture no longer as an anomaly, but as a survivor. The film assumes a new importance when seen not as a curiosity but rather as a clue, an archaeological relic pointing back to an obliterated people and pointing ahead, for us, to a much needed perspective on our current situation.

The first lesson of *Maedchen in Uniform* is that lesbianism has a much larger and finer history than we often suspect, that the film indicates as much, and that we need to do more work on reconstructing the image of lesbian culture that has been so painfully erased. The second lesson is that in looking backward and inward we cannot afford to stop looking forward and outward. The bells and bugles that sound periodically throughout the film, casting a prophetic pall upon the love of Manuela and Fräulein von Bernburg, are waiting just outside the gates for us as well. As I have suggested, the ending of the film can be interpreted as a warning to heed the forces mounting outside our narrow zones of victory and liberation. Such an interpretation, if it was perceived at the time, went unheeded by the film's lesbian audience in 1931. Today, the work in building a lesbian culture cannot afford to ignore the context of such labor in a society veering so strongly in the opposite direction.

Today, we must begin to consider the contemporary gap between "personal" (or lifestyle) freedoms and "collective" (or legal political) rights. We must begin to examine what the links and coalitions are, in our own time, among lesbian, gay male, and feminist organizations. We must learn strategy and remember that when the pre-Weimar misogynist, F. Eberhard, wanted to attack the women's movement, he accused the emancipated women of being lesbians and, therefore, depraved. The women's groups of the late Weimar period exhibited a distressing willingness to take such attacks to heart and try to accommodate themselves accordingly. Polite cooperation sapped the strength of the groups. Too late, many lesbians must have learned that patisseries do not grant asylum.

Struggle was postponed to a fatally late date due to false perceptions of homosexuality as a "private" issue that was being adequately handled and of lesbians and gay men as somehow more protected than others because of the history of social tolerance. The celebrants of the staircase must listen hard to the rallying cries outside the school and take heed. Today, we cannot afford to ignore history, nor to repeat it. Though lesbianism and feminism are certainly "revolutionary" (to quote the principal yet again), the history of Weimar politics demonstrates that they are not inherently so unless linked to a pragmatic political strategy and set of principles. In the eighties, our struggles for sexual freedom and gender flexibility must be integrated with the ongoing fights against economic injustices, racism, growing militarism, and all such forces that have an impact on every individual in our society. We have to do better.[35]

Opening night at the
Woods Hole Community
Film Society, June 1972,
with Florrie Darwin and I
selling tickets and $1
memberships. (photo:
Warner Wada)

Warner Wada, cofounder
of the Woods Hole Com-
munity Film Society, gazes
into the Cape Cod sun-
shine to dream up the next
poster. (photo: B. Ruby
Rich)

The Woods Hole Commu-
nity Film Society posters,
all drawn by Warner and
written by me, then hand-
inked by the whole group,
were collectors' items
coveted by Woods Hole
patrons. (photo: Warner
Wada)

Gunner and I pose in our Bonnie-and-Clyde guise for Margie Keller's camera, circa 1974. (photo: Marjorie Keller)

Laura Mulvey, her then-husband Peter Wollen, their son Chad, and their niece pose against a symbolically twisted tree in the Kew Gardens after the 1974 Edinburgh conference on the avant-garde. (photo: B. Ruby Rich)

Touring the Scottish highlands after the Edinburgh conference, Yvonne Rainer and Gunner Piotter puzzle over castle life and the history of the Clearances. (photo: B. Ruby Rich)

In Havana in 1978, the *Jump Cut* gang poses in front of ICAIC's film wall: John Hess, Julianne Burton, Julia Lesage, and I. Note my version of fellow-traveler chic. (photo: n.a.)

In the poster workshop in Havana where workers silkscreened film posters, my pals go crazy from the effort of having to narrow down their choices in a Leftie game of kids in a candy shop. Front and center: Cheryll Greene, Joan Braderman and Martella Wilson with the treasures of the moment. (photo: B. Ruby Rich)

Jorge Fraga, Myra Villasis, Gloria Martinez, and Joan Braderman debate the place of women in Cuban society. (photo: B. Ruby Rich)

The organizing committee of the Northwestern University "Feminar" pose in front of a typically august campus building just before the conference itself. Michelle Citron is front row center. Gina Marchetti is the first on the left, front row, and that's Jane Gaines in the third row, second from right. (photo: n.a.)

On the streets of New York City, "No More Nice Girls" demonstrated agit-prop style in the reproductive-rights march of March 1980. Gagged are Roz Baxandall on the far left and Yvonne Rainer second from left; I'm in profile in front of the "No Forced Labor" banner, and that's Joan Braderman on the far right in sunglasses. (photo: Jerry Kearns, from the collection of Joan Braderman)

Karola Gramann and Heide Schlüpmann, with a bit of their friend Monica Neuser camp it up in front of Munich's Cinema of Women theater. (photo: n.a.)

Hertha Thiele, beloved star of *Maedchen in Uniform,* interviewed by Karola Gramann and Heidi Schlüpmann during their interview with her for a special issue of *Frauen und Film* following a retrospective of her films at the Kommunales Kiro. On the back was a special inscription they had her write for me. (photo: Amadou Seitz)

Amy Taubin and Marjorie Keller at the Collective for Living Cinema's "Imaging Women" panel. (photo: Hali Breindel)

Same panel, this time with everyone: Sally Potter, Bette Gordon, Karen Kaye, Amy Taubin, and Margie Keller, in varying moods, mid-discussion. (photo: Hali Breindel)

In a more casual pose: Sally Potter with badminton racket, ready for a game, in some random field in the British country-side, soon after screening *The Gold Diggers* for the BFI production board. (photo: B. Ruby Rich)

Taking a break from the NAMAC conference at the Walker Art Center to mug for the camera: *Jump Cutter* Chuck Kleinhans, long-distance driver Martha Gever, organizer Bill Horrigan in a typically skeptical mode, and mischief-maker Lynn Blumenthal. None of them attended the performance of *The Threepenny Opera,* to my knowledge, though we were all Brechtophiles. (photo: B. Ruby Rich)

The author herself, holding the Canadian journal *Fuse* aloft and lecturing the NAMAC audience on the importance of an alternative press to champion oppositional work. Ah, brave old world that had such convictions in it! (photo: Walker Art Center)

Karola Gramann again, here outfitted as the executive director of the Oberhausen short film festival, a post for which she took her fashion responsibilities seriously. (photo: B. Ruby Rich)

Laura Mulvey, happily jurying the Oberhausen festival. In the foreground: Fernando Birri. Also on the jury was Philippine filmmaker Nick Deocampo; see us all jurying away in his film of this period, *Revolutions Like Refrains of a Song.* (photo: B. Ruby Rich)

Back in Cuba again with a different crowd. It's Havana 1986 this time: left to right, Lita Stantic, the Argentine producer of Maria Luisa Bemberg's *Miss Mary;* her daughter Alejandra, whose father had been one of Argentina's tragic "disappeared"; Sheila Whittaker of London's National Film Theater and London Film Festival fame; Julie Christie, star of *Miss Mary;* and yours truly. (photo: Nereida García-Ferraz)

Prologue.

Softball,

the Goddess,

and Lesbian

Film Culture

Filmmaker Michelle Citron was living in Grand Rapids, Michigan, when we both took part in the 1978 discussion of women's films and aesthetics organized by the *New German Critique* editors. By then I'd already heard about her from Julia Lesage and Chuck Kleinhans, who'd made her part of their farflung *Jump Cut* network. She'd done an early film about her sister's violin lessons as her Ph.D. thesis project and, though I didn't like the film very much, I liked Michelle herself immensely. Soon I was traveling from Chicago to Grand Rapids to visit her, my frequent trips facilitated by a tiny prop plane that took off from Chicago's wonderfully antiquated downtown airport, Miegs Field, and charged a mere $10 for standby passage. I experienced a thrill equal to any roller-coaster ride when flying low across Lake Michigan, the towers of downtown Chicago disappearing over the horizon and the relatively tiny town of Grand Rapids looming into view.

Grand Rapids in the late seventies was a hothouse of lesbian culture, a fact that must have appalled the Calvinist city fathers. The women's community there prided itself on having more women's softball teams per capita than any other city in the United States, a statistic that in those days (pre-Martina, pre-women's basketball teams) was a reliable indicator of lesbian presence. The presence was real enough to make Grand Rapids a stop on any tour of lesbian interest. Thus it was that in 1978 I boarded the prop plane to hear Adrienne Rich read from her as yet unpublished lesbian love poems in a sold-out church packed with what Jill Johnston had already dubbed the "lesbian nation."

This was cultural invention at its boiling point: the effect was somewhat like being present in the laboratory at the moment of some momentous scientific experiment that will change everything in its wake. Lesbians in the seventies were starved for cultural representations of emotional realities, and equally starved (then as now) for heroines, stars, and celebrities. For Adrienne Rich, a mainstream poet of considerable reputation, to have come out as a lesbian was major news; for her now to be touring the country with love poems written to her real-life, flesh-and-blood woman lover was an action downright stratospheric in its implications and effects. The audience was euphoric, transported into the kind of fervor nowadays reserved for concerts by k.d. lang, Melissa Etheridge, or Ani DiFranco. But, remember, this was poetry. And it was before all that.

Michelle fulfilled her promise to take me along to the faculty lunch with Adrienne Rich. It took all my courage to hand Rich the manuscript copy of my "Naming" piece, then in progress; when she wrote me later in praise of it, I was thrilled. I stayed in touch with her for several years after. Even though it became fashionable in the eighties and nineties for a younger generation of theorists to fault her — and particularly her essay on "Compulsory Heterosexuality and Lesbian Existence" — for desexualizing lesbianism, exactly the opposite was true of these texts and speeches in their original contexts. Rich injected both eros and politics into lesbian culture at a crucial moment and should be recognized for doing so.

In Grand Rapids, high and low culture were being conscripted into lesbian service. While softball and poetry prospered, goddess worship was also in full swing. Local artist Jerri Van Syoc, herself an escapee from a Moody Bible Institute upbringing, created a house packed with altars to Her Most Worshipful. One week, L.A. art critic Arlene Raven arrived in town with her then lover Cheryl, who liked driving around Grand Rapids with a machete under the seat for defense against any "weenies" that might hassle her. (Cheryl went on to appear in Jan Oxenberg's classic *A Comedy in Six Unnatural Acts* as the tuxedoed butch who picks up another butch on a date; later still, I heard she was working as a bodyguard and roadie for Lily Tomlin.)

Lesbian culture was full of appealing bravado. At an aesthetic level, though, a lot of work was needed: the "community," then as now, showed an alarming tendency to settle for crumbs as long as certain political requirements were met. It was in this environment that Michelle Citron started work on *Daughter Rite,* informed on the one hand by the community within which she functioned in Grand Rapids, on the other hand by discussions with *Jump Cut* and our Chicago circle. By the time the film was finished, she'd been offered a teaching position at Northwestern University; by the time it premiered at Edinburgh in 1978, she was packing her bags to leave Grand Rapids. The film fit perfectly the aim of the Edinburgh conference as expressed by its organizers ahead of time: to address "the dilemma facing feminist theory and practice: while attempting to build a new language of film, relevant and comprehensible, the very project of challenge and change restricts the audience reached." Michelle Citron and her film were taken up by *Time Out* conference reporter Mandy Merck and profiled in the festival coverage. She was the perfect Exhibit A for an event that claimed it wanted to "grasp the realities of this dilemma, the problems associated with political film-making on the one hand and particular problems facing women in film work (production and theory) on the other."

Throughout this period, Michelle and I tried to bridge the gap (Edinburgh's "dilemma") that we saw widening between feminist film theory, as it was developing in the academy, and the on-the-ground audiences and concerns of the feminist and lesbian communities within which we were moving. It was a time when the National Women's Studies Association conferences were major events. We went to one at Indiana University in Bloomington, stayed with Claudia Gorbman, and lectured on these new films that were beginning to integrate feminist theories into new aesthetic strategies. The room was packed; there really was a great hunger and enthusiasm on the part of women to follow new developments.

Then as now, the problem was a kind of class difference between town and gown. We kept trying to talk to both sides of the divide; the closer we could move them toward each other, the less isolated we ourselves would feel. For me, the split cut close to the bone. I was trying to figure out how to make a living as an itinerant critic and sometimes envied my academic friends their security. But my earlier decision still held: I needed to demonstrate that it was possible to think creatively and rigorously outside of the university. It was still a time of social movements and energy. Knowledge wasn't only for students. Why settle for communicating only in the classroom when everyone needed to be (re)educated?

Arlene Raven invited Michelle and me to edit a special section on feminist film for *Chrysalis,* the magazine she coedited out of the influential L.A. cultural-feminist institution, the Woman's Building. We were thrilled with the opportunity, figuring the work would be worth it: we could influence women to take independent film seriously and maybe we could drum up enough business for the filmmakers we cherished to keep them solvent. Alas, after we'd rounded up all our friends to produce a guide to current feminist film, *Chrysalis* ceased publication one issue before our section was scheduled to run. (Like other lesbian and feminist enterprises of the era, it was shut down less decisively by its chronic fiscal difficulties than by the breakup of its founding couples.)

Once Michelle was in Chicago and coming to *Jump Cut* meetings, we managed to collaborate again more productively on a Lesbian Special Section for *Jump Cut*. Organized with Julia Lesage (our designated non-lesbian collaborator) and my former student Edith Becker (today a film-maker), it was published in a double issue, number 24–25 in 1981.[1] This section marked the first consideration of lesbians in cinema to appear anywhere since Caroline Sheldon's pioneering essay, "Lesbians and Film," in the BFI monograph edited by Richard Dyer.[2] A special issue of *frauen und film* came out around the same time. Our introductory essay, crafted by the four of us over long afternoons of collective argument and editing, attempted to elaborate a theory of lesbian cinema, an oasis as we saw it in the desert of heteronormative feminist film theory. The very first sentence told the tale: "It sometimes seems to us that lesbianism is the hole in the heart of feminist film criticism."[3]

We were determined to redefine the rules of the film-analysis game. For instance, we asserted: "Gossip provides the unofficial unrecorded history of lesbian participation in film. . . . If oral history is the history of those denied control of the printed record, gossip is the history of those who cannot even speak in their own first-person voice."[4] We urged the use of subtextual readings to tease out lesbian meaning in film, called for the development of a lesbian film language similar to the writing strategies implemented by Wittig and others, and catalogued the representation of lesbians in a range of independent and commercial films. We devised a chart to illustrate how phobic Hollywood films were about showing even friendship between women, in contrast to the buddy movies then preva-lent. We even called for attention to be paid to aspects of lesbian life that hadn't yet made it into film. Our example? The bars! Little did we know that the nineties were coming. Chris Straayer, Chuck's student and a *Jump Cut* protégé, became the heir to these early inquiries.

Naturally, I reviewed *Daughter Rite* for the Chicago *Reader* when Michelle premiered it there; Linda Williams, then still living in Chicago, introduced the screening and delivered a short lecture to the audience. Our approaches were different but complementary. We decided to col-laborate on a piece for *Film Quarterly* that incorporated the gist of her lecture and my review, reworked to include more theoretical material. I still think of it as a model collaboration. Linda later borrowed part of our title for the *Re-Vision: Essays in Feminist Film Criticism* volume (but of course we'd borrowed it from Adrienne Rich in the first place).

Michelle went on to make another film mixing documentary and fiction elements, *What You Take for Granted,* concerning women in the labor force. She continues to teach at Northwestern, where in recent years she's served as chair of the film and television department and developed feature film scripts.

12.

The Right

of Re-Vision:

Michelle Citron's

Daughter Rite

(1979/1981)

Linda Williams, coauthor

The vast majority of literary and visual images of motherhood comes to us filtered through a collective or individual male consciousness. . . . We need to know what, out of that welter of image-making and thought-spinning, is worth salvaging, if only to understand better an idea so crucial in history, a condition which has been wrested from the mothers themselves to buttress the power of the fathers. — Adrienne Rich[1]

Perhaps our current responsibility lies in humanizing our own activities so that they will communicate more effectively with all women. Hopefully, we will aspire to more than women's art flooding the museum and gallery circuit (and screens). Perhaps a feminist art will only emerge when we become wholly responsible for our own work, for what becomes of it, who sees it, and who is nourished by it. For a feminist artist, whatever her style, the prime audience at this time is other women. — Lucy Lippard[2]

Within the form of the melodramatic Hollywood "woman's film," the mother-daughter relationship has been a favorite theme, from *Stella Dallas* to *Mildred Pierce* to *The Turning Point*. But even though they focus on the complex of emotions contained in the mother-daughter bond, such films are characterized by a hidden misogyny. Pretending to sanctify the institution of motherhood, they more often merely exalt its ideal while punishing and humiliating the individual women who participate in it.

At the heart of all these representations of the mother-daughter bond is a psychological truth that has been much discussed in recent writing.[3] It has perhaps been best described by Nancy Chodorow in *The Reproduction of Mothering*.[4] According to Chodorow, a son must ultimately repress or deny his original attachment to and identification with the mother's body to take on a more abstract and less primally connected identification with the father. But a daughter undergoes no such shift in gender identification; her primary identification with the mother remains with her always. This "oedipal asymmetry" causes the daughter to continue to experience herself as unseparated, continuous with others, making it difficult for the daughter to separate off from her mother to claim her own life. It is not surprising then that so much melodrama has centered on the contradiction of an idealized mother love, which, when actually made into a component of an ongoing relationship, turns into a smothering influence that the daughter seeks to escape (as in *Now Voyager*).

The mother fares no better than the daughter in Hollywood's unraveling of this mother-love knot. The mother usually must learn to renounce her love for her daughter to suffer nobly for a supposedly higher good: the daughter's increased social status achieved through marriage (*Stella Dallas*) or even the daughter's entrance into a career (*The Turning Point*). Thus, narrative resolution usually occurs through the mother's sacrifice — a sacrifice that unhappily perpetuates a patriarchal definition of motherhood *as* sacrifice.

Given these problems, what are the alternatives for a radical feminist filmmaker who chooses to represent this most crucial relationship? In the past, the most popular format has been the cinema verité documentary. But despite its efficacy as record, testimony, and organizing wedge, the documentary form has begun to be reexamined by critics skeptical of its neutrality. The use of the documentary as a form of social evidence has rested on the misconception that film can be equated with "truth." This assumed truth is negotiated through an unspoken contract with the spectator, necessitating both an acceptance of the film's subjects as real persons and of the film's narrative as a spontaneous recording of a candid situation. *Daughter Rite*, Michelle Citron's film about mothers and daughters, avoids misleading notions of truth by, first of all, subverting the audience's expectation of the documentary form. This subversion overcomes the limitations of identification and culminates in analysis. The filmmaker's central problem was how to make a film about relations between women within the family without producing either a first-person confessional film or a fictional portrait of a representative family. By reconstructing and juxtaposing four different forms (cinema verité, soap opera melodrama, home movies, journals), Citron challenges identification itself—its false and easy notions of unity and truth.

Instead of representing a single mother and daughter in a single representational mode, *Daughter Rite* represents a plurality of interwoven subjective approaches to two different mothers in a variety of modes. Significantly, neither mother is directly represented in any of the film's sections; they appear to us only in the form of their daughters' desires, angers, and memories of them. Thus, Citron replaces conventional and unitary "representation of" with multiple, overlapping, and contradictory "relations to." All of these "relations to" are characterized by very specific problems of identification with the mother that radically affected each daughter's sense of self.

The film opens with several sequences of home-movie footage: flickering 8mm shots of a mother and two daughters at various stages of mother-and-girlhood, smiling and waving at the camera in typical poses of coy and narcissistic femininity. In an early scene, the mother and daughters ride a swan boat. The mother sits in the middle, a protective arm around each daughter, smoothing the hair of one, leading both in cheerful waves at the camera.

These movies have been taken, as are most home movies, by a father-cameraman who is never seen. Nothing could seem more true to life, more acceptable as unmediated reality, than a family's home movies. Yet by her techniques of rephotography, slowing down and repeating actions and gestures, Citron questions the neutrality of even this form of movie making, uncovering a more problematic picture of family life than these domestic scenes of family outings might suggest. Just as feminist historians have called attention to the dilemma of searching out women within written history, which itself is patriarchal, so Citron calls attention to a similarly patriarchal vision of domestic life captured in home movies.

Where the father's camera portrays the mother as a happy Mother Goose, instinctively leading her flock to fulfill their natural destinies as daughters, wives, and mothers, "the daughter's" slow-motion re-editing of these haunting happy memories of the family album reveals a process of socialization that is neither very natural nor very happy. Optical step-frame printing repeats and slows the telling gestures with which the mother teaches her daughters their roles as proper young ladies. Repetition renders the gesture unnatural, constraining, obsessive.

In a striking scene that begins the film, one of the daughters repeatedly races with an egg balanced precariously on a spoon held in her mouth to her mother at the far end of a field. As the film continues, we begin to understand that it is precisely the carrying of this egg—symbol of the daughters' role as the bearer of future generations and of the culture that nurtures them—that is at issue in this film.

Adrienne Rich has written that patriarchal culture depends on the mother to act as a conservative influence "imprinting future adults with patterned values even when the mother-child relationship might seem most individual and private."[5] By making us aware of the ritual nature of this imprinting, the home-movie sections of *Daughter Rite* claim the daughter's right to wrest the image of the mother away from the "power of the father," to filter it back through her own consciousness. A first step in this refiltering has thus been the dismantling of the father's image of both mother and daughter in order to discover the other possibilities that the patriarchal image has long masked. Inevitably, such a dismantling affects the daughter's own identification with images and actions X-rayed on screen, making the acceptance of these previously "natural" truths now problematic.

Accompanying the home-movie images from the past, in counterpoint to them, is the first-person voice of one of the daughters, now an adult filmmaker, speaking as if to a film diary of the troubled, guilt-ridden, ongoing relationship with her mother. Thus, past images of childhood combine with a present voice of adulthood that probes the confusing mixture of love, hate, and guilt so typical of our adult relationship with our mothers.

The daughter's voice begins with the impetus for the film itself: her twenty-eighth birthday and the realization that she herself had been born when her mother was twenty-eight. As we see the egg race in the home movies, the daughter confesses her uneasiness at not following in her mother's footsteps: she is neither married nor having a child. The fear that she will not be like her mother (and will not carry on that egg) is followed in succeeding sections of voice-over by its even more terrifying opposite: the matrophobic fear of, in fact, "becoming" the mother.[6]

Inevitably, the daughter's attempt to claim her own life involves the expression of anger, even hatred, toward the mother. Force is necessary to break through the patriarchal definitions of womanhood that the mother implicitly foists upon the daughter. Unlike the anger of indirect misogyny common in the many so-called woman's films, the daughter's anger is more direct and positive, a necessary exorcism of emotions that have poisoned the daughter's own view of herself. As she explains, "I hate my mother and, in hating her, hate myself."

Anger is equally manifest, though more oblique, in the sections that alternate with the home-movie images and diary-style voice-over. Two women sit, ill at ease in front of the camera. The scene is a familiar one in recent documentary: the "common woman" consenting to share her experiences with a film crew, to communicate with other women. The camera moves in closer, rather clumsily, for effect as the emotional register requires. When the film next returns to the two sisters, they are again facing the camera, speaking this time about their childhood: how they kept diaries, how their mother read those diaries, to what extent their mother denied them privacy to exert her own power over their lives.

It is only when the film returns for the third time to the domestic locus of the two sisters, who have moved from the dining room into the kitchen, that a shift in the style of representation moves the viewer to a shift in awareness. In the kitchen, the sisters, for the first time, ignore the camera entirely: there is no face-front address, nor any particular testimony. Instead, the sisters interact with each other, revealing through conversation and gesture a range of character and emotion (including humor) inaccessible in the more formal interview format. It is this very display of character that signals the artifice that has underlain the sisters' scenes from the start. No cinema verité documentary could ever capture this scene of intimacy, this sudden ease in front of the camera. The scenes have been acted all along: these women, not sisters at all, are in fact actresses engaged in a convincing replica of documentary behavior. And to complicate matters even further, these are not the same sisters who appear as children in the home-movie sections.

Nor, as it turns out, can the voice of the narrator speaking over the home movies be linked to either of the sisters in the apparent documentary footage. Subtle discrepancies in references to the two mothers force us eventually to grasp that what is at issue here is not an individual mother but a synthesis of a number of different daughters' attitudes toward their mothers and a number of different, but typical, experiences of the middle-aged, divorced mother who finds herself at loose ends with all her family gone. This synthesis allows for variations of attitude (ranging from anger to sympathy), tone (ranging from maudlin melodrama to genuine lyricism), and socioeconomic situation. But even within these latter scenes there is an alternation of modes: from quasi-verité to staged fiction. In the second half of the film, these staged scenes come more and more to resemble the stuff of soap opera.

Once the audience has been able to adjust successfully to the film's mixed modes and synthetic approach to character, Citron is able to return to the earlier verité style with stunning effect. The younger sister faces the camera and recounts a chilling tale of incestuous rape. Now the viewer is forced into a contradictory series of reactions: sympathy for the character, whether real-life or constructed; respect for the actress's performance, so true to life; anger at the filmmaker's exposure of this intimate moment, followed by a quick save as its artificiality is recalled. In other words, the film's mixed-mode form of presentation profoundly criticizes the very form in use without sacrificing the emotional connection binding the viewer to its workings. What seemed at the film's start to be a one-dimensional documentary truth has become, by its end, a more complex rendering of truths through these shifts to a more obviously manipulated, fictional style of representation.

Although the tone of the adult sisters' scenes ranges from gossipy anecdote to intense emotion, these scenes are in strong contrast to the voice-over that accompanies the home-movie sections. The filmmaker-daughter's voice has a reflective, often lyrical, tone. Her recollections of her mother freely mix specific events from the recent past with more obscure accounts of dreams. Combined with the flickering images of the already dreamlike slow-motion of the home movies, this disembodied, comparatively detached voice often achieves a more sympathetic understanding of the mother. Perhaps it is due to its dreamlike locus that such a sympathy can be expressed, for on the more realistic bedrock of the sister scenes, daily behavior still lags far behind any such fantasy resolution.

Dreams are used repeatedly by the voice of the filmmaker as one way of breaking out of the repetitive cycle in which the two sisters seem to remain caught. In this cycle, the mother infantilizes the daughter until such time as the daughter can infantilize her in turn. The crippling effects of this infantilization are stressed in a scene in which one of the sisters tells how her mother's babying of her during her own birth-giving sapped her strength. Only when her mother left the room could she regain it.

The filmmaker, on the other hand, uses her dreams to imagine a more mysterious and powerful — though not always beneficent — mother. In the final episode of the film, her dream recounts the story of a mother who has and can give amazing strength, but whose strength is employed to strangely destructive ends. In this dream, the mother helps burn the filmmaker's sister, who is dying of cancer of the jaw and has asked to be set on fire. The dream account tells how the mother takes control, burning and then burying the youngest daughter while the older sister (the filmmaker) stands in awe and appreciation of the herculean task. If this dream offers no solution to the actual relations of mother and daughter, it at least avoids the reductive infantilization of the sister scenes, offering an appreciation of the mother's power to give and take life.

Another of the filmmaker's dreams affords a more positive contrast to the sisters' view of the mother. The younger sister's cinema verité account of her rape by her stepfather is preceded by the filmmaker's dream of an attempt by both her mother and grandmother to get her to accept an injection from a giant needle, "for the good of mankind." In both the dream of the injection and the "reality" of the rape, the mother emerges as the final culprit, tacitly acknowledging her complicity with the power of the father that rapes her daughter in one instance, wielding the phallic needle, symbol of that power, in the next. Here we see most forcefully the mother's role as "imprinter" of patriarchy. But the narrator's dream contains an obvious wish-fulfillment: the power of the daughter to refuse the needle and thus to refuse patriarchy.

As we have seen, this is the daughter's film. The girl who rode the swan boat in the home movies has grown up and taken over from Dad: now it is she who gets to peer through the lens, this time with X-ray eyes, to visualize the family. Toward the close of the film, in the home-movie sections, there are many shots of Mom alone, looking vaguely heroic, extending her arm out over an expanse of water. This near noble portrait, along with the dreams of reconciliation, perhaps constitute an acknowledgment of the other film, the one that could match with positives all the negatives of this film: the mother's film, of course, which no daughter could ever make, but which could speak the flip side of all we have heard as alternative readings of identical actions.

As it is, *Daughter Rite* reflects the generational imperialism whereby a decade of daughters have frequently sought to remake our mothers in our own renovated image. By summing up the emotional quandaries of the moment, Citron has at least opened the way to dialogue. In fact, after the last image fades and the screen goes blank, a voice speaks as though out of the collective memory. It is the voice of the mother, speaking as she might in her daughter's fantasy, in fact taken from a Deena Metzger story about a mother reading her daughter's writing: "Why do you have to say all this?" she asks. For an answer, only the credits appear.

Daughter Rite is an important film for feminists due to the fundamentally new way in which Citron has chosen to rework existing forms. The critique from within of the cinema verité format accomplishes a dual task. On the one hand, Citron is able to criticize its limitations, showing that cinema cannot deliver up the Truth, that character identification may lead only to individualized pathos, that the political is not merely the personal, nor the personal only the private. Yet, at the same time, the film functions to redeem documentary, in that its form is accessible, related to the lives of women, a meaningful tradition and a still powerful taproot into the emotions as well as the intellects of viewers. By combining the mock-documentary with the introspective voice of narration that accompanies the home movies, Citron can validate the personal subjective documentary with qualification; rather than making it the only voice, she provides a multiple approach to the truths of mothers and daughters. And by replacing the usual individual with a synthetic character (whose experiences, in fact, were scripted out of materials derived from some forty interviews with mothers and daughters), Citron is able to break the traditional documentary dependence on the isolated life and extend the individual experience into the social sphere.

In her use of soap opera, home movies, and diary or journal, Citron employs three familiar "domestic" forms, explicitly reviewing the home movies, while the soap opera form is implicitly critiqued by the play-off with cinema verité that disrupts the credibility of both.[7] These disruptions inevitably also bring into question the normally authoritative narrative voice; we begin to subject the narrator-filmmaker to the same kind of distanced critique applied to her characters.

Even more important, because *Daughter Rite* is self-explanatory in its criticisms and priorities, it represents a significant alternative to films that base their forms of subversion on systems of reference with which most viewers are not familiar. Because the documentaries taken as the film's starting point are a mutual resource for both filmmaker and audience, and because soap operas have already entered the home (and women's consciousness) through television's inclusion in the daily rituals of domestic maintenance, Citron's work can offer a bridge of communication between feminist artists and the larger community of women.[8]

Over the past decade, there has been a dearth of work by filmmakers who are both committed to the women's community as an audience and yet equally influenced by the developing theory of feminist critics. By daring to enter into the seeming limbo, Michelle Citron moves beyond the previously acknowledged boundaries of the positive "image" of strong female role models and the avant-garde film's negative lament of women's inscription within patriarchal language. Because her film was made with a woman's movement audience in mind, sharing a common concern with current issues of mother-daughter relations, and because it annexes popular forms by both reviewing and criticizing them, *Daughter Rite* succeeds in opening up a major new direction for feminist filmmaking.

Prologue.

The Allure

of Alchemy

The screening of *Thriller* at Edinburgh in 1979 catapulted Sally Potter into celebrity as the film acquired a certain cult status as state-of-the-art filmmaking that pointed to new progressive feminist strategies. Now she had begun working with two co-conspirators: her longtime performance collaborator, Rose English, who appeared briefly as Musetta in the film, and Lindsay Cooper, the New Music composer and ex–Henry Cow musician, her partner at the time. Marshaling their resources from the worlds of theater, music, and film, the three had scripted a new feature-length film project. If there was anything better than the script itself, it was that trio, all high spirits and wit and adventure, making art out of their energetic responses to life's events and collective fantasies. While it germinated, awaiting a decision from the British Film Institute's production unit, Sally began to tour with *Thriller*. By then I was teaching a class in women's films and feminist theory at the School of the Art Institute of Chicago, and offered her a place to stay and a speaking gig at the school.

I had closely followed Sally's career since our chance meeting back in Edinburgh in 1976 and always regretted not being in London for her fabled live performances with Rose English and Jacky Lansley. One of the most famous of the English/Potter productions, "Berlin," was a series of four consecutive performances in 1976 with varying locations to which the audience traveled at irregularly timed intervals. It had inventive mise-en-scène and background details, such as the "chorus line" of tuxedoed men who appeared on the ground floor of the house where the performance began; a week later, they were on skates in the municipal ice skating rink to which the production had moved; one night later, they were rediscovered, dripping wet atop a diving board, this time at a public swimming pool; finally, a week later, they were back in the original flat for the finale, this time standing on the mantlepiece. In the foreground, throughout, were the central protagonists: two women, one in a crinoline of leaves and the other in a black dress, their scenes accessorized with babies, cradles, candles, and talk. Precinematic, to be sure, but wonderfully prophetic and suggestive of things to come.

Sally Potter's lecture at the School of the Art Institute may not have been quite as formally conceived or presented, but it caused a moderate sensation nonetheless — due to the impact of a film as aesthetically sophisticated as *Thriller* on an audience of art school women, but equally due to the unexpected presence in the audience of Stan Brakhage. A lecture version of a duel followed the screening as Brakhage sought to guard the fortress of the avant-garde against this interloper whose film was so clearly a challenge to everything he and his films represented. How I wish a tape recorder or camera had been present that day, but all I can remember is one exchange about her subject matter. "Do you really think that poor people will see your movie and be changed by it?" he asked incredulously, taking this to be the intent of the film. I recall Potter's careful deconstruction of his question, phrase by phrase ("Let's take the word 'poor,' for instance") and the way his vociferous interventions finally dwindled into silence.

Thriller showed publicly in Chicago that same week in a series at Chicago Filmmakers, and I wrote the review that follows for the Chicago *Reader*. It was a wonderful time to be writing, as I was regularly experiencing moments of euphoria and infatuation in the dark, eager for the movies that suddenly were being made. Distribution of this work was a different matter, though, and Potter's own political and cultural work back in London at the time made such decisions particularly strategic. To my mind, the best distributor at that time in the United States was a little company that went by the name of Serious Business. It had been founded by Freude, formerly Freude Bartlett, ex-wife of filmmaker Scott Bartlett and a filmmaker in her own right. She was gutsy and outspoken and flamboyant, a veteran of the early counterculture days of underground movies and an indefatigable champion of women's work. Her one-woman company specialized in women's films and animation. Freude saw *Thriller* as the future of feminist filmmaking.

Sally agreed to place the film with Serious Business instead of with a British film distribution package assembled by the Museum of Modern Art, hoping that this would ensure its distribution beyond the museum/academic context to a broader range of women. My review became part of the press packet, and I began to use excerpts from the film in my continuous round of lectures and conferences. I recall this history for a purpose. Too often, audiences are underestimated. It is assumed that certain kinds of film are too difficult for the uninitiated to fathom. This snobbery is an unfortunate byproduct of cineaste culture. But it's wrong in virtually all of its assumptions. I have always believed that audiences can respond with passion to a wide range of films if only the critics would do the necessary job of educating and preparing them for what they will see. And if only the distributors get the films out to a wide enough public. Though *Thriller* was a case of that opinion put to the test and victorious, almost any of the essays in this volume could be seen as signing on to the same mandate — and many films could benefit from more optimistic expectations of their ability to connect with audiences.

For Serious Business itself, the experiment was ultimately less successful. *Thriller* did well, but the company suffered from a syndrome that Freude identified without hesitation: the difficulty of doing business when "you always have to create the market first before you can sell to it." The educational work required made the business, finally, unprofitable. Similar problems afflicted Iris Films, founded by Elizabeth Stevens and cinematographer Frances Reid; a pioneering lesbian film distribution company, it was key to a lot of grassroots organizing and documentary exhibition. Today much of the work of those early companies is carried on by the nonprofit but entrepreneurial Women Make Movies, which distributes Potter's early work as well as the work of the generations of women filmmakers that preceded and followed her.

In April 1981, Sally Potter came to New York to show *Thriller* and to participate in Towards a Living Cinema: Issues in Contemporary Film, a symposium organized by the Collective for Living Cinema. Her panel, "Imaging of Women," included Bette Gordon, Karyn Kay, Marjorie Keller, and Amy Taubin. Potter announced that *Thriller* was meant to provide "an image for, homage to, the contradictions within the women's movement" and that it was a statement "against the pessimism of depoliticized psychoanalysis." She went on to offer it up as a sort of manifesto: "It's about the pleasure of political analysis, the thrills of moving forward into feminism as a revolutionary movement, the possibility of unity between women based on difference and ultimate unity between the interests of different oppressed groups toward the overthrow of capitalism towards a new order, all in the spirit of joy." Her intentions and strategies were very different from either Keller's lyricism or Gordon's downtown formalism. I knew and liked them all, and was fascinated at seeing these differences played out on stage.

The panel proceedings were transcribed and published in *No Rose,* volume 3, a slight volume edited by then-director of the Collective, Renee Shafransky, better known today for her long collaboration with ex-husband Spaulding Grey. Besides its archival value, the volume held a surprise: a postscript by Marjorie Keller that sought to clarify and amplify her original statements and then went on to attack unnamed feminists (possibly including me) as well as Kay and Gordon and the kinds of films they made. The volume concluded with their outraged response. Back home in London, Potter didn't participate in these postpanel renegotiations, so her statements were all verbatim from her extemporaneous speech. The panel had been fractious even when it unfolded, composed of participants from radically different traditions of filmmaking who were uniformly uncomfortable at combining into any perceived unity in public, let alone any representative-of-feminist-cinema body. Taubin even admitted that someone had made a suggestion simply to send slides of themselves with an accompanying audiotape and thereby elude all physical association with the event.

The symposium wasn't the only draw that had brought Potter to New York. Music was the other. In her other role as singer, she and Lindsay Cooper were performing as part of a short-lived musical group called the Marx Brothers at Franklin Furnace. It was part of a festival where Rose was presenting a hilarious solo performance. This emphasis on music and self-conscious repartee would go on to dictate the style of *The Gold Diggers,* the film that the British Film Institute would soon announce its decision to fund. Filmed in Iceland in 35mm in the dead of winter with an all-female crew that included Babette Mangolte as cinematographer, it was immediately notorious for Potter's coup in convincing actress Julie Christie to costar opposite Colette Laffont (and for the same paltry salary as the rest of the cast and crew).

Centered on two characters named Ruby and Celeste, in homage to the celestial ruby prized by alchemists, *The Gold Diggers* tracked the effort of one woman (Laffont) to decode via computer a nefarious conspiracy involving economic sabotage enacted by a suspicious cadre of men. Her mission, apart from halting their plot, was to free another woman (Christie) who was held captive and entranced within a mysterious maze of stage performances, ocean liners, and flashbacks to her own emotional traumas.

I traveled to London in the fall of 1982 on assignment for *American Film* magazine, then the major U.S. mainstream film magazine, to report on the start-up of a brand-new television station called Channel Four. I had arranged the trip to coincide with a private screening of the rough cut of *Gold* (as it was then called) that Sally had scheduled for the British Film Institute. It would be the BFI's first view of the film in nearly finished form. When I arrived, she was behind schedule and nervous. Every day I'd journey around London interviewing filmmakers, bureaucrats, and commissioning editors, while Sally locked herself in the editing room with Rose, her assistant editor, frantically working against the clock to get the film ready for the screening.

When the day finally came, it was a disaster. This was a time when the BFI had decided to move from backing short avant-garde films with little market possibility to backing feature films. Peter Greenaway's *Draughtsman's Contract* had just signaled the shift and scored a substantial success at home and abroad. But *Gold* was no *Draughtsman's Contract*. It was a deeply feminist film, for one thing. It was black and white, not color. Its commitment to narrative was minor. And its emotional plunge into the very essence of female being was nothing to be taken lightly. The two films could not have been more different, nor the two filmmakers; as Sally toiled with dwindling cash in the editing room, Greenaway was busy doing a film portrait of Prince Charles.

I thought that *Gold* was emotionally exhilarating and visually and musically brilliant (I still play the soundtrack album); the BFI panel found it problematic, difficult, "not ready." They were all men. Their verdict stuck, sending Sally back into the editing room for many more months. I flew home and filed my story, writing: "With a black-and-white epic timelessness, *Gold* combines the style of Fritz Lang's *Metropolis* with that of Jacques Rivette's *Paris Belongs to Us* . . . and a tone of conspiracy that owes as much to the paranoia of *film noir* as it does to the whimsy of *Alice in Wonderland*."

Alongside my production report I also filed an interview with Julie Christie, who at that time was exercising a near total ban on interviews; she made an exception for me in order to support Sally and the film project. Asked what it was like to work with an all-woman crew, she was unequivocal: "I kept thinking, I'm in heaven." Asked about her earlier film work, which scenes of trauma in *Gold* seemed to invoke, she replied: "I'm pretty amnesiac. I can't really remember very much. I was a very frightened person, allowing other people to control my destiny. I was lucky to have come out of it as I have. It doesn't always work that way." Asked about the likelihood of many films by women being put into production, she was pessimistic: "There's no doubt that women's consciousness is different from men's. Maybe the men just cannot see what is being offered to them by women as very interesting." Christie's words turned out to be prophetic.

When *The Gold Diggers* finally debuted in its finished form, a gender divide pervaded. Sheila Whittaker, newly installed as programmer of the National Film Theatre, dedicated a whole season to the film and its influences. The result? A London press corps that turned positively rabid, savaging Sally and the film. The male critics went ballistic over the perceived hubris of some, ugh, woman presuming to make a feature film at all. How dare she shoot in 35mm? And how dare she put an actress as sexually sacred to them as Christie into an arty, obliquely narrative exploration of ideas that, to them, smelled antimale and anticapitalist. It didn't help that the film performed an elegant critique of mainstream movie making. Finally, most of them hated the BFI's history of production financing anyway and considered the upstart Channel Four, which had put up some of the money, equally suspect. *The Gold Diggers* was a convenient target for all their gripes. If they could turn the premiere into a referendum on the BFI and Channel Four and upstart women, all rolled into one, then their ideological chores for the season would be done. The option was irresistible (not that they cared to resist) and *The Gold Diggers* was the made-to-order scapegoat. They demolished it.

When *The Gold Diggers* finally got a limited release in the United States, I praised it as "one of the most original films to emerge from Britain this decade . . . an adventure movie turned inside out, an antimusical." I wrote that Potter had given us "a black and white laboratory of ideas for the future of cinema." But the British damage was already done. Though *The Gold Diggers* today remains a landmark for its consideration of money and commerce, fame and femininity, and the powerful bonds between women, it's a largely unseen landmark. Potter was ahead of her time and, like so many women directors in film history, she was punished for her vision. Blackballed after one try, she couldn't find backing for her next film, which she wanted to base on a novel by Virginia Woolf.

The rest of this history is happier. Potter fought back by surviving. She went on a BFI-organized trip to the Soviet Union with Derek Jarman and a few other British filmmakers. She met Tilda Swinton. She began writing the script. And rewriting it. She returned to singing and toured the improvisational music circuit. She made a short film and a couple of documentaries for Channel Four. She attracted the support of Michael Powell and Thelma Schoonmaker. She met her future producer, Christopher Sheppard. She went back to the Soviet Union to do a documentary on women filmmakers there. She and Tilda Swinton, in between stumping for film financing, went to Tblisi, Georgia, for the founding meeting of KIWI, a new international organization of Soviet women filmmakers. They'd been invited by Lana Gogoberidze, a wonderful Georgian director whom I'd met at a film festival in Havana in 1986 and who had told me about this great new epoch the USSR had entered: it was called "perestroika." A year later, with Sally and Tilda and Lana all coincidentally passing through town at once, I organized an open forum in New York to drum up support for KIWI and increase international contacts for the Soviet women filmmakers just emerging from years of isolation.

Eventually, of course, Sally Potter did manage to raise the money (some of it, incidentally, from Soviet funds) to make her movie. *Orlando* was an international success, critically and financially, a vindication of the artistic vision she'd harbored for a decade. And enough of a success to win her the chance to make another film, *The Tango Lesson,* featuring Potter this time not only as director and screenwriter but as star, too. But how many films were lost in those lean years? And how many women directors have been lost to us completely, the victims of inhospitable circumstances?

13.

Femicide

Investigation:

Thriller

(1980)

T hriller is the first feminist murder mystery. Working within a tradition defined by such filmmakers as Maya Deren and Yvonne Rainer, Sally Potter synthesizes fantasy, wit, and intellectual rigor into a fresh, startling work. Like Deren and Rainer, Potter began as a performer; like them, she has retained a sense of timing, of entertainment, and of the audience (she still performs, in fact, as a member of the Feminist Improvising Group of musicians).

A most unlikely murder mystery, *Thriller* is based on the Puccini opera *La Bohème*. Yet by its example, *Thriller* points to the vast quantity of female-murdered mysteries waiting for filmmakers with the imagination to decode them. The film opens with the screen black and the timeless music of *La Bohème* filling the space. The first image is that of a contemporary woman laughing hysterically in a bare, unfurnished space, like an attic or garret. The dissolve to a period production of *La Bohème* documented by a still photograph suggests that the bare space is the world of the opera stripped of its props and fantasies, reduced to its basics. It is, in other words, the scene of the crime; in keeping with this realization, the music of *La Bohème* is interrupted by shrill, anxious strains from the *Psycho* shower scene. Again, there are still shots of the woman, her leg, her eye gazing into a mirror. In a heavily accented voice, she begins to speak, while she stares into the mirror as into a reverie, searching for clues, trying to discover what really occurred at that moment of death so many years before. This woman, with her broken English and close-cropped hair and obviously contemporary appearance, is Mimi. Here in the rough, unfinished space of the film, she inhabits the terrain of creation. Not the original Creation, not God's. Rather, she is stalking the hardly less idealized specter of the male artist and excavating the hardly less mythologized process by which art is created.

For those not knowledgeable in opera matters, it comes as some relief when Potter breaks with the hallowed codes of avant-garde ambiguities to tell straight out the "story" of this opera in four acts. Set in Paris in 1830, *La Bohème* describes the bohemian life of four poor artists sharing a studio. The central theme is the love affair between one of the artists, Rodolpho, and a poor seamstress, Mimi, who lives in the same building and dies of consumption at the finale. Musetta, the "bad girl" with whom the other artists consort, brings the dying Mimi back to Rodolpho for the last act. Potter economically suggests the terms of the story through the use of stills from various lavish productions of the opera; her focus is on meaning rather than spectacle. "Can these be the facts?" muses the resurrected Mimi of the film. "Was that the story of my life? Can this be the story of my death?" As the strains of *Psycho* return, Mimi settles in front of the mirror to await a clue. This simple scene of the woman, archetypically staring into a mirror in a room stripped of all elaboration, is repeated at intervals throughout the film. It has all the power of a true symbol, evocative and transcendent. Maya Deren's dangerous search for identity in *Meshes of the Afternoon* comes immediately to mind, as does *Psycho's* ending, with its resolution of false identity and its exposure of the male appropriation of female identity for his own ends. Again and again, Mimi searches the mirror, as Potter moves through the structure of a suspense movie, enlivening her own theoretical search with all the magic and intensity of a seance.

For a long time in feminist filmmaking and film criticism, there has been an apparent rift between works concerned with the representation of women in film and those concerned with the oppression of women in actual society. *Thriller* ingeniously connects the two issues; it shows how smoothly male artists manipulating woman's image naturalize and obscure the manipulation in women's lives. As a result, *Thriller* goes farther than many feminist films. It not only reclaims the past, not only rereads the official history in terms of the present, but also dares to imagine the future. Many avant-garde films dealing with feminist themes have involved deconstruction — the dismantling of oppressive cinematic machinery. *Thriller* begins the work of *reconstruction* in which the personae and materials that once were invisible, omitted, or unspoken become inevitable and get to play out their own evolution on the screen.

The murder suspense story is an appropriate structure. Mimi sifts through the opera's data (people, places, suspicious events, crucial scenes), much as a private eye might in the early stages of a murder investigation. Each retelling of *La Bohème* unearths different sets of implications and clues. Other films have used repetition. In *Celine and Julie Go Boating,* for instance, the heroines return again and again to a suspicious fiction in an attempt to find clues and influence the outcome. Though their awareness progresses, the fiction remains relatively unchanged. In *Thriller,* however, the locus of concern shifts again and again as different perspectives are brought to bear upon it. This is because Potter insists on Mimi's own consciousness and point of view as the only guiding force. The Mimi of the opera is a working-class woman; the Mimi of the film (Colette Laffont) is a foreigner, in keeping with Potter's shift to an English location, and furthermore, she is Black. Her point of view, therefore, can only expose the opera's overwhelming deceptions in dealing with the material of her life. It is not necessary for Mimi to be an exceptional woman for her to achieve a correct analysis of the opera. On the contrary, this analysis is the inevitable consequence of Potter's staged meeting between the "real" Mimi and the opera's. By presenting such a dialectic, Potter radicalizes the previous boundaries of avant-garde art: she assumes the genius of her public.

Meanwhile, back in the attic, Mimi goes over and over the opera as Potter offers various visualizations of her memory and desires. More and more daring questions are asked. Why is it the men who are the heroes? What if Mimi had been the hero? The sight of Mimi whirling a man in a tutu over her head provides the hilarious answer. What if Musetta had been the one to die instead of Mimi? Mimi's increasingly aware voice provides the answer: that wouldn't have been a tragedy, because Musetta was a "bad" girl. Finally, the inevitable question floats to the surface of reminiscence like a code word on a Ouija board: "What if I hadn't died?" Archive photographs of old English needle-women appear on the screen, suggesting the hard life and crowded domestic working conditions of the profession. It is the stuff of which realist novels might be made, or sociological exposés, but not an opera. No, not suitable at all for an opera.

Here, *Thriller* reaches the heart of its condemnation of the opera as a genre and of the bourgeois male artist as an innocent figure. Potter dares to imagine murder in its broadest sense. If the Ford Motor Company can be tried for death-by-Pinto, as it just was, then she can try the artist for death-by-opera.

Motivation? Desire to be a hero. Murder weapon? An opera. Victim? Hundreds of women characters throughout history, plus the consciousness of millions of women subjected to the fiction. Murderer? In this case, one Puccini. Sentence? Fame, immortality, and royalties for his heirs.

However, like any good suspense story, *Thriller* does not rest its case with the resolution of the crime. True, the film follows the lines of suspense-suspicion-solution for much of its forty-five-minute course. Different lines of analysis are pursued. All the clues are amassed, and when the decoding takes place, plot lines and character motivations fall into line as magically as the dénouement of a traditional stateroom scene in a detective book. (To make the analogy with detection even closer, Potter has restricted herself for most of the film to still photographs and slowed-down step-printed actions, giving the visual effect of a microscopic examination of the action.) But at the end of a traditional murder mystery, the victorious private eye might ask the rescued heroine what she plans to do next. In *Dial M for Murder,* for instance, the would-be murderer (the husband) is packed off to jail, leaving the rescued damsel to live on in the arms of her half-hero suitor. In *Klute,* the private eye gets the girl. In any number of film noir resolutions, order is restored either through the death of the woman or through her salvation in the arms of the detective, standing in for the director and his male audience. How, then, is Potter able to end her film in the thriller mode? For a clue, there's the mirror.

Throughout *Thriller,* Mimi's gaze into the mirror has been accompanied by two sets of apparitions, one inside the mirror and the other inside the room. The room contained the contemporary reinventions of the *La Bohème* characters, with Mimi joined by Musetta, Rodolpho, and the others. Inside the mirror there's been the constant suggestion of the door opening ever so slightly, and the figure of a woman (Musetta?) appearing in the crack. In his book *The Simple Art of Murder,* Raymond Chandler defined the thriller novel's standard ploy: "When in doubt, have a man come through the door with a gun in his hand." Potter insists on imagining a thriller ending for a feminist murder mystery: a woman comes through the door without a gun in her hand. If the connections between women were totally obliterated in the male thriller films and in the opera *La Bohème,* then the surfacing of these connections must figure in the dénouement of any feminist reconstruction. With the revolutionary humor that accompanies much of *Thriller,* a final shot even posits the male artists' reaction to such unexpected material occupying "their" work.

It would seem that Sally Potter has raised and dispatched every possible issue of art making in our society in this short, austere film. An analysis of opera as an extreme of the bourgeois art form is never far from

Mimi's lips: "They produce the opera to conceal how I must produce the goods" is one of her many skeptical remarks. An analysis of the nature of art and its creators is similarly present, in such observations as: "They were making something in their cold studio . . . was it work?" The painful contradictions between the subject of the opera and her presence outside it permeate the film as thoroughly as they fail to permeate the opera. As Mimi struggles to "remember" her own history, she follows a route that Potter singles out for inspection as a particular danger to women at this moment. Here Potter poses a second mystery within the film, one that has little to do with *La Bohème* but a great deal to do with Potter's own situation as a filmmaker.

Why is Mimi laughing at the beginning of *Thriller*? It's the unspoken question that underlies the professed unraveling of the spoken one: Why did Mimi die? She is laughing hysterically, out of control, inspired by either grief or pleasure, in a perplexing display that remains a mystery throughout much of the film. The source of her laughter is nowhere apparent, though bits of visual materials resembling subconscious flashes set the stage for its solution. "She was searching for a theory to explain her life, her death. . . . She should be able to understand by reading them why this other woman was watching, listening, to her."

It is the search for a solution in the writings of male thinkers that has prompted Mimi's laughter. Potter shows us Mimi searching the pages of a book of the *Tel Quel* group of French theorists, creators of the very body of theory followed by so many British film critics, even professed feminists. Mimi reads aloud in French from "Theorie D'Ensemble," but Potter makes it eminently clear that her activity cannot be viewed neutrally. As she is reading, the shadowy figures of the attic appear; the male artists carry out Musetta while Mimi is so immersed in the text that she does not even notice. "Mallarme, Marx, Freud," she murmurs, as the apparition in the mirror disappears from sight, removed by the group of men. Only now, just before the film ends, does Mimi begin once again to laugh the bitter, grievous laugh that was our first image of her. Facing the camera, facing this audience of today, Mimi closes the book and laughs. It is hard to imagine a more forceful rejection. For Potter, whose film reflects some of the past year's theoretical thinking about film constructions, the terrible limitations of much of that theory must have become abundantly clear, along with its cost in attention deflected from the more pressing demands of feminist film work. It is only when she reads the French theory that Mimi "loses" Musetta, just as it is only when she realizes her loss that she can break through the web of revisions and with a "No, wait!" create a resolution.

It is not a man with a gun who appears in the mirror and walks in the door at the film's end, but another woman, without one. So does Sally Potter chart a course through operatic form, women's history, and contemporary theory—and skeptically move past them into a vision of women working together at a new kind of art, a new kind of life. By delving into the areas of subjectivity, point of view, humor, and fantasy, *Thriller* becomes an exemplary sign of how pleasurable and how illuminating such a new feminist art might be.

Prologue.

Sour Grapes

In November 1980, Ronald Reagan won the presidential election. My students at the School of the Art Institute, where I was teaching women's films and contemporary art, flipped out: What had happened to America? Who were these people who had voted for this madman? Nowadays, it seems like an element of normative history, but back then it was as though the ground had shifted, especially for my generation. We had barely got over Nixon and now we were stuck with Republicans again. I worried about making a living in my marginal freelance style if the country was about to turn into the cold harsh place I anticipated. And I worried about my friends, too, artists and activists, writers and thinkers, all suddenly marginalized and endangered. So when my friend Carrie Rickey, then the *Village Voice* film critic, told me about a job opening, I jumped at the chance.

In January 1981, Ronald Reagan went to Washington to be inaugurated as president and I moved to New York City to become the director of the Film Program at the New York State Council on the Arts (NYSCA). I wasn't eager to leave Chicago. I'd come of age there in the most fundamental way and had found myself—professionally, sexually, personally—as an adult capable of making her way through the world. But there were no jobs for me in Chicago. It was time to move on. Furthermore, with hard times looming at the federal level, I imagined that I could create a safe harbor at NYSCA for others doing the kind of film work I felt was important to support and vital to preserve.

For half a year, I lived a schizophrenic life between New York and Chicago. I was camping out in a tiny corner of the Tribeca loft where my pals Kate Horsfield and Lynn Blumenthal lived. Every morning I'd walk across City Hall Park to my bureaucratic labors. Every weekend that I could, I'd fly back to Chicago. I was desperately homesick. I missed my girlfriend, my apartment, my friends, my neighborhood, and my whole sense of community there. New York felt impersonal and overwhelming. I could hardly wait for the spring, when Nereida would finish school and join me in New York.

Midyear, everything changed—though not quite in the manner I'd expected. No sooner were the two of us united at last in Manhattan than we broke up in a blaze of drama, betrayal, and tragedy. A long hot summer. I still can't hear the lyrics "Bette Davis eyes" without flashing back to that key-in-the-lock nightmare of love gone sour.

It was back to camping out. This time, I borrowed Joan Braderman's apartment for the summer, cried myself to sleep, and tried to put my life and psyche back in order, all the while working furiously to get the Council's Film Program in shape. I hired a new assistant, Deborah Silverfine. She was my best hiring decision ever and today is the director of NYSCA's Electronic Media and Film Program. We went to work cooking up plans to improve the field and strengthen film production, distribution, and exhibition. Soon we were joined by Claude Meyer when NYSCA reorganized its departments, a quixotic restructuring that so alienated the staff that I referred to the day of its announcement ever after as "Christmas morning in a sadistic family."

I found a magical apartment on Avenue A overlooking the East Village's Tompkins Square Park with a view of the treetops and sky and a walled garden in back. As part of the deal, I got the best neighbor in the world, Loretta Szeliga, a former Communist and rank-and-file organizer, who regaled me with stories about New York in the old days: Harlem rent parties, Greenwich Village clubs, theater premieres, gay and lesbian bohemians, FBI intimidation, turncoats and cowards and heroes. We gardened together every summer. This was paradise enough to make me stop missing Chicago.

My job at the Council was equally enriching and exhausting. But by the New Year, I was worried: I had written virtually nothing since the move. For someone who'd so recently had a weekly column, this state of byline withdrawal was intolerable. Removed from my Chicago context, where both *Jump Cut* and the Chicago *Reader* had provided immediate outlets and spurs to production, it was getting harder and harder to kick myself into gear. I suffered, then as now, from the journalist's vice: copy needs a deadline to coax it into being.

As damaging as the lack of assignments was the Council's own code of ethics. I was having a great time learning the New York film community and designing guidelines, broadening the inner circle to include a full range of progressive artists and administrators with true diversity across race, ethnicity, and sexuality. But the harder the bureaucrat worked, the worse life became for the writer. The Council's rules prohibited my writing about any New York filmmakers (whether or not they'd ever received Council funds), prohibited my reviewing shows at any New York venues supported by the Council (we funded virtually all of them, from the most obscure Upstate library to the Film Forum and the New York Film Festival), and banned me from publishing in any publications supported by the Council (which soon included the full spectrum of journals for which I might want to write). Though I did write my first piece for the *Village Voice* in 1981, one assignment was hardly enough to sink my teeth into. I missed being in the middle of the fray. I was looking for an occasion.

I didn't have long to wait. Roswitha Mueller invited me to come to the Center for Twentieth-Century Studies at the University of Wisconsin in Milwaukee in April 1982 for a conference, German Avant-Garde Film: The Seventies. It was meant to be an important event, bringing together some important German filmmakers (Birgit and Wilhelm Hein, Ulrike Ottinger, Helke Sander, and Straub/Huillet) with key critics and scholars (Thomas Elsaesser, Eric Rentschler, and others); as is the case with this sort of event, lots of participants arrived feeling correspondingly self-important. I spoke on a panel devoted to the work of Helke Sander, moderated by my friend Judith Mayne. Our panel had been preceded by one on Alexander Kluge and *Germany in Autumn,* which was a collaborative, politically committed film by Kluge, Fassbinder, and others that was considered a paradigmatic work of the period.

I couldn't help but love Kluge's work: he had taken the place of Godard as the favored film practitioner for anyone interested in radical form plus radical content, the sine qua non back then. But I had become disenchanted with his sexual politics. I wasn't satisfied with assessing Helke Sander's worth and leaving Kluge untouched. That would have been too easy, too much like performing in some ladies' auxiliary. I decided it was the perfect time to take them both on, together, and see what the consequences would be.

My approach met with mixed success. Kluge was supposed to be lauded on this occasion, not marked down a grade on some unwelcome feminist report card. One eager young academic on his way up the university ladder approached me after the talk to ask whether I could possibly really believe that any cinematic difference could be argued along gender lines. My appeal to the real ideological distinctions between patriarchal and feminist modes failed to convince, and he shook his head. Wasn't this kind of thing already old-fashioned? It was 1982, after all. Why hold onto feminism as an operative category, when intellectual interests had moved so much further along? This was a new decade: feminism was an endangered species, and not just in film studies.

The conference was beset by contradictions and dramas that could barely be termed ideological. Instead, the stresses and strains of academic life in the theoretical fast lane were beginning to take a toll. People were acting out like crazy. For instance, Janet Bergstrom made a lengthy presentation analyzing Ulrike Ottinger's *Ticket of No Return (Portrait of a Woman Drinker)*, illustrated with strikingly beautiful slides. Her talk had been so rambling that another participant attacked her for imprecision. Emotions were bristling. When the print of the film was projected afterward, it skipped wildly in the projector, leaping out of sync constantly, and Ottinger accused Bergstrom of chopping her slides straight out of the print. Bergstrom heatedly denied the charge, but the issue was never settled to anyone's satisfaction. It didn't help the tension that the conference was massively overprogrammed: events started at 8 A.M. and didn't end until 11 at night. Moderators were powerless to rein in speakers who went overboard and used up their copanelists' time slots without apology.

Once again, sexual politics were a constant but unspoken factor, lesbianism at once present but invisible: the lesbians in attendance were many, but we weren't there *as* lesbians, and we never became our own or anyone else's subject. A trip to a local gay bar turned to scandal when two of our prestigious conference colleagues (one male, one female) were spotted necking in a corner: a clear case, some of us thought, of heterosexual privilege insinuating its power even into the inner sanctum of our own sexual sanctum. Heterosexuality, turned on by gayness; how tired, we thought.

Nerves were frayed all around. Common sense and courtesy were so out of balance that, when Kaja Silverman (then a junior professor at Simon Fraser University, today the chair of Berkeley's film program) tried to fulfill an ill-advised request by the conference organizers to deliver a closing address summing up the proceedings, she was banished in tears by conference participants' oppositional harangues. So much for academic decorum. Our essays were eventually published in a special issue of *Discourse* edited by Roswitha Mueller, with mine taking pains to explain itself in the aftermath of my encounter with the careerist young man; all our essays looked considerably more civilized and well-behaved there on the page.

I returned to New York City with a redoubled determination to stay out of academia if this were its level of human interaction and social skills; my ambivalence about being left outside its intellectual richness and relative privilege was shoved into abeyance, at least for a while. I discovered, however, that my commitment to Milwaukee had been a strategic error: it meant that I missed an event transpiring that same weekend in New York, the Barnard conference, The Scholar and the Feminist IX: Toward a Politics of Sexuality.

By traveling to the midwest to assess the German version of the seventies, I had missed the defining event of the eighties. It was this conference, staged by Carole Vance, that catalyzed the explosive confrontation between sex radicals and antipornography forces that would be replayed in varying forms throughout the decade of the eighties. But I wasn't prescient enough. If I'd been more so, perhaps I would also have mitigated my enthusiasm in this essay for Christa Wolf, who was the paramount model of political intelligence and integrity at that time, only to suffer the ignominy of association with the former East German state apparatus and to have her reputation trampled underfoot in reaction, once exposed to the post-soviet nineties. But her work still means a lot to me, for all that the world has changed.

14.

She Says, He Says:

The Power of

the Narrator

in Modernist

Film Politics

(1982–83)

> In the construction of their own new forms, women may well react against some elements in modernism and will almost certainly challenge some current definitions of what an artist does and what her relationship to her audience can be.
> — Ann Barr Snitow[1]

A s the seventies have shifted into the eighties, certain parallel aesthetic and political trends have edged close enough to shed light on one another. In the area of film criticism and filmmaking, this closeness has proved particularly provocative in the juncture of modernist and feminist film practice. In this article, as in the conference presentation that preceded it, I take up two films that together constitute a nearly axiomatic case in point: Alexander Kluge's *The Part-Time Work of a Domestic Slave* (1974) and Helke Sander's *The All-Around Reduced Personality — Redupers* (1977). In their intense similarities and differences, these two films can illuminate for us both the nature of feminist film practice and the implications of a modernist film form. Most pertinent, in both cases, is the role played by the narrator in relation to the central protagonist as well as to the audience — a role that raises serious questions concerning the actual politics of a modernist film practice.

The Part-Time Work of a Domestic Slave examines the contradictions attending the life of one Roswitha, a wife and mother of three who gives up her work as a part-time abortionist and, together with her friend Sylvia, instead undertakes a political investigation of her chemist husband's employer, the Beauchamp Factory, which covertly plans to move its operations out of the country and shut down its present plant. Such is the bare-boned narrative line.[2] Throughout, consistent with modernist film style, Kluge interrupts, inflects, and retards the forward movement of the story by the insertion of other types of materials into the film. These include pictures taken from moralistic German children's books, excerpts from *Kuhle Wampe* and from the Soviet realist film *Chapayev,* songs and rhymes that indirectly comment on Roswitha's situation at various points, intertitles that supply key information at other points and, of course, the ubiquitous voice-over that directs our view of the images and transactions on the screen. The structure of the film is derived, not from any narrative progression or character development, but rather from the course that Kluge's narrator pursues in conjunction with the viewer. It is the voice-over, together with the intertitles that constitute its point of view, that exercises organizational control over the film.

Two questions demand our attention: What is the function of the narrator in the film? and What is the effect of the narration on the viewer? Although Roswitha is not a properly constituted character in the realist sense of character unity and psychological motivation, she *is* the film. Her persona as well as her distillation of the film's narrative and political concerns do lead to an audience engagement with this "Roswitha." In the best modernist style, such an engagement is then distanciated and fractured by Kluge's devices of narration, extrapolated references, and so on. Thus cut off from the characters (who in fact remain a mystery to the viewer, devoid of any visible subjectivity and relieved of all psychology) and from the possibility of identification with these characters, the viewer must turn elsewhere. It is commonly assumed that such a viewer, blocked from character identification, turns instead to the higher strata of non-identificatory responses.

With Kluge's help, I would disagree. The narrator holds a position of omniscience as a deus ex machina privy to information unavailable to the film's characters and inaccessible within the film text. In this guise, the narrator quickly becomes the favored replacement for the viewer in search of identification. The narrator, in his display of wit and wisdom, wins the respect of the viewer over the course of the film. The viewer, in turn, repays this narrative generosity with downright chumminess, uniting in a spirit of smug superiority with the narrator over and against the character(s). In a film such as *Part-Time Work,* in which the filmmaker and narrator are male and the protagonist is a woman, the sexual politics are sharply etched within the film's form. The narrator, in league with the author (Kluge), whose point of view he comes to represent and whose words become inflected through the intertitles, consistently undermines the film's female protagonist by a process in which the audience is actively complicitous.

A simple but clear-cut example of this process can be found in Kluge's presentation of the Beauchamp Factory's impending move. The viewer learns this crucial fact via intertitle. Having discovered the fact with such ease, the viewer then has little respect for the character's diligent uncovering of the same knowledge. The narrator's omniscience undercuts the protagonist's power. The effect is even more decisive later in the film, when Kluge frames Roswitha's investigative efforts with a damning title: "Under pressure from the work-force and the public, the management decides — independently of Roswitha and Sylvia — to scrap the planned closure."

In the context of the film, the title is received as a hilarious send-up, a final jab at the Sisyphean haplessness of Roswitha's mission. We are not told just what did motivate the management's decision, nor why the narrator is so sure that it was made "independently." The film has shown the nighttime raids conducted by the two women, the desperate trip to a newspaper editor for better coverage, the meetings with union representatives, and even Roswitha's solo journey to Portugal to verify the prospective site being readied there by Beauchamp. How can the narrator be so sure that all this work was, not only ineffectual, but totally and utterly without effect? More important, how can the viewer accept this "fact" without question? It is a testimony to how thoroughly the viewer is under the sway of the narrator by this point in the film that, indeed, the assessment is accepted and the character thereby further disempowered. Severe judgments become the rule of thumb, couched in irony and ridicule, proffering jokes to be shared by narrator/author and viewer. A voice-over describes the women's activity in another scene: "Having found no better way of experiencing reality, Roswitha and Sylvia learn a song by Brecht by heart."

All the trouble is not located in the narrator's treatment of the characters, however. Once a reassessment of the role of the narrator (hitherto considered benign) has begun, the film's façade starts to reveal other fissures. A new layer of contradiction emerges.

"The more contradictory a situation, the more contrasts you need to describe it."[3] The words belong to Alexander Kluge, and presumably refer to the sorts of contradictions upon which his films have focused: the contradictions between the interests of the family and those of society, between the private and the public spheres, between the individual and the historical process, between logic and chaos. There are other contradictions, though, within his film's own parameters. They are contradictions that have been lodged there by the author to throw off the balance, not unlike the corrupt merchant's thumb on the scale to cheat the customer. Two central tenets of Kluge's own political praxis provide the guideposts for our inquiry: "It's the spectators who produce their films," and "Materialist aesthetics [is] a way of organizing collective social experience."[4] Both statements demand a consideration of the social context of the time (Kluge made his film in 1974) to assess what relation it might have to its subject and, furthermore, to determine exactly what social experience spectators could indeed find there.

The Part-Time Work of a Domestic Slave was made at the height of the campaign to abolish Paragraph 218 and thereby make abortion legal in the Federal Republic.[5] In the Federal Republic, as in the United States and France and Great Britain, the pro-abortion campaign has served as an index to the force of the women's liberation movement during this period. Curiously for a film that states so adamantly its concern with public and private spheres, this paradigmatic struggle to claim the public right for a previously "private" act has been totally omitted. Indeed, the entire social and political context of the time within which Roswitha can be presumed to be working is omitted. The omission serves a very clear purpose for Kluge: once the evidence of the highly political nature of any abortion activity in the Federal Republic of 1974 has been precluded, then the coast is clear for the narrator's redefinition of Roswitha's abortion work as individualistic and apolitical. Instead, her work as an abortionist is defined by the narrator as one of the film's previous contradictions. "In order to afford more children of her own, Roswitha runs an abortion practice." The memory must struggle to recall that this is not the tale of a backstreet abortionist fleecing customers in the fifties, but rather a woman engaged in supplying crucial women's health care in the midst of a political crisis threatening both her livelihood and the lives of her patients (toward whom Kluge is pained to show her great, if "apolitical," concern).

Omission is but one tactic employed by Kluge to combat the feminist position on abortion. Together with his sister Alexandra, who plays the part of Roswitha and who is credited with substantial input into the film (in particular its handling of abortion), Kluge chose to present a more direct attack on the pro-abortion campaign by including a graphic, emotionally jarring shot within an abortion sequence. At the time of the film's release, a counterattack was launched by the members of the *frauen und film* collective (including Helke Sander). In their published critiques of the film, they questioned its moral and political ambivalence toward the abortion issue and its sensationalistic handling of the mock-clinical surgical sequence that ended with the instruments being tossed onto a slop bucket atop what seemed to be a fetus. Sander et al. censured the film as "a slap in the face" to the women's movement by Kluge.

"It's necessary to have in your nerves a sense of what constitutes a false choice." [6] The words, again, belong to Kluge; once again, they indicate a damning view of his own film. Kluge has constructed a false contradiction between abortion work (apolitical) and political work (workplace organizing). The spectator is led to accept the false choice posed to Roswitha of sleazy abortion profiteering versus the righteous work of combating multinationals. Her abortion work, furthermore, is peculiarly privatized in contrast to the collective struggles that surrounded such work in the year of the film's making. When Roswitha is busted by the police (due to a vindictive tip by a rival abortionist), her case is no cause célèbre. Left with Kluge's depiction, we might well be in the fifties. Further, the most basic politics of abortion are altered. The major villain is the rival woman abortionist who does sloppy work and informs on Roswitha; not a word about the medical profession that has been complicitous in the deaths of countless pregnant women for ideological reasons. The only male doctor is pictured as professional but callous, skilled but fed up with these messy women. It is the women abortionists upon whom Kluge focuses as self-motivated, medically incompetent, and vengeful—this at a time when a number of politically dedicated women running abortion and health clinics were coming under severe (and often physically violent) attacks from the right. Whence this portrayal? Whence Kluge's oft-expressed doubts about abortion rights when there is no such doubt about such "clear-cut" cases as yellow journalism or multinational corporations depicted negatively in the film?

An analysis of the film's perspective can thus clarify the reactionary view of reproductive rights that Kluge has couched with apparent objectivity and ironic neutrality. There is more at stake, here, however. How does the spectator come to accept these views within the experience of the film's exhibition? How is the spectator made into a passive consumer of authorial authority, unquestioningly constituting the film's meaning according to the false choices dictated by the narrator?

The clues are lodged in yet another set of fraudulent contradictions, which are basic to this film and much of Kluge's other work, and are imposed on the audience by the narrator at the very beginning. The very first spoken narration tells us that "Roswitha feels an enormous power within her, and films have taught her that this power really exists." The words are coupled with an excerpt from *Chapayev* (Sergei and Georgy Vasiliev, USSR, 1934), the film that marked the turn from montage to socialist realism as the feature of Soviet cinema. The "power" that "really exists" is one of political abilities as defined in a revolutionary battle situation circa 1917. In the film excerpt, the emotional peasant leader Chapayev, who is obstinate and prone to acting instinctively, is taught "rational" leadership by his comrade Lenin. Roswitha's character in Kluge's film may be seen as a dramatic literalizing of this peasant metaphor. Kluge assigns her to an essentially preliterate, irrational locus, consigned by her sex and her role within the family to act out, without mediation, illogically, and — consistently — ineffectually. The narrator leads the viewer in laughing at this buffoon and her stupid ways. In one case, even a feminist analysis of the film followed this lead in praising the "screwball" comedy effected by Kluge.[7]

In interviews, Kluge himself has denied that the humor ridicules or demeans the character, indeed has denied that Roswitha's actions are necessarily intended as comedic. Instead, Kluge offers a different view of the female characters that populate his films: he idealizes the irrationality he has imposed on them, praises the "chaos" from which new choices can potentially be constituted, and blasts logic as a supreme value. The seeming contradiction between Kluge's praise of irrationality and his film's ridicule of Roswitha's same irrationality provides the clue to the film's most basic problem. The female/male chaos/rationality dichotomy is, after all, a familiar schema. In a discussion of Althusser and psychoanalytic theories, Elizabeth Wilson has characterized the nature of the discourse in a manner fitting Kluge as well. She cites it as "the language used in political debate since time immemorial, whereby anarchy on the one hand and law and order on the other are posed as antagonistic opposites in order to discredit anarchy, i.e., chaos. Feminists should know better than to be taken in by this kind of language which constantly seeks to mask the progressive or revolutionary implications of rebellion; rebellion is always stigmatized as flouting law and order and producing chaos."[8]

With Kluge, we encounter a minor variation on the theme. Rather than stigmatize chaos, he heroizes the stigma with all the fervor of a Noble Savage devotee. Deprived of rationality, derided for this lack within the film even as she is lauded for it by the author outside the film, the character Roswitha must struggle to consciousness like some sort of primordial slug struggling to emerge from the muck into life.

Kluge's true attitude regarding rationality (which Jessica Benjamin has so convincingly characterized as the religion of the Federal Republic's fatherless patriarchy) is revealed in his choice of narrative voice.[9] Despite his fervent support of irrationality, Kluge carefully preserves his narrator and narrative voice from any such taint. In discussing the function of the voice-over commentary in Kluge's film, Miriam Hansen pointed out that "its own status remains unquestioned."[10] Kluge's disembodied voice clearly assumes the position of authority and shapes the film according to its maxims. Chummed and charmed by narrative complicity, the viewer identifies with the narrator, whose role as Kluge surrogate is, by now, clear. Meanwhile, the distanciated clinical treatment of Roswitha blocks her own subjectivity from view, just as the modernist avoidance of any realistic character construction prevents the viewer from making any sense of her motivations, goals, needs, or even identity. A modernist victim, Roswitha can claim no subjectivity in exchange for the rationality she forsakes. Nor does Kluge ever permit his own subjectivity to be at issue. He conceals his own biases and agendas beneath a layer of pseudo-factual contradiction. Behind this cover of false choices, however, he can be found manipulating the viewer into his corner through the use of an authoritarian narrator, completely equipped with voice, titles, supporting texts, and even appropriate snippets of relevant films.

The narrator takes on the guise of a metacharacter, offered up unproblematically for audience identification, smoothing over the real contradictions of the film's form to displace attention upon false contradictions taken to represent impossible obstacles to political consciousness or action. Pretending to offer a sympathetic analysis, Kluge instead offers a frame-up. Caught in it are not only the female protagonists of his films, but the women in the audience as well.

The writer Christa Wolf has called for a prose capable of giving people "the courage of their own experiences."[11] From Kluge, that is impossible. From Helke Sander, whose film quotes the words of Christa Wolf, that is requisite.

Helke Sander's *The All-Round Reduced Personality—Redupers,* like Kluge's film, focuses on the issues surrounding a particular period of time in a woman's life. Like Roswitha, Edda Chiemnajewski is a mother (but not a wife). She is also an artist and journalistic photographer, seen during the time that her women's photography group has received a commission from the city of Berlin. The issues of representation and political meaning that marked the women's project are equally those that dominate Sander's film.

Unlike Kluge, Sander does not construct a character outside the realms of language and logic. On the contrary, the film opens with a demonstration of Edda's mastery of language, as she translates an English message to her postman. Later, Edda is seen in a number of freelance situations. She photographs an old people's party at which—as is typical for someone in a freelance position trying to invest her work with a feminist consciousness — she overinvests her time and emotions. She demonstrably cannot collect enough money to pay for the time spent in this place, nor can she sell the photos she takes other than the banal man-at-podium snaps she's been assigned. Her involvement produces a surplus for which there is no compensation. This imbalance, consisting of the constant inability to tally an emotional and artistic accrual against a photojournalistic ledger sheet, builds throughout the film. It marks as well her other columns of imbalance: her home life balanced against her public obligations, her assignments versus her own photo project, and so on. These imbalances produce the contradictions that permeate the film and that, in turn, form the subject the film seeks to investigate. Unlike the Kluge/Roswitha version, here the contradictions are manifested not by an omniscient narrator's instructions to the audience, but instead through the direct visualization of the material conditions of Edda's life on the screen. The film's leitmotif is its central contradiction: the all-consuming wall dividing the city in half ideologically, it seems, whereas in reality it is walling in West Berlin.

Most critics and viewers would agree that the Kluge and Sander films are both located within a particular area of contemporary filmmaking that could be termed, more or less, modernist. In such a recognized, if vaguely defined, area as contemporary modernist cinema, certain assumptions are operative. The tenets hold that a self-interruptive text provides the appropriate rupture with linear narrative or transparent narrativity; that an uninflected voice-over provides the distanciation necessary to prevent an unmediated identification with a character that, after all, is not a "character" at all; that nonpsychological progressions, furthering formal requirements rather than plot concerns, shape the structure; that such a structure, meditative in tone, combining elements of realist depiction with material drawn from other films and sources of representation, ensures that the viewer will have to construct the film actively from its parts, thus in the process securing liberation from the trap of passive consumption; and that a mix of fiction and documentary modes will disrupt genre conventions, throw the elements of genre into dialectical opposition, and throw into doubt the notion of a fixed "truth" representable on screen, thereby securing the viewer's complete engagement in the labor of producing meaning.

Assuming that these criteria are equally supported by the two films under consideration here, any differences become of paramount interest. Ann Snitow, in the article cited above, called for an investigation into "the problems and contradictions in the way modernism descended in the female line."[12] The comparison of Sander's film with the parallel

Kluge work demonstrates forcefully the causes of such problems, given the nature of modernism, and casts doubt on the radical political claims made for its form once viewed within a feminist context.

The narrative voice-over in *Redupers* is more discursive, self-interrupting, and nonhegemonic than the corresponding voice in the Kluge film. Unlike the male Klugian narrator, the female voice of Sander's film does not set out to control audience response nor to undermine the protagonist with superior wit. There are marked shifts in the narrative locus from scene to scene, opening up the route of identification from an individual bonding to a collective process.

Frequently, the voice-over offers entry into the thoughts of the protagonist, though devoid of any attendant drama or motivational closure. As Edda photographs an anti-rape demonstration, the viewer is told that "she thinks that not enough of her socially significant fotos are bought." At other times, the observations seem less those of an observer than the interior voice of a self-deprecating character: "At age 34 she decides to do something for her body." At certain points, the position of the narrative voice shifts from this sympathetic proximity to a more Klugian, detached, data-prone chronicler, as in one scene of a meeting of Edda's women photographers' project: "The group continued the futile discussion for some time." Shortly after, though, the narrator turns downright low-key, remarking only that "all kinds of people come to her" as a pair of art world hustlers try to con her. Similarly, as her schedule careens out of control with overload, the narrator remarks, "Monday — the Sunday paper — have to keep up to date."

Such jibes are not entirely out of line with those of the Klugian voice, yet the effect of the voice-over in the Sander film is utterly different, in its effect both on the film text and on the spectator. The most reductive explanation, and a persuasive one, focuses on the difference between Sander's utilization of a woman narrator to speak for and comment on a woman character, whereas Kluge imposes a male voice on a female subject. It is a fundamental and determining difference, but for formal reasons rather than simply those of gender identification. The difference arises from the disparate sources of the two styles, with Kluge proceeding from the political base of a post–Frankfurt School modernist aesthetic and Sander proceeding from the feminist political base of writing and filmmaking made by women for an audience of women. At a few points they may coincide, as when Kluge's narrator quotes proverbs and moral tales with a panache of irony, while Sander matches the proverbs with a very different popular-culture source: the radio. Yet Sander's narrator goes on to quote from the writings of Christa Wolf. The difference in film quotations is even more revealing. Kluge picks *Chapayev* as one model, whereas Sander sandwiches three different films made by women onto the screen at once. The three films (by Valie Export, Yvonne Rainer, and Ursula Reuter-Christiansen) are layered atop a newspaper that fills the frame, which is itself overlayed by the words of a letter read on the soundtrack. Over the facts of women's lives asserted within the newspaper, Sander superimposes the private words of women's letters and the unprecedented film images of women's imagination and self-definition of daily life.

The major break with Kluge's narrative model might be pinpointed in Sander's rejection of hegemony and authority as narrative qualities. A clue can be found in one otherwise unexceptional scene: in the home dark-room where she prints her photographs, Edda is finishing up her latest order. A voice-over, assumed to be the narrator initially, turns out to be-long instead to an offscreen character carrying on a conversation with Edda. The same confusion occurs again in a meeting of a women's group, at which a seemingly authoritative narrative pronouncement turns out to be spoken by another character. Such confusion would never transpire in a Kluge film, for there is no possibility of any such case of mistaken iden-tity. Kluge's characters do not share in the narrative authority granted to his deus ex machina. There is no possibility of inclusion: his woman pro-tagonist suffers the same exclusion from her own history within the film that women have suffered for years under patriarchal record keeping. In Sander's films, the other characters do not just share in the narrative au-thority; rather, the authoritarianism of narration is avoided in favor of a relationship that sounds at times more like conversation than like any hierarchical ordering of narrative truth. In earlier writings, I have con-tended that such structuring and narrative voice in the feminist cinema can be termed a "cinema of correspondence," both due to its base in the historical unpublished writings of women and due to the correspon-dences between women's lives and the shape of these works.[13]

As Christa Wolf's writing is quoted extensively in *Redupers,* it is par-ticularly appropriate to refer to an assessment of Wolf in light of the feminist tradition in the United States. Myra Love assesses the narrative style of Wolf's work in terms that fit *Redupers* equally well: "The prose writing of Christa Wolf . . . makes use of the self-interrupting and non-linear methods of communication which characterize conversation. . . . She demystifies authorship by removing it from its traditional position of depersonalized authority and returning it to its function as a means of social communication."[14]

The link between author and viewer is a solid one for Sander. It is a link that proffers an easy crossing to the narrator without any need for pulling rank. After all, *Redupers* was made in the spring of 1977 (not yet the fateful autumn of Kluge's next film contribution), as the state apparatus was coming down soundly on the heads of the women's movement in the Federal Republic. The comrades in arms invisible to Kluge's Roswitha — the feminist health workers — were being busted under the very same laws used against so-called terrorism.[15] Sander was a part of this situation and at one with this world, and it shows. Her narrator speaks *to* as well as *with* both character and viewer. The narrative voice may be fragmented in its identity, free to float from locus to locus, but it is absolutely unified in terms of its sympathies.

Given such a style and voice, *Redupers* is able to pose contradictions to us, not as a trump card of doom, but as an inevitable foundation upon which lives and ideologies may be, however provisionally, constructed. In place of Kluge's false contradiction of privatized political fervor tilting against overwhelming state power, Sander provides a view of collective work in the very area of representation (a women's image-making project) within which the film being seen is itself inscribed.

The differences between the two films are extended and further accentuated when their treatments of the function of "seeing" are examined. In *Part-Time Work,* Roswitha's trust in her own act of seeing is a foolish and naïve one that undermines her political work and diminishes her strength in the eyes of the viewer. This is a key scene. Wanting to prove that the Beauchamp Factory is indeed being built in Portugal and thus expose the denial as a lie, Roswitha drives all the way there to find out for herself. Sure enough, she finds the site of the factory construction. She returns with the knowledge of the site, but she does not think to replicate the knowledge in the form of a photograph. She does not realize that her personal vision, externalized as a photo, would become evidence. The Klugian narrator therefore presents the viewer with this monumental miscalculation as a self-destructive act of political folly. When Helke Sander and the other editors of *frauen und film* (then newly formed) attacked the film, they particularly cited this stupidity that had been foisted on the character. Kluge was prone to justify the choice *not* to make a photograph: in a peculiar fetishization of "lack of access" as a positive value, Kluge has chosen to frame the nonaction as a touching testimony of the working-class faith in words. Thus, with an element of perversity, Kluge transformed exclusion from technology into an act of choice.

Given the chance four years later, Helke Sander redressed the balance. In *Redupers,* the women have an ease with the technology of representation and free access to the world of imagistic "truth," yet the true fundamental problems that had been masked by Kluge's tactic here persist.

First, the women's ability to create photographs carries no assurance that the photographs will be granted legitimacy as any sort of evidence. When Edda visits an editor to encourage the publishing of a photo portfolio in his magazine, she is treated badly and turned away; when a newspaper publishes her photojournalistic photo, she is not credited and most likely not even paid. For Kluge's film to imply a change of fate based on the mere taking of a photograph in Portugal is for Kluge to indulge in uncharacteristic political naïveté. Further, for his film to equate the taking of a photograph with the political understanding of image making is to reveal just how far from a feminist aesthetic we have wandered. To be able to make images, women must still overcome the obstacle of discovering how, truly, to see. In a paper presented in Graz, Austria, in 1977, Helke Sander wrote: "Women today find themselves in a situation which is perhaps best comparable to that of Kaspar Hauser or the wild child. They must first learn to see with their own eyes and not through the mediation of others." [16] Thus Sander draws the opposite lesson from the same comparison motivating Kluge. Whereas Kluge can celebrate woman's exclusion as a sign of purity, Sander is looking for the route out of the situation.

At one point in *Redupers*, the narrator comments that Edda is "obsessed with daily life as other women see it." The emphasis is on the act of seeing, both as a metaphor for, and an acting out of, feminism. Sander is not content to describe woman as inscribed within patriarchy or as, in Kluge's idealist view, outside the gates of the city and the limits of logic. *Redupers* reveals its feminist assumptions within its language, images, and structure. The emphasis on vision is collectivized and thus granted the dimension of a political struggle. The inclusion of the three films by women, all concerned with the surreal banalities of everyday life, represents the shared concern of women artists in the seventies "to see with their own eyes." By including these films in her own, Sander is claiming the political dimension of the filmmakers' work and supporting the claim made by Snitow on behalf of women novelists: that the making of "visionary recombinations" is one kind of political work.

Like all political work, this one carries its attendant risks. The risk, as might be guessed from the vaunting tone of Kluge's narrator, is a familiar one for feminists: ridicule. In one of the key moments in *Redupers*, the women's photography group is preparing a billboard-sized blowup of one of Edda's photographs of the Berlin Wall. They are seen mounting the giant photograph onto a frame to carry out into the streets of the city on a test expedition aimed at evaluating their plan to install a number of such billboards, equipped with their photos. Unsure how successful the images will be on this scale, out in the unsheltered, ungallery-like jungle of representational overload, the women have agreed to try one outing as a test. The narrator intervenes with some added information for the viewer: "a male friend makes fun of them for carrying out their ideas." In other words, the women are ridiculed for literalizing instead of conceptualizing their process. The women's distrust of stopping at working the idea out on paper (of merely *imagining* the effect) is held by this unseen commentator to be a ludicrous deficiency, an inadequacy to be squelched with ridicule. The women's commitment to physical process is perceived by the male friend as a lack of abstract conceptual ability. Such a perspective harkens back to the familiar Kluge narrator, casting a rather jaundiced light on that narrator's smug dismissal of Roswitha's activities as irrational blunders meriting ridicule. Here, male ridicule is subject to containment: it is held to an offscreen account, mediated by a different narrative voice, meant as a necessary reminder of a major patriarchal weapon (ridicule) used against early feminist activity, against women's efforts to embody a new vision, and revived increasingly now as a tactic of the antifeminist backlash.

Through her choices of which material to visualize onscreen, which to sequester offscreen, and which remarks to assign directly to the narrative voice, Sander continually demonstrates an effort to encourage women to see with their own eyes and speak in their own voice. The effort marks the two final points that require attention here: the significance of the term with which the female protagonist is named ("I" or "She") and the significance of the other voices that the narrator/author quotes to substantiate an identity. Judith Mayne, in her extensive analysis of *Redupers,* has concentrated on this issue of articulating an evasive self-definition.[17] Mayne situates Sander's film within a feminist novelistic tradition and follows the film's lead back to the words of Christa Wolf, whose narrator/protagonist in *The Quest for Christa T.* is engaged in a search for "the secret of the third person, who is there without being tangible and who, when circumstances favor her, can bring down more reality upon herself than the first person: I."[18]

The difficulty of saying "I" has been a central subject for many contemporary feminist authors, most notably Monique Wittig. The extent of alienation, silence, and containment has been so vast that women, accustomed to speaking for so long in the voice of a male syntax, have had to undertake a political struggle to reclaim language. In the cinema, of course, this language encompasses the lexicon of images as well as words. The shadowy "I" has to be located, often hidden in the domain of the "she." The narrator in *Redupers* fulfills this very function of struggling to adapt/invent a language. The lack of a hegemonic narrative voice, as pointed out earlier, reflects in all its shifts and contradictions this precise struggle to name the self by finding the voice of that intangible "third person." The shifts between an interior and exterior discourse, between an objective and subjective narration, are precisely the tactics of stalking the self. The narrator may be seen, then, as an active agent working in conjunction with the active viewer; the two become partners in the collective enterprise of fashioning a feminist voice.

Part of this enterprise is the enlistment of allies and sources. In *Redupers,* the narrator refers to the words of Christa Wolf and the films of a trio of women filmmakers, while the characters themselves appeal to friends, old allies, and experts in their quest for reassurance. In the Kluge film, the lessons of *Chapayev* are paramount; Roswitha reads theoretical texts, takes tours of workers' housing, and learns the songs of Brecht; but she never finds the words of other women, nor does the Klugian narrator have any occasion to quote them. The Sander film can be inscribed within a context of feminist writing and filmmaking in part because this context is itself inscribed, by Sander, within the film. The antifeminism of the Kluge film can be discerned, just as plainly, from its exclusions of similar material. Criticism is prone to the same examinations: a feminist critical context depends on the ongoing work of building ideas, quoting sources, extending arguments. If feminist critics sometimes falter on this point, it may be that we suffer from a problem that Myra Love, in her article on Wolf, pinpointed as a trouble spot for feminist novelists. Love hypothesized that the long-time silence of women in literature was due, not entirely to a lack of the means to use written language, but rather to "the lack of practice in occupying the position of authority which has traditionally characterized authorship." [19]

Redupers is a particularly significant film in that Sander takes as her subject the real labor of representation — photography, picture making — and positions that work unambiguously out in the world as collective labor, as political process, as hard and contradictory and inevitable. The usual power relations that dominate the interaction between male narrator and female subject are not replicated, as they are so cleverly by Kluge. More important, neither are the power relations that have long characterized, covertly, the interaction between the male narrator and the female viewer — or female critic.

A feminist modernism insists on holding the narrator to the same codes of anti-authoritarianism and nonhierarchical processes that have long characterized the women's movement. In place of the exempted and fetishized author, there is a demystified author intent at working together with the viewer to construct, not merely the film text, but a new vision, a different society, a feminist locus of production and reception. The least we can do, as feminist critics, is to match this accomplishment with a worthy critical theory. It is an obligation reiterated with some urgency by Elizabeth Wilson in her divergence from current psychoanalytic feminism: "The last thing feminists need is a theory that teaches them only to marvel anew at the constant recreation of the subjective reality of subordination and which reasserts male domination more securely than ever within theoretical discourse. . . . To change the conditions of work—in the world and in the home—might do more for our psyches as well as our pockets than an endless contemplation of how we came to be chained."[20]

The creation and explication of a feminist modernism is important to any further development of a feminist film aesthetic or its theory. It may be that the two dominant modes of contemporary cinema that we discuss today—namely, capitalist escapism and patriarchal modernism—will continue to characterize film culture in our alienated society for some time to come. In the cinematic tradition of patriarchal modernism exemplified by Kluge's *The Part-Time Work of a Domestic Slave,* irony and distanciation replace identification, the absent but controlling author stands in for the invisible father, rationalism is simultaneously deployed and derided, and woman (when such a figure appears) is merely the figment of an idealist imagination. Sander's *The All-Round Reduced Personality (Redupers)* presents an alternative to such a modernist hall of mirrors. In this example of modernist cinema as descended from the female line, the narrative is discursive rather than controlling, the narrator is female and benign, contradiction is an accepted assumption, daily life is a proper subject for visualization, the choice of subject can encompass the political in all its manifestations, humor does not mitigate against the characters, and an engagement with the viewer is an essential requirement. The narrator is not a figure set apart at the top of a hierarchical pyramid, analogous to the absent father-figure signing his name to the movie. Rather, the narrator in a work of feminist modernism problematizes the power relations within the viewing process, much as the earliest works of cinematic modernism first sought to problematize the power relations within the film text itself.

Only by undertaking a study of feminist modernism, in Sander and other filmmakers (especially those engaged in the "cinema of correspondence"), can we assess its true significance and begin to recognize the power of the narrator in a film politics that has gone unexamined too long.

Prologue.

Sex, Gender,

and Consumer

Culture

When I returned to New York City after the temperamental Milwaukee conference, I discovered that history had been made with far more public tumult at the 600-person event at Barnard instead. Still in town after attending The Scholar and the Feminist IX: Toward a Politics of Sexuality was someone I'd always wanted to meet: Elizabeth Wilson. A celebrated British historian and social critic, she was also one of the founding editors of *Feminist Review* and an early member of the British gay liberation movement. More to the point for me, however, was her status as inhabitant of an extraordinary bedroom I'd occupied in her absence in London in 1979 on my way to Edinburgh, when her housemate Angela Martin (then working at the British Film Institute) had offered me lodging.

I was astounded by the room in which I found myself precisely because it combined elements normally never found all together in an American lesbian feminist abode: portraits of Nathalie Barney, volumes of Lacan, Cameron Mackenzie's *Extraordinary Women,* innumerable Marxist texts, and piles and piles of books and photographs alongside wonderful fabrics and actual fashion. Who on earth lived here? Back then, I'd had to leave before finding out. Now I had a second chance—not just to meet her at last but also to find out firsthand what had transpired at the Barnard conference.

Elizabeth Wilson doesn't disappoint. She arrived full of questions about American feminism and the antipornography movement for starters, then sharp observations and theories about the emergent "pro-sex" forces and what they represented. We seemed to agree on the basics and had great fun pooling information and exchanging takes on the controversies.

Because of the central role played by film in so much of the pornography-antipornography histories and debates, I'd already been giving the subject a lot of thought. I was irritated that no one was discussing imagery with any degree of specificity. There had been huge advances made by feminist academics in terms of audience reception, representation, and gender differentiation, yet all of this work seemed left at the door like some kind of prohibited armament when women entered the pornography discussions. Before parting, we urged each other to write something and turn this chat into text.

At that time, I was taking part in an extraordinary biweekly seminar. It was titled the Seminar on Sex, Gender, and Consumer Culture and met at the New York Institute for the Humanities. Initially organized by Edmund White, Richard Sennett, Ann Snitow, and other Institute fellows, it continued for years under Snitow's direction. This seminar became my intellectual home in New York. It's where I first met Ann and Edmund as well as Lisa Duggan, Kate Ellis, Faye Ginsburg, Amber Hollibaugh, Michael Kimmel, Linda Nochlin, Alix Kates Shulman, Sharon Thompson, Carole Vance, Judith Walkowitz, Jeff Weinstein, Marilyn Young, and numerous other intellectual figures who would influence my thinking and, in some cases, become my friends for years to come.

It was there at a seminar meeting that I'd first heard the plans for the Barnard conference and it was there that I heard the postmortem on its dénouement. The conference had been picketed and leafletted by a group calling itself the Coalition of Women for a Feminist Sexuality and Against Sadomasochism, which was basically WAP (Women Against Pornography) members, WAVAW (Women Against Violence Against Women), and a few veterans of other lesbian activist formations. They commandeered the open mikes during the conference to denounce sadomasochism (with slogans emblazoned on their T-shirts). Pressure from this group led to Barnard's losing its traditional corporate sponsorship for the event, thereby impoverishing all future editions of the college's long-established Scholar and the Feminist conferences (the Helena Rubenstein Foundation was not immune to questions of image).

The "antiporn" forces (called by their enemies the antisex forces) had demonized conference participants as pornographers and had struck out in particular against certain women (Gayle Rubin and Dorothy Allison, for example) who had already been associated with texts or practices they were intent on condemning. In the case of Alice Echols, she was attacked for denigrating a shared history, the seventies, and seemingly dismissing out of hand lesbian feminism. Other groups got pulled into the fray. For instance, No More Nice Girls, an abortion-rights group formed by Rox Baxandall, Karen Durbin, Ellen Willis, Joan Braderman, and others, was branded as pro-pornography; I had marched with them already for abortion rights and knew otherwise. A particular target of their wrath was a "speakout" organized as an open forum in conjunction with the conference and titled "Politically Incorrect Sex," organized by a loose-knit group calling themselves the Lesbian Sex Mafia (LSM), described as a "coalitionist group committed to the active support of radical perverts in all circles of society." Fourteen women spoke, including Jewelle Gomez, Judith Butler, Cherríe Moraga, and a number of already-named conference organizers and participants. In that atmosphere, it took a lot of nerve.

By June, *off our backs,* the nearest thing to a journal of record that the self-described feminist "movement" could claim, published a massive report on the conference with coverage by some of its regular writers. Though much of the piece was reasonable reporting, the subjectivity of the scribe shaped its tone ("I was disturbed" was her mantra), and therefore important fears of a new feminist McCarthyism, clearly pronounced in the article, were subsumed under its more hysterical fear of feminism's allegedly being taken over by sadomasochists. For months, indeed years, after the conference, such attacks persisted and escalated, and a siege mentality took over.

Soon enough, all our apprehensions about the antipornography movement proved resoundingly justified when the eighties served up its next course: Andrea Dworkin and Catherine MacKinnon developed the strategy of civil-rights-based antiporn ordinances, which they then shopped around to city councils in the United States and Canada. Their minions did indeed go on to shut down porn shops, or at least try to — including, in their exuberance, gay porn shops, a strategy that led to one of the more absurd dyke-faggot splits and called into question the real motive behind the hatred of explicit sexual imagery, given that no women were around to be exploited or forced into nonconsensual behavior in gay porn.

It was the organizing required around these antiporn ordinances that led Carole Vance to spearhead the formation of an activist group called FACT (Feminists Against Censorship Taskforce) to reclaim feminism from the antiporn movement with which it was being equated by the media, to educate other feminists about the dangers of this antiporn moral crusade, and to have a feminist entity on tap for media interventions to counterbalance the antiporn spokeswomen. As FACT groups sprung up around the country in the wake of ordinance fights, the need for printed materials became urgent. Eventually, FACT formed a book committee and a loose-knit group of overworked volunteers—including Kate Ellis, Barbara O'Dare, Nan Hunter, and other writers and artists—banded together to write and design *Caught Looking: Feminism, Pornography and Censorship*. Published in 1986, *Caught Looking* sought to concretize the imagery of desire and fantasy that seemed to be so hard to pin down, and so unacceptable once pinned, alongside key texts aimed at thinking through the issues at stake. Even though it consolidated many of the positions originally developed before and after the Barnard conference, *Caught Looking* seemed surprisingly tame to anyone expecting a scandalous compendium of antiporn invention; its acceptability quotient was made all the more surprising by the vitriol of the rhetoric that preceded its publication.

FACT and Vance and the Barnard conference participants were already a veritable coven of antichrists in the crosshairs of the WAP forces. Our New York Institute for the Humanities seminar, on the other hand, was more than ever a testing ground for all the new, more inclusive theories of sexuality and representation that were being developed. It was a place to discuss these issues seriously without any ideological pit bulls on the attack, without the simple mutual exclusion of right-wrong, and with plenty of good minds for stimulation. I was impatient to join my voice with theirs and go on record on what had quickly become the defining topic of the moment—though I still thought it was questionable whether the subject that had everybody so fired up was pornography or really just sex.

My chance for a voice came along very quickly. A new Canadian documentary about pornography, *Not a Love Story,* had just been produced by Bonnie Klein for Studio D, the women's studio at the National Film Board. I volunteered to write about the film and the issues it raised for the *Village Voice* when it was released that summer. The film, of course, turned out to be a clarion cry for the antipornography movement. I couldn't have asked for a better platform, and my editor, Karen Durbin, handed me a priceless one: the front page of the paper and thousands of words inside. (For years afterward, the late Renee Furth, queen of the New York publicists, would try to get me to press screenings of movies she thought I might hate in the hope of landing another media blitz.)

Meanwhile, back across the Atlantic, Elizabeth Wilson was preparing her report on the Barnard conference for *Feminist Review* when momentum built so rapidly around these sexuality issues that she decided to devote most of the issue to the subject. She'd already invited Linda Gordon and Ellen DuBois to publish their conference paper there, and now she invited me to submit the *Village Voice* piece as well, which I did with some revision to clear up any lingering ambiguities. Ironically, the issue's noticeboard contained a prominent announcement of the start-up of a new American journal based in Washington, D.C., *The Celibate Woman Journal.*

A further pleasure came when film scholar Scott MacDonald indeed took up my challenge to "feminist men" to own up to their own investment in pornography and wrote his own treatise, "Confessions of a Feminist Porn Watcher," which later was anthologized in Michael Kimmel's landmark volume, *Men Confront Pornography.*

It's been more than a decade since this article first appeared, and the landscape has shifted enormously, the taboos along with the feuds (today, female-to-male transsexuals occupy the position once held by sadomasochism or butch-femme, that is, the "You're not me–I'm not you–how dare you implicate me in your evil identity–damn you" bad object). Analyses, thankfully, were forced to become more complex with the arrival on the scene of woman-made pornography intended to arouse, not demean, women. In March 1983, I went to Washington, D.C., for a panel at the American Film Institute's Women and Movies festival. It was entitled "Pornography for Women? The Female Influence on Erotic Films" and was moderated by Elizabeth Hess; the panelists were Jean Callahan, an *American Film* editor who had written on video erotica for women in *Playgirl,* and Gloria Leonard, publisher of *High Society,* a "men's" magazine. The flyer credited "the advent of cable television and home videocassette players" with bringing erotic films to a new audience that was no longer exclusively male and questioned how the adult film industry would respond to this new market. I made the following introduction to my own remarks:

> I need to disentangle some basic assumptions before addressing the question of new work for the female consumer.
> (1) Men hate women and wish us harm. Porn proves it. So what else is new?
> (2) The representation of women in porn is not just symbolic, not just a fantasy—it oppresses all women, in a concrete way. I agree with this one. Unlike many of my otherwise-colleagues, including here on this panel, I'm not so taken with a free-speech defense of porn. It's another example of how men use representation against women in a complex system of signs reducing us to lesser beings. So what. I

do think that by and large it's pretty wretched stuff. But so is sterilization. But so is incest. So is wife-beating. So is rape. So are the thousands of homeless in our urban streets. What I reject is the priorization of porn as a form of oppression.

(3) Pornography is a multimillion dollar industry. Men make money off the daily exploitation of female (and male) workers. It's an industry. OK. Then I oppose it as much or little as I'd oppose the military buildup or nuclear industry.

(4) And here's the crux of the matter: Pornography is a way to talk about sex. And the discussion of sexuality that it has precipitated, almost as a byproduct of the controversies, is an important one. And *that* I support.

I went on to recommend a number of films that were exciting me at that time for their bravura in taking on sexual themes: Nelly Kaplan's *Nea*, a film that should be revived for its portrayal of a teenage girl who becomes a successful porn author publishing under a pseudonym until she falls for her publisher; Valie Export's *Invisible Adversaries,* for its visual energy and voracious sexual appetite; and Chantal Akerman's *Toute Une Nuit,* for its melancholic tracing of desire, rather than just sex, and the fevered passions that it engenders. Gloria Leonard was the one who zeroed in most successfully on the subject, but then she'd given it serious consideration as her preparation for launching a new company to produce porn videos for women. Her verdict: "The basic difference between pornography and eroticism is the lighting." Remember, Linda Williams had not yet written *Hard Core,* her masterful study of pornography as a genre. This was a good start.

Later that year I had a bizarre experience. I was at an office party when suddenly the subject of Chantal Akerman came up, or more specifically, the subject of *Je tu il elle.* A colleague's husband, drunk and belligerent, began to complain loudly that he'd been dragged by friends to see the film and that it was awful, pathetic, what could women do without the equipment, and so on. So tell me, he raged, since you're a dyke, what do they do? Everyone instantly froze, silence galvanized the room, and they all waited for me to speak. I was furious. Although I was "out" at work, it was not my idea of fun to explain lesbian sexual practices to a drunken man in front of an audience of my bosses, colleagues, and employees. I spat out a refusal: No, I will not explain a damn thing to you. Silence again, and then out of the silence, a plaintive voice. "Oh, please tell him, you could save my sex life." It was his wife. I wasn't surprised to hear, a few years later, of their divorce.

Meanwhile, the inversion of cause-and-effect that had troubled me in the antiporn rhetoric of the early eighties continued to occupy my thoughts. When Nora Sayre reviewed James Gilbert's *A Cycle of Outrage: America's Reaction to the Juvenile Delinquent* for the *New York Times Book Review,* I finally had the ammunition I'd wanted. Analyzing the postwar phenomenon of delinquency, Gilbert traced an evolution of blame: over and over, experts and politicians had fingered outside influences, popular culture, comic books, and (especially) rock and roll for leading patriotic American youth into dissolution and crime. A psychiatrist and author by the name of Fredric Wertham had even testified at a Senate subcommittee's hearings that there were demonstrable links between delinquency and "crime comics." By focusing on the context of a developing "youth culture" that encompassed everything from blue jeans to automobiles, Gilbert was able to make explicit the subtext of many of those panic crusades against comic books and music.

Of greatest interest to me was Gilbert's discovery of a 1959 National Education Association conference statement worrying that "class hostilities" were at work in these kinds of attacks, leading the bourgeoisie to classify as "delinquency" what was "actually lower-class behavior." He had identified the very dynamic that I'd felt was at stake with the antipornography attack on sex-industry workers and consumers.

Morality crusades seem to me to have more to teach us about the nature of phobia and panic than about any of their alleged targets. The antipornography crusade got taken up by the right wing and Christian organizations, this time targeting gay bodies along with transgressive women or suspect men: Robert Mapplethorpe, Karen Finley, Marlon Riggs, Andres Serrano. No doubt the Dworkin-MacKinnon team would disavow any responsibility, but subsequent political crusades were successful precisely because such fertile ground had already been prepared. If rock and roll was the cause of delinquency in postwar America, then it was no surprise that the 1992 presidential campaigns focused on music again to assuage the pain of the cold war's ending: in a rare bipartisan effort, George Bush went after Ice T and Bill Clinton after Sister Souljah.

Like the antipornography movement, such campaigns ironically never work, at least not in the way they claim. Mistaking cause for effect, they operate much like the classic corrupt police sweep in the old Hollywood movies that always ends up framing an innocent ex-con to solve a hot case expeditiously. Moves and movies like these carry a treacherous, faulty message: *This* is the source of all that's wrong, and now that we've locked it up, you're safe. The reality, on the other hand, is always less simple and less comforting. In the seventies, for example, U.S. leftists and feminists who'd read Dorothy Dinnerstein and Nancy Chodorow and been converted to their worldviews proceeded to travel the world scolding any country that didn't have men working in their child-care centers. That was supposed to be the One True Cure, the magic bullet of its day, that would effect gender equity and thereby change all social structures, from the bottom up as it were. Alas, there are never such easy solutions to complex problems. Child molestation won't be cured by shutting down child-care centers, nor will the rape and murder of women be eliminated by shutting down porn. Such proposals for social cleansing become poignant symbols of their epochs, litmus tests for prejudice and fear set loose in the body politic.

Although I did my best to attack the goals and methods of *Not a Love Story,* I myself am not immune to the feelings of outrage and dismay shared by so many women who, faced with a barrage of gender-based violence, would like to shut down the movie emporiums and studios and ad agencies and networks and magazines responsible for purveying it. I have to acknowledge the transformative power of such myths of causality and the craving of women for some force to counteract the seemingly unending exploitation of their/our images onscreen and real bodies offscreen. But at what cost?

An actress of my acquaintance once confessed to me, just as I was writing a piece on the causes of "neoviolence" in recent movies, that the rape and murder of a friend had caused her to shift her position on censorship and movie portrayals of violence against women. I still can't bring myself to support censorship in any way. I tend to agree with those who argue that it always backfires, censoring "us" but not "them." Yet in my heart of hearts, I am not quite the strict First Amendment kid that I used to be. I'm stuck with it until something better comes along, but I now wonder whether the debate doesn't have to evolve beyond an all-or-nothing acceptance-rejection dynamic. So far, the egregious consequences of prohibition still outweigh the mistakes of excessive tolerance. I don't have the new answers, just the sense of some new questions in the air.

15.

Antiporn:

Soft Issue, Hard

World (*Not a*

Love Story)

(1982–83)

Why has the antiporn movement been so popular with the dominant media? My suspicions are not benign. For one thing, in a society that has failed to distinguish between sexuality and pornography, the antiporn movement is a perfect vehicle for lumping all feminists together into one posse, a bunch of sex cops out to handcuff the body politic's cock. The ensuing ridicule can always offset any serious statements. Second, the subject offers the chance to talk about sex, something the mainstream media are never loath to take up. Third, the antiporn movement is probably seen, and rightly so, as profoundly ineffectual, unlikely ever to make a dent in the massive commercial sex industry it would seek to topple. The porn companies don't have to worry about any consumer boycott by women; we're not their customers. It is even possible that the antiporn forces get press because they represent no threat. *Not a Love Story*—portentously subtitled "A Motion Picture about Pornography"—can open at the 57th Street Playhouse in a gala premiere, emblazon *Village Voice* and the *Times* as well with ads, boast a prestige distributor and a first-class PR firm, and even make it onto the evening news. Just in case there's any lingering doubt about its moral fiber, keep in mind that it's showing at the same theater where *Genocide* just ran.

Documentary films, like fiction, have a script. The script may not be written before the shooting, as with fiction, but in that case it gets written in the editing room. *Not a Love Story* is no exception. Director Bonnie Klein, producer Dorothy Todd Henaut, and associate director and editor Anne Henderson seem to have scripted a religious parable.

The pivotal figure in the parable is Linda Lee Tracey, a stripper with a comedic "Little Red Riding Hood" act. She performs the role of the re- formed sinner, without whom no religious faith could be complete. Her redemption seals the film's theme, binds the audience to it, and provides the necessary narrative closure. *Not a Love Story* opens with a series of valentines, ranging from soft-core forties style to an up-to-date hard-core *Hustler* version, but clearly it is the Sacred Heart that takes over by the end.

Linda Lee is the real star of the film. A Montreal media personality famous for her annual "Tits for Tots" charity strips, she was a find for the filmmakers. It is she who accompanied director Klein on all the inter- view sessions, frequently asking the questions herself, challenging the hucksters, haranguing customers from a soapbox on the street. If Klein empathizes onscreen, emoting outrage and concern, it is Tracey who acts, reacts, and takes the risks. Just how much of a risk is made clear toward the end of the film. The audience has already been buffeted by porno- graphic images and film clips, appalled by the attitudes of the porn kings, overwhelmed by the statistics, and alternately inspired and outraged by what has been shown and said. As the culmination of its guided tour, the audience gets to be present at a photo session set up between porn photographer Suze Randall and our by-now heroine, Linda Lee, who has decided "to find out what it feels like to be an object." In her willingness to embrace this risk, Linda Lee becomes the film's dramatis persona, the one character who is transformed, within the film, by the very experience of making the film. As if Christ had come back as a latter-day Mary Mag- dalene, she literally offers up her body for our, and her, salvation.

Halfway through the film, Linda Lee comments, "it's starting to get to me at an emotional level." She means: the pornography. But I mean: the movie. *Not a Love Story* is, for me, more depressing than inspiring, more irritating than enlightening. The film hits its emotional stride early on and stays there, never straying into detours of social analysis, historical per- spective, or questions of representation. Klein sets the tone with her pose of womanly empathy, polite outrage, and respectability. She recounts her decision to make the film after her eight-year-old daughter's exposure to porn magazines at the local bus counter. I suspect many viewers' responses to the movie will rise or fall on the issue of identification with Klein. Mine fell. An aura of religiosity began to permeate the proceedings. Method and message began to blur as the film gained in momentum, upping the emotional ante into a cathartic finale.

Not a Love Story is no call to arms, but rather an exercise in show-and-tell. Gaze at the forbidden, react with your choice of anger or outrage or grief (or the male option: guilt), and leave a changed person. When Linda Lee undergoes her debasement at the lens of Suze Randall and subsequently emerges transformed and cleansed—running on the beach in the film's last frames—she is enacting a ceremony that the audience communally shares. A change in consciousness, a change of heart. Look here and weep. Postscreening goings-on, both at the New York premieres and in Canada, fortify the scenario. After-film discussions have turned the theater into a secular confessional, eliciting testimonials, women's resolutions to confront their mates' porn collections, teenage boys swearing to forgo the porn culture that awaits them, male viewers alternately abashed and exploding in anger, and so on. According to polls of the film's audiences, people are moved from seeing pornography as harmless to viewing it as harmful by the end of the film. Conversion cinema in action.

In this moral tale, each character has a clearly prescribed role. Klein, who appears onscreen to supply an identificatory figure for the audience, plays the missionary in a heathen land. Seeking out the purveyors of porn, she is seen unearthing the sins of the world in order to combat them and save our souls. Blue Sky, Raven, and other peep-show workers and strippers all play the collective role of victim. Porn photographer Suze Randall, who photographs hard-core spreads in her studio, plays the classic madame: she who sells her own kind but probably, deep inside, is a true believer. The porn moguls interviewed are surely the forces of evil, whether represented by the sleezy panache of publisher David Wells or by the endearing just-like-your-Uncle-Henry spirit of one sex emporium manager. The male customers constitute the legions of rank sinners. A San Francisco–based group of men against male violence assumes the guise of penitentes; matching a sixties wire-rim style to an eighties sensitivity, they take the sins of their kind upon their shoulders and expiate them. There is, of course, a roster of saints: Susan Griffin, Kate Millett, Margaret Atwood, Kathleen Barry, and topping them all, Robin Morgan, who, with husband Kenneth Pitchford and young son, presents her own version of the Holy Family. Addressing the camera with a philosophical fervor (except for the more casual Millett), the saints embody the forces of righteousness arrayed against the sinful.

Is the appeal of the film, then, a religious one? A desire to pass through the flames, be washed in the blood of the lamb, and come out a new person? I think not. Instead, the antiporn film is an acceptable replacement for porn itself, a kind of snuff movie for an antisnuff crowd. In this version, outrage-against replaces pleasure-in, but the object of the preposition remains the same. Cries of outrage and averted eyes replace the former clientele's silent pleasure and inverted hats; the gaze of horror substitutes for the glaze of satiation. The question, though, is whether this outcry becomes itself a handmaiden to titillation, whether this alleged look of horror is not perhaps a most sophisticated form of voyeurism. The ad campaign reinforces the suspicion, with its prominent surgeon-general-style warning about the "graphic subject matter" that viewers might want to avoid — if avoidance is indeed the desired goal.

The film's own methods compound the problem. Though it would be unrealistic to ask *Not a Love Story* to solve problems the political movement it addresses has so far ignored, it's reasonable to expect the film to take up those problems relevant to its own medium. A host of issues raised by pornography are applicable to cinema, ranging from voyeurism or objectification to simple questions of point of view. Instead of facing these challenges, though, the filmmakers seem unquestioningly to accept and deploy traditional cinematic practices. Given their subject matter, this decision creates a subtext of contradiction throughout the film.

For example, the early scenes of strippers performing their act are shot from the audience, a traditional enough technique for a rock concert movie, but problematic here. Doesn't such a shot turn the viewer into the male customer normally occupying that vantage point? Doesn't the camera's privileged gaze, able to zoom in and out at will, further objectify the woman on stage? Worse yet is the scene shot in a club equipped with isolation masturbation booths, wherein the women on display communicate with the male customers via a glass window and telephone, with the duration determined by a descending blackout shutter timed to the deposit of money. The cinematographer lines the camera up with this same shutter, positioning us behind the shoulder of a male customer in the booth, protected by shadows even as the woman called Blue Sky is exposed to our view. The cinematographer takes this alignment with the male customer one step further by zooming in for a close-up on Blue Sky — thereby presenting us with an intimate view not even available to the real-life customer. (At such moments, Klein's use of a male cameraman becomes an issue.) Why visually exploit this woman to a greater degree than her job already does? Why make the male customer our stand-in and then let him off the hook, without either visual exposure or verbal confrontation?

Why not let us see what Blue Sky sees? Instead, the filmmaker proceeds to interview two of the women from within this same booth and from the customer's seat. Now the man has departed and we remain sophisticated consumers, out for the show and the facts, coyly paying money when the inevitable shutter descends.

The filmmakers efface their own presence whenever the movie enters the sex emporiums. Although Klein is prominent in the other interview sessions, she does not appear at all in the clubs. Furthermore, no second camera ever shows us the steady gaze of this one filming the scene for us, the performer's "other" audience. True, we see the male audience — but only from the vantage point of another member of that audience. The camera is protected in its invisibility by the filmmaker, just as the male customers are in turn protected in their anonymity by the camera.

This is a serious mistake, but it's a clue to the film's attitude. At no point does the camera offer a shot from the point of view of the women up on the stage. We're never permitted to share their experience while they're working — to inhabit their perspective when they're supposedly being most exploited and objectified. The result is a backfire: we remain voyeurs, and they remain objects — whether of our pity, lust, respect, or shock makes little difference.

Not all the problems arise out of shooting; others occur in the editing room, particularly in the choices of sound/image combination. The key scene is Linda Lee's porn photo session with Suze Randall, whose presence overwhelms us with frequent calls for such props as "the pussy light," and "the pussy juice." Although the scene has Linda Lee speaking as she starts to pose, her voice gives way to a voice-over of Susan Griffin explaining eros. Only later do we get to hear Linda Lee's comments. Why use Griffin's words when the film could have reinforced Tracey's image with her own explanation? Instead, the considerable power she wields elsewhere in the film simply evaporates.

The power of the pornography included as exhibits throughout the movie does no such evaporation act. Why does the film present us with the porn materials intact? Any number of methods could have been used either to intensify their impact or to diminish it. Some kind of manipulation of the image is standard practice in films incorporating preexisting footage. The filmmakers chose not to, with two possible results: either we're made to undergo the degradation of porn or we're offered its traditional turn-on. Klein wants the audience to eat its cake and have it, too.

In sum, *Not a Love Story* is very much a National Film Board of Canada product: concerned, engaged, up to the minute on social questions, but slick, manipulative, avoiding all the hard questions to capture the ready success of answering the easy ones. It may have a different subject from other NFB films, but its methods are inherited. These methods have been developed for decades, and they work. If *Not a Love Story* is successful, that will be because of its emphasis on emotion, the presence of Linda Lee Tracey as a genuinely appealing star, the shock of the porn characters, and the sympathy of Bonnie Klein as our Alice in Pornoland. Not incidentally, the film offers some of the porn its audience wants to see but wouldn't be caught dead seeking out in Times Square. Most fundamentally, though, the film's fate will signal the prospects of the antipornography campaign itself. The basic questions are not, finally, about *Not a Love Story* at all. They concern the past and future of antiporn politics, the reasons for its appeal, and the questions of priority it raises.

Displacement, Confusion, and What's Left Out

There are many unanswered questions in *Not a Love Story,* the title itself not the least of them. Assuming that pornography is not about love, what is it? The film privileges the words of Susan Griffin, who defines one of the central tenets of the antiporn movement: pornography is different from eroticism. Kate Millett says the same thing, as have countless others. But, what is pornography and what is eroticism? One is bad, the other is good (guess which). Fixing the dividing line is rather like redlining a neighborhood: the "bad" neighborhood is always the place where someone else lives. Porn is the same. If I like it, it's erotic; if you like it, it's pornographic. The rules don't seem much clearer than that, so the game gets murkier by the minute. Ready?

Two stories. Back in 1969, when I first started thinking about this distinction, my best friend worked as an artist's model; so, eventually, did I. She would model for painters but never for photographers, because with them you'd have no control over who saw your body. Once she broke the rule and modeled for a mutual friend, a photographer who did a series of nude photographs of her that we all loved. He had a show in a local gallery. One photograph of my friend was stolen out of the show. She went into a terrible depression. She was tormented by the image of an unknown man jerking off to her picture. Test: Was that photograph erotic or pornographic?

Back in 1980, a woman I know went to spend the day with a friend's family. Looking around the house, what should she discover but the father's personal copy of the Tee Corrine cunt coloring book. Made for the women's community, the book usually was found only in feminist bookstores. Test: Is the book erotic or pornographic?

I have other friends and other stories. Surely it is not merely an image that is one thing or the other, but equally (if not foremost) the imagination that employs the image in the service of its fantasy. It is time that antiporn activists stop kidding themselves about the fine distinctions between eroticism and pornography. If any extra test is needed, the film offers us one in its final freeze-frame shot of a bikini-clad Linda Lee, snapped in midair, seaweed in hand. It is meant as an image of "wholeness, sanity, life-lovingness" according to the filmmakers, but it comes out looking more like a soft-core Tampax ad. Is this image, perchance, pornographic as well?

There is no end of definitions as to what pornography is or isn't. For me, that's no longer the point. I have read the statistics, thank you, on whether porn causes violence or violence causes porn, taken part in the chicken-or-the-egg fights, steered clear of the currently chic analyses of porn in academic circles. I'm as fed up with pornography being identified as sexuality (in some circles) as with antipornography being identified as feminism (in other circles). The books, the articles, and now the films have been rolling out.[1] Such widespread acceptance is always a clue that the problem has moved elsewhere. Why is pornography so important, finally? Is it important enough to be consuming all our political energy as feminists? Certainly it is seductive. It offers no end of discourse, arguments, connotations, and denotations in which we can immerse ourselves, no end of soul searching and pavement pounding that we can enact if so moved. But whence comes its assumed political priority, and does the issue deserve it?

The film, like much Women Against Pornography campaign rhetoric, tends to identify porn both by what it is *not* (a love story) and by what it *is* at its most extreme (sadism, torture dramas). The film, like the antiporn movement lately, emphasizes the extent to which sex-and-violence is the contemporary face of porn. But such a focus dodges the dilemma. If violence were the only problem, then why would the film include extensive footage of the strip shows and peep booths? If only violent sex were the object of wrath, then why would any Women Against Pornography group picket a nonviolent live sex show, or girlie line-up? In fact, the reliance on violence condemnation in the rhetoric is a clue to the appeal of the antiporn movement. Women today are terrified at the levels of violence being directed at us in society—and, to take it further, at powerless people everywhere. As one porn actress in the movie eloquently put it, we're "the fucked." Women are terrified at the crazy spiral of rape, assaults on abortion rights, sterilization expansion, domestic battering, and anonymous bashing.

Terror is not an effective emotion, though. It paralyzes. The fear of escalating violence, accompanied by the larger social backlash, has resulted not in massive political action by feminists but rather in a reaction of denial, a will not to see the dangers—a desperate desire to see, instead, their disguises. Turning away from a phalanx of assaults too overwhelming to confront, the Women Against Pornography groups turn instead to its entertainment division, pornography. But whether symptom or cause, pornography presents an incomplete target for feminist attack. The campaign against pornography is a massive displacement of outrage that ought to be directed at a far wider sphere of oppression. Just as the film narrows the hunt down to sinners, villains, and victims, so too does the antipornography movement leave out too much in its quasi-religious attack on the Antichrist.

The hunt for archetypes, darkly submerged drives, and other assorted ghouls of the pornography industry and the pornographic imagination has left livelier culprits out in the cold. So long as the conversion experience is the primary method, then the social, economic, historical, and political determinants get short shrift. As long as they continue, of course, it is unlikely that Dorothy Henaut will get her dream—announced opening night—of seeing the porn industry dry up and "wither away."

The emphasis on violence has masked the central issue of male-female power relations that we see reflected and accentuated in pornography. Any woman is still fair game for any man in our society. Without an understanding of these power relations, no analysis of porn will get very far. It certainly won't be able to account for the prevalence of fake lesbianism as a staple of pornographic imagery (without violence). It certainly won't be able to account for the difference between straight porn and gay male porn, which lacks any debasement of women and must raise complex issues regarding sexual objectification. If an analysis of porn were to confront its basic origin in the power relations between men and women, then it would have to drop the whole eroticism-versus-pornography debate and take on a far more complex and threatening target: the institution of heterosexuality. Here, again, is a clue to the antiporn movement's appeal for some battle-scarred feminists. Is it, perhaps, more tolerable for the woman who might attend *Not a Love Story* to come to terms with how her male lover's pornographic fantasy is oppressing her in bed than to confront, yet again, how his actual behavior is oppressing her in the living room—or out in the world?

Also left out of the picture are all questions of class and race, subsumed under the religious halo of good versus evil. Does it do any good, however, to view the women employed in the porn empire as victims? Linda Lee herself, in the movie, describes having gone to a Women Against Pornography demonstration in New York and feeling the other women's condescension. Or, as "Jane Jones" told Laura Lederer in the *Take Back the Night* anthology, "I've never had anybody from a poor or working-class background give me the 'How could you have done anything like that?' question, but middle-class feminists have no consciousness about what it is like out there."[2] As long as the economic forces and social choices that move these women into the commercial-sex world remain invisible, they themselves will continue to be objectified, mystified, and misunderstood by the very feminist theorists who, wine glass in hand or flowers nearby, claim to have all the answers. The film equally ignores questions of race, even though the porn industry, in its immense codification, has always divided the female population up into racial segments keyed to specific fetishes.

Issues of race and class, here, are particularly troubling in that they divide so clearly the filmmakers from their subjects. One friend of mine, herself a Puerto Rican activist, pinpointed the cause of her outrage at the film: "All these years, she [Klein] was never bothered by my exploitation. Now, suddenly, *she* feels exploited by my exploitation, and it's *this* feeling that really upsets her." The film never acknowledges that there might be a difference between the physical debasement of the women who earn their living in the sex industry and the ideological debasement of all women caused by the very existence of that industry. On the contrary, the antipornography movement has never taken up the issue of class. If it had addressed questions of class with attention or seriousness, then it might have avoided the seeming complicity with the state (like its notorious participation in the Times Square cleanup campaign, evidenced by its acceptance of office space by the forces advancing the street sweep) that has made so many feminists wary of the antiporn movement's real politics. Instead, the total and very apparent isolation of the filmmakers from the women who populate the various sex establishments in their film cannot help but make the viewer uneasy. Empathy? Forget it. To put it bluntly, the antiporn campaigners seem to view the women working in the commercial-sex industry much the same way that the Moral Majority seems to view pregnant teenagers. The powerful sense of identification that has been such a keystone of feminist politics is absent; in its place is a self-righteous sense of otherness that condemns the sex workers eternally to the position of Bad Object (pending, of course, any Linda Lee–like transubstantiation).

Also overlooked is the aboveground face of porn, its front-parlor guise as legitimate advertising. This was the first target of WAVAW (Women Against Violence Against Women) in such actions as the attack on the

Rolling Stones' infamous Black and Blue billboard. The *Hustler* cover image that made the movie audience gasp (a woman churned in a meat grinder) made its feminist debut in the early WAVAW slide shows. Such actions have faded in recent years, as debate, theory, and red-light-district pressure tactics took over. *Not a Love Story* alludes to the intersection of pornography and advertising, even illustrates it at points, but never explicates the connections. The antiporn literature does the same, condemning the continuum without analyzing the linkage. Hasn't anyone heard of capitalism lately? To use women to sell products, to use pornography to sell genital arousal, there has to be an economic system that makes the use profitable. Porn is just one product in the big social supermarket. Without an analysis of consumer culture, our understanding of pornography is pathetically limited, bogged down in the undifferentiated swamp of morality and womanly purity.

Significantly in these cold war times, the differing attitudes of Nazi and Communist societies are not cited equally. The historical usage of pornography by the Nazis (who flooded Poland with porn at the time of the invasion to render the population . . . impotent?) is mentioned by Robin Morgan in the film and has been cited by others in articles and talks. No one ever mentions (with whatever reservations) the contemporary abolition of pornography in Cuba or in Nicaragua. There, it is one part of an overall social program; here, it must be the same if it is ever to succeed in transforming our systems of sexual exchange.

The single-issue nature of the antiporn movement is one of its most disturbing aspects. Once the "final solution" has been identified, there is no need to flail away at other social inequities. I'd guess that its avoidance of social context is another of antiporn's attractions. Racism, reproductive rights, homophobia, all pale beside the ultimate enemy, the pornographer. How politically convenient for a right-leaning decade. It is precisely this avoidance of context, this fetishizing of one sector or one crime, that is the distinguishing feature of life under capitalism. It is also, of course, the same fetishism and fragmentation that characterize the pornographic imagination.

Retro Politics

How can it be that I, as a feminist, even one who objects to pornography and subscribes to many of the arguments against it, can at the same time object just as strenuously to the antipornography movement and to the method, style, perhaps even the goals of *Not a Love Story*? Or that many other feminists share my objections? The answer, predictably enough, is political. It has to do with the conviction that, in the fight against pornography, what gets lost is as serious as what gets won.

Behind the banner of pornography is the displaced discourse on sexuality itself. Indeed, if the antiporn campaign offers a safety zone within which the larger antifeminist forces abroad in eighties America need not be viewed, it also offers a corresponding zone that excludes personal sexuality. This depersonalizing of sexuality is the common effect both of pornography and of the antipornography forces. It is a depersonalization that is all too apparent in the film.

Only Kate Millett speaks with ease, in her own voice, and from her own experience, lounging on the floor with one of her "erotic drawings." It is impossible to connect the other spokeswomen personally to the texts that they talk at us. Both Susan Griffin (with, unfortunately, nature blowing in the wind behind her head) and Kathleen Barry (framed by drapes and flowers) speak abstractly, rely on the third person, and bask in an aura of solemnity that punches all of the film's religioso buttons. When Robin Morgan hits the screen, an even greater problem appears.

It is here that we realize just how much space the film has preserved for men. Not only has its debate been framed entirely in terms of heterosexuality; not only have we been forced to watch always from the seat of a male buyer; but now we are made to accept feminist wisdom from a woman in tears, reduced to crying by the contemplation of the great pain awaiting us all, and capable of consolation only by the constant massaging of a sensitive husband (in a supporting penitente role) and a prematurely supportive son, who flank her on the sofa as she tells of women's suffering, boyhood's innocence, and men's innate desire to do right. Isn't this going too far? Middle-class respectability, appeals to motherhood, and now, elaborate detours aimed at making men feel comfortable within the cozy sphere of the enlightened. Any minute, and the film will go all "humanistic" before our very eyes. Men didn't used to play such a central role in the feminist movement. Nor did women used to put quite such a premium on respectability and sexual politesse.

What has happened here? It has been an unsettling evolution, this switch from a movement of self-determination, that trashed billboards and attacked the legitimacy of soft-core advertising, to a movement of social determination, that urges legal restrictions and social hygiene. When the antipornography movement traded in its guerrilla actions for the more recent route of petitioning a higher authority to enact moral codes, the political trajectory went haywire. I do not agree with those who go no further than a pious citing of the First Amendment in their pornography discussions; although the vision of free speech is a benevolent one, even at times a practicable ideal, I am cynically aware of its purchase power in this society, especially in a backlash era. Although I do not, therefore, agree that WAP can simply be conflated with the Moral Majority and that's that, I do think the notion that a feminist agenda can be legislated in our society is a naïve, and ultimately dangerous, one.

Judith Walkowitz, in her essay on "The Politics of Prostitution," traced the political ramifications of the British nineteenth-century antiprostitution campaigns, cautioning that the feminists lacked the cultural and political power to reshape the world according to their own image.[3] Although they tried to set the standards for sexual conduct, they did not control the instruments of state that would ultimately enforce these norms. Nor do we today. Nor are feminists likely to countenance any such movement to set, let alone enforce, some notion of sexual "norms." This proscriptive tendency in the antiporn movement is not offset by any counterbalancing emphasis on an alternative sexual tradition (except for the elusive eroticism). Is it a coincidence that one of the film's antiporn demonstrators could be a stand-in for Mercedes McCambridge in *Johnny Guitar?* The antiporn movement has a tendency to promote a premature codification of sexuality, and *Not a Love Story* may suffer for that emphasis.

Perhaps the film actually arrived just one season too late in New York. The questions of sexual norms and sexual codification exploded at the 1982 Barnard conference on "the politics of sexuality" with a coalition of WAP and others pitted against women espousing "politically incorrect sexualities." The conference has trailed in its wake a series of attacks and counterattacks, a sensationalizing of the proceedings, and one of the worst movement splits of recent times. Again, my perennial question surfaces: Why pornography? Why this debate? It seems that after a long hiatus, following Ti-Grace Atkinson's polemical assertion that "the women's movement is not a movement for sexual liberation," feminists have come back to sexuality as an issue to discuss, argue, and analyze. It is not, however, clear why this debate should focus either on pornography or on sadomasochism (the two extremes at the conference), why it should short-circuit its own momentum by immediate codification.

It's time that the women's movement got back on track. While Robin Morgan weeps on the sofa, there are worse things happening in the world. It's time to acknowledge the importance of analyzing pornography, assign it a priority in the overall picture, and get on with the fight. Pornography is an issue of importance. But it is becoming much too fashionable to "study" pornography in academic circles to dubious effect. Unlike many of the theorists doing that work, I would agree instead with Monique Wittig in "The Straight Mind" when she stresses that, though pornography is indeed a "discourse," it is also for women a real source of oppression.[4] That said, however, I would suggest that women desist from putting ourselves through the study of it. Finally, here's a proper subject for the legions of feminist men: let them undertake the analysis that can tell us why men like porn (not, piously, why this or that exceptional man does not), why stroke books work, how Oedipal formations feed the drive, and how any of it can be changed. Would that the film had included any information from average customers, instead of stressing always the exceptional figure (Linda Lee herself, Suze Randall, etc.). And the antiporn campaigners might begin to formulate what routes could be more effective than marching outside a porn emporium.

As for the rest of us, it is time to desist, stop indulging in false and harmful polarities, and look around. Outraged at the abuse of women in our society, there are any number of struggles that can be joined on a broad social front. Outraged at pornography's being the only available discourse on sexuality, there is a great amount of visionary and groundbreaking work to do in the creation of a multitude of alternative sexual discourses, a veritable alternative culture of sexuality, that people can turn to for sexual excitement instead of porn. It's about time we redefine our terms and move on, with the spirit of justice and visionary energy that always used to characterize feminism.

As the first mass-audience film to take up the subject of pornography, *Not a Love Story* is an important work. It opens up the issues even if it closes them down again too soon. For the people whom the film makes think seriously, for the first time, about pornography, it is a landmark. It is fascinating to hear that the audience at a recent midweek daytime screening was all single men; is it encouraging that none of them walked out? or discouraging that they could stay? Perhaps the film sins, for all its righteousness, in being simply too little, too late, even though it's the first of its kind.

Because it can help move the political debate on to the next stage, *Not a Love Story* deserves attention. Because it shows all too clearly the stage the debate is now in, it deserves criticism.

Prologue.

Unguided Tours

I n 1983, I traveled to Minneapolis for two very different events that
both took place at the Walker Art Center in Minneapolis, one in the
spring and one in the fall.

Melinda Ward and Bill Horrigan had been hard at work organizing a major conference, The Media Arts in Transition, for the National
Alliance of Media Arts Centers (NAMAC). Although the conference was an
annual event, this one was meant to be more than a mediated gathering:
its title announced its purpose of taking stock of the field and attempting
to chart some strategies for the future. A glossy catalogue offered essays by
a strange combination of foundation and public funding brass, a handful
of founding fathers of the avant-garde, and current curators. It was a very
mainstream selection drawn from the high-art end of the field, but the
conference itself was drawn from the entire media arts constituency — and
NAMAC already had a history and reputation for fractious polarizations.

Now, what I enjoyed about my position as the director of the New York
State Council on the Arts Film Program was that it tended to ensure, at
gatherings like this one, that I be given a seat at the big table, not in the
kids' annex where my point of view would otherwise relegate me. In this
case, that privilege translated into a position on the keynote panel addressing the conference's theme. Ron Green of Ohio State University was
the moderator. To my delight, Brian O'Doherty, the once and future head

of the National Endowment for the Arts media division, preceded me on the dais. His essay had given a hint of his approach as a beltway bureaucrat with liberal white-boy credentials in year two of the Reagan revolution: talk tough, stand tall, no more entitlements, time to grow up. In his essay, he'd asked: "Are these comments too banal? Maybe they're not as exciting as great ideas. But I've never found that a marvelous idea got you across the street." Really? I didn't like his message and decided to give him a run for his money. As a state arts bureaucrat with a film budget second only to the feds, I was uniquely positioned to try to neutralize his influence.

The official catalogue was stuffed full of what might have been dubbed The Men We Admire (barely a quarter of the contributors were women) drawn from the ranks of the patriarchs of the film and video world: Stan Brakhage, Jonas Mekas, Gene Youngblood, Tony Conrad, and so on. What year were we in? I had a strange, time-traveling premonition. Renee Tajima, Jon Alpert, and George Stoney were the activist rabble-rousers that had snuck into the pages, but they were clearly meant to be invited guests at the soiree: behave yourself, or you won't be invited back.

My own essay for the catalogue, "Cultural Democracy in the Electronic Age," had been an anxious one. Concerned that technological "access has evaporated faster than it's materialized," I was worried that "culture, in its electronic phase, seems to be in danger of retreating to an old pre-democratic model." I focused on distribution as a neglected aspect of the field that was crippling filmmakers and audiences alike by its underdevelopment, and I faulted film criticism and journalism for not fulfilling their obligation to bring independent work to the public. I called for an invigorated film criticism, "honestly engaged with the medium, neither defensive about its legitimacy nor didactic about its superiority." In that regard, I had persuaded Carrie Rickey (today the *Philadelphia Inquirer* film critic) to attend and report on the conference for the *Village Voice,* where she was on staff; afterward, she reflected on what an odd experience it had been to be treated like an interloper and pariah when journalists were usually courted by institutions desperate for press coverage.

In the end, I ditched much of my prepared speech in reaction to what Brian O'Doherty had to say. He held up corporate models, demanded that people expand their boards, talked budgets and cutbacks and "economic realities," and generally did a great job of blaming the victim at a moment of political retrenchment and disenfranchisement. I advised the audience to beware of his message. As to the great but vague offers being made to all of us to come in and share resources, I complained: "When we are finally invited in to share the power, it's usually because the real power has already moved elsewhere." As for technology and the way it was being offered as a panacea at the very moment when few in that room had the balance sheets needed to acquire it, I quipped that offering such advice to this field was rather like recommending real estate investment to a group of tenants-rights activists. I advocated political solutions instead.

Whereas O'Doherty thought getting bankers on the board was important, I thought getting back in touch with communities was crucial. I urged the audience to reject the Reaganesque top-down trickle model for a return to the grassroots that could sustain us. The early eighties were a rough time for the independent film field, and I knew people were hurting. I called for more demands to be made on the press, and to emphasize the point I held up a copy of *Fuse* magazine and reminded my audience that the glory days of sixties filmmaking included a glorious "underground" press that had been key to the creation of a countercultural community with a sense of its own identity and potential power. Feminism, too, could never have taken off without *off our backs, Chrysalis, Heresies, Ms, Signs, Feminist Studies,* and other such magazines and journals. My speech was popular enough that O'Doherty, seething, felt obliged to mutter: "Very statesmanlike." He had never spoken to me before and he'd never speak to me again. But he'd given me his ultimate compliment by including me as a "man."

While Media Arts in Transition was busy discussing its serious policy issues in an incubatorlike environment sealed off from any issues of gender or sexuality, some of us at least were aware of the Twin Cities reputation as one of the centers of lesbian activity in the country. Martha Gever arrived in her pickup truck from Rochester, where she was editor of *Afterimage.* Lynn Blumenthal organized an outing to a lesbian bar in St. Paul and we all piled in the back of Martha's pickup. Ecstatic at having escaped the antiseptic world of the media arts, we hung out for hours, some on the dance floor, some around the pool table, until the authenticity of this neighborhood joint exceeded our tastes. A good old-fashioned dyke fight of the stay-away-from-my-girlfriend variety broke out and we reluctantly headed for the pickup truck, the bridge, and the sanctuary of the media arts world at the Walker.

Back in New York City, I decided to break up the long hot summer by throwing a thirty-fifth birthday bash for myself. I cut off my long hair to mark my transition. My friend Carrie was lending her loft on lower Broadway as party central and I'd already sent out invitations with the motto: "No longer precocious." My friend Petra Barreras, at that time married to the son of the Casa Moneo family, contributed Spanish tortillas and other party food. Madonna's great dance record had just come out. It was easily the hottest day of the summer, and when everyone jumped up to dance, the temperature must have risen to nearly 100 degrees. My pal Ana Mendieta introduced us to her weird antisocial boyfriend, artist Carl Andre; she had recently moved out of her tiny, charming Village studio to live with him. Lizzie Borden came with her girlfriend Honey, who starred in *Born in Flames*. Filmmaker Sheila McLaughlin and her girlfriend Telma Abascal were there as well and would become my great friends in future years. After a few rough years in my emotional life, this party was meant as a declaration of a clean bill of health, and became the start of the rest of my life.

A few months later I was back in Minnesota, this time for the Women's Independent Film Festival that had been organized by a group called Iris Video. They'd managed to get a number of different organizations in both Minneapolis and St. Paul to cooperate on the presentation — so there I was, back on the stage of the Walker, but this time my copanelists were Michelle Citron and Lauren Rabinovitz, with the extraordinary Sally Dixon moderating. (Sally Dixon had been instrumental in the early development of the media arts field in her capacity as curator at the Carnegie Institute in Pittsburgh; she then threw away her socialite status in midlife, relocated to St. Paul, and continued as an angel to countless filmmakers and video artists through her work at the Busch Foundation.) Jacqueline Zita, who'd already written about Barbara Hammer's films for *Jump Cut,* was teaching at the University of Minnesota and was part of the planning committee for the symposium.

This time around, there were no fights or controversies. Even though we knew we were in the ideological heart of antiporn country, or perhaps because of that, there were no films in the festival that set off any precipitating tremors. Everyone was very well behaved. At least for a while. When trouble struck, it was in the least likely location: Susan Sontag's film, *Unguided Tour.* To understand the trouble, it's necessary to understand the context. In general, the festival was reaching out not to cineastes but to the women's community. The festival program showed that aim quite clearly in the nature of its selections: for the politically committed, there were documentaries on Peru's Shining Path, lesbians and mothering, and women in Northern Ireland; an emphasis on multiculturalism had brought films by Julie Dash, Kathe Sandler, Sharon Larkin, Trinh T. Minh-ha, and an in-person appearance by Christine Choy; the selected fiction films tended to focus on female friendship or lesbian adventure. In a way, it was an old-fashioned women's film festival that revived the old spirit. Up to a point.

It was surprising to see *Unguided Tour* included because, like Sontag's other films, it had no feminist perspective or thematic relevance for this festival, being less preoccupied with Israel, its subject, than with its own opaque concern for cinema qua cinema. I knew a lot of film curators who'd passed on showing it. Sontag's film work, unlike her writing, tended to be a specialized taste that few people had managed to acquire. In the context of this activist-oriented event, however, the Saturday night screening of *Unguided Tour* was received with outrage, as though its dullness constituted a physical attack on the audience.

Women began to evacuate the theater in a fury and to complain vociferously to the festival organizers — who, in turn, novices themselves, made the remarkable decision to halt the screening in deference to the public's hostility. At about this point, several of us arrived at the theater to see how the audience was reacting to the film and were horrified at what was transpiring. It was absolutely unheard of to shut off a movie during a public screening. But this is censorship! we cried. No, it's not, we were told, they just hate the movie. It turned out that the festival programmers had not bothered to watch it before inviting it, overeager to score the coup of a Sontag film. We could not convince the festival organizers, no matter how hard we tried, that they were acting in violation of all professional standards and artistic ethics. Never a fan of Sontag, I was nevertheless chilled by this feminist mob behavior. What if I delivered a boring paper the next day? Off with her head!

In retrospect, I could see that what happened that night in Minneapolis was definitely linked in spirit and tactic to the events of the preceding year at Barnard (and of following years, as other films and tapes in other exhibitions have been removed or shut down for offending local "feminist" sensibilities). This event is notable, however, for being the only case to my knowledge in which boredom achieved the status of censorable content.

At the symposium, we all felt compelled to address the events of the night before and speak out against this abhorrent film exhibition behavior. We felt compelled to try to explain the necessity of tolerance, respect, diversity of opinion, and so on; then, that part of our missionary work over, we went on to deliver our prepared presentations as planned. Mine, transcribed from a handwritten text, is coming up.

The year 1983 looms large in my memory for other reasons, though. In the spring, Third World Newsreel and Hunter College had organized a big conference on Third World cinema that brought together key players from all over the world. I remember Haile Gerima sitting outside, basking in congratulations for his wonderful new film, *Ashes and Embers*. I remember my friend Lillian Jimenez introducing me to two filmmakers who were hard at work on a documentary about the mothers of the Plaza de Mayo. Nice to meet you, I said to Lourdes Portillo and Susana Blaustein (later Muñoz). My attention was elsewhere.

I hadn't been to Cuba since 1978, but here in person were Jorge Fraga and Hector Garcia Mesa from the Cuban Film Institute. They were scheduled to meet with a group of us who had already been at work for a few months on a program of U.S. independent films to travel to the film festival in Havana that winter. It was an extraordinary group, including the talented filmmaker Jacqueline Shearer (who would tragically die of cancer in the mid-nineties), filmmakers Deborah Shaffer and Ana Maria Garcia, activist and funder Monica Melamid, and my good friend Lillian Jimenez as coordinator.

We had endless meetings over which films to include and whom to invite. Lillian became pregnant and ended up having to resign as coordinator, though she went on to numerous key posts in the field of media arts and community activism, while raising her son Yuis. We managed somehow to raise money and pull off the most extraordinary event: a whole group of U.S. film folks, transported to Havana, along with a slate of films with translated soundtracks that included such early classic works as Charles Burnett's *Killer of Sheep* and Connie Field's *Rosie the Riveter*. We presented a symposium there and published a catalogue. Freude Bartlett, Jim Hoberman, and Richard Peña all attended.

This achievement is particularly notable given the context: between our meeting in New York and our arrival in Havana, the United States invaded Grenada, the cold war had taken over the Caribbean, and nothing about our arrangements for La Otra Cara (The other face) was easy. But we managed to bring Latin Americans the news that there was something happening cinematically in the United States outside Hollywood. For me, it was a healing return to my Cuba work. Monica and I stayed on for a few days after the festival and took a little R&R out at a beach house with a group of our Cuban film friends. (Monica became my good friend; she later married a Cuban and lives today with him and family in Mexico City.) Our friend Hector from the Cinematheque had arranged the outing, in part so that he could maximize his chances of plying young men on the beach with bottles of rum and his great personal charm. He became my best friend and protector in Cuba, even interceding for me when Cuban homophobia erupted. He collapsed a few years later from a stroke and died, such an unjust death (as they always are), given his many projects and pleasures still pending.

Back in the United States, I found myself frequently involved in anti-racist work, as it used to be called back then. Sometimes that involved policymaking, as my team and I worked to open more doors to NYSCA resources and persuade our funded organizations to become more inclusive. But other times it simply involved personal relations. Lillian, Jackie, and I invented an impromptu group for ourselves to talk about race and class. We'd meet every few weeks and discuss class and race, our families, our upbringing, and our perspectives on the current film scene. We had intersecting interests and backgrounds: Jackie and I had both gone to Girls' Latin School, she and Lillian shared a more active political past, Lillian and I were both working in funding while Jackie sought money for her next film. We had hilarious times calling each other's bluff and trying to help each other transcend our class limitations.

It was in this same period that my friends Lynn and Kate and Yvonne Rainer all got involved in an ultimately ill-fated project to create an artists' building in the East Village by leveraging city money. Once I had to leave a meeting about the Cuban film festival up in East Harlem to race down to the Lower East Side to testify in their favor at one of their hearings. Ironically, race politics took over the politics of funding such buildings; the artists were accused of gentrification and in pleading their case frequently ended up proving their enemies right, and the only productive result of a year's work turned out to be Yvonne's use of some of the videotaped hearings in her film, *Privilege*.

Moving around New York, I was constantly made aware of the contradictions of race and class that shaped work in the arts and influenced the kinds of films and filmmakers who would be judged acceptable. More and more, as feature filmmaking took over the field, access to investors enabled a whole different class of filmmaking than earlier public funding had empowered. We were losing the promise of a film meritocracy just as it could become a reality. For women filmmakers, in particular, tough times were about to get tougher. Feminism up to that point had never handled race very well, either, but at least it was learning. The essay that follows, delivered at that festival panel in Minneapolis, shows how hard I was working to try to pull together the different strands of my life into coherent critical positions.

16.

The

Feminist

Avant-Garde

(1983)

In thinking about current feminist film practices, it's helpful to recognize that each decade has been characterized by a preferred site of film production for women involved with the medium. In other words, there has always been one dominant choice operative at any given time. During and prior to the twenties, before the invention of sound, the site was Hollywood. Lois Weber and Alice Guy Blache both gravitated there, as did scores of other women directors whose names and films have been lost to us. Beginning in the twenties and lasting intermittently throughout the sound period up through the sixties, that site was instead the avant-garde. Excluded (with few exceptions) from the industry of film, women instead found an arena of expression within its parallel artisanal universe, the avant-garde.

Technological changes and political transformations in the late sixties shifted the site dramatically to the arena of the short documentary, a genre that could be said to have been transformed by its feminist reworking throughout the seventies. In the eighties, energy and focus have been shifting steadily from documentary over to the feature-length film, either in the form of narrative or some hybrid that grafts dramatic conventions or concerns onto avant-garde roots to create a "new narrative" genre.

If these have been the major trajectories of the century for feminist film work, then what are the implications for a discussion of the history of a so-called feminist avant-garde practice? The first task is to admit that this is a recent term. In the heyday of the avant-garde prior to a women's movement in this country, women were at a singular disadvantage. Most famous was the split between Artaud and Germaine Dulac. But equally relevant was the Derenesque bury-the-mother maneuvers by which the founding fathers of the New American Cinema sought to masculinize their tradition. Take the example of Joyce Wieland, the visionary Canadian filmmaker. Instead of being celebrated in her own right, she has been relegated to the category of Michael Snow's wife and her work pegged well below his in the pantheon, as if it were some quaint hobby, needlework perhaps, begging for indulgence or masculine attention.

In the groundswell and wake of the women's movement, a new film situation has emerged. The documentary became the cinematic voice of feminist ideology. Women committed to the avant-garde were often unsympathetic to feminist concerns, having successfully acclimated to the individualism and elitism of the art world. Maintaining the *artiste* standard of strictly individualistic achievement, they are horrified by the prospect of collective movements and creations. It's an old conflict. Many feminists, in turn, quickly copped an attitude of anti-avant-gardism based on notions of its experimental forms being intrinsically elitist, male-identified, and inaccessible to ordinary women, lacking in graduate school film education, who were assumed, or alleged, to be filling the screens and audiences of feminist cinemas. A classic case of the latter was Cindy Nemser's article in the *Feminist Art Journal* attacking Yvonne Rainer's first film on grounds of virtual collaboration with the enemy. Thus a standoff ruled over the early and mid-seventies, reflected sometimes in the women's film festivals' schizophrenic selections; only the less-polarized features coming out of Europe could contribute the necessary ballast to the programs.

By the late seventies, attitudes were beginning to unfreeze. JoAnn Elam's *Rape* marks one such point on the thaw line. She actively struggled to find a way into the issue of rape, a way beyond statistics into the feelings, gestures, and aftershocks of life lived in the pervasiveness of a rape culture. Her solution was to employ avant-garde techniques to do so: the use of video as a recording medium downplayed the testimonials already so familiar in documentary, while the importance of the words and language was inflated by subtitles emblazoned over the image. The use of street shots out of the verité vocabulary and symbolic games out of an avant-garde tradition of meaningful play further enrich her cinematic vocabulary. The film had arisen out of Elam's work with a rape consciousness group at a Chicago YWCA. That's where it came *from*. But as one of the founders of the Chicago Filmmakers alternative exhibition group, Elam was also pointing her film *toward* an art-informed audience. It is no accident that *Rape* seeks to bridge these worlds. No ivory-tower elitist, Elam actually works a day job as postal carrier.

Other work that appeared within roughly the same time frame has paralleled, continued, or expanded the ground staked out here. Evolution, assimilation, transformation: that's been the cycle of development for feminist film lately. If proof positive that a feminist avant-garde could exist had been provided by Sally Potter's *Thriller* and Michelle Citron's *Daughter Rite,* then recent work by Su Friedrich is important for demonstrating that this is no fluke. *Cool Hands Warm Heart* and *Gently down the Stream* are crucial works of feminist fantasy that, like the other films mentioned here, rely on associative meanings and subjective visualizations to revitalize a feminist film language. Ordinary acts are made strange: a woman shaving her legs becomes a sideshow act; dreams, once voiced and acknowledged, become powerful imperatives.

All of this work utilizes highly self-conscious filmic styles, film that's been worked on and worked over to make its point. These films are a far cry from the realism that had dominated feminist filmmaking before. It is for such reasons, I believe, that we can speak of a truly deliberative feminist avant-garde rather than of feminist implications, subtexts, or rereadings more characteristic of earlier avant-garde films by women. Given the nature of their basic reworking and reconsideration of formal elements, I continue to consider such films part of a "cinema of reconstruction."

If the past few years have brought a resurgence of activity in the area of formal experimentation, it's also true that dramatic feature films with a pressing concern for rewriting narrative have been equally influential. The work of such European and Caribbean filmmakers as Chantal Akerman, Sara Gomez, and Ulrike Ottinger, for instance, has defined, challenged, and often transgressed the existing definitions of a feminist aesthetic. Women's films from other parts of the world have influenced our sense here in the United States of what a women's cinema could be, given the resources. Now, without those resources and against all odds, new filmmakers in the United States have begun to produce films that are pushing the old definitions forward yet again. These new films are bound to reinvigorate the tired debates around feminist aesthetics as well as the more contemporary debate about the relationship of film to its feminist audiences. Two films showing in this festival are exemplary for their courage in trying new approaches to storytelling and cinematic expression: Julie Dash's *Illusions* and Lizzie Borden's *Born in Flames.*

Illusions is a major work that will attract a lot of attention as more

people learn of its accomplishment. It is one of the first attempts by a
Black filmmaker to address, at an imaginative level, the question of the
Black and White representations of Hollywood, the illusions and realities
of Blackness, and the particularly contradictory and painful inscription of
the Black woman within this world of processed images. Dash has moved
beyond the documentary portrait of an exemplary figure that has thus
far been more characteristic of Black women's filmmaking. Furthermore,
her film delineates the limits of identification between Black and White
women united in an imaginary sisterhood of solidarity: it's clear that race
is more determinant than gender even as it's also clear that gender can
never be ignored as a site of struggle. It's at once a brilliant riff on Hollywood's "passing" films and a definitive response to what Adrienne Rich
has called "snowblindness."

Born in Flames is already controversial as one of the least assimilatable
films for male viewers (they hate it) due to its assumption of an all-
woman nonracist universe. I suspect the film will be called many things:
naïve, utopian, separatist, violent, antisocial. With the typical displacement practiced by critics and curators who don't want to own up to the
real sources of their discomfort, the film has already been called techni-
cally flawed or, worst curse of all, falling below professional standards.
But *Born in Flames* demonstrates the most dynamic use of film seen in recent years — a use and critique of so many kinds of media (news coverage,
verité documentary, New Wave improvisation) that it becomes downright
voracious in its consumption of styles necessary to fuel its feminist science fiction tale of repression and revolution.

The feminist avant-garde, "the cinema of reconstruction," of the late
seventies and early eighties has thus paralleled feminist work in the fields
of literature and history in its commitment to formulating a feminist language, finding a feminist voice, and creating — in filmic terms — methods
of looking and speaking that are adequate to uncovering the truths, problems, and possibilities of our lives and our psyches. Why do we need such
a cinema? Why aren't documentary (with its presentation of evidence)
and traditional fiction (with its playing out of character and story) sufficient? Why risk the perils of inaccessibility for a seemingly less urgent,
more abstract purpose? For me, the answer lies in our very urgent and
hardly abstract need, in 1983, to begin to confront the relationship, and
widening gap, between behavior (as in fiction) and ideology (as in documentary). And to confront its implicit corollary: the gap between who we
are and who we wish to be.

This is a critical time. I have been engaged all year in a project to bring
U.S. independent films to Havana this winter for the annual Latin Ameri-

can Film Festival. This may seem like a different subject entirely, yet the words of Cuban director Tomás Gutiérrez Alea are applicable to the challenge facing feminist film today. Speaking of the challenge faced by the second generation of Cuban directors, he noted: "We can no longer film the process of the revolution with a candid camera." New tactics have to be devised to address new problems, for any movement anywhere.

In the desire to make everything PC (politically correct), we have too often sidestepped ambiguity and privileged the ideals of ideology over the ideals of behavior. Today the feminist community is suffering the consequences of that attitude in the battles over pornography and perversity, over WAP and lesbian sadomasochism, over censorship and role-playing, repression and expression: the battle of the Sex Cops and the Sex Criminals. As a film critic, I believe in the illuminating potential of cinema as an art form. As a committed critic of feminist cinema, I actually believe that the films I've been discussing today — if used, viewed, discussed — can assist us immeasurably in the difficult but unavoidable task now confronting us: the elaboration of a feminist aesthetic and political trajectory for the eighties.

Prologue.

Attacking the

Sisters, or the

Limits of

Disagreement

Feminism had significant roots in the New Left politics of the late sixties. That's a given. What's equally clear to me but less remarked upon is that feminist film activity had similar roots in the New Left politics of internecine warfare and rancorous internal debate. I had begun tracing such histories and genealogical feuds in my "Naming" piece back when I first entered the field and wanted to sort out the players. In the eighties, the field evolved significantly but was still organized according to the battle lines—now monolithic—that were set back in the seventies.

Arguments had a long history grounded in differing and antagonistic approaches to cultural politics. Well, it wasn't quite Bosnia, but the level of symbolic violence achieved toxic levels of intensity. For example, back in 1974 Julia Lesage had published a critique of the British journal *Screen*'s special issue on Brecht, questioning its investment in psychoanalysis. Her piece, "The Human Subject—You, He, or Me? (Or, the Case of the Missing Penis)," launched a feminist attack on Freud and also took Stephen Heath and *Screen* to task for using "he" as a neutral third-person term.[1] The editors of *Screen* responded by inviting Julia to join in debate. They reprinted her piece in *Screen* along with a longer retort by Ben Brewster, Stephen Heath, and Colin MacCabe, in which they complained of confusion in her article "created by the conflation of 'phallus' and 'penis'" and spoke of the difficulty of applying sociological concerns to theory: "If 'phallic' is simply made to mean 'masculine' and hence 'repressive,' and then pushed back onto psychoanalysis as a monolithic orthodoxy, it will be easy to dismiss Freud, but what gets dismissed along with this is, again, the whole question of the process of the subject."[2]

Yet the *Screen* editorial board was evidently not homogeneous. An editorial in the same issue noted that "not all of *Screen*'s Editorial Board are convinced" of the usefulness of "psychoanalytic concepts exemplified by the articles we publish in this number" and further complained that the "esoteric way the articles drawing on these developments of psychoanalysis have been presented in *Screen* represents a lack of real engagement with the politico-cultural issues which should form the context of *Screen*'s work."[3] Arguments and counterarguments persisted for many years, and intensified after the *Jump Cut* boycott of the Center for Twentieth-Century Studies conference that Stephen Heath and Teresa de Lauretis organized.

If today such reactions and counterreactions look like an absurdly excessive response to theoretical differences, two things should be kept in mind. First, the seventies were an intensely politicized era: intellectual positions were still identified as part of political activity and, as such, fair game for dispute. They were viewed as principled stands that should be taken at their word(s). Second, *Jump Cut* in its heyday was influenced as much by Maoist and Leninist principles as feminist ones, and rightly identified institutional power as a site of contention. If *Screen* or the Center in Milwaukee were setting an agenda for the field, then it was the field's responsibility (as embodied by *Jump Cut* and other interested players) to take up positions for or against that agenda. It was a sort of last hurrah: within a few years, the Center, *Screen,* and *Jump Cut* had all lost their positions of primacy in the field. Seventies-style politics were finally receding and giving way to new concerns.

By the mid-eighties, psychoanalytic feminism was consolidating its position as the only cinematic approach to carry weight in the academy. Its opaque language and narrow assumptions were becoming, astonishingly to me, the lingua franca of feminist film theory. I was feeling increasingly isolated and disheartened as many of my former allies fell by the wayside, switching careers or disciplines or else succumbing to the siren call of academic fashion. Even worse, those of us who had been committed to grassroots organizing, film activism, and accessible language were spread too thin to turn out books, while those whose academic track required publications were suddenly turning out volumes that not only guaranteed their own job security but significantly advanced the primacy of their approach in the world of film studies. I decided, typically, that something had to be done. I was a journalist, I had access to mainstream publications, and it was my job to fight the good fight. That's how I thought in those days.

Peter Biskind, whom I'd met on my trip to Cuba, had become an editor at *American Film* magazine; it was he who'd sent me to England to write about Channel Four. He now called with a new assignment. Two new books by Annette Kuhn and E. Ann Kaplan were about to be published and he wanted me to take them on as a referendum on the state of feminist film criticism. I thought I could use the opportunity to figure out just what bothered me so much about this new development and to try to analyze what the psychoanalytic filter did to feminist perspectives. For different reasons, then, our interests coincided and I accepted the offer.

I decided to speak my mind, knowing that *American Film* would reach a broad audience and could perhaps stimulate a debate on the status of the field. Naturally, I was also nervous about the repercussions. I was no longer in Chicago, where the Sunday afternoon *Jump Cut* editorial meetings (and paste-up sessions) could provide a safe haven for individual daring. Nor was I part of FACT or any other group organized to put forward a particular position. The film world was fractured and individualized by now, so I'd be stuck bearing the brunt of any reaction personally. Only my long-distance phone calls to Judith Mayne at Ohio State University reassured me; she had invited me to do my first lecture after I left the Film Center and was a consistent voice of support and respect from the world of academia. One year we'd even shared a room at a Society for Cinema Studies conference. The room happened to be adjacent to a rooftop from which our window could easily be entered and I was halfway through dialing the front desk to request a change when she stopped me: she had a black belt in karate and had always wished for a chance to test her training. Judith took the bed by the window and seemed a little disappointed that no prowler ever arrived to test her expertise.

Back in New York, as luck would have it, around the time that the issue containing my article hit the streets, I went to a dinner party for Teresa de Lauretis hosted by Margie Keller and P. Adams Sitney, timed to follow her lecture at Cooper Union, which he'd arranged, with a meal cooked by Margie at her Forsyth Street apartment in the heart of the Lower East Side. Though the dinner party would mark the end of the enmity between Teresa and me and the start of the friendship that replaced it, the guest list made it a delicate evening for me.

Seated near me at the small table was Annette Michelson, reigning diva of NYU, *October*, and a post-Trotskyist cultural legacy. Annette and I had met in the seventies in Chicago through Noel Carroll; he and Joan Braderman had been a couple while enrolled in the Cinema Studies Department at NYU and had occupied favorite-protégé status in the Michelsonian universe. But I had committed two cardinal sins in her eyes: starting a friendship with Joan as hers was waning and having the hubris as a mere reviewer to dare to try my hand at theoretical writing. Annette's attitude toward me had changed from paternalistic curiosity to hostility. "I don't know why Ruby is so cold to me," she had recently told Joan. "Someone must have told her that I think she's stupid. I don't know who it could have been. I've only told five or six people." Annette was the archetypical phallic mother, famous at that time for demolishing young women unlucky enough to land in her domain. Some failed to complete their Ph.D.s, others gave up writing altogether. One friend told a story of months spent with a therapist working on "her" problem. Then the therapist happened to see Professor Michelson on a local television show discussing film. "We're not spending any more time on this matter," the therapist told her. "You're not the one with the problem."

Annette was cordial that evening, but E. Ann Kaplan was also there and had just seen my article. She ambushed me in the kitchen mid-dinner and gave me hell for attacking another woman in *American Film,* the patriarchal press. I, however, thought that *American Film* was a neutral zone where I could try to rescue the work and reputations of women who'd been trashed and erased by the kind of history that Kaplan had written. Luckily, we were interrupted by the guest of honor's chance appearance in the kitchen and had to shelve the argument.

Though it was the scars from old battles that had led me to write the piece, new battle lines were soon played out in reaction to its publication. Sharon Thompson, who was coediting a special feminist issue of *American Book Review* (and also busy, as it happened, coediting the landmark anthology *Powers of Desire*), solicited the piece for the *ABR* issue. She performed an edit that enhanced the subtleties of the original argument, so it's that version I include here. Thompson was witnessing the expansion of feminist psychoanalytic rhetoric into adjacent areas of feminist scholarship and activism and wanted to initiate a debate over its consequences. This 1984 issue was a special number of the *ABR* focusing on "Feminist Issues: Writing ·& Criticism Today." After the isolation of my *American Film* publication, I was happy to have a context of community this time around and activist editors to back me up. Here's how they defined their mission in an editors' statement explaining their project: "Our hope for this issue is that people who never read feminists will read the criticism here and find it alive, a voice from a distant and developing position in American letters, and that the people who do read feminists will find the writing here unconstrained by the various forms of orthodoxy which sometimes structure feminist reviews."

Various forms of orthodoxy, indeed. I was disciplined by E. Ann Kaplan herself, who called me an "essentialist." I suppose that was preferable to the older tag line for delegitimizing the opposition: "anti-intellectual." Still, I became convinced in the eighties that "essentialism" was not really the term for a category of backward reified thinking, as it was portrayed to be, but rather a derogatory dismissal of any woman still holding onto an earlier decade's political engagement. Or, to be perfectly frank, I began to suspect it might even be a codified homophobic sneer at any unrepentant lesbianism that resisted the postmodern siren call to shed all such categories of "identity" for a theory (rarely a practice) of polymorphously fluid positions of sex and gender.

Today the wounds of feminist fights of earlier eras have healed and their force has diminished. The "value-added" advantage of shared memories wins out for many of us, even when the nostalgia held in common consists largely of battles joined on opposing sides of lines once etched in stone. The feminist-film cold wars have dissipated and we old warriors have become congenial veterans, not unlike the CIA and KGB spies who now meet to reminisce and do each other favors. Annette Kuhn, who always took my complaints in stride and went on to do a series of substantive theoretical and historical books, has remained a friendly colleague and warm presence across the Atlantic. She and Pam Cook and I once spent an evening reminiscing in a London café, laughing so uproariously and contagiously over the old days that all plans for the evening had to be repeatedly postponed and finally called off in favor of maximum storytelling.

Teresa de Lauretis has become a friend and prized colleague. Strolling down a street in Milan some years ago, killing time en route to a conference at the Rockefeller Foundation's Bellagio Center, we began to speak of long past events and battles. Teresa turned to me and said: "You know, I used to hate you." We both laughed at the intensity of our faded enmity, then went on to dinner at a women's restaurant. Though Ann and I have yet to hold any such postmortem, she once invited me to present a lecture in a series at her Institute for the Humanities at the State University of New York at Stony Brook. I accepted, and we enjoyed each other's company, so perhaps even our swords have been beaten into ploughshares at last. I still hear occasionally from Chuck Kleinhans, Julia Lesage, and John Hess, and my name still runs on the *Jump Cut* masthead, but our paths have long since amicably diverged over the intervening decades.

17.

Cinefeminism

and Its

Discontents

(1983–84)

After a long famine in the book trade, two new works devoted to feminist film theory have now appeared: Annette Kuhn's *Women's Pictures* (Routledge & Kegan Paul) and E. Ann Kaplan's *Women and Film* (Methuen). Actually, feminist film books have always had a propensity for pairing off. A pair of such books in the early seventies defined the popular notion of feminist film criticism for some time. Marjorie Rosen's *Popcorn Venus* and Molly Haskell's *From Reverence to Rape* both focused on the analysis of "images of women" in Hollywood cinema. They set the tone for a half-decade of film classes and discussions, only to be called into question by the next pair of books. In the middle to late seventies, two anthologies expanded the parameters. Karyn Kay and Gerald Peary's *Women and the Cinema* and Patricia Erens's *Sexual Stratagems* collected essays that update image analysis, introduced work on films made by women filmmakers outside of Hollywood, and began the Long March of cinefeminists toward the trinity of structuralist-semiotic-psychoanalytic theories of cinema that currently hold sway as academia's reigning fashion.

In this newest pair, Kuhn and Kaplan push on into the domain of psychoanalytic theory, leaving virtually all other analysis and approaches invisible or even (in Kaplan's case) unacknowledged. Both books are divided, like their predecessors, between Hollywood and woman-made movies, a range of product pitched to the broadest possible readership interest. Both offer the ignorant reader an intense crash course in the newest fashions in film theory. Tired of panicking when your departmental rival inquires after your "cinematic apparatus"? Anxious to understand the "erotic cathexis" in next week's Raoul Walsh film? Hip to "processes of signification" but still behind on the "male gaze"?

The paradox of both books is their explicit dedication to the general reader (replete with glossaries and chapters of introduction to the field) tied to an insistence that such reader come already prepared to speak their language. The tone differs: Kaplan pitches her book for student use, while Kuhn dedicates hers to "my teachers." In both cases, however, the dedication to psychoanalytic theory is paramount and the reliance on its specialized language is absolute. Each book, therefore, is likely to perplex the reader naïvely interested in "feminist" theory or curious about the links between psychoanalytic analysis and feminist ideology. The basis for such similarities or disparities, alas, goes relatively unexamined.

In the early days of feminist film criticism and theory, there was a chaotic and diverse arsenal of approaches examining both classical works and the emergent works of women filmmakers of the time. Since the early seventies, however, the drive for coherence and methodology has led many of the cinefeminist academics into narrow chambers of Lacanian analysis. Emphasizing the film "text" and dedicated to close textual analysis, concerned with film's "specularity" and thus building a corpus of theory on the exchange of the "look" or the "gaze" in cinema to the point of a full-fledged fetish, psychoanalytic film theory today is feminist mostly because those feminists practicing it say so. As practiced by its feminist adherents, indeed, the Lacanian-derived systems of analysis can yield useful results regarding the inscription of the figure of woman within cinema, the exercising of power as a male prerogative within the uniquely cinematic power play of the gaze, and the operative nature of voyeurism as exemplified in the darkened quarters of the movie house. However, the Lacanian crowd never emerges sufficiently from the dark hothouse of the text to take into account the key determinants of context, audience, or even aesthetic fashions (let alone such remote factors as history, economics, or even feminist history and ideological directions apart from the filmic). More and more, the Lacanian cinefeminists are the pathologists of the feminist film world. Their engagement with contemporary cinema is long overdue. A new politique ought, by its nature, to generate new texts by which its points are proved and its development sustained. When the psychoanalytic cinefeminists veer toward the same classic Hollywood texts long used by a succession of "forefathers," the transformative nature of their analysis is called into question. When their theories, glancing at women's work, must reduce the field disproportionately, then the reader must beware.

Annette Kuhn's *Women's Pictures* synthesizes the past decade of film theory, largely of French invention and British derivation, through a series of chapters that sketch a metatheory of "meaning production." The chapters acquire a sense of distance from the subject, as Kuhn refers always to preexisting theory rather than to issues or films directly. She is modest about her role and minimizes her own presence, preferring to marshal, explicate, and oversee the theories of others to which she has clearly paid close attention. Kuhn is often wittier than her sources, with such chapter titles as "Passionate Detachment" or "Trouble in the Text." She is also, happily, more generous than her mentors, crediting an eclectic range of divergent opinions and refusing the job of Theory Cop so eagerly assumed by most of the Brit purists and U.S. counterparts working this particular theoretical turf.

Most of *Women's Pictures* is concerned with tracing the history and value of a pantheon of texts and masters: Metz, Lacan, Kristeva, Irigaray, Barthes, and, of course, Freud. Films themselves are discussed only insofar as they pertain to the explication of the theoretical positions and processes in the first three-quarters of the book.

Subsequently, Kuhn does open up her Masterpiece Theory of the film universe to discuss a number of feminist films, delineating realist cinema within the feminist tradition and examining many exemplary works of feminist cinema. It is unfortunate that she introduces her first example of women's films in the chapter on pornography. Still, in the final chapters of analysis of women's films, the book appears to be freshest and most eclectic. Paradoxically, precisely here the contradictions between the theory that Kuhn espouses and the feminist texts become sharpest, threatening to collapse her entire project. The closing chapters of the book inadvertently make it clear to the reader that psychoanalytically based film analysis is best suited to dealing with classic Hollywood films, for only they embody the codes that its analysis is empowered to deconstruct. As applied to feminist films made under an entirely different rubric, or as applied to feminist issues in current Hollywood practice (or pornography), its inability to incorporate context, and its marginality when faced with films that have themselves addressed and changed the classic codes, combine to render this particular avenue of psychoanalytic research singularly inadequate.

Throughout the book, indeed, Kuhn evidences an awareness of the fatal contradictions lurking beneath the surface of her text. At one point, she concedes that "a purely text-based criticism does have a number of limitations that should be signalled" and that psychoanalytic approaches have the "drawback" of posing "a totalising model of the cinematic apparatus which appears to be somewhat impervious to analysis [of] . . . concrete conditions of production and reception." She finally postulates that "we will not know whether a semiotic-based contextual analysis of the institution of cinema from a feminist standpoint is possible until it has been seriously attempted." My agreement with Kuhn's hypothetical optimism is tempered by the unavoidable recognition that a full decade of work has yet to yield any such attempt. Instead, the decade's focus and concern have continually narrowed, so much so that even the most stalwart adherents are beginning to chafe under the stress of cul-de-sac thinking.

It is unreasonable to expect Kuhn to strike out on this mission in what is, after all, a book of synthesis and foundation building. With her recognition of the limitations of this context, and with her concrete steps toward expanding her sphere of reference beyond its previously acceptable limits, Annette Kuhn represents the most open and conciliatory of the British psychoanalytic cinefeminists. Anyone who footnotes Julia Lesage as often as Julia Kristeva deserves credit. Moreover, she goes so far as to include other figures in passing and in the useful index.

It is likely, however, that Kuhn's seemingly natural constituency will turn against the book. For a world that has thrown itself wholeheartedly into "fetishizing the text," the conversion of hallowed xeroxes into a comprehensively assimilated text will be anathema. What will become of the professor no longer privileged as the sole source of reprints? The fervent attachment to the original pieces approaches the Talmudic, even though none of these original theorists have ever approached the Talmud in their level of prose accomplishment. Those who will carp at Kuhn's synthesizing would do well to reconsider the lucidity of the synthesized. One complaint that is justified, though, concerns the volume's new style of footnoting that leaves the reader with a mere name and date in parentheses, unguided as to where exactly the reference has begun or ended, without page references, and with a vagary of delineation that, in lesser hands, would invite plagiarism. Whether the fault of author or publisher, it is unfortunate.

Women's Pictures is limited by its narrow sphere of allegiance. It will be further limited in its readership by its ultra-academic vocabulary and syntax. To the extent that Kuhn has gathered together the strands with even-handed care and comprehensiveness, its publication sets out a challenge to all those continuing to travel the increasingly crowded thoroughfares of psychoanalytic criticism: it is now necessary to go further, to essay more, or not bother. To the extent that she has displayed a greater intellectual generosity and a more sincere concern with the politics of feminist praxis than all of her sources put together, Kuhn provides an important example to all her readers. If she can take some of her own cues and push past her theoretical barriers, Kuhn's future work will prove rewarding.

More attentive to women's films than the Kuhn text and more committed to explicating terminology, E. Ann Kaplan's *Women and Film* is useful in part, but marred overall by a stolid dogmatism that shows little interest in dialectic, making it seem more concerned with closing down dialogue than with opening up questions. It has the advantage of clear-cut organization (not one of Kuhn's strong points) even though the tone is off-putting and sometimes defensive.

Unlike Kuhn, who gathers up a wide range of films, Kaplan applies her version of a psychoanalytic model to a sequence of "case studies." Selection principles for feminist criticism in general have tended to combine formal qualities with subject matter. For psychoanalytic feminists, selection has often hinged on the match between analytic apparatus and film text. Kaplan never lays down her criteria of selection at all. As a result, the case studies seem too arbitrary to be educative. Her Hollywood choices include *Camille, Blonde Venus, Lady from Shanghai,* and *Looking for Mr. Goodbar.* From Europe, she picks Marguerite Duras's *Nathalie Granger* and Margarethe von Trotta's *Marianne and Julianne.*

She conducts a summary dismissal of the "realist debate" in feminist film documentary history: whereas many feminists in the seventies looked to documentary as a way of making visible the shape of women's lives and writing women back into history with the camera, Kaplan goes overboard with the legitimate antirealist critique, holding realism of this sort (film equals life, problems on screen equal our real lives, image of woman on screen equals real woman, etc.) to be itself a form of delusion that stupidly conflated images with reality and exploited its audience by such a gross manipulation of the cinematic apparatus.

Having theoretically bombed one category of feminist film construction, Kaplan goes on to speed through Yvonne Rainer's work and to create a new-fangled category of her own, "avant-garde theory films," which comprises almost entirely films made via male collaboration. She includes appreciations of *Daughter Rite* and *Riddles of the Sphinx,* but ties both to her own stake in a motherhood theory rather than to their opposite formal strategies.

Faced with the explication and application of her theoretical concepts, Kaplan falls into multiple contradictions. Terms like "phallus" and "penis" are nearly interchanged; "realism" is derided as it appears in U.S. feminist documentaries but exempted when it shows up as *Marianne and Julianne;* the use of "he" as a nonspecific pronoun turns up at distressing moments, even where feminine usage is clearly called for; the Dietrich–von Sternberg relationship is exhumed at length, while von Trotta's past under Schlondorff is never even mentioned; and potential untouchables — like lesbianism — are ignored even where the film text (*Blonde Venus*) practically cries out for some mention. Also unfortunate is Kaplan's frequent use of the inclusive "we" (common to nurses and primary school teachers), except for cases of lesbian films, where "they" is substituted. Though in much feminist writing, the use of "we" is an encompassing, community-creating gesture, here it is clearly Kaplan who is laying down the law.

If Kuhn can be faulted for lack of bravery in not moving beyond her sources, Kaplan must be criticized for lack of intellectual generosity. She expunges all mention of those with whom she disagrees, slurs nonspecific "sociological" critics mercilessly, and gives little sense that anyone in the U.S. feminist film universe might challenge her vision of psychoanalytic cinefeminism.

When Kaplan applies her methodology to women's films in the later sections of the book, she encounters the same problem that afflicts Kuhn: the overdetermined systems of analysis do little to illuminate works not created within dominant cinematic practice, and Kaplan is thrown back upon thematic discussions and old-fashioned character analysis. Precisely because Kaplan has commendably devoted so much of her volume to a consideration of contemporary feminist cinema, the breakdown of her theoretical model becomes starkly visible.

Kuhn's and Kaplan's mutual avoidance of history and process leaves both authors wide open to the traditional challenge to their methodology: that it is irresponsibly ahistorical. But it is too easy to misdirect a critique of this pair of books into a simplified history-versus-theory debate. Both pose as histories of theory, yet chronicle only a partial history of one branch of theory. Both then jettison this theoretical history in favor of close textual analysis — in Kuhn's case, of the theorists; in Kaplan's case, of the films. Neither sufficiently credits the evolution of their own positions; for all the championing of deconstructive analysis, neither turns that beacon on her own trajectory. Kaplan's strategies leave her open to an even more serious challenge: not merely the avoidance of history, but telling it selectively to hide differences and erase aspects of past development.

Reflecting on this pair of books, anyone familiar with the past decade or so of feminist film activity (and, indeed, with feminist scholarship in general) must wonder not so much at what they contain as at what they have so conspicuously left out: the history of feminist film theory, the range of feminist cinema, feminist theory in its many nonfilm manifestations, and the arena of feminist politics in general.

Slighting feminist film theoretical history is probably the most grievous problem, leading to the sort of manipulations mentioned above. Kuhn falls into omissions or misrepresentation; Kaplan opts for total erasure or fabrication. In a discussion of Yvonne Rainer's work, for example, Kaplan cavalierly notes in passing that Rainer's first film, "made in 1972 . . . preceded any coherent feminist film community in New York." Nonsense. The first issue of the national journal *Women and Film* came out in 1972. The same year marked the first New York International Festival of Women's Films (the result, clearly, of a long collective-planning process) and the publication of a special feminist film issue of the New York–based *Film Library Quarterly* and of a feminist filmography in *Film Comment*, also New York–based. Add to all this the release of some half-dozen feminist documentaries (the genre reviled by Kaplan) in the city and the theatrical release of Kate Millet's *Three Lives*. Given such evidence of community, it may be that "coherent" for Kaplan might be loosely translated as "academically institutionalized," as her text goes on to imply.

During the late seventies and early eighties, the most intensive feminist film theory could be found in small-circulation journals or at conferences in both the United States and Britain. There was a virtual battleground established at conferences, through position papers, conference boycotts, and debates, all centering on objections and alternatives to theoretical constructs striving for hegemony. Although Kuhn is better than Kaplan at acknowledging certain feminist "pressures" or political disagreements, she never documents the conferences and alludes only occasionally to the journals. Kaplan ignores the conferences and journals, never mentions any differences, tries to create a field that would appear to center on her own work, and generally comes off acting like the AMA when faced with a plague of chiropractors. (Kaplan is the worse culprit here, because she has been a resident of the United States throughout this period, has herself been a participant at many of the conferences and a warrior in many of the battles, and certainly knows whereof she does not speak.) Both authors try to erase the struggle for supremacy associated with the psychoanalytic theories, and both construct a falsely placid history consistent with their own positions.

The strength and vigor of feminist film theory, in fact, has always been its continual testing in the crucible of debate. Any history that fails to mark this characteristic diminishes itself accordingly. Political arguments about the political implications of psychoanalytic theory as applied to feminist analysis have been a basic feature of film debates. In the past decade, Canadian Barbara Martineau first clashed with Claire Johnston over definitions. Julia Lesage of *Jump Cut* was involved in a long-notorious debate with *Screen* magazine that resulted in dueling editorials; Lesley Stern chronicled the battles at the Edinburgh feminism and film conference; such British critics as Christine Gledhill and Elizabeth Wilson published critiques of psychoanalytic assumptions; the *Jump Cut* special section on lesbianism and cinema tried to challenge the way "sexual difference" has been defined in psychoanalytic theory; critics like Judith Mayne, Linda Williams, and, most recently, Mary Gentile have tried to create a critical middle ground. There is more vigor in these debates than in either of the books sidestepping them.

The impoverishment of Kaplan's and Kuhn's work caused by their isolation from the mainstream of feminist thinking in our time is incalculable. But it is all too characteristic of the psychoanalytic branch of feminist film theory, which has always held itself in abeyance, never connecting with feminist work in other theoretical areas, rarely crossing the discipline of cinema studies except as they lead into the well-traveled pathways of semiotics, linguistics, or psychoanalysis. There is no triumph, only a sadness and missed opportunity, in that absence.

Finally, taking the books on their own terms, one is left with Kuhn's own final rallying cry. Why not essay more? Even within the limitations of a psychoanalytic framework, there is much to be learned that could profit feminist struggles in film and other disciplines, particularly regarding the spectator-film relationship (and its application to pornography), the fixity or variability of the image in relation to meaning, or the playing out of liberation-repression dynamics in cinema. Neither Kuhn nor Kaplan ventures out of the Lacanian shadows.

If these books display the current, arrested states of psychoanalytic feminist theory clearly enough, then perhaps, finally, scholars and students can move on to alternatives. The task of joining sophisticated visual analysis to enlightened feminist perspectives has begun in the byways of articles and sessions. Now it is time, finally, for *that* book to appear.

Prologue.

Libel Threats

and Exile

Tactics

By the early eighties, the documentary field had entered a cul-de-sac with no escape in sight. The committed, straightforward documentary had been the medium of choice not only for New Left filmmakers in the sixties and seventies but equally, throughout the seventies, for women filmmakers bent on exposing oppression and charting women's lives from the perspective of the new feminism. By the eighties, however, these films had been effectively (if excessively) discredited by academic theories that claimed all realist practices were rendered inherently contaminated and retrogressive by their willful reliance on filmic "transparency."

Filmmakers were generally oblivious to such theoretical concerns and—well insulated from them by the near-absolute gulf between the academy, which as usual was more focused on canonical classic narratives that could accommodate their analytic structures, and the production community, eternally consumed by funding crises and distribution quandaries—continued to devote themselves to the production of documentary films that mixed "reality" footage with interviews and archival materials to tell the stories of the past to the present.

In part, this repetition of form was the result of National Endowment for the Humanities influence, which made large-scale funding available for such documentaries that conscripted history as a legitimizing token;

that came to an end, of course, when Reagan replaced Carter and William Bennett politicized the NEH. Nevertheless, the reliance on public television as an outlet and the straight-ahead nature of the U.S. production process created a situation wherein economic scarcity discouraged innovation in favor of bankable consistency and formulaic genres. A sameness set in. The predictability began to undercut the efficacy of the films, at least in the view of many critics. What good was this stale form that could no longer deliver anything new; that was the reasoning. At the same time, stories continued to present themselves, urgently, for the telling (as, for instance, in the Central American solidarity films of the eighties or in the underrepresented communities of color in the United States) and audiences continued to respond with intense emotional engagement.

Despite the stagnation that had set in aesthetically, very little reevaluation was going on. One major exception, that would prove prophetic, was the film that Jill Godmilow was then in the process of making: bent on filming the Solidarity struggle in Poland but unable to secure an entrance visa at the last minute, she jettisoned verité in favor of staged sequences exploring the issues of both her subject and her filming process. Appearing at the same Minneapolis conference with many of us on the future of media, she had named her new film a "dramedy" to distinguish it from the docudrama genre and called for a new approach to documentary. (I guess Michael Moore heard the cry.) In 1984, however, *Far from Poland* was still in postproduction and the tenets of cinema verité were still well enshrined in U.S. documentary practice.

What better place to carry out a little guerrilla warfare against these suppositions than in the belly of the beast (or so I figured)? On a panel at the annual Socialist Scholars Conference, I decided to carry my new documentary message to the heart of what was left of the left. The audience of non-film-specialists saw us as enemy agents nefariously determined to deprive the left of a valuable weapon in a dwindling arsenal. Too bad about our gripes regarding the retrogressive nature of realism and identification and the "movement" documentary films' archaic formal strategies. They liked them just fine, they worked, get a life. Joan Braderman and Martha Rosier were partisans easily equal to the task of challenging crowds, so we had fun nonetheless trying to win them over. But people are fond of their fetish objects.

I tried again a few months later, this time at the Marxist School with a panel composed of documentary filmmaker Deborah Shaffer and New Left stalwart Stanley Aronowitz, who of course didn't exactly agree with my position. Remembering a lesson I'd learned long ago from a Norwegian feminist on feminine decorum and how to stake out space in public,

I decided I needed some immediate bulking-up to compete with Stanley's girth. I settled for crossing my hands behind my head to enlarge my physical space, then used a lot of gestures and tried to speak as loudly as he and address him by his first name. It was fun.

Still, whenever any of us tried to make arguments in academic film circles to support the political utility of such work, which was thoroughly disparaged by this time by the forces of *Screen* magazine and its followers, we were characterized as vulgar Marxists (or vulgar feminists or, more recently still, vulgar essentialists). Theoretical positions condemned such work as unconscious, unaware of its own devices, pathetically simplistic, "transparent." And this orthodoxy was enforced with vigor as a corps of theory cops roamed the land, laying down the law at film conferences far and wide, endorsing a monotheistic film religion whereby only one theoretical god could reign and all else was idolatry.

I should explain, then, that the criticisms launched with such vigor in this piece were clearly positioned "within" the communities that I take to task, much as the charge of "political correctness" was once a charge leveled only within left or feminist circles to curb internal excess. I wasn't signing on to some *Screen* style of antitransparency; rather, I was trying to continue the line of thought begun by Linda Williams and me in our response to *Daughter Rite,* here carried over to a different filmmaking community with other political issues. So I charged ahead, arguing that the success of the documentary format had led not merely to its own exhaustion but more dangerously to its appropriation, first by Hollywood in its telling of history and then by the right in its quest for credibility.

This particular piece has another history as well. Since my first trip to Cuba in 1978, I had become very involved in Cuban cultural work. I had Cuban American friends in the Antonio Maceo Brigade and the Cuban Cultural Circle, I regularly read *Areito* magazine, and I was immersed in U.S.-Cuba cultural dynamics. By then, I was busily collaborating with my friend, Cuban American scholar Lourdes Arguelles, on a series of articles that dealt first with Cuban exile politics in the age of Reagan and next, more intensively, with issues of homosexuality in Cuba and in the Cuban American enclave communities. In 1983–84, we published in both the popular and university press, the *New York Native* as well as *Signs,* in an attempt to reach both the gay/lesbian communities and academics. Such activity guaranteed that I'd be subjected to the intense recriminations and attacks characteristic of any and all participation in any aspect of Cuban exile affairs, but the letter writing that accompanied these interventions was nothing compared to the reaction when I published my views in a mainstream, crossover magazine.

In the summer of 1984, I published an attack on the documentary *Improper Conduct* by the late Nestor Almendros and Orlando Jimenez-Leal in *American Film* magazine. Retaliation was immediate. I later wrote that "a campaign of intimidation unprecedented in cultural circles has accompanied the release of this film." Within days of my article's publication, the film's distributor sent out national press releases denouncing me to major newspaper editors. Almendros himself told mutual friends I was a "foreign agent." And the filmmakers and distributors immediately threatened me and the magazine with a libel suit. *American Film* dropped me like a hot potato, as magazines and publishers tend to do with nonstaff writers whenever trouble breaks out, and brokered its own deal with Almendros and Jimenez-Leal. They received a space greater than my original article to rebut it and attack me, an editorial privilege never granted any filmmaker bristling from a bad review before or since. I was left to face the libel suit threat alone, a crisis I survived only due to the generosity of the Center for Constitutional Rights, its offer to defend me free of charge, and its assurance that no such case would come to court because the mere threat of such suits was currently a favorite right-wing tactic for silencing opposition, intimidating critics, and generally chilling free speech.

The pattern was repeated wherever anyone dared to write negatively about the film, and pressure was brought to bear with almost universal success to gain equal space in the papers for filmmakers who'd supposedly had their say already on screen. The controversy continued for several months, spreading from *American Film* and *The Native* (where Ed Sikov managed to shoehorn a negative review between the paper's pandering to the filmmakers), *Christopher Street*, the *Village Voice* (where Andrew Sarris and Jim Hoberman faced off over it, followed by Richard Goldstein's interview with Tomás Gutiérrez Alea about the film). By autumn, the controversy had entered the pages of *Commentary*. Thus did film criticism and sexual politics intersect with the thuggery of the anti-Castro community.

By the fall of 1984, I needed a break—and Rio de Janeiro sounded perfect. Brazil's military dictatorship was coming to an end, the country's new constitution was about to be approved, Fabiano Canosa was programming the first Rio film festival to take place in years, and I had an invitation to come down and show Lizzie Borden's *Born in Flames*. What a great moment for cultural tourism! For my first few days, I stayed with Sonia Diaz, the actress whom I remembered from her role as a journalist in Nelson Pereira Dos Santos's classic *Tent of Miracles* ("You want to see a mulatta? Here's a mulatta!" she'd said, ripping off her clothes to beat her rivals to the punch and secure exclusive access to the American anthropologist studying race in Brazil.) I met actors and actresses and all kinds of girls. I went to an amazing lesbian bar with hundreds of gorgeous Brazilian women dancing samba and disco on a giant dance floor surrounded by private alcoves that opened into dark walled gardens for couples that wanted even more privacy. I discovered Rio's tradition of "fuck motels," which were respectable by-the-hour places that often had private garages to prevent any unwanted disclosures — should a husband and wife show up with different partners, for instance. Sonia's apartment was an informal salon where interesting Cariocas gathered almost every night to play poker, exchange gossip, and indulge in caipirinhas or something stronger.

I was in heaven. It wasn't just the women or the actors or the drinks. It was that particular political moment in Brazil. The highlight of the festival was the world premiere of Brazilian director Eduardo Coutinho's new film, *Twenty Years After*, or *A Man Marked to Die*. On the evening of its premiere, I had dinner with Tom Luddy and Hector Babenco, who patiently explained to us the significance of this film that took up where Coutinho had left off in the sixties, when he'd been filming a story about land rights with the actual peasants who'd been involved in those very struggles. The shoot was interrupted by the military coup and the star of his film went into hiding. Years later, unexpectedly, his footage was rediscovered and he'd thrown himself back into the fray, tracking down his star and telling the story of her life during the intervening years. It played to a packed house where the audience nearly held its breath for two hours, then leapt into standing ovations. Coutinho made me think about documentary and politics again.

The Americans at the film festival were a ridiculously diverse bunch. I joined them once I moved over to the official festival hotel, and I consider it one of the crowning glories of my career that I was able to introduce John Waters to Esther Williams (during a reception at the U.S. Consulate). I'd been hanging out with her all week, as my roommate was in charge of entertaining her in between her retrospective screenings. One night we ended up closing out a Brazilian restaurant at 3 A.M. as Esther serenaded us with "Some Enchanted Evening" and her friend Francesca, who'd accompanied her from Los Angeles, downed another round of drinks and passed Sonia her phone number on a matchbook. By the time the reception rolled around, John Waters was begging to be introduced: "Please, you must, I stand for everything she most hates in modern films." I obliged, but to our disappointment, his name elicited no recognition.

I returned to New York from Brazil to find myself with a houseguest: Lindsay Cooper, my British composer/musician friend, had arrived to visit. I floated in on a cloud of Brazilian afterglow and promptly got myself into trouble. Our friendship escalated into something more, and I spent the next two years flying over to London or other parts of Europe. Once we combined my trip to a women's film festival in Florence with her trip to a concert in Zurich. It was there that I got to meet Irene Schweitzer and a lot of other improvisers who were retooling music with great panache. Another time, we went to the Oberhausen Film Festival together. Karola Gramann had taken over as director and put together a dream jury (Viennese filmmaker and artist Valie Export, Laura Mulvey, Argentinean director Fernando Birri, the young Philippine director Nick Deocampo among them). She brought me there as a juror and scheduled a concert for Lindsay. During my stays in London, I met her friend and great jazz photographer Val Wilmer and saw a lot of Sally Potter, Rose English, Mandy Merck, and our other friends, all beginning to come into their own.

Back home, though, the recurring battlefield over Cuban politics had stimulated my thinking about documentary film, the forms it was taking, and the interests it served. I finally turned my obsession into an expanded lecture with film clips from *Reds, Seeing Red,* and *Improper Conduct* and delivered it at the La Jolla Museum and the University of California, San Diego. The lecture in turn became an article that I sent off to *Jump Cut,* but when it was returned for the usual round of revisions, I gave up. Here it is now, another time capsule from a long-gone era. Consider whether the preceding account of political wrangling, travel, and love is as relevant to deciphering my philosophy of documentary aesthetics as any texts I was then reading.

18.

Truth, Faith, and the Individual: Thoughts on U.S. Documentary Film Practice (1983–1986)

ny examination of documentary film history reveals a complex trajectory by which differing strategies, traditions, or styles were privileged at differing historical moments.[1] Before and after World War II, in Britain and the United States, Robert Flaherty and John Grierson produced very different films than those sparked in the revolutionary Soviet Union in the work of Dziga Vertov. Different Germanys gave rise to different cinemas, with the films of Leni Riefenstahl emerging from the Third Reich and those of Andrew and Amalie Thorndike from the postwar DGR. France after the war took shape in Marcel Ophuls's opus very differently from that taken by Allende's Chile in the classic by Patricio Guzman. Revolutionary Cuba in the films of Santiago Alvarez virtually christened a whole genre of documentary that influenced all of Latin America, though in Cuba it became formulaic. Jean Rouch and Chris Marker, on the other hand, have constantly refined their engagements with "truth" in an effort to keep pace with history. In the eighties, in turn, evolving stylistic approaches, political perspectives, and historical conditions have contributed to European documentary films as divergent as those by Arthur McCaig (*The Patriot Game*) or Peter Kreigman (*September Wheat*) or the Cinema Action group (*So That You Can Live*) or the films of Raul Ruiz. All have continued to develop divergent documentary essayist strategies.[2]

The situation in the United States is something else. Despite a few glimmers of change on the documentary horizon, the trajectory has been a narrower one. In the United States of the seventies and eighties, it sometimes has seemed that the only documentary tradition that ever really took hold was the one unleashed by *Candid Camera,* the fifties television show that caught so-called real people off-guard.[3]

To be sure, there were updates on its strategies inevitable to the development of a form. Film went portable with the invention of sync-sound equipment. Drew Associates and its gang, Leacock, Pennebaker, the Maysles brothers, et al., went about confronting their subjects and bringing home the goods. Frederick Wiseman continued the shaping of so-called real life into mediated documentary form in what has most recently been termed the "macho fetishization" of pure cinema verité.[4] Some people smelled a rat: Shirley Clarke made *The Portrait of Jason* as a send-up of this kind of truth-mongering. Revisionism came in the form of unmasking the camera (more honest). Round about 1971, the feminist commandeering of documentary resulted in the further modification of the cinema verité legacy, unmasking not merely the camera but also the filmmaker, and reversing the prior exploitation of the subject to create an empowerment of the subject. Other movements (Black, Latino, gay/lesbian, labor, etc.) built upon similar models of empowerment within a basic direct-address format.[5] The speaking subject had arrived.

To consider U.S. documentary filmmaking in the eighties, then, is to confront a highly developed yet fairly homogeneous set of practices. Reduced to the most common denominator? Sync-sound. Punning on the "kitchen sink" school of socially relevant realism, it could be said that current documentaries admit nothing but the "sync" (the synchronous-sound process that allows the simultaneous projection of sound and image). The style is characterized by a "talking head" format, interviews either spontaneous or staged, the provision of personal testimony, the demystification of cinematic spectacle (via the strategy of allegedly eschewing "manipulation") coexistent with the frequent mystification of either filmmaker or subject, and the constant presence of the above-mentioned Speaking Subject. It could be termed a style of "engaged documentary" for the usual participation of the filmmaker in the politique of the subject. Or the "documentary of identification" for the obligatory identificatory participation of the viewer with the subject of such films. Generally, the transparency of film is key to the style, with a close film-reality correlation actively promoted. There are a number of positive and negative consequences to this dominant documentary tradition. Both sets of consequences bear examination, for the documentary as now practiced has come to stand for a progressive cinematic style, one particularly suited to the expression of progressive goals.

Pro and Con

Four components immediately present themselves as crucial positive results of this engaged documentary of identification. First, the subject hereby enters into history. Ordinary people, never before represented in cinema, now can constitute their own record, not as a fictive or misappropriated persona, but in the fullness of self-determination. Second, ordinary people (i.e., an audience apart from film buffs or university students) are able to see them/ourselves on screen, leading to an identification with and understanding of social movements past and present via the lives and personal experiences of the film's protagonists. By means of such demystifications of history and historical process, viewers are empowered as participants in a future process. Third, such documentaries counter the lies of dominant media by representing the eternal "other" — whether welfare mother, gay man, prisoner, sterilized woman, Vietnam veteran, Black activist — as concrete and comprehensible persons. By freeing such figures from the bonds of stereotyping, the documentary can recuperate them into the boundaries of feasible identification and lessen the chance of objectification. Fourth, these documentary films are key to political organizing, successful precisely because their methods pose no stylistic obstacles and structure material with maximum efficacy in mind. Other critics have devoted greater attention to the value of progressive documentary as detailed here, to which the reader is referred.[6]

Five components of negative consequence, however, are equally ever present. First, history is reduced to the individual. In this, the documentary follows the lead of print journalism of the seventies and eighties in producing a *People* magazine version of history. Second, dangers of ahistoricity inevitably set in, as the speaking subjects define their own terms independent of other forces. Third, information comes to replace, and stand in for, analysis. Although "the facts speak for themselves" has an undeniable resonance, its empiricism is no substitute for contextual analysis that helps situate the viewer in history. Fourth, such documentary practice creates an identification *uber alles* requirement, whereby those subjects with whom the audience's identification is less accessible are likely to find the entire film project undermined. Fifth, such documentary filmmaking may inadvertently produce a "cinema of the rhetorical question," in which the film never moves its audience past tacit, predetermined zones of agreement.[7] Such films pose merely rhetorical questions: Women should be allowed to conduct orchestras, shouldn't they? Homosexuals are just like us (*sic*), aren't they? And so on.

Further consideration of these disparate claims, though relevant, is not the focus of this article. To be sure, other routes could be taken. One would explore the current status of the "realism" debates that have marked the past two decades (and more) of film theory and dogged anyone committed, or foolhardy, enough to try representing the chimera of "truth" on the screen. Another might explore the filmmakers currently mixing fact and fiction, inspired in part by the great Cuban director Sara Gomez's fiction/documentary, *One Way or Another,* and in part spurred on by their own increasingly overdetermined genre limitations. But these would be different articles. This one, instead, seeks to follow another trajectory, one suggested by a sequence of films released in the eighties, all concerned with history, all presenting individual testimony as a key to that history. Three films, posing a convenient tryptich. A sequence of three, narrative in its progression, disturbing in its conclusion.

Friendly Witnesses

Many progressive documentaries of the seventies relied on witness-participants who had undergone the experience or lived the historical period in question and thus could speak, usually in direct address to the audience, of what it was "really" like. This article seeks to trace the peculiarly eighties evolution of the witness tradition through three successive permutations: (1) the prologue to Warren Beatty's *Reds* and its reappearance at key points during the rest of the film as a "documentary" counterpoint to the fictional epic; (2) Julia Reichert and Jim Klein's *Seeing Red,* illustrative of the classic use of the technique by two of the most influential practitioners of contemporary progressive documentary; and (3) Nestor Almendros and Orlando Jimenez-Leal's *Improper Conduct,* which updates documentary tradition by reversing its politics and, in so doing, raises new questions about its form.

When first released, *Reds* raised plenty of controversy. In part, it was the predictable controversy of a Hollywood dramatic film daring to interpret the Russian Revolution within the framework of a fictionalized romance, where the love affair tended inevitably to erode the politics. However, of equal concern to me at the time were the film's sequences of testimonies by survivors of the era under fictionalization. Did they represent a bastardization of documentary? The basic form of the seventies documentary was replicated yet transformed. There they were on the screen, the by-now-familiar type of real people, face-front to camera, telling their stories.

Yet the change was indisputable. In the shift from 16mm to 35mm, from low-budget lighting to high-budget chiaroscuro, from identified players to anonymous ones, from memorable recollections to unreliable memories, the sum of the parts combined to make a new whole. Differences of degree and scale seemed to lead to a difference in genre. The allegedly real was turned fictional. People became "characters." Beatty succeeded in fictionalizing history, even "living" history.

In the process, something seemed to happen to documentary as well. It was striking how thoroughly a shift in production practices could transform documentary into fiction. Even when *American Film,* upon the film's release in 1981, published an exhaustive guide to who-was-who in the coy guessing-game sections of the film, the fictional fabric was not rent. Instead, the dramatic whole, *Reds,* swallowed up and incorporated the documentary sequences: historical figures, stripped by time of memory and by celluloid of identity, metamorphosed into dramatic elements of an organic whole.

Far from desecrating the altar of documentary with this creation, however, Beatty might well have understood the central truths of the documentary totem when he set out to cast Personal Testimony as his updated version of a Greek Chorus. If the real people had never been "real" in the first place, as so many critics had argued, then their fictionalizing was no transgression. If history, as remembered even by participants, was a fiction constructed at will by the individual at hand, then surely a documentary interview was an appropriate fictional component. Further, if by its elevation of the individual—the bearer of history—the seventies documentary had inadvertently removed the individual from the context of that very history, then *Reds* could be seen as merely formalizing that isolation. Imbued with experience, opaque as an oracle, the Greek Chorus of witnesses commanded our unswerving reverence, suffered our gaze, and demanded allegiance. Like the ancient oracle, however, they offered no facts. No analysis. No guidance, apart from that we might have conceived before encountering them.

With *Seeing Red,* however, it could be argued that the facts were restored to documentary and that the genre, once again, got down to business. But just what was the business? Once again, the film was composed of witnesses. Of course, these figures were not witnesses in the fifties McCarthy sense of the term; indeed, they were McCarthy's objects of investigation. Following the precepts of seventies documentary, however, the film is not concerned to carry out any counterinvestigation. Rather, à la the seventies, the filmmakers are interested in them as people.

Wisely, for a film released in 1983 (a vintage late–cold war year, with both the Korean Airline 007 downing and the Grenada invasion), the film seems to anticipate an anti-Communist audience and is edited accordingly. It plays against that anticipated reaction, and seeks to convince otherwise. Fundamentally and obviously, the film is not concerned with The Party, but rather with its ex-members. As a result, while it contextualizes its Reds as people within a social setting and cultural milieu, it decontextualizes them as Communists. The objective? Well, I would argue: to make us like them. And, in liking them, no longer to hate them. In this sense, *Seeing Red* fits neatly into the earlier category of the "cinema of the rhetorical question" by virtue of posing the unlikely, or perhaps perverse, question: Communists are just folks, aren't they?

The film's paradox, of course, is that the audience's affectional switch depends totally on the reception of the individual testimonies within the film. Thus, the film's ability to convince the audience to rethink its line on former Party members is dependent on these same protagonists' ability to be photogenic, likeable, good raconteurs, believable. In other words, more or less the same qualities necessary for a presidential candidate in the media age. The audience's identification with a Bill Bailey or Dorothy Healey depends on its affection for them — despite, as much as because of, their politics. Though the audience may exit the theater liking these ex-Communists, will it like Communism? Or even understand its historical, let alone current, appeal?

Psychology has met ideology on the playing fields of documentary, and the result is a soothsayer cinema. History has come to reside within the individual, not the individual within history. Individual testimony has come to occupy that privileged zone outside of history or ideology (much like individual fantasy within the sex debates) where something pure, untouched, can supposedly be found: there for the seeker, who has only to overturn the rock to find the fossil that tells it all. Meanwhile, on other fronts, oral history itself has begun to come under reexamination. Memory is as strong as the rememberer. False consciousness, a desire to please, class or race bias, trace elements of received ideology or mass culture, all have seeped into the allegedly once pure waters of truth. Finally, the skepticism to which "history" and "truth" have always been subjected is being applied to oral history as well, so that we can begin to learn to sort the histories that can lead us from those that might mislead us. If the documentary has been as strong as the force of its individual witness, well, perhaps it is also as weak as each witness.

Seeing Red, unlike *Reds,* makes a point of adhering to seventies tradition via the inclusion of the filmmaker in the film (unlike Reichert and Klein's own earlier films, in which they always edited themselves out).

Not surprisingly, however, the filmmaker is as decontextualized as the various protagonists. In trying to provide an identificatory figure for the audience, Reichert assumes a "just folks" pose and comes across as a naïf learning from her making of this film the knowledge necessary to present it to us — rather than a political sophisticate with clear goals and objectives shaped long before picking up a camera and microphone. I would argue, however, that this sort of dissemblance, or manipulation, is germane to the genre. Like the Olympics, the progressive documentary permits no "professionals," and each character, filmmaker included, is presumed to arrive on the scene unencumbered by political alliances or agendas that might interfere with the "truth" that she or he has to tell us.

Like *Seeing Red,* Nestor Almendros and Orlando Jimenez-Leal's *Improper Conduct* assumes an anti-Communist audience. Instead of playing against it, however, the film plays straight to it, counting on anti-Communism to reinforce its characters and message.[8] The documentary purports to be an exposé of the oppression of homosexuals in Cuba, as told from the point of view of Cuban exiles opposed to Fidel Castro. It combines past and present in a litany of injustices described to the audience by a cast of Cuban exiles speaking from Miami, New York, and Paris, as well as testimony by the eighties arch antitotalitarian, Susan Sontag.

Despite its opposite politics, *Improper Conduct* has many elements in common with the seventies progressive documentary. It employs personal testimony, with the usual spice of selected archival footage, to convey history to the audience. It bases its appeal on an absolute audience identification with the film's protagonists, and for that reason heavily favors individuals who are White (or light-skinned), intellectual, upper middle class (or appear to be), and either queen-styled gays or heterosexual, with men generally preferred to women. As a result, the film provides identificatory comfort for the largely white-skinned, gay male, and/or Cuban homophobic audience that has appeared to constitute its dominant public. Like the seventies documentaries, this film seems to claim its own particular rhetorical question: Fidel Castro is a monster, isn't he?

Like *Reds,* the film has upped the ante on cinematic practices. Almendros, the renowned Academy Award–winning 35 mm feature cinematographer, shoots for theatrical release despite the documentary's television funding, with the speaking subject always face-front to the camera, modulated lighting, comfortable or picturesque settings, smooth-as-silk editing, and the confidence of dominant cinema practice. Unlike *Reds,* however, the filmmaker is included in the frame (Jimenez-Leal, that is, the heterosexual codirector), questioning the subjects and commenting on their answers. Like Reichert, Jimenez-Leal is supportive and encouraging of his subjects' testimonies, even prompting with leading questions where necessary. Like Reichert, he is disingenuous about his own political affiliations. Again, this is permissible precisely because of the decontextualization of the individual within such documentary. The filmmaker is treated no differently than his subject.

In *Improper Conduct,* the potential faults of the seventies progressive documentary style are spectacularly realized. The tendency to eulogize individual oral history becomes particularly problemmatic when the individuals in question are émigrés, offering what is in fact refugee testimony. Where does personal memory stop, and legally necessary material (for an entrance visa, that is) begin? Due to the burden on the would-be refugee to support contentions of persecution back home, and the extensive coaching of Cuban émigrés historically by both fellow émigrés and U.S. security officials, such testimony must be analyzed most carefully. Yet the form of seventies documentary encourages the opposite treatment: acceptance, unquestioning, free of contextualizing factors.

Similarly, the fetishization of the individual over and against politics and/or society is a characteristic of the seventies documentary subject to a variety of manipulations. Originally, the voice of the individual was seen as a corrective to a partial, erroneous official history. The effect, however, particularly in the absence of an analytic cinema, is to elevate the individual above the body politic. It is this cinematic individualism that serves Almendros and Jimenez-Leal so well.

Improper Conduct follows the path of the seventies documentary in other ways, too. It marshals the personal testimony of an oppressed group (homosexuals in Cuba, in this case, via émigré experiences). It uses film as evidence (footage of a map of a UMAP (Military Units for the Aid of Production) camp, or footage of a Valladares news conference). It is edited for emotional impact, culminating in an outpouring of feeling directed at Communist conformity as equivalent to the death of the spirit. White liberals swoon and Cuban right-wingers cheer. Ah, freedom of expression.

The Suspension of Disbelief

What is the problem? Is this just another case of liking tactics when "we" use them but deploring the same tactics when "they" do? If so, this article would not be worth the writing. Another, more elemental problem is at hand. I would suggest that the lesson is a more painful one still: the documentary form that arose out of a progressive impulse, and has long been linked to progressive movements, has in 1984 shown itself equally suited to fascist needs. Indeed, the elements of the seventies political documentary are now revealed to constitute the essential shape of a fascist cinema:

ahistoricity, the valorization of the individual, and the acceptance of testimony as truth. Our beloved documentary cinema stands revealed as a suitable fascist medium, equipped to meet the needs of "myth" and its making.

To understand the current state — and implications — of documentary, it is necessary only to retrace the sequence of assumptions that has led us here, through four basic phases.

1. Film-as-evidence began to bypass plastic filmic techniques (whether montage, rephotography, reenactment, or other devices) and, in the development of the seventies documentary style, to focus on "the word" as the ultimate, absolute evidence. What people had to say became the most persuasive of filmic evidence, as though the movie theater had become a courtroom and the audience could trust the witness to appear in (on?) the box.

2. The authority of the word, however, rested not on demonstration or proof but, unobtrusively and inexorably, on the audience's willingness to believe the speaker. As a belief system, the kind of Greek chorus used in *Reds* became a natural development — a collective version of the individual and a veritable casting director's dream of how innocents, ignorant of the script, might yet play the part. With the audience complicit in its suspension of disbelief, the acceptance of the words spoken within documentary became a token of faith. Thus did the efficacy of the word come to depend on belief.

3. With faith and belief as the foundation stones of audience identification, the diminishing and disappearance of facts and analysis went undetected. As a result, the documentary fabric weakened. The whole notion of "truth" (however religious or atheistic we may be in our regard for its existence) became the hostage of "credibility."

4. This last point incorporates the three just mentioned, for all three — the word, belief, and credibility — are qualities accruing to the central element of the documentary form under investigation: the individual. It is the word of the individual that constitutes the truth. It is the audience's belief in the word of the individual that legitimizes that truth. It is the credibility of the individual to the audience that results in the acceptance of that spoken truth.

Unfortunately, the individual as ultimate authority is a political notion cozily consonant with fascist beliefs. Unless the individual is part of, subject to, and accountable to her or his community, then the word of the individual can exercise an illegitimate tyranny. Alas, the individual — for all such fascist potentials — is also the lynchpin of seventies democracy and the star of eighties cultural life.

Combined with an acceptance of documentary as "truth," the filmic focus on the individual has created a dangerous cinematic tradition, subject to manipulation and resistant to analysis. We need to examine the assumptions that have brought progressive documentary to this state. I am not arguing for an abandonment of the form, not at all. Manipulation is an inescapable component of documentary, while the focus on the witness satisfies this country's idolatry of individualism. Its use value is undeniable. Rather, I would argue that we must begin to analyze current documentary form and understand its limitations—and that means first forsaking the illusion of aesthetic and political purity that once prevailed.

Prologue.

Disempowerment

and the Politics

of Rage

Marleen Gorris's debut film, *A Question of Silence,* premiered in March 1983 in the New Directors/New Films festival in New York. I immediately put in my bid to be the one to write on the film for the *Village Voice* when it opened. I thought that would happen soon, but instead the kind of lengthy delay ensued that so often attends transgressive work by women directors (sometimes, of course, the films never get released at all). It would be more than a year before *A Question of Silence* finally arrived in theaters. In the interim, I had plenty of time to think about the film and simmer with impatience.

In my folder from that period, I kept a copy of Susan Jacoby's "Hers" column from the *New York Times* in which she worried about something that was just becoming labeled "post-feminism," our gender's gift from the Reagan years. Jacoby begins her column with a lament: "For many young women today, 'feminism' is a word with a shady reputation." Explaining that she'd made this discovery by talking to her NYU class, she lets us in on her research data: "My students told me they objected to feminism because it made women bitter, angry and unattractive to men. They said they felt that feminists had placed too much emphasis on careers at the expense of both romance and family life. . . . Most significant, my students told me that any form of sex discrimination could be overcome by individual effort and that older feminists tended to blame personal inadequacies on 'the system.' "

Convinced that the whole point of social movements is to ensure that each new generation inherit change rather than relive the same struggle over and over, Jacoby despaired of the predicament of women in their thirties (like herself, like me at the time) faced with such barriers to handing over a legacy. As Jacoby wound down her essay with an admonition to women not to delude themselves that semantics was the problem, she linked this rejection of feminism to the recent defeat of the Equal Rights Amendment.

I saved the article because it accurately reflected my sense of the period as one in which feminism was under siege and in which gains of the past were being rolled back and potentially lost. I was desperate for a shot of inspiration. I thought that, if anything could reconnect women with their capacity for rage and empowerment, then *A Question of Silence* had a good shot. (Yeah, I know, it was only a movie.) I stayed in constant contact with its distributor, and when I heard rumors that the film might be dumped straight to video, I kept up the pressure for a release by reminding him that a guaranteed rave was waiting in the wings at the *Voice*. Was its release ever really in danger? Dunno. But one part of the rumor was true: *A Question of Silence* became the first film by a woman with widespread video distribution and as a result entered widespread curricular use.

I got to meet Marleen Gorris a year later when her second film, *Broken Mirrors*, came to New York as part of a special week of Dutch cinema. A fascinating study of the intersection of gender, sexuality, and violence, the film told its story in two parallel sections: one traced the fate of a woman abducted by a serial killer whose need to control women completely has already led him to kill three others; the second interwoven section traced the life of a woman working in a brothel, the daily mundane details of which Gorris subjected to a sardonic treatment. Though I had a few minor criticisms, I filed a positive review in *Ms* and was upset when the film was totally overshadowed by Lizzie Borden's next film, *Working Girls*. Borden's movie was a much more upbeat view of prostitution, one much more palatable to men, and it consumed all the media attention. *Broken Mirrors* failed to find a distributor; eventually it was sold to cable, dubbed into something called "mid-Atlantic" English, and never heard from again.

Gorris at that time was particularly phobic about doing press and tried to avoid journalists as much as possible. I had no assignment to interview her, despite my hero-worship, because I was pretty interview-phobic myself. To our mutual delight, we went to lunch without notebook or tape recorder and just talked and gossiped off the record. What struck me about Gorris was how phenomenally devoid of defensive reactions she managed to be: she was eager for responses to the new film, wanted details of my reactions whether negative or positive, was curious to learn what worked and what didn't. She also gave me the greatest compliment that any filmmaker has ever given this critic, saying that my piece read as if I'd been there in the room with her when she wrote the script.

Life in New York went on. My little Avenue A apartment became a stopover for friends traveling east or west, north or south. One week, the Mexican filmmaker Maria Novaro and her producer/distributor husband Jorge Sanchez occupied the sofabed and basked in the full sun that they thought they'd have to leave behind when they left Mexico City for New York. Friends from London would stop by: Sue Steward, who was doing a documentary on salsa music, and Robyn Davidson, recovering less from her book on crossing the Australian desert with her camels than from her nightmarish love affair with a famous writer. I was also enjoying my work at the Arts Council. I had great colleagues. Jewelle Gomez had come to work in the literature program and her office was right across the hall from mine. Life wasn't half bad.

I lost track of Gorris for a while. Her next film, *The Last Man*, misfired. It was never released in the United States, though I saw it at the gay and lesbian film festival in New York where my friend Sande Zeig had loyally arranged a screening. An odd tale of fascism, spiritualism, and self-defense among a shipwrecked group on a deserted island, *The Last Man* led Gorris to disappear off U.S. radar. Over the years, I heard an occasional rumor about a script in progress or a television series, but nothing concrete.

I was delighted, then, to discover Marleen Gorris staying on the same floor of the same hotel with me in Toronto in 1995. She'd come to the Toronto International Film Festival with her new film, *Antonia's Line*. The rest, like everything else in this volume, is history. In this case, of a particularly pleasurable sort. Carole Meyer, who had been in charge of publicity for Sally Potter's *Gold Diggers*, had brought Gorris to the Cannes market and invented a publicity stunt (a woman-only screening; where had I heard that before?) which set off the all-important buzz. The film went on to win the audience award in Toronto and more awards at the Hamptons Film Festival the next month.

The normally reticent Gorris overcame her dread of the press and rose to the occasion, giving interviews like never before. In one, she disclosed that her original inspiration for making films had come from seeing *Jeanne Dielman*. She had tracked down Chantal Akerman and presented her with her first script, only to be told: make it yourself. That's how *A Question of Silence* came about.

Driving up the California coast after a tough press junket in Los Angeles, Marleen and her girlfriend Maria stopped in San Francisco to relax and we met for dinner. We discussed the odds of the film's actually getting an Academy Award nomination. Remote, thought Gorris, though her distributor was surprisingly optimistic about it. Well, get it she did. And that's not all. She went on to make history by winning the Academy Award for Best Foreign Language Film for 1995 (only the second woman director ever to win an Oscar) and delivered a gracious acceptance speech in which she even, discreetly, thanked Maria. How satisfying it is when prizes are so very well deserved and how rare that women get those moments. My friend Marti Wilson now runs the YWCA in Boston, where she recently started an annual set of awards for women of accomplishment in the Boston area. She was afraid that some women might be too jaded to want to bother with the Y's ceremony, but to her amazement, it turned out that every woman selected accepted with gratitude. Many had never been recognized before, and everyone seemed to need the attention. Should we really be so surprised that still, in the late nineties, women's talents are inadequately rewarded?

Marleen Gorris confided to me over dinner that *Antonia's Line* represented the end of the line for her, as it was the last of four film ideas she'd originally developed together, all of a piece, back in the early eighties; she thought she might now be ready for the first time to direct someone else's story. And so she did. Her first gig as a hired director, *Mrs. Dalloway,* starred Vanessa Redgrave and premiered in the fall of 1997.

19.

Lady Killers:

A Question

of Silence

(1984)

Many years ago, in a decade called the seventies, there used to be women's film festivals in which extraordinary and previously unimagined films, made somewhere in the world by women directors against all odds, lighted screens in the dark and changed the lives of the women who came out to see them. Then, everything seemed to settle down. All was well, it was said. Women's films could be seen everywhere, sometimes. Women's work was integrated now. No special need for special festivals. Such an old-fashioned idea—ghettoizing women's work—wasn't it? No longer fashionable at all.

And even the films themselves seemed to have changed, at least those that still managed to get shown here. No reason that *Entre Nous* couldn't have been seen and loved by one and all, or *Smithereens*, or *Sugar Cane Alley*, all well-wrought films genuinely pleasing to man and woman alike.

Marleen Gorris takes us back to our roots. *A Question of Silence* works on its viewers as forcefully as water on dehydrated food, reconstituting its proper audience even as it unreels upon the screen. But the audience formed is not a harmonious whole. It is a gendered audience to which Gorris appeals, a subversive audience of women scattered throughout the movie theater, rising up in instinctive laughter to greet the clarifying truths there beckoning. *A Question of Silence* is so revealing of women's anger and men's fear that it may well shatter the complacency of the so-called postfeminist eighties. But this is getting ahead of the story.

The story? Three women, strangers to one another, happen into a clothing boutique on a busy afternoon. One is caught shoplifting and confronted by the male proprietor. All three — spontaneously, collectively, brutally — murder the man as four other women shoppers look on, implacable in their endorsement. As the film opens, in a smooth triptych of portraits, the three women are viewed in the milieu of daily life as the arresting officers arrive to take them away. When the police realize that these women knew neither each other nor their victim, a psychiatrist is summoned to assess their fitness to stand trial. All concerned legal parties anticipate a finding of insanity with a plea to match. The psychiatrist is the quintessence of the New Woman: well-groomed, well-married (to a lawyer of similarly enlightened views), well-suited to the task of finding three impulse murderesses of a different class and arcane motive to be insane. Yet as the film progresses, our shrink becomes less and less sure. And thereby hangs the tale.

A Question of Silence is the first film by this young Dutch director, who wrote the screenplay after seeing a news item about a working-class woman's arrest for shoplifting. Thanks to the Dutch production subsidy system and a sympathetic male producer, Gorris was able to direct her own script despite her lack of experience. Neither entirely literal nor wholly allegorical, her film assumes the tone of a ritual drama and the pace of a comedy. Though it may seem perverse to call such a work comic, A Question of Silence easily qualifies in its use of audience reaction as a lever to its own movement, coasting on laughter where a less bold movie would settle for lengthy exposition or tedious cross-cutting. It is precisely the smoothness of its execution that makes the film so effective: this is that rare sort of comedy that takes your breath away when you realize why you're laughing.

Laughter may be the ultimate device of deconstruction, yet A Question of Silence is neither self-conscious nor particularly intellectual despite the ideas it sets off. Gorris has the production standards and dramatic look of mainstream European art-house movies: clean structure and an unruffled surface. It is the motive, not the crime, that forms the subject of her investigation. Armed with style and wit, she sets out, much like an updated Brecht, to try not the criminal but the society that created the crime.

Gorris has drawn her women with a sense of symbolic fitness that avoids the formulaic, partly owing to the script's insistence on their very ordinariness, partly owing to the fine acting, which approaches the documentary in its fusing of actress with character. One woman is a frazzled housewife, trying to cope with an active toddler and brusque husband. One is a hearty coffee-shop waitress, dishing wisecracks to her male customers alongside the food. One is a cool executive secretary, taking dictation with an unmistakable air of insubordination amid a posh corporate suite. Each woman seems to have made her own truce with the compromises and indignities of daily life.

Unexpectedly, the boutique is the last straw in an invisible, unacknowledged tally of abuse. When the housewife is caught shoplifting, the male proprietor is smug and supercilious, ridiculing her attempt at crime, refusing to take even this act seriously (as though shoplifting were not, in itself, an ideologically charged crime: the traditional "woman's" crime, the consumer's inchoate attempt to break her fraudulent contract with an economic system that denies her significant power and prohibits direct satisfaction of desire or need).

The scene of the crime is made up of its parts, examined and reexamined in flashbacks that slowly reconstruct the sequence of events. The film moves back and forth in time, before and after the murder, before and after the incarceration, before and up to the trial. There are earnest jailhouse sessions between the probing psychiatrist and her subjects. There are strung-out, night-long sessions between the psychiatrist and her tape recorder, in which she torments herself with replays of the waitress's irreverent laughter at her sober, off-the-mark questions. There are polite but increasingly awkward dinner parties at which the psychiatrist begins to confront her lawyer husband and their guests, as she comes to doubt the women's insanity and to understand their motive as potentially, hypothetically, her own. It is this fundamental sense of identification—an ideal that triggered the women's liberation movement but later sank under the weight of its own naïve expectation—that Gorris develops in her characters and sparks in her audience.

Gorris waits until the middle of the film to show us the actual murder. It's a literal scene, explicitly setting out such weapons as a coat hanger, an ashtray, a broken mirror. Yet it's also the very opposite of a literal movie murder, for at no point is the body visible. Gorris has set her frame just above that imaginary line, so that each blow rains down upon an unseen figure, thereby transforming the acts into a horrifying ritual and this one proprietor into an Everyman, a generalized figure who, by dint of his very typical behavior, becomes an arbitrary target of a rage set free.

The flashbacks to the boutique and to the women's lives create a sense of action, but the drama resides in the series of confrontations between the psychiatrist and her subjects. They meet within the metaphoric space of the prison—an actual Dutch prison, the most modern in the world, which replicates the society outside its walls in offering the women inmates an illusion of freedom (bright colors, no bars, smiling guards) that sugarcoats the reality of unchanging captivity.

The confrontations are as various as the women. The housewife is catatonic, expressing herself only through childlike drawings. Her catatonia provides the film with its title and most elemental metaphor: she has stopped talking because no one listened. Like an amphibious creature giving up gills on dry land, she has dispensed with speech as no longer necessary to her life. The waitress is boisterous and industrious, fixing up her cell (which looks like a dorm room), knitting, and taking on the psychiatrist's questions with feisty disbelief and a scorn for her rational ignorance. It is the secretary who most consciously articulates the film's ideology, as she reads Doris Lessing and spars outright with the psychiatrist, ridiculing her analytic worldview and pushing her toward an emotional watershed. "Don't you know anything about women?" she finally asks. Unlike most movie attempts at such debate, these conversations are riveting. They're as upsetting and suspenseful as an argument running out of control on live TV.

If *A Question of Silence* liberalizes feminist thinking on woman's place in society, its tactics in doing so have already come under attack as unfair to men. Janet Maslin, in her *New York Times* review last year on the occasion of the film's premiere at the New Directors/New Films festival, complained that this sort of movie gave the women's movement a bad name. Others have criticized the one-dimensionality of the male characters or attacked them, on aesthetic grounds, as stereotypical. I'm not so sure. The male characters are more unimaginative than unimaginable. In an interview with the *Village Voice*'s Carrie Rickey, Gorris herself argued— perhaps disingenuously—that stereotypical or incomplete characterization has been cinema's routine way of dealing with women characters, so why the fuss?

Surely this is not the point. The men aren't the focus of the film; maybe that's what's so startling. The psychiatrist's husband is the most sympathetic (in the New Man mode, he is rational, a good cook, lets his wife seduce him, and appears frontally nude), but even he's left behind once his wife moves beyond the safe confines of liberal consensus. The boutique proprietor is unctuous but otherwise a cipher. The prosecutor is a cartoon chauvinist, yet hardly unlikely. Perhaps, finally, the men in this film are incompletely drawn because they're irrelevant to the narrative. Gorris isn't concerned with these male characters, nor with women's personal relations with men. *A Question of Silence* addresses the force of women's energy and the social containment of that force, the nature of women's rage and the threat of its eruption, the potential bond between women and the circumstances that can bring it into play.

"If they wanted to kill the guy, they should have done it more professionally," insists the psychiatrist's legal colleague. "Of course they're crazy . . . you can spot women like that a mile away." Of course, you can't. The film is absolutely subversive in its insistence upon this point; it is precisely these women's ordinariness that is so unnerving to the male order assembled within the courtroom. Ann Jones, in her landmark book *Women Who Kill,* documented the male criminologist's obsession with this issue. Jones traces the work of Cesare Lombroro, the "father" of modern criminology, who devised studies in 1893 to distinguish between the "born female criminal" and the "normal woman." Jones offers an astute synthesis: "Common sense and Lombroso's own experience told him that there were only these two kinds of women in the world—bad and good—but he seemed haunted by the fear that an apparently good woman might, at any unexpected moment, turn out to be bad. Thus, he devoted a large part of his career to marking once and for all the difference between them." Such male anxiety may hardly be said to have lessened in this century. It is just such a dread that motivates the demand, within the film, for the finding of insanity by the psychiatrist and court. And, in a catch-22, the psychiatrist need only rule the women sane to have her own sanity called into question.

Gorris barely makes a false move as she uses the mundane details of her women's lives to suggest a fairly outrageous hypothesis: that, although no exceptional provocation set off this unpremeditated murder, there is motive enough in the daily life of any woman to create the conditions conducive to just such a murder of just such an arbitrary man. To be sure, the film is a fiction. A fantasy, if you will. As innumerable studies testify, women do not kill men in our society; overwhelmingly, men kill women. But what if women did? And what if men feared such a deed? Mutiny, revolt, uprising: such words appear in no feminist lexicon of the eighties. What then, has become of the impulse? To what do the oppressed turn when revenge is unimaginable? Where does anger go when it's forced underground?

A Question of Silence has come along at a perfect time, because it addresses women's subterranean rage and the intense humor, strength, and sheer power available to us if we can only acknowledge—and accept—its existence. After all, anger was the engine propelling feminism in the late sixties and early seventies. Yet, in the eighties, in the age of professionalism, women's anger has become illegitimate—or worse, unfashionable. In this decade of accommodation, anger is the red-flag word that lesbianism was a dozen years ago, with all the same accusations attached: it is "regressive" or "immature," or simply "unproductive" or even "self-destructive."

The causes of women's anger, however, have not disappeared; indeed, during the Reagan administration, they have multiplied. Such a situation leaves women in a state of double jeopardy, still angry yet deprived of any socially acceptable form of expressing it. There is no choice but to direct the anger inward, as women have done for centuries, against the self. It is a neat solution for the status quo, and a terrible choice for women.

In her book, *The Invisible Drama,* Carol Becker traces the phenomenon of women who, in a sense, have made the opposite choice from that detailed by Ann Jones, opting for implosion rather than explosion. Though her study is concerned with anxiety and its consequences (rather than anger), Becker analyzes the literally debilitating effect on women of emotions driven underground, forced into somatization — pains and diseases of various kinds — as a means of expression.

If the shape of contemporary life actually makes women sick, then *A Question of Silence* is a crucial antidote. Its appeal to instinct and fantasy succeeds in making palpable many of the prescient observations of more than a decade of feminist thinking. Gorris takes the ideological and renders it downright visceral. No wonder the film makes people nervous.

Whence the nervousness, though? Is it the murder that is so unsettling, or is it the laughter? Gorris leads us out on just this tightrope with her controversial ending. I have no intention of giving away her cagey bit of wish-fulfillment, except to say that, on the climactic day in court, the men rant and the women laugh, and the legal system is subjected to an insubordination as threatening as shoplifting is to commerce.

At the New Directors preview in New York, the audience recapitulated the film's own ending: man after man rose to confront Gorris with hostile or garbled questions, only to encounter raucous laughter from most of the women in the audience. Gorris wasn't surprised; she had observed this pattern everywhere the film had shown. In Holland, women had confided to her that they wouldn't take their husbands to the film ("I didn't want a fight"), going with a woman friend instead. Gorris acknowledged the discomfort the film provoked in many male viewers: "The men felt threatened at the women's laughing so hard, when they [the men] didn't know what they were laughing about." It is precisely this laughter that forges a bond among women — and between women viewers and the film — for this transgressive laughter that overflows its boundaries and manifests itself to excess is intimately connected to its flip side, the rage that does the same.

To the extent that men have always suspected and feared some sort of preternatural tie among women (a tie fiercely disowned by many eighties feminists as "essentialist"), then the film's turning upon just such a tie is likely to be alarming. Not only to men, but to some women as well. The laughter mows down the opposition and shatters the illusion of consensus. To anyone committed to rationality, good manners, and political prudence, the film must seem an outright disaster — if only because it's so much fun.

A postscript. With the usual vagaries of marketing and distribution in play, *A Question of Silence* has had the misfortune of opening two weeks after the Democratic Convention. I didn't realize this was a misfortune until I sat down to write this piece. I didn't feel very interested, at first, in women's anger; I knew I had been, but then I'd watched Geraldine Ferraro's acceptance speech, and something shifted. What? I offer you the clue I found in the foreword to *Women Who Kill*, published in the year of Reagan's election: "A baby girl born tomorrow stands a chance of growing up to stick a kitchen knife into an assaultive husband; but the chances of becoming President are too slim to be statistically significant." The links between the psyche and society, between so-called personal freedom and the body politic, should never be taken for granted. Now I've begun to understand why, all over the United States, women seem less angry this summer. There's nothing like a whiff of power to make the powerless surrender their rage. But, of course, if the powerful understood the necessity of surrendering power, the history of revolutions would be quite different.

Meanwhile, though summer is benign, autumn and winter inexorably follow. The squirrels gather nuts against the cold. Me, I've registered to vote. And I'm off to see *A Question of Silence* for the third time.

Prologue.

Film Star as

Outstanding

Human Being

W hen I first met Julie Christie in London in 1982 for an interview arranged through Sally Potter in connection with her film *Gold Diggers*, it wasn't an auspicious occasion. Though both Christie and I were full of the requisite bravura that interview situations inevitably demand, we were actually scared to death: she of granting interviews, I of conducting them. (I could understand her fear after preparing for the interview by looking through her file in the Lincoln Center Library for the Performing Arts, where profile after profile exposed the gossip-mongering downside of celebrity.) Fiercely, palely, we plodded through our alotted time. Dozens of questions later, we finished. "Oh, good," she said. "Now that it's over, would you like some tea?"

With relief, then, began the second stage of our friendship and professional interactions. I attended her birthday party in New York one year, when she was starring opposite Richard Gere in Sidney Lumet's *Power*. Christie, playing a journalist, was concerned that they get her wardrobe right; she asked me where I bought my clothes. This story sent my *Village Voice* editor into peals of laughter, because she thought I dressed like a downtown arts gal and nothing at all like a reporter.

This same editor, Karen Durbin, was as much of a Christie fan as I, so when she heard that Christie was due to show up for a benefit in Washington, she thought the *Voice* could capitalize on our acquaintance by sending me down to capture twenty-four hours in the life of a film star. It was the most pleasurable of assignments, made even more so by the good company of photographer Sylvia Plachy, who was assigned to shoot the goings-on. We got to stay in a swanky hotel and even, thanks to Christie's ever democratic instincts, got to ride in her limousine.

I had never done this kind of reporting before (just call me "Hedda Firestone," I told my friends, grafting the famous gossip columnist's name onto the feminist revolutionary), but I couldn't resist witnessing the incongruity of Christie's integrity colliding with the Machiavellian configurations of beltway society. I wasn't disappointed: I came away from the encounter admiring Christie more than ever for her inimitable brand of dogged commitment, her optimism in the face of overwhelming odds, and her conviction that it's worth fighting the lazy corruption of routine thinking to do things better.

Our paths crossed for a long time afterward, thanks to the vagaries of film festivals and transatlantic intrigues. Thanks to my involvement with composer/musician Lindsay Cooper (who'd written the score to *Gold Diggers*) in the mid-eighties, I was in London often and never missed the chance to visit with Christie.

Back in North America, we shared a riotous dinner at the Toronto Film Festival in 1986 at the premiere of *Miss Mary,* the film directed by Maria-Luisa Bemberg and produced by Lita Stantic in which Christie played a British governess who discovers sexual and political repression in pre–World War II Argentina. The dinner table was filled with Argentine film directors and producers, talking politics with habitual passion.

A few months later, we all met up in Havana—with the casual preplanning of inveterate festival aficionados—when they brought *Miss Mary* to the Latin American Film Festival (it won second prize, losing out to Suzana Amaral's extraordinary *Hour of the Star*). We wandered the streets of Havana and celebrated her journalist beau Duncan Campbell's birthday at dinner in the Hotel Capri. Best of all, the group of celebrants was enlarged by the presence in Havana of Delphine Seyrig, one of world cinema's all-time great actresses and, like Christie, someone who had turned her back on easy fame to work with women. Not only had she appeared in the films of Chantal Akerman and Ulrike Ottinger, but she'd founded the Simone de Beauvoir Center in Paris and championed the feminist use of video as both expressive and archival medium. It was hilarious to watch both of them navigate the waters of patriarchal Cuban hospitality. Seyrig was there for the same symposium on women's film and video work that had brought me there, but her fame made her a crossover guest and before long she was invited to dinner with Gabriel García Márquez. She had admired some chairs at his house and, with a gentlemanly flourish, he'd immediately promised to ship an identical set to her house in Paris. "I know that male style," she told us. "They'll never arrive."

From time to time, Christie and I touch base by phone or letter. Once she asked my opinion of a script for which she'd been offered the leading role of a lesbian character; much as she wanted the part, she felt the script sold out the character's sexuality at the end and didn't think she should lend herself to that. She was right, and it was a shame, because the film was meant to be directed by an interesting woman director. She didn't do it, and as far as I know it never happened. For a long time, she wouldn't accept any role that failed to meet her moral and political standards for representing women's lives on film. She tended to do projects by young filmmakers, women, Third World directors, and other creative people outside the loop of dominant cinema. It was a career of solidarity with marginalized voices and a reaction against the flash success of her earlier years.

At one point, Christie took time out completely to go back to school, enrolling at the Open University to study Eastern religions (she actually spent much of her childhood in India). More recently, she's relaxed and is working again. When I last saw her in London, she was no longer in flight from acting and, shedding her sometime ambivalence, was relishing the idea of returning to the screen, which gives me cause for optimism.

Christie is that rarest of beasts: a woman's woman as well as a man's woman, an actor's actor and artist's artist. Her integrity is unassailable. What a shame that she's in a profession that values such a quality so little. A year ago, I wrote: If only a director with even one-twentieth of her level of consciousness would come up with a suitable role, now that Susan Sarandon and Catherine Deneuve have proven that being over forty is no barrier to being brilliant and sexy on screen. But then her stage career suddenly took off, she went on to appear in Kenneth Branaugh's *Hamlet* where she won raves as Gertrude, and I got my wish after all. Alan Rudolph, of all people, recognized what was going on and cast her as the fabulously complicated character Phyliss Mann in *Afterglow*. Playing a has-been actress haunted by marital betrayal and the loss of her daughter, Christie delivered a phenomenal performance that seems to have led to one of those born-again, where-has-she-been-all-my-life moments with the critical establishment. Savagely intelligent, beautiful, sexy, and endlessly tragic, her character provides the kind of platform that actors live for (and climb to Oscars upon). Maybe Christie will now finally get to make the kinds of films she so deserves. God, I love happy endings.

20.

Julie Christie

Goes to

Washington

(1985)

All posh benefits for worthy causes are contradictions, glittering oxymorons of the night whose only justification is money. I didn't expect this one to be any different. Julie Christie was coming to Washington to help out a women's film festival to be held in March. Her recent film, *The Return of the Soldier,* would premiere for the rich friends of the Washington-based professional group, Women in Film and Video, who stage the biannual festival. The film's producer, Ann Skinner, production designer Luciana Arrighi, and costar Ann-Margaret would be there. There would be a cocktail party ($250) at the home of George Stevens Jr., chairman of the board of the American Film Institute and the bête noire for most of what I value in cinema. The screening would be followed by an elegant champagne reception ($100) at the elegant Regent Hotel in newly elegant downtown Washington. Who could resist?

How did a women's film festival ever score an evening like this? Why was Julie Christie, notorious for her avoidance of public appearances, flying in for this particular fete? And even in a town where politicians do show up on cultural bills of fare, what on earth was Casper Weinberger doing on the list of patrons?

· · ·

The Regent is indeed elegant. It's the kind of hotel that has a concierge in the lobby and three telephones and four kinds of soap in every room.

Done up in today's postmodernist style, the lobby is all overstated under-statement, soaring marble and discreet porters (Asian, like all of the hotel staff, perhaps in a bit of California influence ascribable to the president or to Hollywood, if there's any difference). Beyond the marble formality was a bar that felt like an homage to the Algonquin, with wooden columns and comfortable chairs, a fire going full blast beneath a newly age-old mantle, and businessmen conversing (I swear) in French. Complimentary tea was served in the room to arriving guests with courtesy just short of full ceremony.

I was impressed with the festival organizers' taste and clout. One of their advisory board members, it turns out, is part owner of the Regent. More than any other town, perhaps, Washington runs on who you know.

• • •

Julie Christie was getting ready for the evening, recovering from jet lag and, as the *New York Times* avidly reported, ironing her own shirt. Christie left Hollywood in 1977 to return home. Involved for the past several years with journalist Duncan Campbell, she lives in London and spends as much time as possible with the group of friends she regards as her ex-tended family at her farm in Wales. She hasn't stopped making films, not at all, but she's restricted by the limits of the ailing British film industry.

Why was she here? Well, to support women working in film, of course. And Ann Skinner in particular.

"I knew Ann when she was John Schlesinger's continuity girl, many years ago. She was always very impressive. But I certainly had no idea that inside her lay a driving producer—and driving is what you have to be. There are hardly any women producers in Britain."

Would Christie herself ever produce? "No, I'm no good at that. You have to have a very enduring, sustained energy. I'm more like a flea." In fact, she's trying to get two projects off the ground right now: one about the beginning of labor unions in Britain, and the other still secret.

She has made other films in the three years since shooting *Heat and Dust.* She starred in Sally Potter's avant-garde epic, *The Gold Diggers,* shot in Iceland by an all-woman crew. She played opposite Alan Bates in the Schlesinger-directed *Separate Tables,* a British TV drama that was shown here on cable, and has recently done another television series. Now she's coming to New York for the new Sidney Lumet film.

"People act as if I'd gone away from movie making, and now I've come back. Well, I didn't leave, and I haven't come back."

But she announces a change. "I think I've decided to stop being so fussy. There was always some reason or another. Either I thought the woman character was slightly insulting to women of her sort, or else the film was about something abroad, and there'd be that awful thing by which a country and a race become background for the European white carryings-on. Oh, there's always something." And now? "Now I've decided, just screw it, and just be part of it all. If you want to be perfect — ideologically perfect, that is — you can just tie yourself up into a little knot."

However ideologically imperfect, as the sixties girl of the moment in *Darling* and *Petulia* or the later, more sexualized woman of *McCabe and Mrs. Miller,* Christie was the key icon of a time when women's expression of sexuality became, in itself, a route to rebellion. The strength and intelligence she projected on screen kept the potential victim in her vulnerable women at bay. I think of her as an actress who refused to succumb to the Hollywood model, who insisted on taking her career in hand and making of it something different than it might have been. But Christie rejects the compliment.

"I don't think it's a question of taking my career in hand. Because I always felt that way. There are lots of actresses who do that — Glenda Jackson certainly does, for instance. In a way, it's just simply personal choice." After a pause, she adds, "I think it's also that making films just isn't the be-all and end-all of my life. Sometimes I wish it were, but it isn't."

And with that, Christie turns to the political issues she's been concerned with these past few years, ranging from antinuclear work to Central America. She has been studying U.S. foreign policy and despairs of her country's links to Reagan. The hotel table is cluttered with books about Nicaragua, which she visited twice last year.

What effect did her visits have on her? "Well, you come back informed. But then, you always come back informed, wherever you go, unless you just travel in an air-conditioned bus. I didn't expect to like it as much as I did. I thought it was going to be too totalitarian for my liberal views. You see, I did believe a lot of the stuff I'd read."

Christie is passionate on the subject. She talks about the Nicaraguan elections and how fair they were, what Reagan is up to, why the United States won't leave Nicaragua alone, and similar thoughts likely to be in the mind of any sane person perusing *The Washington Post* at inauguration time. I am beginning to wonder how these attitudes will fare during the coming evening. Which Julie Christie are the patrons and benefactors expecting? Which will they see?

The inevitable "photo opportunity" is scheduled for the marble lobby at six. The hour of contradiction is drawing near.

• • •

The huddle of photographers waited, as the stars were late and the producer was trapped in the elevator. Then there was the usual flashing of strobes and flashing of smiles. It might have been a scene out of *Darling* twenty years later, with the rank aggression of photographers attacking their subject and the ironclad rule: Face the camera or else. I found it horrible. Christie was good-natured but seemed baffled by the once-familiar rite.

• • •

The residence of Mr. and Mrs. George Stevens Jr. was most tastefully colonial, probably dating to the late 1700s or early 1800s. The patrons and benefactors were just beginning to arrive, the only filmmakers in eyeshot were passing canapes, and the remark most often in earshot: "I was a Carter appointee."

Meredith Burch, the chair of the festival, had worked hard to put together an advisory board that could draw this kind of money crowd. It was the first big upscale benefit for Women in Film and Video, a trade organization of women trying to break into the industry, and they sometimes seemed incredulous as they circulated through the crowd offering hors d'oeuvres.

"Do you think there's something to a name? We named our daughter Julie, and now she's grown up and wants to be an actress."

A few people pressed on through the crush to case the house or seek words with a particular congressman, but most had clearly come to ogle Julie Christie and Ann-Margaret (accompanied by husband Roger Smith), and ogle they did.

"Do you know, the last good movie I saw was *Heat and Dust.*"

Christie tried to figure out what she was supposed to do and settled for retiring to a sofa in a side room. The procession into the room immediately began. Meanwhile, Ann-Margaret held court in another room.

"One of your films changed my life. It taught me that a woman could leave a marriage and still live."

Though the men might have come to ogle, the women had come to talk, and talk they did, to Christie. They remarked on how small she was, compared to on screen. On how thin she was, compared to on screen. On how that screen image had "changed" them. And, eventually, of who they themselves were.

"When I first met Liv, I said to him: 'You work so hard for the arts, but no one knows who you are.' And he said: 'That's fine; I just want to help.' Wasn't that sweet? So I married him."

She was Mrs. Livingston Biddle, and her husband went on to become quite well known in the arts, thank you, by writing the legislation that founded the National Endowment for the Arts and, later, running it. He, too, was a Julie Christie fan. She described herself as a painter, who worked in every style and medium we could mention, tolerant of all, decked out in an elaborate Zuni necklace wildly displayed against a print blouse, fiercely eccentric in the manner peculiar to old WASP money. She was the sort of woman who, had she been born into a different class, might well have become a tenant leader, or an ex-CP stalwart, or even a bag lady, but who in her own time and place often represented the best her class had to offer: the flinty matron, unafraid and unabashed, loyal to her principles. Talk turned to Reagan and the just-announced cuts in store for the NEA, and a neighboring dowager began wondering out loud what the president could possibly be thinking.

"How should I know? You're the Republican. You ask him. He's your president."

Mrs. Biddle was not about to tolerate such nonsense, even at a cocktail party. The house was packed with politicians. It was also packed with people who were focused on Christie and determined to get what they'd paid for.

"She looks so thin. Doesn't she look terrible? She must be on drugs. She looks decadent."

Everyone seemed to be getting what they wanted. Except for the senator who decided to take Christie on politically.

"So you went to Nicaragua, eh? Did you meet the editor of *La Prensa?*" Yes, she had, and didn't like him one bit. "You know, they're giving him a lot of trouble down there." Well, his paper's still coming out, isn't it? But facts weren't what the senator was after. He walked away from the conversation while Christie was in midsentence. He would be the only person to walk out on her all evening.

· · ·

"Oh god," said Julie Christie back in the limousine, "I'd forgotten how they turn out to look at you."

· · ·

At the movie theater, the national press was out in force, complete with television cameras and obstinate interviewers. I looked forward to someone addressing our theme of the evening, women in film, which so far, of course, no one had mentioned.

George Stevens Jr. was once again our host. George had some words for us: he thought that "mercy and tolerance" were the most important qualities he hoped for in people who assume power. This was a quip for the ladies, not a protest to the newly rethroned administration.

Nancy Dickerson, our keynote speaker, had even more startling news. Dickerson, the first woman to break the television news barrier, a protégé of LBJ and the first woman political correspondent, is now a television producer. And what did Dickerson have to say? "We could identify with Jeane Kirkpatrick when she said that there's a long way to go with sexism, even in her field."

It was time, finally, for *The Return of the Soldier*, starring Christie, Ann-Margaret, Glenda Jackson, and Alan Bates. All the film-connected guests were led onto the stage briefly, for what seemed to be another photo opportunity, and then the film began. The movie manor looked just like the rooms we'd left behind in Georgetown—minus the Gainsboroughs and the grand staircase, but still, the Anglophilia of the Stevens house had been the perfect dress rehearsal. Even the dinner party in the film, filled with guests struggling to maintain decorum while ogling the center curiosity, seemed a replay.

· · ·

There wasn't much to be learned about women or film that evening, but I sure learned a lot about men. The reception at the Regent Hotel was the site of male fantasy's decisive victory over superficial social decorum. This was where Christie was really expected to pay for being a star.

"I just want to tell you that Kay won't be jealous at all if I fall in love with you . . . just for tonight."

Christie avoided the buffet (she's become a vegetarian) and found a café table off to the side, where she faced, for the next two hours, a nonstop stream of well-wishers, fans, verbal aggressors, and physical interlopers.

"What was the name of the character you played in *Doctor Zhivago*? Laura? I remember when I was 18, my father told me: every man has Laura in his mind. And so that's how I always think of you."

One fan has brought his own personal photographer, who spends all night clicking photos of his employer within the same frame as Christie. Another fan has come all the way from Amish country, bringing Christie a Shoofly pie from Bird-In-Hand.

"Don't get up, just let me kneel at your feet."

He wasn't kidding. I felt like Conrad, traveling into the dark heart of American men's fondest fantasies. They need to approach, to make contact, somehow to appropriate whatever bit of her they fancy is available to them in that setting, within those rules.

"I want to be able to go to the office tomorrow and say: I was at a party last night talking to Julie Christie."

They are not shy, not like the women at this party, who approach usually for only a moment and then retreat, flushed with daring. The men are honest about the enactment of their desires.

"I'm leaving now and I'll probably never see you again, but if you ever come back to Washington and want to have lunch—I mean, I'm not promising anything—but here's my name and address."

And Christie is the consummate trouper, enduring it all, smiling and gracious. More champagne is sipped, as the men keep testing their mettle against this icon, showing off for their wives or establishing a beachhead of bravado they can expand the next morning. The women are more likely to share autobiographies, or simply to bear witness to her. Christie's take on the evening is one only a European could conceive. She likes it.

"Americans are so generous! They are willing to sublimate their own egos, to come up to you and say, 'I am so-and-so,' which is so humiliating. In England, no one would speak to me."

Christie stays until the party ends, past one in the morning. Even two weeks later, the Women in Film and Video organizers can't get over this. Dyan Cannon stayed for only a few minutes the last time.

· · ·

We retire to Ann Skinner's room for the last champagne of the night and a private celebration of her American debut as a producer. It had been her first film.

The perfect aplomb of the Regent was breaking down. The night staff in room service had only a rough command of English and some clear cultural problems. A request for "English breakfast tea" had produced a bizarre delivery. No tea, only someone's very peculiar notion of an English breakfast: lots of jam and sugar and honey, but not a crumb of scone or cracker in sight. After all the Anglophilia of Washington, it was somehow reassuring.

· · ·

The next morning, Christie is up early and impressively intact. She is philosophical about the evening and beginning to decide she'd enjoyed it. We discuss the contradictions of her role: how she steadfastly refuses to play the star, and yet that's exactly what she must do to support the things that the more private Julie Christie believes in. But she balks at my analysis.

"It isn't really turning yourself into another person. It's being yourself. Well, you're much more tolerant than you'd ordinarily be, and of course, it's not quite normal what's required of you. But I never ordinarily do it. It's just like being on a roller coaster: you just go on trying to be nice, trying to be nice . . ."

And she breaks into exactly the smile she had dispensed all evening long. She regrets that she didn't give a better answer to the newscaster who'd asked: What makes you support an event like this? "I didn't understand his question. Anyone would support women in film, I thought. Unless you realize that it was viewed as a sort of fringe event. But I couldn't imagine that it was a fringe event, because of all those people there."

Christie had no idea Casper Weinberger was a patron of the night.

"Why? Why would anyone ask him? What would he be doing there? God, it's a funny country. Everybody mixes up together. Well, I suppose it's this equality business."

But mention of Weinberger brings the morning paper again to mind, and soon Christie is expressing her alarm at the United States turning itself into "a crusade" for the rest of the world, her dismay at the senator who had walked away from her retort and wanted to use censorship as a pretext to destroy Nicaragua. She offered news of the miners' strike in Britain and the repression being used against them. And news of a creepy fan who has been hanging around her house in London, a threatening presence the miner-alert police have no interest in.

· · ·

Women in Films and Video netted $25,000 on this benefit and came away with improved morale and a new reputation for success in Washington circles. It had been a power crowd, there at the Regent Hotel that night, and I doubt if very many gave a damn about the women's film festival they were benefiting. Is this the face of savvy feminism in the eighties? Or is it just Washington?

It's not my kind of feminism. Indeed, the latest festival program announces the opening-night film as Marisa and Dina Silver's *Old Enough,* a choice certainly in honor of making it, a film that speaks to the virtues of having the right parents and getting shown at Cannes—the very formula to which women's film festivals are supposed to provide an alternative.

And yet . . . I can't dismiss these women or this event. Certainly, it's the oldest debate on the books: women making it within the system versus women rejecting the existing system to create a new one. Do we need solidarity with other women to produce someone quoting Jeane Kirkpatrick? Do we want Mrs. William French Smith as our patron? But then, some small voice speaks up for the contradictions again, the value of reaching even these women where they can be reached, the value of getting this kind of clout for a women's film festival. Remember, back in the days of ideological purity, Julie Christie probably wouldn't have been invited either. And I'm not alone in valuing, however bittersweetly, this odd night in Washington. A card arrives from Julie Christie:

"In retrospect, I'm so impressed by the people I met—the businesslike drive of the Women in Film, the forthrightness and generosity of spirit of most of the people who came up to chat afterwards, and those doughty, tough matrons I met beforehand. There's a lot in America to be proud of. I needed that reminder."

The note was written on a *Land to the Peasants* note card, put out by the Nicaragua Solidarity Campaign in London.

Prologue.

Blaming

the Victim

By the mid-eighties I had become a bit worried about the state of feminist filmmaking and feared that a condition of stasis had set in. Then a film came out that convinced me that I was wrong, that in fact something much worse than stagnation had set in — namely, backlash. What was unexpected for me was that the agent of this cinematic retrogression was one of the same women who'd been identified with its feminist beginnings, one Joyce Chopra.

Chopra's *Joyce at 34* had been one of the early classic documentaries of the first wave of feminist filmmaking, though for me it had represented the least interesting tendency of that era in its self-valorizing portrayal of its maker's life and quandries. Taking the age of thirty-four as an occasion for midlife crisis — a sign of its times, to be sure — the film examined the options for a young middle-class career woman (Chopra herself) in terms of balancing work and family. In the years since, Chopra had left the incubatory New Day Films zone and moved on to Hollywood. There, as I chose to interpret it, she'd sold out her earlier, feebly feminist signature for a crack at the big time: genre, formula, a movie director career.

What I thought I saw in her movie *Smooth Talk* was a generational move by an ex-feminist into motherhood and a maternalistic repressive response to teenage female sexuality. I was aware that something important was changing in the status of feminism in women's lives in the mid- to late eighties, although I couldn't yet know that feminism itself would soon become the mother-figure that a new generation would rebel against. (Katie Roiphe hadn't yet published her book, "do me" feminism wasn't yet a term, and the "queer" reaction against women's studies departments founded by feminist foremothers hadn't yet materialized.) Still, I identified Chopra's film as not only significant but symbolic, as any gloss on female sexuality in that period was bound to be, and therefore important to contest. And I obviously had a hunch about "postfeminism," a trend already waiting in the wings.

At that time, my friend Sharon Thompson was in the early stages of the work that would become her opus, *Going All the Way: Teenage Girls' Tales of Sex, Romance and Pregnancy,* an extraordinarily nuanced study of adolescent female sexuality that has tried to combat the Christian campaigns against young women's sexuality. I convinced her to accompany me to the screening and it's thanks to her that I resisted a totalizing attack and assigned the film's first half so much value.

One of a critic's most important tasks is to turn the consideration of any particular film from the expected consumerist referendum of go–don't go into a more far-reaching consideration of the meanings, intentions, and functions of the film in question. In the popular press, of course, this is damnably hard to accomplish. In the scholarly press, where the spinning out of meanings is not only welcomed but required, the accomplishment is less difficult but the size and kind of audience sacrificed to the choice of publishing location is considerable.

For a time in the eighties, the *Village Voice* offered me an ideal situation: a venue with a broad readership open to contributions that would contest the usual reviewer's four-star system of movie appreciation. In this same period, though, Andrew Sarris was still on the staff of the *Voice* and clearly didn't appreciate my interventions on his turf. He repeatedly attacked my pieces and, to be fair, vice versa. When the following critique of one of his favorite films appeared, he counterattacked:

> The issue here seems to be teenage female sex. Is it truly liberating? Or is it threatening, dangerous, and even possibly fatal? Rich's defiant rhetoric has the ring of the seventies still preserved in some of the "sugar walls" rock lyrics of the eighties. And many mothers of young girls are alarmed. . . . François Truffaut once told me (in French) that he was still one of the Original Sin boys. And so am I, I suppose. I don't think sex is ever "easy" or "zipless" or even "life-enhancing." The French expression for orgasm — "le petit mort" — is much closer to the mark. I don't happen to think that kids can handle sex, and

young girls, especially, seldom find the Promised Land in the libido. Too often nowadays they are left holding the bag and the baby, while their elders keep wringing their hands and Prince keeps beckoning to them with his falsetto.

Sarris argued that *Smooth Talk* was simply "a story of one girl, not all girls" and that I had "overreacted."

For me, his comments replicated the neoconservative morality that I had spotted in Chopra's film. The controversy between the two of us was played out in the Letters column, once again, with readers weighing in on both sides. My old pal Patricia Erens wrote in support of my point of view, arguing that the message of *Smooth Talk* was as easy to discern as any gangster movie's crime-doesn't-pay moral. She decoded Chopra's message as spelling out that " 'trashy dreams' and sexy clothes will get a young girl in trouble" and then complained that "the double standard is still alive and well." And so the debates over sexuality and its representations continued, and have continued to this day in the form of V-chips, censorship, internet legislation, and perennial attacks on the National Endowment for the Arts.

It was 1986 and one's feeling of membership in an embattled minority was constant. At the same time, I was still at the New York State Council on the Arts. Our chairman was Kitty Carlisle Hart, a fine role model for any modern woman living through difficult times. She had already had a film career, playing, among other things, the romantic lead in the Marx Brothers' *A Night at the Opera;* a television career, as a permanent member of the quiz show *To Tell the Truth;* and a major off-camera role as first the wife and then the widow of playwright Moss Hart. She'd been the chairman (no chairperson for her, please) of the Council for many years and would stay in that post, seemingly for life, until a punitive Republican governor forced her resignation. Wonderfully for us, she is the last of a breed: not only a true grande dame of class and taste, but also a spirited liberal Democrat who really believed in freedom of speech and subsidies for the arts. She is fearless and she is charming: her only personal defeat came about when she was unable to persuade Mario Cuomo, then governor of New York, to accept a lobbying call from Sophia Loren.

Working for Kitty could be a pleasure as well as an education. Once I had to attend a very difficult meeting with her, to which she wore a wide-brimmed straw hat. At times I couldn't see her face clearly to assess her reaction to the proceedings. Afterward, in the car, I complimented her on the hat. "Well, dear," she replied. "It's always helpful in a meeting like that to have a little privacy." Though she's been written up often in the popular press, the writers tended to play up the society-lady angle and sell her short as an arts leader. Yet I knew how hands-on she actually could be, sitting in our committee meetings, with an uncanny ability to find something potentially troublesome hidden away on a back page of some magazine or book. She had a knack for opening right to the spot. She hated having things hidden from her, but as long as we could supply a decent explanation or defense, she'd go to bat for the artists. Thus it was that she led the Council through serious censorship battles with the state legislature, falling back on the classics to support our choices. Michelangelo was a homosexual! The opera is full of violence! These were her favored defenses. Why is that art? Because the artist says it is. She was our very own "Teflon" chairman.

Being the director of the Film Program also gave me a sort of bully pulpit from which to shape a climate different from the federal one within which filmmakers and film exhibitors could function. Two events aimed at creating a progressive and strategic film environment took place in 1986 and confirmed my belief that I should stay at the Council a while longer because the work that my staff and I were able to do there really mattered.

Premiere: The First New York Conference on Film Exhibition was an event I organized with my staff, Deborah Silverfine and Claude Meyer, and with the Crandall Library up in Glens Falls, New York. We staged the conference in Saratoga Springs off-season, at a hotel usually frequented by the horse racing crowd. The conference coordinator who had to navigate all the horrific details that arose was Carmen Ashhurst, who had just finished running the Film Fund, a key national organization funding "media for social change" that had recently had to shut its doors. Before that, she'd been a reporter in Grenada during the New Jewel Movement and would later go on to become the president of Def Jam Records. In the meantime, she ran a great conference, including negotiating with a hotel that initially refused to accept any room bookings for pairs of people of different genders without a shared surname.

I moderated an opening plenary titled "Censorship, Boredom, Outrage" to address the crises of the moment. Amos Vogel spoke about modes of censorship and puritanism in the fifties and sixties when he ran Cinema 16 as a brave pioneer in film exhibition in an era when scenes of childbirth, for example, were considered obscene and liable to police seizure—even when the film in question showed a cat giving birth to kittens. Joanne Koch, executive director of the New York Film Festival, talked about its history of controversies and detailed which sectors had objected to which offerings; just coming off a national mobilization aimed at suppressing Jean-Luc Godard's *Hail Mary,* she detailed the kinds of parish-generated handwritten letters she was receiving. From San Antonio came

Rolando Rios, who described the censorship campaign waged against the Guadalupe Cultural Arts Center for including Cuban films in its annual festival of Latin American and Latino cinema: his story traced how a community-based facility victimized by red-baiting fought back by marshaling popular support to defeat an anti-Communist agenda. To underline the themes of censorship and repression, the closing night was dedicated to a screening of Lourdes Portillo and Susana Muñoz's film, *Las Madres: The Mothers of the Plaza de Mayo.*

Another important conference that year was Viewpoints, a collectively organized feminist film conference at Hunter College, which I funded. The organizing committee had included Fina Bathrick, Martha Gever, Charlayne Haynes, Renee Tajima, Debra Zimmerman, and others. They'd worked hard to make the event inclusive. Of course, what that meant was that they survived endless disagreements in the planning process only to be attacked by a new round of objections and inflated expectations at the event itself. Bruised feelings aside, it turned out to be a provocative event that was notable for that time in being neither academically generated nor academically aimed. Somewhat in the style of the Northwestern University Feminar seven years earlier, critics, scholars, graduate students, artists, and filmmakers all attended this conference.

Moderating a panel entitled "Cracking the Media Mystique," I presided over a group comprised of Serafina Bathrick, Ayoka Chenzira, Mary Helen Washington (who discussed the work of Euzhan Palcy and Sharon Larkin), and Trinh T. Minh-ha. This panel has the distinction, I believe, of being the first time that Trinh T. Minh-ha was recognized in a star-making capacity, speaking in a quiet voice from the podium while slides of her images and words flashed on the screen behind her. She had just made *Naked Spaces: Living Is Round* and quickly went on to become a major figure.

The conference was prophetic in many ways. Carrie Mae Weems, then a little-known photographer, showed her sharp critique of racism, "Nothing but Jokes," and "Family Pictures and Stories." Sheila McLaughlin and Lynne Tillman came with their film collaboration, *Committed,* a remarkable exploration of the life of Frances Farmer "as starlet, icon, leftist, and victim" with McLaughlin in the role of Farmer. (Especially in the light of recent work on Jean Seberg, *Committed* deserves to be remembered and revived today.) From London, Martina Attille brought *Passions of Remembrance,* an ambitious film by the very active and talented Sankofa collective, which included Isaac Julien among its members. And my friend Joan Braderman brought her soon-to-be-classic *Joan Does Dynasty* (in addition to a cameo appearance in one of the "Family Pictures").

Viewpoints collected a remarkable flowering of feminist film and video energies and marked the fruition of many trends that had gathered force through the seventies and survived into the mid-eighties. Meant as a tonic for feminism in a period of attack, Viewpoints also broke open assumed alliances to show growing disagreements over questions of race, ideology, and theory. In its insistence on activism, embrace of multiculturalism, and respect for theory, it looks today like a unique springboard from the seventies into the eighties.

The fall of 1986 also marked the first anniversary of an event that would shape my life throughout the eighties and influence my view of the art world forever. My friend Ana Mendieta, the Cuban American artist, had fallen to her death under suspicious circumstances in September 1985. I was convinced that she'd been pushed out that window by her husband and ungrieving widower, Carl Andre, who was walking around freely claiming that she'd committed suicide. On the first anniversary of her death, I published an article in the *Village Voice* calling for Andre to be indicted. He eventually was and even stood trial, albeit without a jury. His defense attorney had the temerity to introduce Ana's art as evidence against her, patching Cuban Santería and performance art into an argument that she was suicidal. Andre was acquitted for lack of sufficient evidence after a trial that not only lacked the appeal to emotion that a jury would have afforded but also included tainted testimony from a key witness who mysteriously disappeared back to Hong Kong. The courtroom was divided into a bride and groom section: on our side, the feminists and Cubans and other people of color who cared about Ana and wanted Carl to do time; on the other side, empty seats testifying to his success in persuading the main art world not to lend legitimacy to the proceedings.

I eventually wrote a series of articles for *Mirabella, Sulfur,* and the WARM journal in Minneapolis in the late eighties, laying out the facts of the case and putting forward the substantive circumstantial evidence for his guilt. Two factors particularly bothered me. One was the extent to which the art world turned its back on Ana and drew up the wagons in a circle to protect Carl. The other was the argument by Andre's defense attorney (and by most of the art world establishment) calculated to demonize Ana as a hot-blooded Latina who, well, you know, would just do a thing like that. Elizabeth Lederer, the assistant district attorney who tried the case (and who later would go on to try the notorious Central Park jogger case), told me that the only time she'd ever experienced this level of cover-up in a murder investigation was in dealing with the Mafia. My sense of injustice and my outrage at women being blamed for their own misfortunes at the hands of men were deeply rooted for the rest of the eighties.

I think that my *Smooth Talk* critique is related both to the debates over sexuality that dominated the early eighties and the art world debates over Ana's death that occupied New York in the mid-eighties. When Elaine Showalter reprinted this piece in her collection of essays on the Joyce Carol Oates story, "Where Are You Going, Where Have You Been?," I learned something chilling: that the peaceful all-American small town where *Smooth Talk* had been shot was Petaluma, California, site a decade later of the dreadful Polly Klaas kidnapping. I could have asked for no better verification of my thesis that blaming young women's sexuality for whatever fate befalls them at the hands of murderous men is wrong, vindictive, and dangerous.

21

Good Girls,

Bad Girls:

Joyce Chopra's

Smooth Talk

(1986)

There is a wonderful movie called *Smooth Talk*. It ends when its teenage protagonist, Connie, has a fight with her mom and stays home alone. There is a horrible movie called *Smooth Talk*. It starts when a psychopath in a gold convertible comes looking for Connie, alone in an empty house.

If you want to see one of this season's finest films, walk out of the movie theater when Connie's family drives off to their barbecue. If you want to see one of the most pernicious pieces of moralism to emerge from a woman director in the eighties, then stick around.

Smooth Talk is Joyce Chopra's critically acclaimed new movie, but, its boosters to the contrary, this film offers neither the screen's most delectable seduction nor the definitive female coming-of-age portrait. No, what Chopra offers, with the help of the predictably nasty Joyce Carol Oates story that is her springboard, is a punishment to fit the crime of sexual desire. *Smooth Talk* may be the first genuinely postfeminist movie, unless it's just a belatedly prefeminist one.

The first half of *Smooth Talk* is indeed an engaging and finely observant study of adolescent female sexuality and narcissism, relations between a family and its pubescent girl-child, and most astonishingly, the combination of fear and desire (what used to be called "thrill") of virginal sex. It provides the grand drama of going, not All The Way, but at least a ways down the road. We see Connie rehearsing come-on lines in front of her mirror, cruising the mall boys with her girlfriends only to dissolve into giggles if any come close, and infuriating her mom and stay-at-home sister with the omnipresence of her newfound sexuality. Her make-out scenes, in the parked cars of a succession of teenage boys, are so hot they'll define the genre.

But watch out. This movie is made by a moralist. For pleasure like that, Connie — and the audience — must pay.

The second half of *Smooth Talk* is a nightmare. The film drags two red herrings across our path: scary moments in a deserted parking garage and a dark road abuzz with overamplified crickets and a car of drunken boys. But these are mere plot embroidery. It is broad daylight when Connie's family heads out with the charcoal and Arnold Friend pulls up in his golden chariot, intent on having his way with Connie, and mesmerizes her into rape by verbal coercion. In this half of the movie, Chopra uses the whole bag of cinematic tricks. Every time Connie is onscreen, she's shot in close-up, tightly, claustrophobically, with no space around her, pinned into that tiny unmovable frame. Every time Arnold is onscreen, he's a middle-shot, framed against an ample landscape, lots of space around him, master of the territory. The music surges on the soundtrack. It isn't long before the high-spirited Connie is a quivering puddle on the hall-way floor.

What has happened here? *Smooth Talk* softens up its audience with lust and flirtation, then slices through its gut with a knife of horror. It turns into a familiar product, the stock-in-trade of the horror genre: woman alone, trapped in empty house, terrorized, raped or killed or left insane. In Chopra's hands, the knife has a twist: Connie is punished for sex with sex. Connie is singled out for rape because she's guilty of being pretty and flirtatious. She was asking for it, wasn't she? Just looking for it, right? We're back in the familiar terrain of Blame the Victim land.

Smooth Talk is an insidious movie, and a curious one. Thirteen years ago, Joyce Chopra made a name for herself as a feminist documentary filmmaker with *Joyce at 34,* a self-portrait of her pregnancy. Now, she's the forty-eight-year-old mother of a teenage daughter. And she's made a movie with a message for teenage daughters everywhere: Keep a lid on your sexuality, don't you dare express it, don't you ever act out those "trashy daydreams" (as Connie's mother puts it) or you'll get it. Like a grown-up bogeyman, Arnold Friend will come and get you. *Smooth Talk* is a movie that means to teach teenage girls the perils of sex. Worst of all, the film carries out its mission with a massively mixed message. Connie is terrorized with words, reduced to dumb paralysis, abducted from her home, returned to her doorstep after an offscreen rape . . . and this is praised by some critics as a masterful cinematic "seduction." Joyce Chopra is praised as a major new talent. But a talent in the service of what? The phenomenon of a feminist filmmaker from the seventies emerging in the middle of the eighties to put young women in their place does not, for me, go down easy.

Even more disturbing than the critical raves and festival accolades was the reaction of the movie theater's posh audience the night I went: overwhelmingly middle-aged, they laughed all through the first half and then kept on laughing right through Connie's disintegration. I suspect the lure of *Smooth Talk* is a simple one: the spectacle of lust delivered unto the audience, and then the punishment of its female embodiment, again for audience pleasure. If people tell you they like this film, be skeptical. Ask who they were in high school. The desexualized Good Girl? The nerd that so many Connies rejected? *Smooth Talk* provides vicarious retribution for a wide audience. Meanwhile, if you know any teenage girls, keep them away from this movie just on the off chance that the antiporn crowd might be right and that movies really can affect behavior. *Smooth Talk* is an old-fashioned mother's dream: fleeing the consequences of her sexuality, Connie returns to the bosom of her family, right into the literalization of Mama's arms. That's what Joyce Chopra might call a happy ending.

Prologue.

The Berks

and the

Sex Wars

During the eighties, I began to attend the Berkshire Conference on Women and History, a national event that gathers together women professors, graduate students, and historians from all over the United States for an intensive meeting of the minds. Continuing a tradition that began with the first such conference in 1928, the event took place approximately every three years, usually but not always in the geographic environs of New England's women's colleges. Though it inevitably acquired a dimension of job hunting as the field matured, the conference really was dedicated to the exchange of information and the mutual support of research and projects by women historians — a task that the more mainstream professional associations by nature could not fulfill.

Filmmakers and film scholars were notably absent. The decentralized organization of the event made it very hard for anyone outside of informal historian networks to participate, while there was a parallel lack of interest among many feminist film scholars and filmmakers who were more concerned with entering their own professional associations. Interested in amending this situation and in stimulating the use of film by historians, my friend Martha Gever and I eventually began curating film sidebars for the conference, introducing the historians to the work of Joan Braderman, Julie Dash, Sherry Millner, Michelle Parkerson, Valeria Sarmiento, and others.

I was first introduced to the Berkshire Conference in 1984, when it was held at Smith College and I was recruited to chair a session entitled "Violence against Women in the Twentieth-Century United States." This invitational post turned out to be terribly problemmatic, for the conference organizers wanted me to try to control a panel that they suspected was already out of control. The panel had been proposed by its two members, Laura X from the National Clearinghouse on Marital Rape and Elizabeth Pleck of the Center for Research on Women at Wellesley. Trying for a balanced roster, the conference had added a commentator, Susan Schecter of the Women's Education Institute, who had dedicated her life to working in and writing about the shelter movement for battered women and women at risk. And then there was me.

Well, the session began and my heart sank. Laura X, who had been key to making marital rape a legal category, sounded as though she considered virtually every male-female sexual encounter to be a case of forced intercourse. Elizabeth Pleck, not a film critic or scholar, offered a reading of movies as case studies in rape, using *Gone with the Wind* as a clear-cut example. I couldn't let this go by and took it up in my rebuttal, where I tried to argue that power differential might sometimes be an intrinsic component of sexual attraction and that, well, perhaps dating styles had changed over the years. Schecter, with her years of experience on the ground with women who'd encountered real-life violence, disputed the overarching categories put forward by Pleck and X, arguing that they flattened out women's experiences and claimed a victim affiliation that was unearned and probably insupportable. Good try. But when the question-and-answer session began, I found myself chairing a feminist academic version of an AA meeting, with women rising to testify teary-eyed about representations of violence. (I would recognize the same phenomenon years later when debating Michael Medved, cinematic moralist.) The session was out of my control. I left shaken by the irresponsible forces set loose, as I saw it, by the MacKinnon-Dworkin arguments.

Later that day, walking around the serene Smith College lake with Marilyn Young and Martha Vicinus, we talked endlessly of the sexuality debates and the seemingly unbridgeable abysses separating the different communities. It was an invigorating and inspiring discussion. When Martha Vicinus, whom I'd met for the first time there at the lake, returned home to her duties on the *Feminist Studies* editorial board, she suggested I do their upcoming review essay on what by then we were calling "the sex wars." I agreed, as long as I could make humor a part of it. With a Lynda Barry "Foxy Lady" cartoon on the cover and Nicole Hollander's "Sylvia" cartoons included inside, I contributed the following meditation on the state of the debates.

The only anecdote of any importance in the editorial process concerns the title. I had originally titled the article "From the Vagina to the Clitoris and Back," only to have it returned to me with my title turned into a section heading and a new, more generic title in place. Why? The editorial board assured me it wasn't censorship at all; rather, they felt that the article was destined to be a classic reference, but that, with my title, it wouldn't be footnoted to the extent it ought to be. Scholars supposedly would be ashamed of citing my sassy title. So I went along with their market-research claim and the equally hypothetical promise that I'd get my footnote in history.

Unlike the other essays in this volume, "Feminism and Sexuality in the Eighties" does not have film as its subject except parenthetically. I have included it, nonetheless, because it so neatly summarizes and positions so many of the issues surrounding feminism, sexuality, and representation that have formed the substance or background to so many of my discussions of film until now. In the monumentality of its scope and the summing-up tone evoked, this essay seems at once a fitting conclusion to this volume and a fitting end to a period that was more or less obsessed with these issues—issues that have yet to be resolved, of course, but no longer command quite the attention they once did.

22.

Feminism

and Sexuality

in the Eighties

(1986)

From the Vagina to the Clitoris and Back:
How Times Have Changed

Had the earnest scholar conducted a survey of feminist literature or women's studies courses during the boom days of
the seventies, the issue of sexuality would not have emerged
as particularly significant. Absence was its strongest evidence. Thus, when Martha Vicinus published her astute review of the
literature on sexuality in *Feminist Studies* in the spring of 1982, she could
not have known that her article would appear simultaneously with the
disappearance of the landscape it described.[1] That same spring, the ninth
edition of the Scholar and the Feminist Conference, Toward a Politics of
Sexuality, was held at Barnard College. Today, this event provides a convenient before-and-after landmark delineating the terrain of feminism
and sexuality.

To be sure, there had been signs and stirrings beforehand. Audre Lorde
spoke out against the silence and willful repression in her historic 1978
essay, "Uses of the Erotic: The Erotic as Power."[2] Today, this essay seems to
occupy a vanished middle ground. Lorde may speak out against pornography, but she speaks up far more forcefully against the self-censorship of
the erotic. Yet, even then, she was attacked as "antifeminist" for valorizing
the erotic.[3]

Lorde's statements coincided with the beginnings of movements that have persisted and gained force. The year 1978 marked the first Women Against Violence in Pornography national conference, attracting women from over thirty states to San Francisco.[4] Vigilance against pornography was an expanding movement in the United States by the mid- to late seventies, although the battles of hegemony mounted for and against porn as a feminist issue had not yet begun. Similarly, lesbian sadomasochism made its public debut in 1978 with the S/M contingent of Samois members marching in the Society of Janus contingent of the San Francisco Gay Freedom Day Parade, followed in 1979 by the printing of the first Samois booklet.[5] Although the two groups were adversaries even then, at least locally, it took several years of diffusion and decentralization throughout the country—via demonstrations, conferences, and countless journal articles—for the focus on issues of pornography and sadomasochism to reach its current level of interest and polarization.

By 1981–82, the first years of the Reagan administration, feminist issues of sexuality began to undergo a series of shifts in style and intensity. In 1981, *Heresies: A Feminist Publication on Art and Politics* published its "Sex Issue." The collective had tried its best to make the issue as "politically incorrect" as possible, from the hot porn-playing graphics to the choice of the word "sex" (the thing itself) instead of "sexuality" (the academic/scientific issue) as title. By all rights, the *Heresies* open meeting I attended in June of that year should have been a fractious gathering; instead, the editors outnumbered readers in attendance and the discussion never took off.

Less than a year later, in April 1982, the Barnard conference got the response that *Heresies* had invited. Fueled in part by attacks on the conference as one-sided by New York's Women Against Pornography (WAP), internal attacks by the Barnard administration, and leafletting outside the conference by WAP forces, sexual issues that had been free-floating suddenly became charged into their respective magnetic fields. The conference diary, seized and impounded by the Barnard brass, featured much the same catchy graphics and outspoken personal experience that had been characteristic of the *Heresies* issue, with some of the same players. More public attention was focused on one event, an accompanying "speak-out on incorrect sexuality," than on all the official panels and speakers.

This heating-up of the discourse never cooled down, although, as of this writing, some aspects have faded into the limbo of last year's fashion. This article seeks to trace a few of the trajectories of the eighties' Sex Wars through the literature of the past several years. In so doing, other directions may surface, other silences be signaled, so that the current battle lines may be redrawn and the stalemated debate may move forward.

The *Heresies* "Sex Issue" had all the spunk and sass deserving of a magazine founded by feminist artists. The visual carried as much weight as the verbal. In fact, the journal was most controversial in its choice of unacceptable images, all rendered in neutral or celebratory presentation — porn cartoons, nearly naked women wrestlers, a hand in a zippered glove, a woman's leg poised over a cactus, strippers — all alongside a wide array of images of lesbian couples as Black and White, able-bodied and disabled, butch and fem.

What stands out most clearly in the "Sex Issue" is its spirit of *daring* in both senses of the word, the taking of a risk and the accepting of a "dare," here requiring a jump across the old boundary of respectability. Articles consider sex across a broad range of concerns: incest, trauma, celibacy, sadomasochism, fag hagging, Black sexuality, heterosexuality and lesbianism, power relations in general. One editorial acknowledges the collective discomfort: "Taking risks with our desires, with our bodies and our conceptions of self, in the pursuit of erotic pleasure feels frightening. . . . If we have known ourselves as sexual magnets, waiting, waiting for the pull, then altering our relationship to activity feels uncomfortable" (p. 39).

This sense of fear at the brink of a brave new world would come to be characteristic of the "liberationist" text of the eighties that sought to expand the parameters of sexuality with a full consciousness of the possible price. There was another characteristic as well: a spirit of rebellion, a kicking up of the collective heels. In "Pornography and Pleasure," Paula Webster makes the target clear when she tracks morality back to the nuclear family: "Television, film, and our mothers all reinforce the notion that only bad girls like sex. . . . The training we received as girls encouraged us to renounce acting on our own behalf and for our own pleasure. Our . . . desires threatened Mom and Dad, and they told us how dangerous sex was, especially curiosity or experimentation" (pp. 50–51). Webster identifies contemporary feminism with this same maternalistic morality, whereby love replaces marriage as a prerequisite for sex. I suspect that, in creating this respectable sexuality, feminism has become a mother-figure and what we are seeing is a daughter's revolt.[6] Nowhere has this Manichaean struggle between updated bourgeois respectability and its opposite become more attenuated than in the debate over lesbian sadomasochism.

Coming to Power: Writings and Graphics on Lesbian S/M combines theoretical essays, personal narratives, and fiction, all treating the subject of lesbian sadomasochism. The book's theoretical pieces are largely reasoned and articulate, but lest the reader fall into an accepting rational mode, the photographs of women in full leather regalia insistently confront us with the facts of the matter. Above all else, the Samois contributors scorn the socially sanctioned image of seventies lesbian feminism. One story even features a protagonist, just back from a National Women's Studies Association (NWSA) conference, who is forced to dress in pink fluff as her lover's rite of humiliation. Although there is no attempt to soft-pedal S/M for the public, there is a concerted effort to convince the reader that consent is real and that roles are not fixed.

Coming to Power is at once a coming-out book, a how-to guide, a text of pleasure for anyone open to it, a text of persuasion or polemic for anyone not. The book's greatest strength is its boldness. As a result, it offers a visceral, vicarious experience of S/M as well as an ideological justification of the practice. The fiction ranges from the silly to the discomforting to the utterly erotic. Ideally, the anthology should desensitize the knee-jerk anti-S/M reader and thereby prepare for a more productive debate, cleared of false preconceptions and honest enough to confront the continuum of sexual practice that links S/M to a more common experience. However, it is equally possible that the exercise will backfire and reinforce the horror show already in the head of the unsympathetic reader. The book's coming-out penchant for bravado and nose-thumbing escalates just that response.

Anyone caught in such a response of outrage can turn to the book's antidote, *Against Sadomasochism: A Radical Feminist Analysis*. This is a remarkable document: an entire anthology marshaled *against* something, that something being other women's sexual practices. The texts are almost all theoretical or polemical, spiced with a few confessionals by former S/M "addicts." The contributors (Robin Morgan, Kathleen Barry, Alice Walker, and others) are much better known than those in its counterpart, but the overall effect can be rather numbing.

Essay after essay takes on the subject of sadomasochism with various weapons of attack, aimed at the lesbian variant (the heterosexual kind seems to exist only in literature or history) and often Samois by name. Among a welter of testimony and rage, two objections predominate. One, advanced best by Hilde Hein, in "S/M and the Liberal Tradition," takes on Gayle Rubin's civil liberties arguments, with the retort that "it is a fallacy of liberal individualism that any behavior is purely personal. . . . To degrade someone, even with that person's expressed consent, is to endorse the degradation of persons" (p. 87). The other major objection demonstrates the links between the antipornography campaign and this anti-S/M project, as Diana E. H. Russell, in "Sadomasochism: A Contra-Feminist Activity," complains that the Samois proselytizing is "undercutting the gains feminists have made in conveying to the public our view that pornography is dangerous, anti-woman propaganda" (p. 180). Thus, the opposition to violence that motivated many of these contributors (such as Susan Griffin) to oppose pornography now motivates the related opposition to lesbian sadomasochism, with a virulence heightened by their outrage at the practice's being labeled feminist.

There are numerous points of fascination and numerous problems in the stated philosophies and underlying assumptions of both volumes. The "nonpartisan" reader is bound to alternate between agreement and outrage when reading either volume. For the generation that came of age in the late sixties, the assumption of an active sexuality was generally accompanied by a hybrid of post-Freudian, post-Reichian, post-Marcusian thinking that saw repression as evil and the throwing off of bourgeois restraints on sexuality as inherently liberatory, if not revolutionary. The women's liberation movement, emerging from that environment, began by calling the lie on such practices as liberatory for women, thus creating new sets of values that persisted through the seventies.[7]

More recently, the primary theorist of sexuality has been Michel Foucault, who stands quite apart from the repression-explosion model to posit a different dynamic, based on a free-floating system of powers and desires, mediated by institutions and formed by social constructions.[8] Gayle Rubin has frequently used Foucault to explicate the construction of sexuality, yet she and other Samois writers contradict this allegiance by their frequent reliance on the earlier antirepression model of libidinal release: If it feels good, do it. Just as the late sixties saw this release tied to a contempt for the restrained, so too the defense of lesbian sadomasochism is linked to an attack on seventies lesbian feminism and its assumed orthodoxy (nonexploitation, equal power relations, and so forth).

Although the tendency to see this period as an asexual "vanilla" wasteland is ridiculous (not everyone claimed perfection, and anyway, what about hypocrisy?), there is indeed justification for alarm at the evolution of feminist attitudes toward sexuality in the late seventies and early eighties. The lesbian moved from a position of outlaw to one of respectable citizen. Yet, in the pre-Stonewall era, prior to 1969, the lesbian was a far more criminal figure, her very sexuality criminalized in many laws, her desires unacceptable, and her clothing taboo (at least for the butch, who was the only visible lesbian in this period). For many women, the drive toward lesbianism was not only sexual but also a will to be the outlaw, the same drive that moved other subcultures, like the Beats, to cross to the "wrong" side of the tracks, if only metaphorically. Thus, there was a very real sense of loss associated with the hard-won respectability: a loss of taboo and its eroticism.

In these two anthologies on sadomasochism, the essence of sexuality, whether soul or drive, whether social or symbolic, is variously advanced and compounded by contradiction and confusion. Within the sadomasochistic context, the argument holds up social construction yet veers off in the direction of nature: this is who I am, this is how I have always been, this was my true nature from the beginning. Nature takes on a different identity in the antisadomasochist context, where the writers appear pre-Reichian or even — as in Robin Morgan's "Politics of Sado-Masochistic Fantasies" — pre-Freudian. Nature is called to substitute for the subconscious, instead. "I lay sunbathing on a dock in the middle of a small pond. I suddenly imagined what it would be like to see someone dressed in black leather and chains, trotting through the meadow. . . . I started laughing as one of the parameters of the theatre of sadomasochism became clear: it is about cities and a created culture . . ." (see Susan Leigh Star's "Interview with Audre Lorde," p. 66).

The attempt to hold on to an imagined "natural" sexuality, that is, one that excludes sadomasochism, leads to an exclusion here of all urban realities from the natural world and a rekindling of old-fashioned romanticism that identifies the city with the forces of so-called perversion. On the other hand, the attempt by Samois to recuperate the sadomasochist into the feminist community leads to an equally extreme gesture of inclusion, whereby all practices become acceptable simply by virtue of being carried out by women and situated within a self-conscious ideological context. The category of perversity is denied and sadomasochism is recast as a "healthy" process. According to Susan Farr, in "The Art of Discipline: Creating Erotic Dramas of Power and Play" from *Coming to Power*, the "working out of play and power between our bodies has served to keep clean and fresh and comprehensible the working out of play and power between ourselves" (p. 183).

There is a curious standoff at work here. Both sides to this debate have definite and useful points to make, yet both suffer from the extremes of their adopted positions, falling into pitfalls forced upon them by the overextension of their arguments. At the same time, both seem oddly deterministic about fantasy and tend to equate it unproblematically with lived experience. For Linden et al., fantasy is meant to be kept in line, rationalized to fit ideological determinants. For the Samois writers, it is meant to be acted out, translated into daily life in the form of sexual rituals. Neither group seems to recognize fantasy as a sphere apart, shaped by social and psychological factors but lacking any inherently linear relationship to action itself, positioned finally in a more complex dialectic with the active life than contributors to either anthology care to acknowledge.

A second wave of anthologies sought to create a less polarizing discourse while remaining committed to the disruption of "natural" ideas of sexuality.[9] The first, *Powers of Desire: The Politics of Sexuality,* avoids some of the extremes of the debate by omitting both WAP and Samois articles. The editors stake out their own political ground in the introduction: they are clearly pro-expression, antirepressive, race-aware, class-sensitive, sticklers for historical precedence, and more apt to fall into sexual liberationism than sexual dogmatism. The anthology is successful in marshaling much new information, hard-to-find classic pieces, and suggestive bits of fiction and autobiography. Four key texts, all reprinted there, by Jessica Benjamin, Adrienne Rich, Ann Barr Snitow, and Judith Walkowitz, reproduce the shape of key arguments that may predate the binarism of the current cops-or-criminals feuds, but they nevertheless provide precedents still germane to the contemporary debate.

Benjamin's "Master and Slave: The Fantasy of Erotic Domination" is notable for its injection of psychoanalytic insights into the subject of sadomasochism. Indeed, Benjamin is one of the few writers to bring psychoanalytic theory to bear upon issues of sexuality.[10] She locates the eroticism of domination in the earliest mother-child dyad and in the need for recognition, mediated by the opposing forces of autonomy and dependence, which first motivates our actions and feelings. Benjamin is adamant that we "take this fantasy as fantasy" and put aside moral judgment, advising attention to the material that exists, regardless of how it measures up to ideological criteria. Too often in the debates, the injunction of what *ought* to be takes over, plundering the expression of a wide range of fantasy that has flowered unbidden, the product of forces that we've yet to develop an adequate language to explain. Benjamin's essay is important for its explication of the erotic attraction of domination-submission scenarios, which she ultimately ascribes to the need for transcendence: "The experience of losing the self . . . is increasingly difficult to obtain except in the erotic relationship. Consequently, sexual eroticism has become the heir to religious eroticism" (p. 296). Masochism and submission become, then, the new road to epiphany.

The emergence of lesbian sadomasochism may be redefining relations between heterosexual and lesbian feminists. Adrienne Rich's "Compulsory Heterosexuality and Lesbian Existence," in this same anthology, poses a continuum of affection between women that leads, at one point, to actual lesbianism, which hypothesis stands in direct contrast to the model posed by the gay male community in the seventies and eighties. Male gayness was self-identified and clearly demarcated from heterosexuality, so much so that this identifiable gay community began to constitute a sort of ethnic group in terms of community base, clothing, and institutions. What a relief this ethnicization must have been to heterosexual men, freed of the fear of being "latent." Gayness became a matter entirely of choice and proclamation: if you didn't say you were, then you weren't. This distinction permitted heterosexual men to develop characteristics (sensitivity, passivity) that may have been shunned previously lest they be interpreted as gay.

Heterosexual women, on the other hand, had no such "luck." Despite the National Organization for Women's purge of lesbians from the organization circa 1970, feminism has always carried the accent of lesbianism. Rich's article formalized what had always been felt: that the boundary between heterosexual and lesbian was not fixed but fluid, that a woman could cross over at unpredictable moments, and that sexual identity in this sense was not necessarily stable. It is this continuum that has dragged both attraction and fear into the history of female gay-straight relations. Lesbian sadomasochism may offer heterosexual feminists their own sigh of relief: if the lesbian turns out to be that creature in black leather leading her girlfriend by a dog collar, then the heterosexual woman need never fear being mistaken for lesbian again. And yet, for years, many lesbian feminists had argued that all heterosexuality was by definition sadomasochistic. By this strategy, heterosexual feminists can expect no differentiation but rather a new identification based on the acceptability of sadomasochistic relationships. Whatever the ultimate explanation, it is indeed peculiar that the debate on sadomasochism should have arisen as a lesbian issue when the practice is so widespread among heterosexuals. The debate needs to be broadened and the differences (or similarities) aired.

In the old days, before behavior was dictated by political correctness, emotional sadomasochism was a staple of women's sexual life. Heterosexual romance in this period was shaped by fantasies of domination, seduction, powerlessness, and force, which continue to be reworked in Harlequin romances, gothic novels, and television soap operas.[11] For lesbians, the novels of Ann Bannon and Valerie Taylor, Claire Morgan and Jane Rule were all about being in thrall, surrendering to the pull of a stronger force: another woman. Once feminism took hold, however, these models were shelved (supposedly). For lesbians, the earlier model was dismissed as internalized oppression or, at best, an unfortunate earlier stage in the great forward march to self-realization. In a sense, then, the emergence of sadomasochism is lesbian feminism's own "return of the repressed," as the uneven power relations that had to go sub rosa in the emotional life have returned at the level of the body to be acted out physically.

Pleasure and Danger: Exploring Female Sexuality, edited by Carole S. Vance, who had organized the Barnard conference, is an anthology that emerged from a specific historical moment. Vance has enshrined that moment by the design and structure of the anthology, which follows the original conference chronology with an epilogue of aftereffects and consequences. The volume thus acquires the semblance of a sort of intellectual autobiography, recording as well as reflecting back upon its own genesis.

In her introduction, "Pleasure and Danger: Towards a Politics of Sexuality," Vance usefully threads her way through the delicate analysis necessary to understanding "symbolic context and transformation" in the realm of sexuality: "Sexuality poses a challenge to feminist inquiry, since it is an intersection of the political, social, economic, historical, personal, and experiential, linking behavior and thought, fantasy and action. That these domains intersect does not mean that they are identical. Feminists need sophisticated methodologies and analyses that permit the recognition of each discrete domain as well as their multiple intersections" (p. 16). Given its inherent ambiguity for a field always more comfortable with the quantifiable or verifiable, it is not surprising that sexuality took so long to enter into the feminist discourse.

Vance significantly warns against "the overemphasis on danger" that she fears is impeding speech about sexual pleasure. Although the question of danger is clearly of central concern to any consideration of female sexuality, some feminists see the focus on danger as itself alarmist, a form of collusion even in women's powerlessness. This point is made retrospectively by Linda Gordon and Ellen Carol Dubois in "Seeking Ecstacy on the Battlefield: Danger and Pleasure in Nineteenth-Century Feminist Sexual Thought," in which they chart the exaggerated views of prostitution held by "social purity" campaigners.

Despite Vance's justifiable suspicion of an autovictimization perpetuated by threats and fears, the link for women between sexuality and danger must also be recognized as a real one. For some, the sensation of risk can accelerate eroticism. For others, the prospect of losing (or gaining?) control can be inhibiting. Danger is both psychic and physical for women. The extent to which female children have to repel male sexual invasions is considerable; the extent to which adolescents must cope with unwanted male aggression is equally vast. Such an experience of sexuality as an uninvited intrusion influences a young woman's development of her own desire and sense of her own sexuality. In a recent discussion in Rio de Janeiro, one Brazilian woman commented on the numbers of women she had found to be "asexual," meaning that their expressions of sexuality were severely repressed. She argued that this would be inevitable so long as women had to form their sexual selves in a patriarchal society, where sex could only with difficulty be separated from male aggressions.[12]

Silence over sexuality has its basis in fear. The opening of discussion, then, is likely to restimulate those same fears, even if the goal is to allay and dispel the fears through knowledge and understanding. Many of the essays in *Pleasure and Danger* bear the scars of their authors' fight to be heard, such as Joan Nestle's article on "The 'Fem' Question," her reminiscence of her struggle to be accepted as a fem outside of purdah, and Amber Hollibaugh's "Desire for the Future: Radical Hope in Passion and Pleasure," a gutsy and class-wise assessment of the state of affairs: "We can never afford to build a movement in which a woman can 'lose her reputation' " (p. 409). Both essays display courage ringed by defensiveness, revealing the real limitations of the dialogues so far: debate must be able to proceed without inflicting pain. If conferences and journals prove too rugged an environment for productive growth, then perhaps the late eighties will bear witness to a revival of consciousness-raising groups among women.

Sense and Sensibility

If the four anthologies have addressed the theory and history of sexuality, they have nonetheless frequently employed rhetoric to mask an absence at their heart: the act itself, sex itself, "it" itself. Frequently, then, the discourses on sexuality have come to seem exercises in displacement, advancing with all the stealth of a narrative in melodrama, with the outcome continuously deferred, the pleasure of closure infinitely postponed, until the deferral itself becomes the pleasure.

It is impossible to overemphasize just how basic the problem of sexuality is for many women. At the 1983 NWSA conference, Frances Doughty opened a panel on sexuality by distributing questionnaires on the sex life of the audience. One woman in my row was visibly perplexed, unable to answer the very first question about lovers because she had no idea how to define the act of sex. "Does necking count?" she asked an embarrassed friend. At that point, I began to reconsider my attitudes toward the sexuality debates and to wonder just how much had been submerged alongside the words, as though literary style were being discussed in a land of illiteracy.

Sapphistry: The Book of Lesbian Sexuality entered the world embroiled in notoriety, sold under the counter in some bookstores, prohibited from others (as were other Samois texts). In retrospect, however, this sex-help book by Pat Califia seems endearingly straightforward. Unlike its best-known predecessor, *The Joy of Lesbian Sex* (1977), this volume takes care to be nonjudgmental regarding the variety of sexual practices it inventories. Poignantly, Califia tries hard to counteract the layers of guilt and self-abnegation lying between so many women and sexual fulfillment by reassurances and quotes from scores of women to expel the chimera of "normality" in the realms of fantasy and sexual practice. Occasionally, she becomes glib or unduly flip (such as in the bestiality section), but the lapses can be excused. Califia emphasizes the need for her own book: "Sex is treated differently from other human needs. Nobody assumes you should know 'intuitively' how to cook or 'automatically' how to build a shelter. Sex is the only skill we are expected to possess without receiving any instruction. Women are led to believe that good sex happens magically and naturally if you are with someone you love" (p. 45).[13]

If sex is to be found on paper, it is necessary to look at the margins of the feminist discourse, the world of how-to books or the kiss-and-tell volume, *Pleasures*, which has emerged from the "other side" of the debate. The display of the editor's Ph.D. on the cover and the subtitle, *Women Write Erotica*, establish a position within the politics of the sexuality debates: serious "erotica," not pornography, and certainly no hint of sadomasochism, as a carefully worded note on "power," in Lonnie Barbach's "Equalities of Erotic Moments" (p. 76), makes clear. Because a key point in the debates has always been the exact identity of erotica, that tantalizing utopia of sexual turn-on hailed as delivering all the goods of arousal without any of the exploitation, violence, or objectification of conventional commercial porn, *Pleasures* may be seen as a test case. In addition, editor Barbach's prohibition of fantasy in favor of real-life experience (all stories are true, although not all authors' names) gives *Pleasures* the alluring aura of a "true confessions" piece.

The collection is largely white and heterosexual, although there are some lesbian tales. Stories genuinely concerned with celebrating peak sexual experiences alternate with others more occupied with emotional relationships and responses. Overwhelmingly, they demonstrate to what extent emotion plays a role in these women's sexual responses and excitement. If, too frequently, physical details overwhelm (or fall short of) sexiness with the minutiae of anatomical realism, then the problem may be due as much to the inexperience of these erotic writers as to the careful, no-fantasy and no-rough-stuff rules evident in Barbach's solicitation. To accept Richard Dyer's definition of pornography as any material intended to create sexual arousal in its reader/viewer is to acknowledge one of the book's aims, but not, in sum, its achievements.[14]

In part, this failure results from a misunderstanding of what sparks female desire. In "Mass Market Romance: Pornography for Women Is Different," from *Powers of Desire*, Ann Snitow pointed out how carefully Harlequin romances manage to balance the factors requisite to reader satisfaction, weighing the explicit details against an ambience underserved by these feminist tell-all writers: "Getting romantic tension, domestic security, and sexual excitement together in the same fantasy in the right proportions is a delicate balancing act" (p. 259). Although few of Barbach's contributors succeed, as their emotional dramas crowd out the physical or the physical description wipes out the erotic, their forays are nonetheless instructive.

What does turn women on? Little concrete information has been amassed, so it's still the land of I-may-not-know-much-but-I-know-what-I-like. One original interpretation has been advanced by Australian writer Beatrice Faust, in her *Women, Sex, and Pornography: A Controversial and Unique Study*, in which she connects the erotic to both cosmetics and fashions. Arguing that Elizabeth Arden and Helena Rubenstein "founded a multimillion dollar industry on women's need for epigamic display and haptic stimulation," Faust promotes tactility itself as women's form of pornography: "There may be method in the madness of women who resist rational dress. . . . Walking in high heels makes the buttocks undulate about twice as much as walking in flat heels, with correspondingly greater sensation transmitted to the vulva. Girdles can encourage pelvic tumescence and, if they are long enough, cause labial friction during movement. . . . Fashions are for men to look at and women to feel" (pp. 53, 54, 58, 59).

Faust unfortunately carries her argument too far. After contending that men are visual and women are tactile, she pushes on into truly dubious areas of gender difference drawn from medical writings by John Money and others, sources as disparate as Margaret Mead and Kinsey, and finally approaches flat-out biological determinism. Still, she succeeds in moving us past the established choices of categories, neither celebrating pornography as it exists nor working to outlaw it, but groping instead toward alternative explanations.

Faust is original on the issue of pornography as well, diverging from the well-worn path of free speech defenders to delve again into her favorite source of authority—scientific studies—to rupture belief in the stimulus-response cycle that antiporn forces customarily cite (pp. 78–80). Despite its drawbacks, *Women, Sex, and Pornography* marks an adventurous foray into new directions for exploring female sexuality.

Attitudes toward pornography have changed little in the United States during the eighties, although the *politics* of pornography have changed significantly.[15] The WAP forces moved on from their peepshow-of-horror tours and demonstrations to legal initiatives with the antiporn legislation drafted by Andrea Dworkin and Catherine MacKinnon, adopted by the City Council of Indianapolis and argued in hearings in a number of other cities. Opponents of WAP and its antiporn tactics, meanwhile, moved from merely holding conferences to founding activist groups like FACT (Feminist Anti-Censorship Task Force), engaged in countertestimony, friend-of-court briefs, and similar actions aimed at thwarting legal maneuvers and reopening debate.[16] The Supreme Court decision ruling the Indianapolis law unconstitutional should precipitate a new phase of activity.

Pornography itself still hovers between two inadequate definitions: either a conscious degradation of women, ideologically aligned with misogyny and psychologically linked to actual violence against women; or one of the few expressions of explicit sexuality in a repressive culture lacking in sex education and opposed to the taking of pleasure. The debate is severely hampered by the lack of honest testimony by politically aware users of pornography and by the absence of empirical studies apart from the Pavlovian stimulus-response type. Other views are just beginning to surface.

In his "Confessions of a Feminist Porn-Watcher," Scott MacDonald traces the needs and desires that he believes inspire the user of pornography, bravely drawing on his own experience.[17] To counter the view of porn as a celebration of male mastery, MacDonald argues that it serves, instead, to allay deep-seated male fears of inadequacy: the fear not only of a sexual performance that won't measure up but also of a body that in its very design and mechanisms must evoke women's revulsion or even repudiation. He suggests that pornography functions as a repetitive reassurance machine for a male psyche far more fragile than generally acknowledged — so tenuous, indeed, that it requires a continual assertion of its powerfulness to neutralize incipient physical and spiritual impotence. He sees pornography, in other words, functioning as ritual: "From a male point of view, the desire is not to see women harmed, but to momentarily identify with men who — despite their personal unattractiveness . . . despite the unwieldy size of their erections, and despite their aggressiveness with their semen — are adored by the women they encounter sexually."[18]

MacDonald's article confirms my belief that pornography has less to do with deliberate sociocultural functions than with the shadow world of Oedipal and pre-Oedipal fears and desires. There may be an audience of grown men there in the theater, but buried only skin-deep are little boys, trapped in the prison chamber of the flesh, desperate for a release more profound than the physical one delivered for the money. This is not to say that pornography is a fabulous balm (and MacDonald can stray too far in this direction). Particularly in its commercialized form in eighties America, it is a degraded medium, trafficking in women's bodies for the dubious benefit of men's souls or cocks, depending on your perspective.

362

Pornography is a symptom. Like a nightmare, it embodies and encodes the social corpus in its fully diseased state. Not a system complete unto itself, pornography serves a particular and circumscribed function within a much larger and more important ideological system. Pornography itself is neither the problem nor the solution.

Pornography is also not the only example of the male propensity for reducing psychological or emotional problems to their physical manifestations. Leonore Tiefer, a psychologist in the urology department of New York's Beth Israel Medical Center, has reported on her work in conducting entrance interviews with men suffering from erectile dysfunctions and seeking surgical remedies.[19] Hospital tests demonstrated that no anatomical problem exists in a majority of cases and that the problem is psychogenic. Yet most men reject the suggestion of psychological factors and recommended therapy, insisting instead on a surgical solution and turning elsewhere after the hospital's refusal. Their reaction is all the more striking in that the surgery is irreversible: all future erections will be artificial, dependent on a facsimile created via implant or manual pump system.

Whether exploring the emotionally uncharted territory of male sexuality or the physically uncharted territory of female sexuality, it is important to balance any view of conscious behavior with some account of unconscious mechanisms. In his "Three Contributions to the Theory of Sexuality," Freud suggests how fundamentally difficult sex remains for both genders. As one friend remarked on reading it: people need all the help they can get. The interdictions of morality and ideology may be inevitable, but the need for compassion and invention is urgent. In reviewing the current literature, it is imperative constantly to interrogate the materials; to work to imagine a future course encompassing the fullest possible pleasure; and to emphasize that the defensive postures and brash pronouncements often conceal a terror, pain, or confusion hiding behind the facade.

Although these self-help books, confessional articles, and data-based studies provide alternative routes toward sex, the "it" missing in so many of the theoretical pieces, there remains a boundary line beyond which no discussion centered on "sex" can move us. For beyond this boundary lies the land of romance, a very different "it" that, nevertheless, continues to be a determining factor in our debates.

What's Love Got to Do with It?

Tina Turner is not alone in her critique of the relationship, for women, between the physical and the emotional, nor is she alone in trying to break out of its grip. Contradictions abound. What to make of the Ann Landers survey indicating that 72 percent of her women readers found hugs and cuddling adequate, if not preferable, sexual expression in their marriages or relationships?[20] What can one make of the liberal demand that pornography can be improved by including "relationships" in its narratives to humanize the objectified representations of sexuality? The long-touted puritanism of the female sexual psyche persists as a present and documentable stereotype, right alongside the new breed of sexually explicit literature (not just *Pleasures,* but the more daring lesbian magazines like *On Our Backs* and *Bad Attitudes*). The revival of the Ann Bannon novels of the fifties by Naiad Press suggests yet another direction, one that answers Tina Turner's question with a synthesis of powerfully suggestive (if not always explicit) sexuality and a double-whammy of romance. The Bannon material makes especially clear our need to inquire seriously into the connections between women's emotional life and their sexual responses.

Ann Snitow was one of the first to begin this reconsideration of the emotional dimensions of sexuality—and the sexual components of romance. In her landmark essay, "Mass Market Romance: Pornography for Women Is Different" (reprinted in *Powers of Desire*), Snitow put forth a theory that romance novels not only represent an alternative to pornography for women but also embody a sort of pornography of the emotions. Using the word in its most value-free sense possible, Snitow essays a description of the infantile pleasures of pornography as being "the joys of passivity, of helpless abandon, of response without responsibility . . . all endlessly repeated, savored, minutely described." She goes on to distinguish the products according to gender: "In a sexist society, we have two pornographies, one for men, one for women. They both have, hiding within them, those basic human expressions of abandon. . . . The pornography for men enacts this abandon on women as objects. How different is the pornography for women, in which sex is bathed in romance, diffused, always implied rather than enacted at all. This pornography is the Harlequin romance" (pp. 256, 257).

Snitow is able to dissect the attractions of two very different sorts of material. In the first case, she characterizes the infantile dimension of pornography's appeal in a manner consistent with the revelations of Scott MacDonald's "confessions." In the second, she analyzes the Harlequin romance's efficacy in providing its readers with a functional sexual fix: a seemingly contradictory sum of the parts needed for an orgasmically directed fusion of abandon and safety.

Snitow's argument might be taken even further along its provocative trajectory. For years, pornography has been attacked as a representation of the male objectification of women. Do women not objectify men as well, albeit in a different manner? In fact, if the male form of objectification is degradation, then perhaps the female form, as demonstrated by the Harlequins, is idealization. Both forms ignore the totality and integrity of the other person in favor of a disassembling of parts, an appropriation of fetishized qualities or attributes (physical in the male version, emotional in the female); both generate a fantasy that, based in real-life desires and unconscious fears, can only be oppressive to an actual person. A tendency toward degradation in male homosexual literature, toward romantic idealization in lesbian literature, is a product of this split.

The popularity of the Harlequins leads Snitow to the conclusion that "romance is a primary category of the female imagination" (p. 261). Her insight is taken up and given shape by Sharon Thompson in the first article drawn from her ongoing work with teenage girls, "Search for Tomorrow: On Feminism and the Reconstruction of Teen Romance" (also in *Pleasure and Danger*). Tracing the development of adolescent girls of disparate racial, class, and geographic backgrounds, Thompson finds a striking similarity in all the narratives marshaled in answer to her questions, the element that she terms "the romance quest." So frequently did romance occupy center stage in the teenagers' narratives that Thompson realized that, "like the murder in a detective novel, sex makes it a story worth telling." Thompson devotes part of her report to the intergenerational split that she sees increasingly separating teenagers from the ideas of second-wave feminists; parallel to this split, and in some senses occasioning it, is the gap separating the rituals of romance from mainstream feminist thinking on sexual objects. Thompson decries the myopia of feminist thinking insofar as it has served to derogate romance: "The rationalistic tradition that feminism is heir to viewed romance as a variety of superstition that would vanish in the light of reason and free love, and ... feminists have distrusted romance as one of the chief ways that women 'do it' to themselves. Romance, we have said, is a trap too charged with misogyny and domination for women to risk. But can a field so magnetized with Oedipal material be simply written off?" (pp. 355, 375).

Indeed, if one version of the history of contemporary feminism is the history of the struggle between ideology and behavior, then a major theme would be the effort to exterminate the practice of romantic love through the prohibition of any acknowledgment of its attraction or, ultimately, its very existence. The recuperation of romance as an issue, at least, requiring attention is an important benefit of the sexuality debates of the eighties.

Building on suppositions similar to those of Snitow and Thompson, Elizabeth Wilson has begun a reevaluation of romance from a lesbian and feminist perspective. Taking the argument into a more personal direction, Wilson complains that the *Heresies* "Sex Issue" might as well have been the "General Motors catalog" for all the attraction it held for her. Instead, Wilson confesses that it is romance that holds the "erotic charge" for her, that she had begun to realize was her illicit turn-on: "Operatic, star-crossed, forbidden loves were the silent movie backdrop to my sexual forays. My secret life was peopled with Fatal Strangers, vampiric seducers, idealized violators. Nothing so crude as flagellation or bondage . . . rather the refined thrill of psychic pain, the 'real thing' of rows, reconciliations, parting, absence. . . . The magic of dominance and submission is written into romance as it is written into pornography."[21]

The current debates reflect complex attitudes toward romance and toward the underpinnings of power relations that it stirs up. Wilson goes on to both criticize and reclaim psychoanalysis as a tool for understanding sexuality and gender construction. In a sense, the articles by Snitow, Thompson, and Wilson point toward a decisive break with an earlier attitude represented by such classic, influential works as Adrienne Rich's "Compulsory Heterosexuality" and Carroll Smith-Rosenberg's "Female World of Love and Ritual."[22]

The Rich and Smith-Rosenberg articles are key to any consideration of romance precisely because of their foundation in a base of historical romanticism from which to construct a model for sexual relationships between contemporary women freed of the constraints of romantic love. The contemporary feminist resistance to romantic love is founded, in part, on revived notions of romantic friendship. For heterosexual feminists in the seventies, this model implied companionate marriage or cohabitation, shared housework, contracts of responsibilities. The model for lesbian feminist relationships seeking to avoid the romantic love trap was somewhat different: the utopian ideal of equal power relations, the romanticism of "democracy" that has led in other eras to revolutions or ecology movements or utopian communities.

In the eighties, however, the principle of utopian equality has lost some of its hegemonic status. Inherited from the primal inequality of the infant's relationship to the mother, all sexual relations seem to concern some kind of power disequilibrium, some kernel of psychic domination or surrender, some terror of dependence fighting a wish to depend, a simultaneous desire for, yet horror of, merging. These counterforces of omnipotence and vulnerability persist from the earliest relations with the mother and father. The infantile aspects converge with a presentday sense of the real social consequences facing any woman who dares to be powerful.

Within the sex debates, complex positions have been deployed in specific battles. Groups arguing for lesbian sadomasochism or a revival of butch-fem relationships have attacked the romantic friendship model for turning lesbians into eunuchs by desexualizing lesbianism. At its worst, this revisionism has resulted in "vanilla bashing" and exaggerated caricatures of lesbian feminist prudery. (The question of lesbian feminist hypocrisy, which sustained a rhetoric often unsupported by actual sexual/emotional practice, has yet to be addressed.) At its best, the new energy has produced witty reevaluations of lesbian feminist history. For example, Wendy Clark's "The Dyke, the Feminist, and the Devil" employs fictional motifs as well as autobiography to assess the feminist enthusiasm for "woman power" and to question the way in which the "woman-identified woman" model actually resulted in a loss of "the specificity of lesbianism."[23]

In the 1980s, feminist lesbians have begun to create a new model of romantic love out of revivals of old standards. Perhaps there is a nostalgia at work here, an attachment to the *temps perdu* of subcultures, dress codes, and relationship rules. Still, in an era of popular culture that takes "the new romantics" to signify a British style of clothing and rock'n'roll, it is hardly surprising that the new lesbian romantic heroine should be a figure adapted from the Harlequins and cross-dressed: the stone butch, the S/M dominatrix, the idealized "top" of every bottom's dream.[24] The figure of the outlaw, mentioned at the start of this article, has returned to assume her position at the center of an updated scenario of romance. Shorn of the romanticism of lesbian feminism, the new feminist lesbian fantasy replays the Harlequin formula: she is hard, not soft; controlling, not power sharing; dominating, but still kind; and absolutely unrecuperable despite her partisans' use of civil liberties arguments to win her respectability (when the lack of it is the whole point).

The sexuality debates play out a battle between romanticism and romance, in which issues of control and identity vie for expression. The debates may also mask yet another, equally basic, division: a fundamental disagreement over penetration itself. In this sense, the eighties' furor over dildos is a significant event, implying more than a position on plastic accessories.[25] For many lesbians, the dildo has been inadmissible evidence, a sort of Exhibit A proving lesbian recuperation into the phallic order. For both lesbian and heterosexual feminists, however, the emergence of the dildo into the light of day also implies a new attitude toward the vagina. After all, in the seventies, the sexual frontier moved from the vagina to the clitoris as decisively as the art world moved from Paris to New York after World War II. The shift was connected, often dramatically, to assaults on heterosexuality itself and the emergence of the "political lesbian." The emergence of such a long-tabooed item as the dildo threatens to realign the rhetoric and assumptions of the past decade, centered on the ascendancy of the vagina as sexual site but pulling much more in its wake.

The sex debates of the eighties would seem to be proceeding in a world far away from the grim gay-straight splits of the feminist community's earlier stages of development. But are they? On both sides of the debate, the catcalls are sometimes homophobic. In New York, at least, the universal object of scorn seems to be the lesbian feminist, who, as "last year's model," is spurned by a variety of sectors, including the editors of several of the anthologies and many heterosexual feminists. At the same time, antiporn forces are sometimes treated with homophobic overtones by the mainstream press. It is possible that feminism has not transcended its own straight-gay splits at all but has simply relocated them within the rhetoric of each section of the movement. There may be a lasting bedrock of self-loathing or anxiety that finds relief in the chance to live in glass houses and throw stones.

In an era in which we are all, rapidly, becoming outlaws within an increasingly repressive society, we would do well not to make outlaws of each other. If we can agree that sexuality is more than the sum of its parts and that its construction owes as much to fear as to desire — as much to Mommy and Daddy as to the boy or girl of our dreams, as much to infantile pleasures as to adult preferences, as much to trauma as to personality — then our critique of sexuality must begin to consider our own moment in history, in the culture of 1986.

The Geopolitics of Sexuality

To avoid isolating sexuality from its sociocultural moment, it is necessary to assess the impact of this moment both on the inner workings of the current debate and on the shape in which the debate itself has been constructed. At first glance, the women's movement's racism would seem to have been transcended, as women of color appear on both sides of the sexuality arguments. *Against Sadomasochism* boasts Alice Walker and Audre Lorde among the names on its cover. In addition, there is an article by Yoruban-influenced Vivienne Walker-Crawford and another entitled "Racism and Sadomasochism: A Conversation with Two Black Lesbians," by Karen Sims and Rose Mason. Yet, when Sims and Mason concur with another woman's statement on sadomasochism — "That's not my issue whatsoever. That's for white people to deal with" (p. 99) — then the entire relationship of Black women to these sexuality debates is called into question. Indeed, women of color are noticeably absent from the Samois anthology.

In *Powers of Desire,* the contributions by Black writers parallel the collection's overall tendency toward the historical. Asked to address sexuality, Rennie Simson and Barbara Omolade address themselves to the past, concentrating on slavery and the Reconstruction period. In "Hearts of Darkness," Omolade points to the very particular dynamic linking Black women's sexuality to history: "History would become all that (white) men did during the day, but nothing of what they did during the night" (p. 364). That is the history that Omolade and Simson seek to write.

In *Pleasure and Danger,* Oliva Espin's analysis of sexuality and assimilation in Hispanic/Latina women within the United States and Hortense J. Spillers's consideration of Black women's sexuality constitute the important but sole articles by women of color in the anthology. In "Interstices: A Small Drama of Words," Spillers herself supplies the explanation, not only for this volume but for the larger debate as well: "The nonfictional feminist work along a range of issues is the privileged mode of feminist expression at the moment, and its chief practitioners and revisionists are Anglo-American women/feminists in the academy. . . . The nonfictional feminist text is, to my mind, the empowered text—not fiction—and I would know how power works in the guise of feminist exposition when 'sexuality' is its theme" (pp. 74–75).

Women of color do enter into the two anthologies in the poetry sections: Jayne Cortez, hattie gossett, Cherríe Moraga, even the blues lyrics penned by Porter Grainger for Ida Cox, "One Hour Mama." More to the point, however, women of color make their contribution to issues of sexuality outside the nonfiction books that constitute the official discourse, in texts that exist on the margins of the debate, as currently constituted, if not entirely apart. Sexual concerns fill the novels of Toni Morrison and Alice Walker, the blend of fiction-autobiography-nonfiction in Cherríe Moraga's *Loving in the War Years,* the autobiography of Audre Lorde's extraordinary *Zami,* and the poetry of Cheryl Clarke's *Living as a Lesbian.* These works, together with those essays that touch on sexuality in the context of investigating such larger issues as race or class or literature, such as the *Home Girls* and *But Some of Us Are Brave* anthologies and the ongoing journal *Conditions,* constitute as meaningful a contribution to questions of sexuality as the analyses produced by certified theorists within the official debate.[26]

Spillers has noted that Black women's major voice of sexuality has always been the blues, quoting critic Michele Russell on the blues as a fulcrum of experience: "Black women have learned as much (probably more) that is positive about their sexuality through the practicing activity of the singer as they have from the polemicist" (p. 87). How explicit is the color line in the sex debates? Spillers surveys the territory and concludes that "black women are the beached whales of the sexual universe, unvoiced, misseen, not doing, awaiting their verb" (p. 74).[27]

In her introduction to *Home Girls,* Barbara Smith even questions whether that dynamic is worth fighting: "Until now, Black women have been peripheral to these debates and I am not sure that it will be helpful to us to step into the middle of 'white-rooted interpretations' of these issues."[28] The history of sexual exploitation of Black women, at the level both of myth and of daily life, by a White culture has understandably made many women wary of participating in this particular controversy. Similarly, Latina women struggling to come to terms with La Malinche may not care to embrace her quite yet. Until the debate is widened beyond its current scope, women of color may well continue to prefer the blues to the polemicists.[29]

It is the polemicists who still reign, however. They are backed by the historians and by the autobiographical testimony of nonacademics who use their own lives as an alternative form of currency in this theoretical economy. Spillers's point concerning the fetishizing of the theoretical text could be taken even further, beyond the sexuality debates. Why have certain issues proven to be theorizable, and others have not, thus producing the inevitable dominance of the theorized issues, rightly or wrongly, within feminist debates? An investigation of this question could well provide a redirection of feminist energies into a world far broader than the academy now containing them.

To address the larger world of sexuality in the eighties, it is necessary to leave the current literature behind. The global context of contemporary life rarely enters into the theoretical debates, as though to indicate that sexuality is not really as socially constructed as claimed, as though sexual issues were not so deeply affected, after all, by history, the economy, the cold war, disease, the new conservatism, or even fashion. If, as considered, the feminist exchanges on sexuality have transcended neither racism nor homophobia, replicating portions of each by displacement or absence, then it's especially crucial to examine our sociocultural context and its political implications. Only then will change be possible.

The sudden debates in the early eighties over lesbian sadomasochism or butch-fem roles, for example, make little sense if viewed solely as feminist issues, rather than within the milieu of contemporaneous heterosexual society. After all, the turn of the decade had marked a swift reestablishment of gendering in fashion. Women went "fem" wholeheartedly for the first time since the fifties, men went butch, and gender became secure enough to permit exceptions (Boy George's clothing, Calvin Klein's models). In such a context, the revival of butch-fem codes into a lesbian version of retrofashion would appear to be eminently reasonable, as a sign both of creativity and of an accommodation to social trends. (See Amber Hollibaugh and Cherríe Moraga's "What We're Rolling Around in Bed With" and Joan Nestle's "Butch-Fem Relationships: Sexual Courage in the Fifties," both in the *Heresies* "Sex Issue.") Just as the lesbian debates paid attention to behavior (especially in bed) as much as to clothing, so, too, has mainstream culture been occupied with the reification of traditional female roles, caused as much by disease (such as herpes) as by ideology.

Similarly, the rise of lesbian sadomasochism as an issue should be analyzed in the context of the sadomasochistic trend of mainstream society in this same period. The late seventies and early eighties were the era of punk, a world dominated by exaggerated S/M trappings in clothing and song lyrics, and by the punk influence on the art world. Unlike in Britain, where punk carried a political charge of class rage, here in the United States in the early Reagan age, punk had an aura of celebratory nihilism, a coming-of-age with no Age coming, an end-of-the-empire abandon. Punk made seventies lesbian feminist styles awfully old-fashioned, whether measured by clothing or behavior or simply cultural sensibility. Some sort of change or renovation of the image would clearly be appealing.

Such strategies as butch-fem roles or lesbian sadomasochism, in turn, suggest another dimension that is just beginning to take shape in some of the psychoanalytic work on lesbian relations: the issue of differentiation. Joyce P. Lindenbaum's "The Shattering of an Illusion: The Problem of Competition in Lesbian Relationships" is a major contribution toward understanding the dynamics of merging, identification, and differentiation in relations between women. She sets out a number of observations: "There is a tendency toward overidentification in lesbian relationships. The same-sex nature of the relationship, women's comfort with 'less-differentiated' relational modes, the recapitulation of primary intimacy and merging, and the social oppression that locks the lesbian couple in the closet contribute to this overidentification."[30]

Lindenbaum goes on to argue that lesbian couples cope with the "recreation of primal intimacy" and the "excruciating terror of primal loss" through a number of steps that culminate in "the sacrifice of sex." Her hypothesis may well have repercussions for the debates over sexual behavior. The adoption of butch-fem roles or lesbian sadomasochism may well constitute an alternative remedy to the problem of merging identified so acutely by Lindenbaum. In adopting these roles, women are constructing and insisting upon the *otherness* of the partner, in direct contradiction to the identification that has long been the basis of lesbian feminist relational ideals. To be sure, these roles may offer only a superficial remedy in that they can also block the route through to the underlying traumas or needs, providing a mechanistic acting-out at the physical level in place of a deeper acting-through of actual pains and desires. Nevertheless, their emergence in the eighties has widened the parameters of sexual possibility and debate, leading, it is hoped, to a much broader reinvention of the terms of discourse, drawing from the world of psychoanalysis and the secular world of manners and mores.

In the spirit of the world at large, it would be irresponsible to conclude this article without noting three contemporary factors that must intrude upon any attempt to examine contemporary female sexuality. First, any study of sexuality in the eighties would be myopic indeed if mention were not made of AIDS, which has already touched off an epidemic of panic (particularly concerning the infection of children). Reactions to AIDS have made homophobia mainstream again in a fashion unprecedented for nearly two decades. Although AIDS has inevitably altered the sex life of gay men, it has dealt just as severe a blow to the fluidity of sexual identity that had been sparked by the sixties and still survived in the culture, until now. In the wake of AIDS, bisexuality has suffered a greater setback than the ideological brickbats could cause in the seventies. Polymorphous perversity? The theory has become fashionable in inverse proportion to the practice. The laissez-faire economy has been restructured in the sexual zones, where the principles of deregulation are being reversed and where morality is once again dictated by fear. The result is the increasing rigidity, not only of gender roles, but of sexual identity as well.

Second, it would be folly to consider any theories of sexuality without reference to the eighties baby boom. The aging of the "second wave" of feminists has contributed to major changes in feminist notions of sexuality, but this maturation has also brought a susceptibility to intense pressures (whether hormonal or familial or cultural) to reproduce. If a rupture seemed to have been made between sexuality and reproduction back in the sixties and seventies, then the lesson of the eighties is that no rupture is permanent; the two are once again joined. It is clear that the change to being mothers, accompanied often by being married, will require feminists to develop new identities and new approaches to sexuality. For lesbians, too, the eighties baby boom is a reality, though in this case the rupture between sexuality and reproduction is further widened.

The theorizing of artificial insemination has not yet taken place, yet the widening practice of "alternative insemination" by lesbians will certainly have consequences far in excess of anything ever written about hypothetical parthenogenesis. Changes in sexual identity are an inevitable corollary to such major alterations.

Third, sexual issues can no longer be separated from politics—and not simply the politics of the feminist community, but the larger left-right skirmishes of U.S. society in the eighties. Most commonly, political influences are recognized as the attempt by the New Right to control and contain female sexuality through such mechanisms as the attack on abortion (see Faye Ginsburg, "The Body Politic: The Defense of Sexual Restriction by Anti-Abortion Activists," in *Pleasure and Danger*, p. 186). In addition to controls on reproductive rights, the right has catalyzed a large-scale backlash that has affected a sweeping range of women's activities and feminist concerns—from the control of sexuality to the attack on day care centers, civil rights, affirmative action, and so forth. The enormity of the backlash affects the core of our life, and in turn, our sexuality. Furthermore, the Dworkin-MacKinnon antiporn legislation has occasioned alliances with sectors of the right, setting off a replica of right/left politics within feminism, with the right lining up to contain or ban pornography and the left holding to its traditional First Amendment position. The Supreme Court decision finding the law unconstitutional and the recent report from Edward Meese's pornography commission may provoke manifestations of right agendas on new feminist fronts. Although the pragmatic allies on these issues would seem to share few goals with their feminist allies, the division has forced the issue of politics within the feminist community in a manner never before seen in a movement that has always taken its "progressive" credentials for granted.

Right/left alliances of a different sort have arisen out of the cold war politics of the United States in the eighties, involving the U.S. relationship to Cuba and placing U.S. lesbians and gay men in an untenable position. With the release of the anti-Castro documentary *Improper Conduct* in 1984, alliances were formed between the right and the gay community; the U.S. gay and lesbian community was cynically manipulated by the right to neutralize support for Cuba and to strengthen cold war policies.[31] For an alternative example of cold war dimensions to feminist debates, consult the chapters on Cuba, other socialist or communist countries, or the absence of any chapter on Puerto Rico in Robin Morgan's anthology, *Sisterhood Is Global*.[32]

These examples are given, not as a definitive survey, but as a suggestion of the broad range of factors that account for the shape of sexuality as a feminist issue in the eighties. Some sort of "geopolitics" of sexuality is necessary if we are to develop the understanding to carry us past the current dead end of polarized and frozen positions. In a sense, we have failed to develop an active feminist theory of sexuality, which all our fidelity to Sigmund Freud, Michel Foucault, Jeffrey Weeks, Jacques Lacan, or even Juliet Mitchell, Nancy Chodorow, or Angela Carter, cannot counteract.

I agree with Hortense Spillers that sexuality must be linked to power in its broadest meaning and scope. Like others, I have sometimes felt that the emphasis on sexuality in the feminist communities of the eighties was just a dodge: a way of turning away from the hard questions, a retreat from the horrors of Reaganism, a terrible wasting of energies and factionalizing of unities in hard times. During the long struggle with these ideas, however, and the writing of this article, I have come to feel differently. It has become apparent just how deeply sexuality is linked to the other issues confronting women in the eighties, so much so that the goal must not be to sever that connection even further but to insist on the relatedness of it all. The sexuality debates have always been too narrowly focused, too turned in upon themselves; the claustrophobia of self-reflection can be dispelled by opening the gates to the many connected issues, to the ways of other cultures, to the full span of the historical moment in which we find ourselves.

Just how deeply sexuality cuts as an issue may also be seen in the remarkable vitriol that has infected the debates. Humor would be a welcome interjection. Both Lynda Barry and Nicole Hollander have the ability to pierce the veils of pride and tension that guard the subject of sexuality.[33] Hollander has created her Sylvia as the woman we'd all like to be, while Barry has created characters who, horror of horrors, are the women we really are. Sometimes it seems as though Hollander and Barry are playing out one of the great feminist debates, cartoon-style, of woman-as-agent versus woman-as-victim. Other times, the dichotomy seems more psychological. Hollander's Sylvia offers up the victorious female ego, wisecracking her way through world events, while Barry's protagonists embody the vulnerable female id, exposed to the world and searching alternately for punishment and revenge.

Confirming Scott MacDonald's point about the childlike terrors that motivate our adult patterns of sexual consumption, Barry uses her cartoons to return women to the primordial laboratory where our sexual fantasies and identities were once shaped. Ignoring political imperatives, she stakes her position on the tragicomic inevitability of it all. In *Naked Ladies*, for example, she recreates the tones of adolescent malaise: "Our Home Ec class looked out on the boys' playfield and everyone wanted the sewing machines on that side of the room so we could watch the guys and think about them wearing Jock Straps. We got Bras and they got Jock Straps. Like everything was suddenly going out of control and your mom had to buy you something to stop it."[34]

The body of work created by Barry and Hollander is a necessary antidote to the sobriety and defense-offense postures of the sex debates. In the era of postmodernism, it is easy to forget that humor is the oldest form of deconstruction: it breaks down barriers, shatters polarities, and conducts subversive, or even liberatory, attacks on the reigning order.

Compassion, too, is urgently needed. If any progress is to be made in a discourse that even its participants admit is stalled, then the battlements must come down and the siege mentality be dismantled. Empathy should be heightened across the lines of debate. Right now, the deepest fears are being masked as aggression, and acts of aggression are concealed as righteousness. So long as the discussion of sexuality retains a binary model, then choosing sides will remain more important than creating, thinking, or making progress. In the aftermath of the Supreme Court decision on homosexuality and the Meese Commission report on pornography, we can ill afford myopia or stasis within our own ranks.

Looking back over the sexuality debates of this decade, it often seems that a crowd is gathered in one corner of a very large house, oblivious to the many places still unexplored. Sometimes, I think we need to remember to move, to stretch both our minds and bodies out beyond the cramped quarters currently occupied. Forays have been made, new territories sighted. We need to follow up these initiatives, to open up the debates, to look elsewhere to find different answers and, even, different questions. We are free to move on. We needn't contain ourselves any longer.

Epilogue:

Charting

the Eighties

I've chosen to end this volume in the mid-eighties for a number of reasons that are both historically purposeful and personally signifi-cant. The last essay in this collection, "Feminism and Sexuality in the Eighties," represents for me a logical fault line separating the politics beginning in the seventies that I have traced here from the some-what different politics that would become characteristic of the eighties and nineties. The old ghosts of feminism past tend to fade away as the eighties progress and in their stead we get such contestatory presences as antiporn and pro-sex, or pro-choice and pro-family, and other colloquial but misleading phrases popularly deployed to describe the movements that here take the place of earlier formations. With sexuality as the central fulcrum on which a massive political realignment rests, it seemed appro-priate to end my early history with this essay as a benchmark.

Furthermore, the nature of filmmaking by women changed markedly around the mid-eighties, when the feature-film format decisively became the only choice for directors in need of prestige, investment, and indus-try recognition. The parallel development of video in this same period further eroded the formerly lucrative educational market for 16mm and diminished the status of women working in shorter forms (documentary, personal film) in the United States. The conservative thrust of the fed-eral government throughout the eighties and early nineties had a negative impact on the sector of feminist and progressive filmmaking, with severe cutbacks and political censorship.

As the availability of grant money of all kinds declined, the promise of cultural democracy that they had proferred to the film production sector deteriorated, too. Just as some apertures were closed, however, others opened up. It is notable, for instance, that the world of feminist film activity I have drawn here was overwhelmingly white—a condition that today would be literally unimaginable. The whiteness of those early years was superseded, happily, by a far more diverse sector of filmmakers and theorists of color whose powers of invention and dynamic energies transformed the field sketched herein. While the individual works are well known, the story of the field's transformation still awaits telling.

Nor was all the news bleak in the eighties, as certain sectors did manage to prevail and even flourish. One notable example is Women Make Movies, an organization that underwent a total change of staffing in the early eighties to become an effective and entrepreneurial distributor of films and videotapes by women in the United States and abroad. Its work has been particularly critical for the diffusion of films and tapes by U.S. women of color, Australian women, and women from Latin America. In the same period, the Video Data Bank became established as a major force for new approaches to video, pioneering home-video distribution with innovative series of feminist and AIDS video. And the home video market had another unexpected, extremely positive effect: the proliferation of the camcorder, which ushered in a burst of low-budget production by women and permanently altered the landscape, opening a sort of "video-zine" culture shaped by female, feminist, and lesbian imaginaries. Strategies changed in this period, for non-profit exhibition as well as distribution, and my own stances and strategies begin to change as well.[1]

The period 1985–88 is also, as earlier noted, the period during which my friend Ana Mendieta died under criminally suspicious circumstances and her husband, Carl Andre, subsequently stood trial for her murder and was acquitted. Though I've already mentioned my own involvement in the campaign to bring him to justice, to monitor the trial, and to publicize the facts of the case to those who knew little or nothing of Ana's life and death, what I've left out is the traumatic effect that her death and his acquittal (on grounds of insufficient evidence) had on me.[2]

The mid-eighties are marked for me forever by Ana's death on September 8, 1985, by my work as a member of the group organizing her retrospective at the New Museum of Contemporary Art that opened on November 20, 1987, and by my experience of Carl Andre's trial and its disappointing conclusion on February 11, 1988. Ana's retrospective closed five days before the trial opened. I lost my innocence during those three years as I circulated through the remains of the feminist art world in a vain search for women who would come forward to testify about the past incidents of his violence toward women that others had reported to me. The bravery of a number of art world women — Jayne Cortez, Barbara Kruger, Yvonne Rainer, Nancy Spero, and Ida Panicelli — who spoke out for Ana was the exception that proved the rule of racial splits within feminism and gender splits within the art world. In that downtown courtroom, where the politics of race and gender played out in a memorably ugly fashion with venomous consequences, I lost (at least temporarily) whatever faith in justice I had left. These years and events mark a decisive before-and-after point in my life that no number of pages or arguments could hope to bridge.

There's another major transformation of equal importance that takes place in this same period: the winter of 1986–87 marks the start of my relationship with filmmaker Lourdes Portillo, with whom I've shared my life ever since. Fault lines don't point to tremors in the professional zone alone, as I hope this volume has amply demonstrated. My alliance with Lourdes has had a transformative impact on my life. I have shifted residence between New York and San Francisco, reconnected with my collegiate love for Mexico, and learned about life from the perspective of her sons, the young men who have become my stepsons. We originally met in Havana, where she was the president of the documentary jury and I was a speaker in a symposium on women in Latin American media. We've attended festivals and conferences together, plotted strategy, and argued our differences. We disagree about films about as often as we agree. In 1990, we traveled together to Tijuana for a landmark conference, Cruzando Fronteras, which brought together Mexican, Chicana, and Latina filmmakers from both sides of the border.

For more than a decade, our private and professional lives have mixed, cross-fertilized, and been mutually influential. We've shared values as well as experiences, argued about aesthetics and politics, and done our best to negotiate the treacherous shoals of a cross-cultural relationship with the added burden of an artist/critic divide. I don't think that my critical writing would read the same without her input; perhaps her films would have turned out differently without mine, but that's for her to judge. So consider this another "fault line" separating the work collected in this volume from the work that would soon follow. Intellectual and political change takes place at all levels, whether one believes any longer that the personal is political or not.

The eighties brought lots of surprises and discoveries. It was in 1987 that a young man came to my arts council office for advice, referred by our shared friends in London. He was beginning research on a film about Langston Hughes, the Harlem Renaissance, and homosexuality. His name was Isaac Julien and he became one of my great friends—my transatlantic brother, I sometimes say, only partly joking—along with his partner, the critic and producer Mark Nash. At that time Isaac was a member of the Sankofa film workshop, which had just finished *The Passion of Remembrance*. His own film, completed two years later, would be the landmark *Looking for Langston*. And that moment, which seemed to be so very much about the evolution of a new Black British cinema, turned out equally to be one of the founding moments of the movement I would later term the New Queer Cinema.

Wherefore and Where To: Feminism at the Crossroads

"Feminist film" as a term and a practice has increasingly lost its meaning over the decades. Today it would be hard to describe such terrain apart from the cherished memories of film professors or veteran filmmakers, people who came of age in the seventies and responded to its power back then. Within the academic world, however, it has dramatically failed to redefine itself in terms of cinematic analysis and modes of thinking. The domination of psychoanalysis as a theoretical approach cut off too many avenues of inquiry and invention, all defeated along the way and dealt out of the game. I think that the influence of psychoanalysis as a hegemonic theory with one singular world-view has been a disaster as a literary device and critical tool in literary analysis and feminist studies (though I continue to have the highest regard for the clinical practice, being a much-improved analysand myself).

The feminist filmmaking energy that was so prevalent in the seventies has returned, I'm convinced, in the form of the combustible dynamic of films and videos being produced in the nineties for and by the "queer" communities that have come of age in the AIDS era. If feminist cinema has a legacy today, then, it's in lesbian feature films, documentaries, and videotapes that invent new aesthetic strategies that are akin to alchemy in fashioning something out of nothing. And in the gay male films and videotapes that push the limits of subject matter and form. This gay and lesbian work plays in the ever increasing number of international gay and lesbian film festivals and continually crosses over into theatrical release. It sparks debates as passionate as those that engaged me in the seventies and is moving into the academy and the publishing world at an astonishing speed.

Lesbian culture is going strong in the nineties. It is heterosexual feminism that has lost its way, at least in the world of film theory. The psychoanalytic and poststructuralist agendas, once dominant, fostered a closed-shop atmosphere with an excess of homogeneity, inbred self-referentialism, and a tendency toward stasis and atrophy. Today, the most powerful legacy rests with the women of color who have taken the lessons of earlier feminism and merged them with the specificity of ethnic or national discourses to create new hybrid models with a strength greater than their original parts. The kind of energies characteristic of early feminist film scholarship today can more likely be found in the open, expansionist universes of cultural studies, postcolonial studies, or queer studies than in film or women's studies departments.

In the filmmaking community, the feminist legacy rests with feature filmmakers who have taken on the lessons of power learned in the seventies and the lessons of sexuality learned from the sex wars of the eighties and applied both of them to fantasy and narrative. In the world of video, its power lingers with the women who have combined video with performance and combined the self with the character to produce new hybrid forms of video art that center women within contemporary discourses.

Strategies for the Nineties

My own interests have continued to evolve largely outside the academy and have followed the currents of the nineties that most fascinate me. I have become increasingly interested in the work of actresses ever since these early conversations with Julie Christie and have gone on to do museum and festival tribute shows with Jodie Foster, Geena Davis, and Maggie Cheung and to write about Tilda Swinton. I've returned to my old roots in film exhibition, working with the Sundance and Telluride film festivals. I've become involved with other film cultures in other countries where exciting work is being undertaken, notably Hong Kong and Brazil. I still follow Cuban and other Latin American film, travel to London, maintain ties to Chicago.

My search for places to write that will reach readers outside of academia has taken me from the pages of *Elle* and *Mirabella,* the women's magazines, to newspapers like the *Village Voice* or the *San Francisco Bay Guardian,* and the film magazine, *Sight and Sound,* my favorite venue in the early nineties for serious pieces to argue ideas, albeit without footnotes. I write for the gay and lesbian press, too: OUT, *Curve,* the *Advocate,* and *GLQ: Journal of Lesbian and Gay Studies.* And I've fallen in love with radio, doing film commentary for Canadian and U.S. public radio shows. I've even ventured into academia since resigning my arts council post in 1991, and now teach every spring at the University of California at Berkeley. Old enmities die hard, perhaps: I've never published anything in *Camera Obscura* to this day. Yet it, too, has changed irrevocably, with a new editorial board and a stance of theoretical inclusivity that's the very opposite of its birthright.

As happy as I am circulating through the film world of the nineties, however, I still carry within me the archaeological remnants of the seventies feminist film spirit. I look constantly for its traces. Sometimes I find it in the new work made by my friends: Joan Braderman, Sheila McLaughlin (before she quit filmmaking to become an acupuncturist), Sherry Millner, Sally Potter, Yvonne Rainer. Sometimes I find it in the new film directors: Allison Anders, Tamra Davis, Susan Streitfeld, Lynn Hershman Leeson, and others. Or in the new lesbian artists working in film and video: Sadie Benning, Cheryl Dunye, Rose Troche, Lisa Cholodenko, Ana Kokkinos. Or the veteran filmmakers who have kept working and against all odds creating major bodies of work—Chantal Akerman, Gillian Armstrong, Jane Campion, Marleen Gorris, Agneska Holland, Ulrike Ottinger. Or the men (Ridley Scott, James McKay, P. J. Hogan) who make the gutsy films that the money guys would never allow a woman to make, like *Thelma and Louise, Girls Town,* and *Muriel's Wedding.*

I find it, too, in the dedication of Dolly Hall, Kate Horsfield, Gail Silva, Debby Zimmerman, and Christine Vachon, who, as distributors and producers and administrators, facilitate getting films and videotapes to audiences and who ensure that the exciting work that can inspire us will get made and find a public. I find it in the dedication to exhibition of those non-profit survivors like Kay Armatage, Mary Lea Bandy, Linda Blackaby, Karen Cooper, Kathy Geritz, Jytte Jensen, Edith Kramer, Marie-Pierre Macia, Adrienne Mancia, Barbara Scharres, and Laura Thielen, women of strength and fortitude who keep doors open for women. And to all the forward-thinking men—Bill Horrigan, Bruce Jenkins, Bob Riley, Steve Seid, and others—who've been so instrumental in these same sorts of venues, opening galleries and museums and festivals to films that in other hands would not get a screening. And to the valiant staff of the Sundance film festival—Geoff Gilmore, John Cooper, Rebecca Yeldham, Lisa Viola, Ken Brecher, and the rest of the gang—who have remained steadfast and committed to holding space open for women's filmmaking within an event that's become the most industry-pressured forum in the country.

At times I have become dispirited, as I realize that the kind of riveting, soul-replenishing work that can give girls and women the confidence and spirit to change the world has indeed come about in the nineties, not in film, but in music. It's a peculiar reversal of the old seventies scene. Back then, music was for guys with drums and guitars, and film was where women could take back their own. Today, with independent movies taken hostage by Tarantino-obsessed dealmakers, film has become a sport for guys, and instead it's the music world, with k.d. lang and Melissa Etheridge and Lilith fairs and Ani Di Franco and Tribe 8, that has become an unexpected and unprecedented zone of empowerment for women. Clearly riot girrrl culture plucked feminist energy and made it sexy. Music, and magazines, too. Zines show off that same feisty feminist spirit of yesteryear. So did the teenage-girl mag *Sassy*. Some video is starting to flex its feminist muscles and enliven the club scene. Maybe someday that wild female energy will cross back over the stage and show up on the movie screens again. Or so I like to dream.

The Return of the Repressed

In continuing my quest for the ghosts of the feminist film past, I'm finding its revival in fresh and unpredictable places: new films and videos that are revisiting a past long ignored on screen and monitor. In 1989, Joan Braderman made *No More Nice Girls,* a semiautobiographical videotape that explores, among other subjects, the good old days of the women's movement and the nature of life afterward. I have the role of an extra, seen endlessly walking up and down the streets of the East Village talking incessantly to our friend Telma. Wildly resonating for veterans of those early years, the videotape struck a surprising chord in a new generation of women who saw our lives as history and were eager for access to the legendary time that predated the present of our acquaintance.

In 1993, I wrote an essay on Valerie Solanas and her *SCUM Manifesto* for the *Village Voice,* part of a literary supplement on out-of-print texts that editor Stacey D'Erasmo and we writers thought should be republished. I wrote:

> Valerie Solanas and SCUM Manifesto represent a key moment in the evolution of feminism, a moment when the despair and anger of women still had no name but was about to emerge into the light of day, to coalesce and become the movements that ideologically, practically, and culturally enable and ennoble our lives today. A change of such magnitude required an enormous catalyst, and few of the women who provided it in those early days were left untouched. Many of the early visionaries were permanently damaged by the crucibles in which they were fired. Sure, some flourished and prospered.

But others are still paying for their insubordination, wounded veterans of a war that pays no pensions.[3]

I termed Solanas the "Joan of Arc of feminism." Three years later, in 1996, filmmaker Mary Harron released her extraordinary portrait of Valerie Solanas, *I Shot Andy Warhol,* with Lili Taylor channeling Valerie as though all our lives depended on it. Schooled in the Factory period by years of working on documentaries dealing with the subject, Harron built an eerie time capsule. With its intoxicating depiction of drugs, freedom, art and misogyny, the film replicates the chilling and forgotten preconditions of feminism.

Valerie Solanas first wrote the *SCUM Manifesto* as a sort of zine, cranking out copies on a mimeograph machine and selling them herself on the streets; the year was 1967. At that very moment in Chicago, a young woman with a lot of what used to be called spunk was finishing up a degree in painting and photography at the School of the Art Institute. A group of film students, who had been given a little cash and the assignment to make portraits of the "now" generation, chose to focus one on her. She was all of twenty-two years old. Their low-budget, black-and-white 16mm documentary, *Shulie,* mixed interviews of her views on life with scenes of her in the studio, at her part-time post office job, out taking photographs on the Chicago streets, and finally in a brutal critique session during which the art school instructors put her through hell and suggested she change medium. She did, but not to the filmmaking they advised.

The woman was Shulamith Firestone. She moved to New York, where in 1970 she published her groundbreaking book, *The Dialectic of Sex: The Case for Feminist Revolution,* dedicated to Simone de Beauvoir. Today, Firestone is famous as one of the premiere philosophers of modern feminism and a prophetic voice, predicting not only changes in gender and sex roles but also the cybernetic future (which she called "cybernation") and ecology movements.

I know about this documentary because I once begged a private viewing from Jerry Blumenthal, one of its original makers, keeper of the archival print, and a life-long cornerstone of the Kartemquin group that produced so many important documentaries. I was enthralled by this historic view of someone who would go on to become so famous and so influential, here captured in all her vulnerability, in a world that couldn't imagine what she would become. I wanted to program the film, but it was not to be, for Jerry had promised Firestone never to show the film in public.

Enter one Elisabeth Subrin, young video artist and curator, a woman possessed when it comes to the early history of feminism and the sixties and seventies in general. With the fetishistic reverence of a true believer, she has remade *Shulie* as a 1997 restaging of the original. Almost shot for shot, with an actress uncannily adept at reproducing the rebel-art-girl essence of the original "Shulie," Subrin manages to convey simultaneously the quality of the sixties and the quality of contemporary obsession with it.

Subrin's *Shulie* is uniquely satisfying to me because it completes a certain cycle: the first generation of feminist theory as revisited, fetishized, and worshipped by the new generation. Damn but the clothes look good, and those eyeglasses are really fresh and, oh, the angst of her confusion, that searching for something that was not yet there, just a dim glow on the horizon that could have made you feel crazy if you didn't know you were right. Subrin has created a document within a document: she makes us feel what used to be, makes us remember what we actually never knew, and then makes us realize all over again how much we've lost. It's a fascinating exercise. For me, the arrival of *Shulie* on my doorstep on the eve of my completing this text is one of those serendipitous events that proves history is just a series of accidents writ large.

What will happen when the circle closes? How will I feel when the cinematic/videographic telling of history catches up finally with my moment of living it and arrives on the doorstep of feminist film? Perhaps then we will be able to claim and honor some of the women I've mentioned here.

Ana Mendieta is gone for more than a decade now, but in 1992, when the Guggenheim Museum opened its snazzy new Soho branch, hundreds of women demonstrated outside with signs protesting Carl Andre's inclusion in the opening exhibition. Carl's in the museum, read their placards, but where is Ana? Those with tickets to the opening scattered cards with the same message onto his pieces on display. Today it is Ana's niece, Raquel Harrington, who carries on: she's a filmmaker.

Joyce Wieland, the important Canadian filmmaker, deserves a retrospective of her films. When I was in Toronto in the late nineties for the film festival I attend every fall, I read a local newspaper article on a retrospective of her painting being held at the Ontario Museum of Art. Considered one of the foremost contemporary Canadian artists, she was only then receiving her first museum retrospective which, further, was billed as the first museum retrospective of a Canadian woman artist. The article, however, explained that it wasn't clear if she would attend, due to her engulfment by Alzheimer's disease. I sat in my hotel room and cried.

Once I published an article in *Mirabella* and got a fan letter from Anne Severson, whose films *Near the Big Chakra* and *Animals Running* I had written about so long ago. She had stopped making films, changed her name to Alice Anne Parker, moved to Hawaii, and worked as a psychic, doing dream analysis in the local newspaper, on the radio, and in a series of books inspired by dream images. Since I had written about her work in the seventies, she wrote, she reasoned that her legacy in film was safe as long as I kept writing. I like this idea, and I do my best to honor it, for her and all the other women of that generation. As this text moved for the final time off my desk into the typesetter's hands (or, more accurately, into somebody's hard drive), Alice Anne Parker herself materialized at the Pacific Film Archive for the first time in years, another linkage manifesting itself.

Epilogue to an Epilogue

When fate intervened yet again into the writing of this conclusion, I began to wonder if there were spirits that didn't want my digging in the ruins of this period to come to an end. After deciding that I'd finally left the reader with the requisite sense of closure, I managed to locate someone I'd never met before but whose spirit I had encountered over and over as I worked on these texts, and whose meeting perforce opened this text up again: Siew-Hwa Beh.[4]

The cofounder and editor of *Women & Film* magazine, Siew-Hwa Beh had been a major figure in the development of seventies feminist film culture, yet she seemed to have disappeared without a trace. I heard rumors that she was still in the Bay Area but no longer working in film. I dialed the number that might possibly be hers, holding my breath that it hadn't changed, and found myself talking to Siew-Hwa herself—but only for a moment. I had reached her at the worst possible time: her husband had died that morning after a three-year battle with cancer. The following week, however, we met and she took the time to tell me some of the stories of those early years.

Siew-Hwa Beh had come to California from Malaysia, disowned after refusing an arranged marriage, but with a terrific spirit and a determination to find another kind of life. Studying for a while at Mills College, she'd hopped on a bus and stumbled by chance into the Love-In in Golden Gate Park. "I've found paradise," she wrote back to a friend in Malaysia. She didn't know anything about drugs, just thought that these Americans were miraculously friendly and welcoming and generous.

Possessed by the desire to become a filmmaker, she transferred to UCLA and later enrolled in the American Film Institute's directing program for women. But here the narrative of her life takes a downward turn. When she proposed a road movie with women as the protagonists, her all-male class laughed at her. "What? Who do you expect to go see that?" It was 1970. All the students crewed for each other's films, but on the morning of her shoot, none of the men showed up. She never was able to make her film. The teachers refused to take girls seriously as students. The men who were her fellow students would actually hide the equipment, passing it to each other in a year-long game of keep-away. One invited her to be in *his* film instead: she was supposed to appear naked, representing one of the seven ages of man.

When she received the AFI opportunity, her hopes were high. But the man in charge of the funds, an "Italian macho," wanted her to spend the weekend with him. She refused, then and ever after. She never saw a dime: he transferred her money to another account, reportedly for a more pliant female. She never made that film either. When she got a woman lawyer to represent her, she discovered that in the legal framework of 1972 there was no such category as sexual harrassment.

Meanwhile, the frustrated filmmaker became an editor. Originally intended as a special issue of *Every Woman* (a local L.A. women's magazine) *Women & Film* was launched by Beh with the help of coeditor Saunie Salyer, who'd worked for the *Every Woman* collective. Siew-Hwa Beh describes the distribution of the first issue. She drove in her beat-up VW from Santa Monica to Hollywood's central newstand, the one where everybody went to buy their copy of *Variety.* She begged its owner to take a few copies, cajoled and finally talked him into it, even though he didn't want to deal with anything not carried by a proper distributor. He took a few and stuck them in an out-of-the-way spot. She hoped someone would notice.

By the time she got home, her telephone was ringing. "I'm sold out," he shouted. "Bring me all you've got." In a matter of days, if not hours, the 600 copies of the first issue of *Women & Film* magazine sold out. The fever for it was incredible. Women sent it to their friends, copies passed from hand to hand. "Women were the best distributors," said Beh. She began to receive letters from Italy, Germany, Sweden. And they didn't come just from filmmakers or students. Ordinary women, housewives, secretaries, all wrote to the magazine about the images of women they were seeing and wanted to see on the screen, about their lives and their aspirations. There in Hollywood, women were desperate for support. "*Women & Film* was the first magazine to articulate the contradictions of sexual politics in the industry." Beh and Sawyer even organized the very first meeting of women working in the industry, attracting actresses and tech crew members as well as would-be directors; the Women and Film organization grew out of it.

Eventually Beh moved from Los Angeles, first to Canada and then to the Bay Area. Problems dogged the magazine, lack of money foremost among them because their ideological purity precluded accepting any ads. The couples involved with administering things were fighting. Nobody really knew how to keep personal problems out of the editorial process. There were no models for how to do this kind of magazine. When internal ideological battles combined with the other interpersonal difficulties, the jig was up. Of course, by then it was the mid- to late seventies, when feminism itself was in crisis.

Comrades who had never met, Siew-Hwa Beh and I reminisced about the glory days of feminist film activity, the rabble-rousing days of *Jump Cut,* and how exciting that epoch had been. "That was the happiest time of my life," recalled Beh. "I felt so alive." And so it was, for so many of us. It's the period that gave rise to today's newer, more modern women filmmakers and theorists. It's a period that deserves to be remembered, not only out of respect to those foremothers but equally out of the need for those models that they invented out of thin air and bequeathed as a legacy to the future. "I'm so pleased that someone still remembers that magazine," she'd said when I first called. At the end of our meeting, she reflected on how she'd always blamed herself for her failure to save the magazine in the end. "But I never gave myself credit for creating it."

I hope that the facts and figures, hypotheses and confessions, memories and gossip all contained in these pages can begin this necessary process of giving credit and remembering. If my narrative has sometimes drifted into a sort of *bildungsroman,* which tells the life writ large of the usually-male protagonist who reflects back on the vagaries of his life, then perhaps it's time to claim this form, too, as a suitably feminist one. Women need to be more willing to claim our lives as inherently eventful and noteworthy, and to acknowledge our friends as worthy of attention and recollection, not only when talking about anorexia or abortion, but in the broader discourses of history and cinema and cultural movements. It's time to place words of remembrance into the hold, ballast for the ships that sail still through troubled seas. Turn the spotlight onto that woman over there, please. And her. And her. And you.

In Memoriam:

Lynn Blumenthal

Marjorie Keller

Ana Mendieta

Delphine Seyrig

Jacqueline Shearer

Notes

Prologue. I Found It at the Movies

1   I make only minor apologies for introducing this first piece outside the chronological progression that I otherwise follow throughout this volume. I wrote it because I wanted to please my editor, Lisa Kennedy, who was spending her days in the hospital at this time in 1991: her brother Kevin was fighting (and would soon lose) a life-or-death battle against AIDS. Merely invoking such a context inscribes the raw facts of difference between the era that produced this essay and the era that inspired it. Given the relevance of its details to my own coming of age, I think it deserves its placement here in violation of chronological order.

Prologue. Hippie Chick in the Art World

1   For the full text of the scroll, see Carolee Schneemann, *More Than Meat Joy: Performance Work and Selected Writings* (Kingston, NY: Documentext, 1997), 238.

2   Ibid., 194.

*Prologue. Angst and Joy on the Women's
Film Festival Circuit*

1   Bernice Sandler et al., *Women and Film: A Resource Handbook* (Washington, D.C.: Association of American Colleges, 1972), 1.

2 "Women on Women in Films," *Take One* 3, no. 2 (Feb. 1972): 11. The note appended to the piece explains: "The object of this symposium was to offer a forum for women filmmakers to talk about their experiences. A questionnaire was sent to many women directors, producers, screen writers, editors, and critics. The majority of the responses came from women who seemed interested in the concerns of women in the profession and in society as a whole." Among those who responded were Eleanor Perry, Stephanie Rothman, and Sylvia Spring. For context, included in the collage of quotations was the following one from Roman Polanski, then very much the hot director: "Well, you must admit that most women one meets do not have the brain of Einstein . . . I do dominate them. And they like it! I know, I know, this is regarded today as a Neanderthal attitude. But I know one women's lib leader who, friends tell me, is a great cocksucker. By the way, what exactly is the women's lib position on fellatio? That it's OK, but only on an equal-time basis?" One wonders if he'd ever seen Carolee Schneemann's *Fuses.*

3 Susan Rice, "Shirley Clarke: Image and Images," *Take One* 3, no. 2 (Feb. 1972): 21–22.

4 Bernice Sandler et al., *Women and Film*, 1–2.

5 Kay Armatage and Linda Beath, *Women and Film Catalogue* (1973), 5.

6 Stephanie Goldberg, *Films by Women/Chicago '74* (1974), 3.

7 "Programme Notes" from *The Women's International Film Festival '75 Catalogue* (1975).

8 "Festival Handout" from The Women's Event: Edinburgh International Film Festival, 1972, as quoted in *The Women's International Film Festival '75 Catalogue.*

9 Marien Lewis, Lisa Steele, Ann Bingham, and Ruth Hartman, *Women and Film Catalogue* (1973), 7.

10 Joan Braderman, "Report: The First Festival of Women's Films," *Artforum* 11, no. 1 (Sept. 1972): 87.

11 See *The New York Review of Books* (6 Feb. 1975): 23.

12 See *The New York Review of Books* (20 March 1975): "Feminism and Fascism: An Exchange."

13 Ibid.

5   *In the Name of Feminist Film Criticism*

This article benefited from tough but sympathetic criticism by Joan Braderman, Regina Cornwell, and Linda Williams. It was strengthened by the opportunity to test my ideas in a winter program at the Walker Art Center, Minneapolis, and at the 1979 Edinburgh Film Festival, where the last section on "Warning Signs" comprised a portion of my talk.

1 Adrienne Rich, "It Is the Lesbian in Us," *Sinister Wisdom* 3 (1977), and "The Transformation of Silence into Language and Action," *Sinister Wisdom* 6 (1978). See also Mary Daly, *Beyond God the Father* (Boston: Beacon Press, 1973), for her pioneering analysis of naming as power.

2   "Melodrama" and "structuralist" cinema were the two names analyzed in papers presented by my copanelists, William Horrigan and Bruce Jenkins, at the 1978 Purdue Conference on Film, where the ideas in this paper were first presented.

3   Women artists working in film continued, as before, to make avant-garde films, but those without feminist material lie outside my present concerns.

4   Monique Wittig, *Les Guerilleres* (New York: Avon, 1973), 112–14.

5   See *Soho Weekly News* (18 Nov. 1976): 36; (25 Nov. 1976): 31; and (9 Dec. 1976): 35.

6   Brian Henderson, paper presented at the International Symposium on Film Theory and Practical Criticism, Center for Twentieth-Century Studies, University of Wisconsin at Milwaukee, 1975.

7   Cindy Nemser, "Editorial: Rainer and Rothschild, an Overview," *Feminist Art Journal* 4 (1975): 4. The same issue contained Lucy Lippard's "Yvonne Rainer on Feminism and Her Film." Lippard, however, is the exception in her ability to handle both the formal value and feminist strengths of Rainer's work.

8   *Women & Film* 7 vol. 2 (summer 1975): 86. Also, *Camera Obscura* 1 (1977).

9   Here I am considering only English-language feminist film criticism. There are other complex issues in French and German criticism, for example.

10   Gilles Deleuze, "I Have Nothing to Admit," *Semiotexte* 6 vol. 2, no. 3 (1977): 112.

11   See Barbara Halpern Martineau, "Nelly Kaplan and Subjecting Her Objectification, or Communism Is Not Enough," in *Notes on Women's Cinema,* ed. Claire Johnston (London: Society for Education in Film and Television, 1973).

12   See Claire Johnston, "Women's Cinema as Counter-Cinema," in *Notes on Women's Cinema,* ed. Claire Johnston (London: Society for Education in Film and Television, 1973); and Laura Mulvey, "Visual Pleasure and Narrative Cinema," in *Women and the Cinema,* ed. Karyn Kay and Gerald Peary (New York: Dutton, 1977), 412–28.

13   Quotations are taken from E. Ann Kaplan, "Interview with British Cine Feminists," in *Women and the Cinema,* ed. Karyn Kay and Gerald Peary (New York: Dutton, 1977), 400–1.

14   Barbara Charlesworth Gelpi and Albert Gelpi, *Adrienne Rich's Poetry* (New York: Norton, 1975), 115.

15   Barbara Halpern Martineau, "Paris/Chicago," *Women & Film* (7: 11).

16   Mulvey, "Visual Pleasure and Narrative Cinema," 414; as well as personal communications. See also E. Ann Kaplan, "Aspects of British Feminist Film Theory," *Jump Cut* 12/13 (1976), for an in-depth examination of the British theories and their implications.

17   Sheila Rowbotham, *Woman's Consciousness, Man's World* (London: Penguin, 1973), 33. See also her statement that language is always "carefully guarded by the superior people because it is one of the means through which they conserve their supremacy" (p. 32).

18 *The Compact Edition of the Oxford English Dictionary* (1971 ed.), s.v. "correspondence."

19 Hélène Cixous, "The Laugh of the Medusa," *Signs* 1 (1976): 888.

20 Paul Mazursky, interview by Terry Curtis Fox, *Film Comment* 14 (1978): 30–31.

21 These remarks by Burton are taken from my memory of her talk at the 1979 Purdue Conference on Film. As stated, they are a simplification of complexities that she was at pains to elucidate without distortion.

22 Christine Gledhill, "Recent Developments in Feminist Criticism," *Quarterly Review of Film Studies* 3 (1979); and Myra Love, "Christa Wolf and Feminism: Breaking the Patriarchal Connection," *New German Critique* 17 (1979).

23 Carolyn G. Heilbrun, introduction to *Mrs. Steven Hears the Mermaids Singing* (New York: Norton, 1974), xii.

9   The Films of Yvonne Rainer

1   Don McDonagh, *The Rise and Fall and Rise of Modern Dance* (New York: Outerbridge and Dienstfrey, 1970), 144.

2   Yvonne Rainer, *Work: 1961–73* (Halifax: Press of Nova Scotia College of Art and Design; and New York: New York University Press, 1974).

3   Yvonne Rainer, quoted in *Terpsichore in Sneakers: Post-Modern Dance* (Boston: Houghton Mifflin, 1980), 224, 229.

4   Ibid.

5   Rainer, *Work: 1961–73*, 189.

6   Ibid., 209.

7   Ibid., 238.

8   Yvonne Rainer, script to *Kristina Talking Pictures*, *After Image* 7 (summer 1978).

9   See Lucy Lippard, *From the Center: Feminist Essays on Women's Art* (New York: Dutton, 1976), 266–67.

10 According to Rainer's script notation: shots no. 9a through no. 23.

11 Rainer, *Work: 1961–73*, 238.

12 Ibid., 278.

13 Molly Haskell, "Madame de: A Musical Passage," in *Favorite Movies*, ed. Philip Nobile (New York: Macmillan, 1973).

14 Thanks to Sharon Russell for help in formulating this definition.

15 Rainer, *Work: 1961–73*, 263; from the performance "This is the story of a woman who . . ."

16 Rainer, *Work: 1961–73*, 117.

17 John Berger, *Art and Revolution: Ernst Neizvestny and the Role of the Artist in the U.S.S.R.* (New York: Pantheon Books, 1969), 98.

18 Annette Michelson, "Yvonne Rainer, Part Two: 'Lives of Performers,'" *Artforum* (Feb. 1974): 32.

19 Roy Schafer, "Abstract: Narration in the Psychoanalytic Dialogue," paper

presented at Narrative: The Illusion of Sequence conference, University of Chicago Extension, October 1979.

20   Maya Deren, "Letter to James Card," in *Women and the Cinema,* ed. Karyn Kay and Gerald Peary (New York: Dutton, 1977), 226.

21   Alan Williams, *Max Ophuls and the Cinema of Desire: A Critical Study of Six Films, 1948–1955* (New York: Arno Press), 66–67.

22   Berger, *Art and Revolution,* 138.

23   Ibid.

11   *From Repressive Tolerance to Erotic Liberation:*
Maedchen in Uniform

Acknowledgment is due here to two people who contributed the very heart of this article: Karola Gramann, who has written me extensively from Frankfurt and shared her own knowledge and research on *Maedchen in Uniform,* and Bill Horrigan, who brought numerous sources to my attention and even located copies of rare materials like the original playbill and published play script; his materials improved my work immeasurably. In addition, I owe thanks to Ramona Curry, who provided encouragement and translations, and to Rennie Harringan, who offered background information and suggested avenues of research. The section of this article that deals with specific textual analysis of the film was originally presented as a paper at the 4th annual Purdue Film Conference, March 1979, on a panel devoted to early German cinema. Thanks to Jim Franklin for his encouragement at that time. This article was first published in *Jump Cut* 24/25 (Mar. 1981): 44–50, as part of a special section on Lesbians & Film; without the context and spirit of that special section and my coeditors on it, this article could not have been written. A shorter version was published in *Radical America* 15, no. 6 (1982).

1   Jonathan Katz, *Gay American History* (New York: Avon Books, 1976), 843.

2   Lotte H. Eisner, *The Haunted Screen* (Berkeley: University of California Press, 1969), 326.

3   Siegfried Kracauer, *From Caligari to Hitler* (Princeton: Princeton University Press, 1947), 227.

4   Alex de Jonge, *The Weimar Chronicle: Prelude to Hitler* (London: Paddington Press, 1978), 138.

5   Gayle Rubin, "The Traffic in Women: Notes on the 'Political Economy' of Sex," in *Toward an Anthropology of Women,* ed. Rayna R. Reiter (New York: Monthly Review Press, 1975), 180.

6   The comparison with *Persona* is made by Nancy Scholar as well, in an article that marks the seventies revival of the film. See her "Maedchen in Uniform," in *Sexual Stratagems: The World of Women in Film,* ed. Patricia Erens (New York: Horizon Press, 1979), 219–23.

7   It should be noted that *Don Carlos* appears to be yet another innovation of the film, as opposed to a borrowing from the play. In the published play

script of *Girls in Uniform,* the production (which takes place entirely off-stage) is described as a light French drama of courtly love, with Manuela featured as a knight in armor. Apart from the clearly delineated statements on forbidden love that I outline in the text, the choice of *Don Carlos* also serves to throw into relief the differing consequences for the outlaw lovers of both periods. In the Schiller drama, death by ritual burning awaited heretics of the reigning order. By the time of *Maedchen,* however, the lover marked by the heresy of lesbianism already faced a modern narrative expectation: in the absence of a functioning Inquisition, she is expected to perform her own execution via suicide. The quotation recited by Manuela about death as the payment for Paradise thus accrues additional meaning.

8   For a fuller discussion of this issue, see my article, "The Crisis of Naming in Feminist Film Criticism," *Jump Cut* 19 (Dec. 1978), and a considerably revised version, "In the Name of Feminist Film Criticism," *Heresies* 9 (spring 1980).

9   Variations on the theme of a double ending have been repeated by a number of critics, including Nancy Scholar and Sharon Smith, *Women Who Make Movies* (New York: Hopkinson and Blake, 1975); Caroline Sheldon, "Lesbians and Film: Some Thoughts," in *Gays and Film,* ed. Richard Dyer (London: British Film Institute, 1977); and Parker Tyler, *Screening the Sexes* (New York: Holt, Rinehart and Winston, 1972). Though American and English critics display a striking unanimity on this point, the German critics of the period of the film's release make no such acknowledgment. Both Eisner and Kracauer specify the averted suicide at the end of the film they are discussing, while neither makes reference to any such "home market" alternative ending. In private correspondence, Karola Gramann wrote me that she was unable to find anyone in Germany who had seen the alleged suicide ending. However, in a recent interview with the still lively Hertha Thiele (living in East Berlin and still active in theater), Gramann discovered that a suicide ending was indeed filmed—but never included in the final film, for the reason that the scene was too pathetic-looking to the filmmakers. As best as can be determined, no one in Germany ever saw the film with such an ending.

10   Rubin, "The Traffic in Women," 183.

11   Quotations and data are derived from personal copies of the original playbill, "Beginning Sunday Night, March 11, 1934," Blackstone Theatre, Chicago, and the published play: Christa Winsloe, *Girls in Uniforms: A Play in Three Acts* (Boston: Little, Brown, 1933).

12   Elaine Marks, "Lesbian Intertextuality," in *Homosexualities and French Literature,* ed. George Stambolian and Elaine Marks (Ithaca: Cornell University Press, 1979), 357–58.

13   Ibid., 357.

14   I refer here to Leontine Sagan alone, but that is inaccurate. Carl Froelich is listed as "supervisor," but other sources of the period make claims for codirector or even director status for Froelich, although there is no film evidence to support such a claim. It should be noted that Froelich stayed in

Germany after Hitler's ascendancy and directed films that met the standards of the Third Reich. In addition, there is a fascinating detail for speculation. According to Erwin Leiser's *Nazi Cinema* (New York: Macmillan, 1974), Carl Froelich directed a film about Frederick the Great, *The Hymn of Leuthen*, which showed for the first time on February 3, 1933, four days after Hitler became chancellor of the Reich—suggesting that the intelligence that created *Maedchen* must have belonged to Sagan and not to Froelich. Given the analogy of the principal to the Frederick stereotype, however, the progression is fascinating. It has been said (by none other than the Reich actor Emil Jannings) that a historical line may be drawn "from Frederick the Great to Bismarck to Hitler." Given that, here is the fascinating detail: a 1942 film on Frederick (Veit Harlan's *The Great King*) detailed the episode of the Prussian king's defeat at Kunersdorf in 1759 and in particular showed the disdain that Frederick manifested for one regiment that "preferred life to victory" and had not thrown itself into suicidal combat. Stripped of stripes and insignia for this action, the regiment's colonel commits suicide. The name of the colonel and his regiment? Bernburg. Such a detail makes one wonder what Froelich's contribution could have been, as Sagan seems so clearly to have had her way thematically.

15 At one point, in the first locker-room scene, the model of heterosexuality comes under discussion and, obliquely, attack. There is a photo of a male actor in Ilse's locker, a male pinup some girls are giggling over, and finally, highlighted, an illustration in Manuela's book that depicts a woman being rapaciously carried off by a swashbuckling man on horseback—a rather dark statement on the power of principles of heterosexual fantasy and reality.

16 Kracauer, *From Caligari to Hitler*, 229.

17 Blanche Wiesen Cook, "'Women Alone Stir My Imagination': Lesbianism and the Cultural Tradition," *Signs* 4 (1979): 722.

18 Information on *Anna and Elizabeth* is taken from David Stewart Hull, *Film in the Third Reich* (Berkeley: University of California Press, 1969), 37–38, and also from private correspondence with Karola Gramann.

19 Erika Mann and Klaus Mann, *Escape to Life* (Boston: Houghton Mifflin, 1939), 50–51.

20 Katz, *Gay American History*, 841.

21 Marion K. Sanders, *Dorothy Thompson: A Legend in Her Time* (Boston: Houghton Mifflin, 1973), 190.

22 Ibid., 193.

23 Ibid.

24 The three basic texts to consult on issues of feminism and homosexuality in Weimar Germany are Richard Evans, *The Feminist Movement in Germany 1894–1933* (Beverly Hills: Sage Publications, 1976); Lillian Faderman and Brigitte Eriksson, *Lesbian-Feminism in Turn-of-the-Century Germany* (Tallahassee: Naiad Press, 1979); and James D. Steakley, *The Homosexual Emancipation Movement in Germany* (New York: Arno Press, 1975). Relevant

information in this article is culled almost entirely from these sources. For a superior review and perspective piece, see Carol Anne Douglas, "German Feminists and the Right: Can It Happen Here?" in *off our backs* 10, no. 11 (Dec. 1980). She discusses at length the political crosscurrents I have barely managed to summarize here.

25 Interestingly enough, Hirschfeld appeared in a film he must have taken a part in producing. *Different from the Others* (directed by Richard Oswald in 1919) starred Conrad Veidt as a homosexual blackmail victim who is "saved" by the intervention of a philanthropic doctor played by Hirschfeld himself. It was widely banned, but evidently more for reasons of anti-Semitism (directed against Hirschfeld) than homophobia, if such a distinction can indeed be made. The film was remade in 1927 as *Laws of Love*, again starring Veidt, but minus Hirschfeld, whose absence in this version led to Veidt's character's suicide.

26 Steakley, *The Homosexual Emancipation Movement*, 78–79.

27 Louise Brooks, "On Making Pabst's Lulu," in *Women and the Cinema*, ed. Karyn Kay and Gerald Peary (New York: Dutton, 1977), 81.

28 De Jonge, *The Weimar Chronicle*, 140.

29 Ilse Kokula, "Die urnischen Damen treffen sich vielfach in Konditoreien," *Courage* 7 (Berlin: July 1980); copy courtesy of Karola Gramann.

30 Vito Russo, *The Celluloid Closet: Homosexuality in the Movies* (New York: Harper & Row, 1981), 56–59. Russo's book came out after this article's initial publication. It is an important work, beautifully researched and filled with primary data, but unfortunately marred by a bit of misogyny. Nevertheless, the photograph of a very butch Dorothy Arzner arm-in-arm with Joan Crawford on the 1937 set of *The Bride Wore Red* is itself worth the price of the book.

31 A print of *Different from the Others* survives in an East German archive. A print of *Anna and Elizabeth* survives in an archive at Koblenz. A special print of *Different from the Others* was made for screening in Montreal and New York City in 1982; *Anna and Elizabeth* has yet to be seen here.

32 The French subtitles and a preface explaining Colette's role in writing them can be found in *Colette au cinéma*, ed. Alain Virmaux and Odette Virmaux (Paris: Librairie Ernest Flammarion, 1975). Unfortunately, the entire *Maedchen in Uniform* section has been omitted from the English-language edition (trans. Sarah W. R. Smith [New York: Frederick Ungar, 1980]).

33 Salka Viertel, *The Kindness of Strangers* (New York: Holt, Rinehart and Winston, 1969), 175. Viertel's memoirs are discreetly restrained on virtually all topics of sexuality and therefore shed no light on the nature of her relationship with Greta Garbo. Viertel wrote the screen treatments for Garbo's films and was her frequent companion. In his dirt-digging *Hollywood Babylon* (San Francisco: Straight Arrow Books, 1975), Kenneth Anger wrote: "Garbo's genuine reserve held the gossips at bay for the most part. There was, however, occasional speculation about how close her friendship really was with Salka Viertel" (p. 172).

34 The event was the International Center of Photography's symposium, Avant-

Garde German Photography: 1919–1939, held at the Guggenheim Museum. Quotations are based on notes.

35 As this volume was going to press, I received a copy of an extraordinary book in the mail. *Lights and Shadows: The Autobiography of Leontine Sagan,* edited and with an introduction by Loren Kruger, (Johannesburg, South Africa: Witwatersrand University Press, 1996) was compiled with the assistance of Sagan's niece and heir, Helga Kaye. Containing accounts of much of Sagan's life, the book provides a wealth of information not available to me at the time of writing this article. I did not know, for example, that Sagan had been born in Budapest, lived in Vienna, then attended a German school in South Africa during the Anglo-Boer War. She was Jewish, from a cosmopolitan middle-class family.

Sagan left South Africa to try to make her way as an actress in German theater, starting in Frankfurt and Vienna, then settling on Berlin. She was a theater director as well: it was her direction of the Christa Winsloe play, "Yesterday and Today," that led to her hiring on *Maedchen.* (But she didn't entirely give up acting: she played the role of Fraulein Von Bernburg in the 1933 South African touring production of the play.) Later, she spent time working in theater in London, New York, and Australia before resettling in South Africa, where she worked in theater until her retirement in the fifties. She wrote these memoirs in 1966 in her "little house in Pretoria," where she retreated after the death of her husband in 1950. She herself died in 1974 — which means that she was still alive in South Africa when the first women's film festivals revived her most famous work.

Prologue. Softball, the Goddess, and Lesbian Film Culture

1 The introduction to this section was finally republished and reclaimed in the context of nineties queer writing. See Edith Becker, Michelle Citron, Julia Lesage, and B. Ruby Rich, "Lesbians and Film," in *Out in Culture: Gay, Lesbian, and Queer Essays on Popular Culture,* ed. Corey K. Creekmur and Alexander Doty (Durham, NC: Duke University Press, 1995), 25–43.

2 Caroline Sheldon, "Lesbians and Film: Some Thoughts," in *Gays and Film,* ed. Richard Dyer (London: British Film Institute, 1977), 5–26.

3 Becker et al., "Lesbians and Film," 25.

4 Ibid., 30–31, 36.

12   The Right of Re-Vision:
Michelle Citron's Daughter Rite

1 Adrienne Rich, *Of Woman Born* (New York: Bantam, 1976), 45.

2 Lucy Lippard, "The Pink Glass Swan: Upward and Downward Mobility in the Art World," *Heresies* 1 (1978): 85.

3 See Nancy Friday, *My Mother/Myself: The Daughter's Search for Identity* (New York: Dell, 1978); Rich, *Of Woman Born.*

4 Nancy Chodorow, *The Reproduction of Mothering* (Berkeley: University of California Press, 1978).

5 Rich, *Of Woman Born,* 45.

6 "Matrophobia can be seen as a womanly splitting of self, in the desire to become purged once and for all of our mother's bondage, to become individuated and free" (ibid., p. 338).

7 This recasting of familiar domestic forms parallels issues under discussion by feminist film and television critics regarding the function of soap opera as a "woman's" form. Just as critics like Molly Haskell were able to find certain positive values in the "woman's film," so now there is an ongoing reexamination of soap opera's emphasis on domestic life, its spinning out of conversation, and the relegation of events to offscreen space to provide an endless verbal replay that retards the forward movement of the narrative in order to explore the lateral repercussions of each action on individual lines. See Tania Modleski, "The Search for Tomorrow in Today's Soap Operas: Notes on a Feminine Narrative Form," *Film Quarterly* (fall 1979): 12–20.

8 Citron is working in quite a different direction, for example, from that taken by Laura Mulvey and Peter Wollen in *Riddles of the Sphinx.* Like *Daughter Rite, Riddles* takes its subject matter directly from the women's movement but takes its formal strategies from theories of avant-garde film, placing itself within an ever-widening gap between the avant-garde and the women's movement. Citron, however, begins with forms familiar to the women's movement and builds from there.

14 She Says, He Says: The Power of the Narrator in Modernist Film Politics

Thanks are due to Ramona Curry, who first prompted my thoughts on this subject by inviting me to give a lecture at the Chicago Goethe Institute as part of the Kluge retrospective she programmed there in 1980. Readers should note that due to my lack of fluency in German, all seeming quotations are actually taken either from printed texts or from the subtitles on the screen (a notoriously unreliable referent).

1 Ann Barr Snitow, "The Front Line: Notes on Sex in Novels by Women, 1969–1979," in *Women: Sex and Sexuality,* ed. Catharine R. Stimpson and Ethel Spector Person (Chicago: University of Chicago Press, 1980), 161.

2 Space here obviously does not permit a full discussion of the film. For that, see Jan Dawson, *Alexander Kluge and the Occasional Work of a Female Slave* (Perth: Perth Film Festival Publication, 1975).

3 Ibid., 40.

4 Ibid., 31.

5 See, for example, Monica Jacobs, "Civil Rights and Women's Rights in the Federal Republic of Germany Today," *New German Critique* 13 (winter 1978), and other articles in the same issue for background information.

6 Dawson, *Kluge,* 42.

7 The best example of this is the piece written by Karyn Kay, originally appearing in *Film Quarterly* and available as "Part-Time Work of a Domestic Slave, or Putting the Screws to Screwball Comedy," in *Women and the Cinema,* ed. Karyn Kay and Gerald Peary (New York: Dutton, 1978).

8 Elizabeth Wilson, "Psychoanalysis: Psychic Law and Order," *Feminist Review* 8 (1981): 76.

9 Jessica Benjamin, "Authority and the Female Revisited: Or, A World Without Fathers?" *New German Critique* 13 (winter 1978): 35–58.

10 Miriam Hansen, "Cooperative Auteur Cinema and Oppositional Public Sphere," *New German Critique* 24–25 (fall–winter 1981–82): 55.

11 Christa Wolf, "The Reader and the Writer," in *The Reader and the Writer: Essays, Sketches, Memories,* trans. Joan Becker (New York: International Publishers, 1977), 193.

12 Snitow, "The Front Line," 161.

13 See "In the Name of Feminist Film Criticism" in this volume.

14 Myra Love, "Christa Wolf and Feminism: Breaking the Patriarchal Connection," *New German Critique* 16 (winter 1979): 34.

15 See the materials presented in *New German Critique* 13 (winter 1978), as well as the summary of the *frauen und film* critiques of Kluge quoted and summarized in Dawson's *Alexander Kluge.*

16 Helke Sander, "Feminism and Film," trans. Ramona Curry, *Jump Cut* 27 (1982): 50. From a talk originally given at Grasz, Austria, 1977, entitled "I Like Chaos, but I Don't Know Whether Chaos Likes Me." See the entire special section in this issue of *Jump Cut,* "New German Women's Cinema," especially the contextualizing essays by Renny Harrigan and Mark Silberman, for a sense of German feminist film activity.

17 Judith Mayne, "Female Narration, Women's Cinema," *New German Critique* 24–25 (fall–winter 1981–82): 155–71. Mayne goes into far more detail on the film than I have been able to cover here, and is the best source for a coherent description of both its narrative and stylistic qualities. See especially her comparison of the film with its Godardian counterpart.

18 Christa Wolf, *The Quest for Christa T.* (New York: Delta, 1970), 170.

19 Love, "Christa Wolf," 41.

20 Wilson, "Psychoanalysis," 76.

15 Antiporn: Soft Issue, Hard World
(*Not a Love Story*)

This article owes its existence in part to the encouragement and fantastic editing of Karen Durbin, my *Village Voice* editor. In addition, the article benefited from extended conversations with Fina Bathrick, Lillian Jimenez, and Sande Zeig.

1 See, for example, Irene Diamond, ed., "Pornography and Repression: A Re-

consideration" in *Women: Sex and Sexuality,* ed. Catharine R. Stimpson and Ethel Spector Person (Chicago: University of Chicago Press, 1980), 129–44; Bertha Harris, "Sade Cases," *Village Voice,* (18 May 1982): 46; Gina Marchetti, "Readings on Women and Pornography," *Jump Cut* 26 (n.a.): 56–60; Varda Burstyn, "Pornography and Eroticism," interview by Lisa Steele, *Fuse* (May/June 1982): 19–24; Ellen Willis, "Feminism, Moralism, and Pornography," in *Beginning to See the Light* (New York: Knopf, 1981), 219–27.

2   Laura Lederer, "An Interview with a Former Pornography Model," in *Take Back the Night* (New York: Bantam, 1982), 45–59.

3   Judith Walkowitz, "The Politics of Prostitution," in *Pornography and Repression,* 145–47, or see the updated version, "Male Vice and Feminist Virtue: Feminism and the Politics of Prostitution in Nineteenth-Century Britain," *History Workshop Journal* 13 (n.a.): 77–93, with an introduction by Jane Caplan.

4   Monique Wittig, "The Straight Mind," *Feminist Issues* 1 (summer 1980): 103–12.

Prologue. Attacking the Sisters, or the Limits of Disagreement

1   Julia Lesage, "The Human Subject — You, He, or Me?," *Jump Cut* 4 (Nov.-Dec. 1974), and *Screen* 16, no. 2 (summer 1975): 77–83.

2   Ben Brewster, Stephen Heath, and Colin MacCabe, "Comment," *Screen* 16, no. 2 (summer 1975): 89.

3   Editorial Board, Editorial, *Screen* 16, no. 2 (summer 1975): 5–6.

18   Truth, Faith, and the Individual: Thoughts on U.S. Documentary Film Practice

1   See, for example, Claire Johnston's landmark essay, "Women's Cinema as Counter Cinema," in *Notes on Women's Cinema,* ed. Claire Johnston (London: Screen Pamphlet 2, Society for Education in Film and Television, 1973): "In rejecting a sociological analysis of woman in the cinema we reject any view in terms of realism, for this would involve an acceptance of the apparent natural denotation of the sign and would involve a denial of the reality of myth in operation. . . . A sociological analysis based on the empirical study of recurring roles and motifs would lead to a critique in terms of an enumeration of the notion of career/home/motherhood/sexuality, an examination of women as the central figures in the narrative, etc. If we view the image of woman as sign within the sexist ideology, we see that the portrayal of woman is merely one item subject to the law of verisimilitude, a law which directors worked with or reacted against. The law of verisimilitude (that which determines the impression of realism) in the cinema is precisely responsible for the repression of the image of woman as woman and the celebration of her non-existence."

2   See recent appraisals of documentary; for example, Bill Nichols, "The Voice of Documentary" *Film Quarterly* 36, no. 3 (spring 1983).

3   Admission: I am oversimplifying to make a point. Emile De Antonio, for example, is the big exception and provides an extraordinary, intelligent example of how to do things differently. But I believe that the underrecognition of his achievement is symptomatic of the dominance of the form to which I here pay attention. Some of the U.S. documentary films that departed from this dominant tradition in the seventies and early eighties have included those by Michelle Citron, JoAnn Elam, Errol Morris, and Jean-Pierre Gorin. Compilation films like *Atomic Cafe* have introduced yet another format, dispensing with interviews entirely à la De Antonio.

4   See Tom Waugh, "Lesbian and Gay Documentary: Minority Self-Imaging, Oppositional Film Practice, and the Question of Image Ethics," in *Image Ethics: The Moral and Legal Rights of Subjects in Documentary Film and Television,* ed. Larry Gross, John Katz, and Jay Ruby (Philadelphia: Annenberg Communication Series, 1985).

5   I explored this concept further in "The Aesthetics of Self-Determination," an unpublished paper that I presented at the fifth International Festival of Latin American Cinema, ICAIC, Havana, Cuba, Dec. 1983, at The Other Face U.S. film symposium there.

6   The most important articles include Eileen McGarry, "Documentary, Realism, and Women's Cinema," *Women & Film* 2, no. 7 (1975); Julia Lesage, "The Political Aesthetics of the Feminist Documentary Film," *Quarterly Review of Film Studies* 3, no. 4 (fall 1978); Christine Gledhill, "Recent Developments in Feminist Film Criticism," *Quarterly Review of Film Studies* 3, no. 4 (fall 1978); and Waugh, "Lesbian and Gay Documentary."

7   The term "the cinema of the rhetorical question" was developed in conjunction with Chuck Kleinhans for a paper that we coauthored, "Avant-Garde Cinema and Its Relationship to Political Cinema," originally presented at the Society for Cinema Studies conference in Syracuse, New York, in 1979, and published in French in *CinemAction* 10/11 (spring–summer 1980).

8   For a full description of *Improper Conduct* and the controversy, see my article, "Bay of Pix," *American Film* 9, no. 9 (July–Aug. 1984). Also, see my two-part article, coauthored with Lourdes Arguelles, "Homosexuality, Homophobia and Revolution: Notes Toward an Understanding of the Cuban Lesbian and Gay Male Experience," pts. 1 and 2, *Signs: Journal of Women in Culture and Society* 9, no. 4 (summer 1984), and 11, no. 1 (autumn 1985). See, too, the attacks on both parts (and our replies) printed in subsequent issues: Carlos Alberto Montaner, "Comment on Part I," *Signs: Journal of Women in Culture and Society* 11, no. 2 (winter 1986), and Roger Lancaster, "Comment on Part II," *Signs: Journal of Women in Culture and Society* 12, no. 1 (autumn 1986).

This article has benefited from the influence and criticism of a number of people whom I would like to acknowledge. For a lifetime of discussions on sexuality that inform this piece, thanks to Carol Becker, Joan Braderman, and Kate Horsfield. For extended conversations on issues of sexuality and/or critical readings of the manuscript, thanks are owed to Telma Abascal, Serafina Bathrick, Jewelle Gomez, Eunice Gutman, Martha Gever, Judith Mayne, Sharon Thompson, and Marilyn Young and to the members of Ann Snitow's Seminar on Sex, Gender, and Consumer Culture at the New York Institute for the Humanities. As usual, errors and failings are entirely my own doing in this and other articles.

Aside from footnoted sources, publications discussed in this review essay include "Sex Issue," *Heresies* 12 (1981); Samois, *Coming to Power: Writings and Graphics on Lesbian s/m* (Boston: Alyson Publications, 1982); Robin Ruth Linden, Darlene R. Pagano, Diana E. H. Russell, and Susan Leigh Star, eds., *Against Sadomasochism: A Radical Feminist Analysis* (East Palo Alto: Frog in the Well Press, 1982); Ann Snitow, Christine Stansell, and Sharon Thompson, eds., *Powers of Desire: The Politics of Sexuality* (New York: Monthly Review Press, New Feminist Library, 1983); Carole Vance, ed., *Pleasure and Danger: Exploring Female Sexuality* (Boston: Routledge & Kegan Paul, 1984); Pat Califia, *Sapphistry: The Book of Lesbian Sexuality* (Tallahassee: Naiad Press, 1983); Lonnie Barbach, ed., *Pleasures: Women Write Erotica* (Garden City: Doubleday & Company, 1984); Beatrice Faust, *Women, Sex, and Pornography: A Controversial and Unique Study* (New York: Macmillan, 1980).

1   Martha Vicinus, "Sexuality and Power: A Review of Current Work in the History of Sexuality," *Feminist Studies* 8 (spring 1982): 133–56.

2   Audre Lorde, "Uses of the Erotic: The Erotic as Power," published originally as a pamphlet (New York: Out & Out Books, 1978), and reprinted in *Sister Outsider* (Trumansburg: Crossing Press, 1984), 53–59.

3   Audre Lorde, "An Interview: Audre Lorde and Adrienne Rich," *Sister Outsider* (Trumansburg: Crossing Press, 1984), 102.

4   Laura Lederer, introduction to *Take Back the Night: Women on Pornography* (New York: William Morrow, 1980), 15.

5   The first Samois booklet was *What Color Is Your Handkerchief?* See also Pat Califia, "A Personal View of the History of the Lesbian s/m Community and Movement in San Francisco," in *Coming to Power* 249–62, for the sequence of events.

6   See also Lucy Gilbert and Paula Webster, *Bound by Love: The Sweet Trap of Daughterhood* (Boston: Beacon Press, 1982), for a groundbreaking analysis of the roots of submission and femininity.

7   Any number of texts could be cited here. See, for example, Anne Koedt, "The Myth of the Vaginal Orgasm," in *Voices from Women's Liberation,* ed. Leslie B. Tanner (New York: New American Library, 1970), 157–65; Alix [Kates] Shul-

man, "Organs and Orgasms," in *Woman in Sexist Society: Studies in Power and Powerlessness,* ed. Vivian Gornick and Barbara K. Moran (New York: New American Library, 1971), 292–303; and Ti-Grace Atkinson, *Amazon Odyssey* (New York: Link Books, 1974). For an overview of this period and its shifts in attitudes, see the introduction to *Powers of Desire,* 9–47.

8   See Michel Foucault, *The History of Sexuality: An Introduction* (New York: Pantheon Books, 1978).

9   For more extended discussion of both these anthologies, see my reviews of *Powers of Desire* and *Pleasure and Danger* in *In These Times* (Nov. 1983): 16–22 and (Feb. 1985): 20–26.

10 This article concerns itself with the main currents of the feminist debates on sexuality. However, the development of U.S. psychoanalytic feminism has taken an entirely different route, largely concentrating on gender rather than sexuality, and derived almost exclusively from the work of Jacques Lacan, with further influences from British and French psychoanalytic critics. See, for example, Jane Gallup, *The Daughter's Seduction: Feminism and Psychoanalysis* (Ithaca: Cornell University Press, 1982); *Difference: On Representation and Sexuality,* exhibition catalogue, (New York: New York Museum of Contemporary Art, 1985); and a number of other texts that owe allegiance to such British sources as Mary Kelly, Laura Mulvey, and the *m/f* journal. For a more promising and productive direction, see Teresa de Lauretis, *Alice Doesn't: Feminism, Semiotics, Cinema* (Bloomington: Indiana University Press, 1984), especially "Desire in Narrative."

11 For an incisive and elegant analysis of these genres, see Tania Modleski, *Loving with a Vengeance: Mass-Produced Fantasies for Women* (Hamden: Archon Book, Shoe String Press, 1982; reprinted, New York: Methuen, 1984).

12 Personal communication, Rio de Janeiro, Nov. 1984.

13 For a more recent book that combines sex manual frankness with lesbian feminist principles, see JoAnn Loulan, *Lesbian Sex* (San Francisco: Spinsters Ink, 1984).

14 Richard Dyer has defined pornography in cinema as "any film that has as its aim sexual arousal in the spectator" in his essay "Male Gay Porn: Coming to Terms," *Jump Cut* 30 (1985): 27. See the entire special section, "The Politics of Sexual Representation," in the same issue of *Jump Cut,* particularly the introduction by editors Chuck Kleinhans and Julia Lesage, 24–26.

15 See, for example, my own piece, "Antiporn: Soft Issue, Hard World," in this volume, and Ann Snitow, "Retrenchment vs. Transformation: The Politics of the Anti-Porn Movement," in *Women against Censorship,* ed. Varda Burstyn (Vancouver: Douglass & McIntyre, 1985), 107–20.

16 See Lisa Duggan, "Censorship in the Name of Feminism," *Village Voice* (16 Oct. 1984); Lisa Duggan, Nan Hunter, and Carole S. Vance, "False Promises: Feminist AntiPornography Legislation in the United States," in *Women against Censorship,* ed. Varda Burstyn (Vancouver: Douglass & McIntyre, 1985), 130–51.

17 Scott MacDonald, "Confessions of a Feminist Porn-Watcher," *Film Quarterly*
    36 (spring 1983): 10–16. See also Philip Weiss, "Forbidden Pleasures: A Taste
    for Porn in a City of Women," *Harper's* (Mar. 1986): 68–72.

18 MacDonald, "Confessions," 15.

19 Leonore Tiefer, presentation to the Seminar on Sex, Gender, and Consumer
    Culture, New York Institute for the Humanities, 1983–84. See also Leonore
    Tiefer, "In Pursuit of the Perfect Penis: The Medicalization of Male Sexu-
    ality," *American Behavioral Scientist* (May 1986).

20 The controversy began in Ann Landers columns of March 27, July 11, and
    November 4, 1984, in correspondence regarding penile implants. Columns
    on January 14 and 15, 1985, of the *Chicago Sun-Times* (and other papers carry-
    ing the syndicated writer) presented the cited survey, based on the response
    of thousands of women, that "the act is unnecessary."

21 Elizabeth Wilson, "Forbidden Love," *Feminist Studies* 10 (summer 1984): 220.

22 Both texts are too well known and discussed to bear recapitulation here. See
    Carroll Smith Rosenberg, "Female World of Love and Ritual: Relations be-
    tween Women in Nineteenth-Century America," *Signs* 1 (autumn 1975): 1–29,
    reprinted in her *Disorderly Conduct: Visions of Gender in Victorian America*
    (New York: Knopf, 1985), 53–76. The Rich article was published in *Signs* 5
    (summer 1980) and is reprinted in *Powers of Desire*, 194–95.

23 Wendy Clark, "The Dyke, the Feminist, and the Devil," *Feminist Review* 11
    (summer 1982): 38. See this entire "Sexuality Issue" of *Feminist Review* for a
    number of important articles on such subjects as sexual violence, jealousy,
    and the history of ideological politics.

24 For an illuminating look at the myths and realities of the original "stone
    butch," see Madeline Davis and Elizabeth Lapovsky Kennedy, "Oral History
    and the Study of Sexuality in the Lesbian Community: Buffalo, New York,
    1940–1960," *Feminist Studies* 12 (spring 1986): 7–26.

25 See, for example, Peg Byron, "What We Talk about When We Talk about Dil-
    dos," *Village Voice* (5 Mar. 1985: 48–49).

26 Key works include Cherríe Moraga, *Loving in the War Years: Lo que nunca
    paso por sus labios* (Boston: South End Press, 1983); Audre Lorde, *Zami:
    A New Spelling of My Name* (Trumansburg: Crossing Press, 1983); Cheryl
    Clarke, *Living as a Lesbian* (Ithaca: Firebrand Books, 1986); Barbara Smith,
    ed., *Home Girls: A Black Feminist Anthology* (New York: Kitchen Table,
    Women of Color Press, 1983); Gloria T. Hull, Patricia Bell Scott, and Barbara
    Smith, *All the Women Are White, All the Blacks Are Men, But Some of Us
    Are Brave: Black Women's Studies* (Old Westbury: Feminist Press, 1982); and
    numerous others that space precludes listing.

27 See also Michele Russell, "Black Eyed Blues Connections: From the Inside
    Out," *Heresies* 2 (1979): 99–104; reprinted in *All the Women Are White*, 196–
    207.

28 Smith, introduction to *Home Girls*, xlv.

29 The ethnocentrism of the sexuality debates remains acute, not only in terms

of a sexuality constructed to exclude the experiences and perspectives of so many women of color in the United States but also in terms of its blindness to cultural differences at the international level. For a useful corrective, see the important anthology New Internationalists Publications Cooperative, ed., *Women: A World Report* (New York: Oxford University Press, 1985), especially Elena Poniatowska's and Angela Davis's chapters on sexuality.

30 Joyce P. Lindenbaum, "The Shattering of an Illusion: The Problem of Competition in Lesbian Relationships," *Feminist Studies* 11 (spring 1985): 93. For all the importance of this article's analysis, however, Lindenbaum's concluding argument for competition as a cure for lesbian ills seems overdetermined and simplistic.

31 For a full reckoning of the film, see my article, "Bay of Pix," *American Film* 9 (July–Aug. 1984): 57–59. For a detailed history of Cuban attitudes toward homosexuality, both in Cuba and in the U.S. Cuban émigré communities, see Lourdes Arguelles and B. Ruby Rich, "Homosexuality, Homophobia, and Revolution: Notes toward an Understanding of the Cuban Lesbian and Gay Male Experience," Pts. 1 and 2, *Signs* 9 (summer 1984): 683–99, and 11 (autumn 1985): 120–36.

32 Robin Morgan, *Sisterhood Is Global: The International Women's Movement Anthology* (Garden City: Doubleday, 1984). Again, see its antidote in *Women: A World Report*.

33 Lynda Barry, *Girls and Boys and Big Ideas* (Seattle: Real Comet Press, 1981; 1983); Nicole Hollander, *Ma, Can I Be a Feminist and Still Like Men?* and *Never Tell Your Mother This Dream* (New York: St. Martin's Press); of her nine books, these deal the most with sex.

34 Lynda Barry, *Naked Ladies* (Seattle: The Real Comet Press, 1984).

Epilogue: Charting the Eighties

1 For further information on this period, see the following articles that I wrote to try to understand for myself the cultural shifts taking place between the eighties and the nineties: "The Future of 16mm," *The Next Step: Distributing Independent Films and Videos,* ed. Morrie Warshawski (New York: Foundation for Independent Video and Film, 1989), 17–23; "Don't Look Back: Independent U.S. Video and Film Production in the Seventies and Eighties," *Breakthroughs: Avant-Garde Artists in Europe and America, 1950–1990,* ed. John Howell (New York/Columbus: Rizzoli Books in association with the Wexner Center for the Visual Arts, 1991), 165–176; "The Movie, The Critic, and You," *Tonantzin* vol. 8 no. 1 (February 1991), 15–16; "In The Eyes of the Beholder," *Village Voice* (28 January 1992), 60; "Rivalries of Representation," *Banned in the USA: America and Film Censorship,* ed. Steve Seid (Berkeley: University Art Museum/Pacific Film Archive, November 1993), 6–12; "The Authenticating Goldfish: Re-Viewing Film and Video in the Nineties," *1993 Whitney Biennial Exhibition* (New York: Harry N. Abrams, 1993), 86–99.

2   For further information, see Robert Katz, *Naked by the Window: The Fatal Marriage of Ana Mendieta and Carl Andre* (New York: Atlantic Monthly Press, 1990).

3   See my article "Manifesto Destiny: Drawing a Bead on Valerie Solanas," *Voice Literary Supplement,* October 1993, 16–17.

4   Thanks to Bill Nichols for providing Beh's telephone number and encouraging me to call. He is part of this history, too, since he was on the editorial board of *Women & Film* magazine and, not incidentally, married to Siew-Hwa Beh at the time.

Index

B. Ruby Rich is an independent scholar and cultural critic.
She has served as the Associate Director of the Film Center
at the School of the Art Institute of Chicago and as Director
of the Electronic Media and Film Program of the New York
State Council on the Arts. She worked as a film critic for the
Chicago *Reader* for several years before moving to New York,
then contributed regularly to the *Village Voice* in the eighties
and *Sight and Sound* in the nineties. Today, she is a film commentator for the national program "The World" on public
radio and is adjunct Associate Professor at the University
of California, Berkeley. She is also a member of the selection advisory committee of the Sundance Film Festival. During the preparation of this volume, she was a Distinguished
Visitor at the John D. and Catherine T. MacArthur Foundation and a Rockefeller Fellow in the Humanities at New York
University's Center for Media, Culture, and History. She continues to contribute to both the popular and scholarly presses,
and lives in New York and San Francisco.

Library of Congress Cataloging-in-Publication Data
Rich, B. Ruby.
Chick flicks: theories and memories of the
feminist film movement / B. Ruby Rich.
A collection of the author's essays from the 1970s and 1980s.
Includes index.
ISBN 0-8223-2106-8 (alk. paper).
— ISBN 0-8223-2121-1 (pbk. : alk. paper)
1. Feminism and motion pictures. 2. Feminist motion
pictures. 3. Women in motion pictures. 4. Feminist film
criticism. I. Title.
PN1995.9.W6R47 1998 791.43′082—dc21 98-12052 CIP